Landmarks

HBJ Reading Program

Margaret Early

Bernice E. Cullinan
Roger C. Farr
W. Dorsey Hammond
Nancy Santeusanio
Dorothy S. Strickland

LEVEL 11

Landmarks

HBJ **HARCOURT BRACE JOVANOVICH, PUBLISHERS**
Orlando   San Diego   Chicago   Dallas

Printed in the United States of America

ISBN 0-15-330511-8

Acknowledgments

For permission to reprint copyrighted material, grateful acknowledgment is made to the following sources:

Arnold Adoff Agency: From "How Jahdu Became Himself" in *The Time Ago-Tales of Jahdu* by Virginia Hamilton. Published by Macmillan Publishing Company, 1969.

Margaret Walker Alexander: "Lineage" from *For My People* by Margaret Walker Alexander. Copyright 1942 by Yale University Press; copyright © 1972 by Margaret Walker Alexander.

T. D. Allen, on behalf of Alonzo Lopez: "Direction" by Alonzo Lopez.

Curtis Brown Ltd.: Adapted from *From Scrolls to Satellites* (Titled: "Signals and Messages") by William Wise. Copyright © 1970 by William Wise. Published by Parents' Magazine press.

James E. Cook: From "You're It! Games Kids Played on the Frontier" by James E. Cook from *Arizona Highways* Magazine, June 1984.

Coward, McCann & Geoghegan: Adapted from *The Little Riders* by Margaretha Shemin. Copyright © 1963 by Margaretha Shemin. Abridged from *On the Frontier with Mr. Audubon* by Barbara Brenner. Copyright © 1977 by Barbara Brenner. Adapted from *The Cabin Faced West* by Jean Fritz. Copyright © 1958 by Jean Fritz.

Andre Deutsch Ltd.: Adapted from "Cherry Ripe" in *The Phantom Cyclist and Other Ghost Stories* by Ruth Ainsworth. Published by Scholastic Book Services, 1971. Originally published by Andre Deutsch Ltd., London, 1971.

Doubleday & Company, Inc.: Adapted from *Donna deVarona: Gold Medal Swimmer* by Bob Thomas. Copyright © 1969 by Doubleday & Company, Inc.

E. P. Dutton, a division of New American Library and Blissymbolics Communication Institute: Adapted from the text, photographs, and the poem "Blast-Off!" (Titled: "The Story of Kari") by Kari Harrington in *Blissymbolics: Speaking Without Speech* by Elizabeth S. Helfman. Text copyright © 1981 by Elizabeth S. Helfman. Blissymbolics derived from the symbols in *Semantography*. Original copyright by C. K. Bliss, 1949. Blissymbolics Communication Institute exclusive licensee, 1982.

Farrar, Straus & Giroux, Inc.: Adapted from *The Cricket in Times Square* by George Selden, illustrated by Garth Williams. Copyright © 1960 by George Selden and Garth Williams.

Garrard Publishing Company, Champaign, IL: From "Nat Love: 'Deadwood Dick'" in *Saddles and Sabers* by LaVere Anderson. Copyright © 1975 by LaVere Anderson.

Harcourt Brace Jovanovich, Inc.: From pp. 69–70 in *HBJ Health,* Level Purple, Grade 5. Copyright © 1983 by Harcourt Brace Jovanovich, Inc. Abridged from p. 225, and from pp. 447–448 in *HBJ SOCIAL STUDIES, The United States: Its History and Neighbors,* Level 5. Copyright © 1985 by Harcourt Brace Jovanovich, Inc. Pronunciation key from p. 33 and the short key from p. 35 in *HBJ School Dictionary.* Copyright © 1985 by Harcourt Brace Jovanovich, Inc. Abridged from pp. 29–31, 103–105, and 180–181 in *HBJ Science,* Level Purple, Grade 5 by Elizabeth K. Cooper et al. Copyright © 1985 by Harcourt Brace Jovanovich, Inc.

Harper & Row, Publishers, Inc.: Foreword and pp. 19–30 from *The Big Wave* by Pearl S. Buck. Copyright 1947 by the Curtis Publishing Company; copyright 1948, 1976 by Pearl S. Buck. Published by Thomas Y. Crowell. "Introduction" poem (Titled: "Where Do You Get the Idea for a Poem?") from *NEAR THE WINDOW TREE: Poems and Notes* by Karla Kuskin. Copyright © 1975 by Karla Kuskin. Text from pp. 62–63 in *Charlotte's Web* by E. B. White. Copyright 1952, 1960 by E. B. White.

Holiday House: From *High Elk's Treasure* by Virginia Driving Hawk Sneve. Copyright © 1972 by Virginia Driving Hawk Sneve.

Henry Holt and Company, Inc.: "The Old Woman and the Rice Cakes" from *The Maid of the North: Feminist Folk Tales from Around the World,* edited by Ethel Johnston Phelps. Copyright © 1981 by Ethel Johnston Phelps.

iv

Photographs

The following abbreviations indicate the position of the photographs on the page: *t,* top; *b,* bottom; *l,* left; *r,* right; *c,* center.

Illustrators

Design, Production: Kirchoff/Wohlberg, Inc.

Contents

Unit 3 Dialogues 275

Unit 4 Heirlooms 429

Landmarks

Unit 1

Serendipity

Have you ever set out to find something and along the way, quite by chance, found something else even more interesting? Something you weren't even looking for?

There is a word we use for this kind of unexpected discovery — **serendipity**. It's a relatively new word in our language. It was made up by the English writer Hugh Walpole, who lived from 1717 to 1797. He made up the word after reading an old folktale, "The Three Princes of Serendip." (Serendip is the old name for the island of Ceylon. It is now called by still another name — Sri Lanka.) In this story, a king sends three princes to look for a secret way to kill dragons. The princes wander for years. They have adventures far and wide. Although they never find the dragon-killing formula, they discover many other wonderful treasures — ones they were not even looking for.

Serendipity does not happen only in folktales. It happens in everyday life. And it happens to all of us. You will see how adventures and serendipitous discoveries are experienced by some of the characters in the stories you are about to read. Some of the adventures and discoveries are quiet and personal. Some are record-breaking and grand. As you read these stories, think about what you are discovering. Perhaps one of the stories will lead to an adventure or a serendipitous experience for you.

Realistic Fiction

A story that is fiction is one that is made up. A story that is **realistic fiction** contains events and characters that seem real. In this kind of story, you read about characters who are like the people you know in real life. They live in apartments, shop in stores, and have problems just like real people. They speak, act, grow, and learn from their experiences just like you. Even though the characters and events are made up by an author, they are believable and seem real.

A realistic fiction story has never really happened. It only seems as if it could have happened. Because it seems so real, realistic fiction can give you a look into the lives of others. It can also show you something about your own life.

Another kind of fiction, **fantasy**, is very different from realistic fiction. The world in a fantasy story is never mistaken for our world. Fantasy characters are clearly not real. They are characters of the world of imagination. They may be elves, princes, or people of a time to come. Characters in fantasies live in worlds of magic where anything can and does happen. Animals talk, people fly, and things appear and disappear. Nothing is impossible in the world of fantasy.

Nonfiction is the opposite of realistic fiction and fantasy. Nonfiction stories tell about *real* people, events, and subjects. Nonfiction stories may tell about anything from the first climb of Mount Everest in 1953 to the way that a handicapped girl today is learning to communicate.

Sometimes nonfiction stories give information about a subject. This kind of nonfiction story may help the reader to learn about everything from computers to the habits of a particular animal. We read this kind of nonfiction not for the story, but to learn factual information.

Practice recognizing realistic fiction, fantasy, and nonfiction. Read each of the groups of sentences below. Identify what kind of story each group of sentences is from.

1. One of the first electronic computers was called ENIAC. It was a 30-foot by 50-foot giant that filled a room as big as a school gym.

2. It was exactly two months since Chester Cricket had arrived in New York. He and his two friends, Tucker Mouse and Harry Cat, wanted to celebrate the anniversary.

3. Jess's straw-colored hair flapped hard against his forehead as he ran. His arms and legs flew out every which way.

As you read the stories in this unit, think about whether they are realistic fiction. Do the characters in the story seem like real people? Do the characters remind you of anyone you know? What is realistic about their experiences? If the story is not realistic fiction, why not? What is it about the story that makes it fantasy or nonfiction? An awareness of these things will help you to better appreciate and understand what you read.

Victory gets a homework assignment to do over the weekend. How does serendipity help her do her assignment?

"Dreams of Victory" is a realistic fiction story. But it is through fantasy that Victory manages to complete her assignment. As you read, look for what is real and what is fantasy.

Dreams of Victory

by Ellen Conford

Vicky—short for Victory—is sure that she is a loser. Her very name seems a cruel joke because nothing ever seems to come out right for her. At home her parents pester her about doing her homework. In school things are no better. In the class election for president, she gets an embarrassingly small number of votes. In the class play, she does not get a good part. Instead, she gets a ridiculous role—she has to be *litter* and lie on the floor. And she can't even do that right.

To get away from her failures, she daydreams . . . that she's the first woman President . . . that she's a gold-medal Olympic skater . . . and other wonderful things.

Are her daydreams silly? Or can daydreams lead to very real success?

"All right, class," Mrs. Friedman said, "your homework for the weekend is—"

"Aww," everybody groaned. Homework on a weekend is a crummy idea. Homework on a week-day is bad enough, but at least it only louses up one evening. On a weekend it louses up three nights and two days, because if you don't do it right away Friday afternoon (and who wants to come home Friday afternoon and do homework?) you *think* about having to do it all through Friday night, Saturday and half of Sunday, and it ruins whatever else you're doing while you're not doing the homework. And when you finally *do* get to it, on Sunday night, your parents stand over you and say, "Why do you always leave things for the last minute? You had all *weekend* to do it. . . ." At least mine say that.

"Your assignment for the weekend," continued Mrs. Friedman, ignoring the groans, "is to write a composition—"

"Yucch," said Kenny Clark.

"—about one of these qualities."

She turned to the blackboard—which is not black, but green, and you're supposed to call it the chalkboard, but only Mrs. Friedman calls it that—and wrote:

HUMOR
INTELLIGENCE
IMAGINATION
BEAUTY

"Now what I want you to do is pick the quality that you think is most important, and tell me why."

"I don't get it," Kenny Clark said sullenly. "Most important for what?"

"For whatever you want," Mrs. Friedman replied. "That's up to you to decide."

"I still don't get it."

"It can be the quality you think is most important in your own life, or it can be the quality you feel you like most in other people, or the quality you feel is most necessary to be a success in the world. You decide how and why it's important to you."

Spider Webb raised her hand.

"Should it be a quality you have?" She smoothed her hair behind her ear as she lowered her hand. I could see she was eyeing beauty and trying to figure out a way to write about being beautiful without sounding even more conceited than she already was. I tried to picture her

blown up, like a yellow balloon, puffed out from face to feet with hot air. Then I stuck a pin in her.

"No," Mrs. Friedman said, "as I explained, it can be a quality you admire in somebody else. It all depends on how you approach the idea."

The bell rang.

"How long does it have to be?" Kenny asked as we leaped out of our seats.

"I'm interested in quality, not quantity," Mrs. Friedman said wearily. She must have said that at least fifty times already that year. "Make it as long as it takes to say what you want to say."

"I don't want to say *any*thing," Kenny complained.

"I hate weekend homework," I grumbled to Janey as we climbed onto the bus.

"I hate compositions worst of all," Jane sighed. "I never can think of anything to write."

"Which quality are you going to do?" I asked as we took our seats.

"I don't know," she shrugged. "Who cares, anyway? How do you know what's important? It depends on what you want to be. If you want to be a movie star, beauty's important. If you want to be a scientist, brains are important. It's a dumb assignment."

Spider Webb leaned over the back of our seat.

"I'm writing on Beauty," she announced.

"No!" I gasped, opening my eyes wide. "Really?"
She nodded.

"Don't you think you ought to write about something you know from personal experience?" I asked.

"But I *am*," she said patiently.

I think it's impossible to insult someone who refuses to realize she's being insulted. I guess it never occurs to Spider that she's insultable.

"Why don't you write about intelligence?" I suggested, turning back to Jane. "You're intelligent, and besides, that covers everything. I mean, no matter what you want to be, it always helps to be smart."

"Oh, I don't know," Spider said doubtfully.

"I wouldn't expect you to," I said.

Well, like I figured, that composition ruined my whole weekend. I couldn't write it until I figured out what to write about, and I couldn't figure out what to write about. So I kept putting it off until I could think of what quality I was going to write on, and then, suddenly, it was Sunday night.

"I don't understand it," my mother said, watching me

sitting at the dining room table, staring at a blank sheet of loose-leaf paper. "You had *all weekend* to do this. Why do you leave it for the last minute?"

"What are you doing?" I asked nastily, looking pointedly at the book she was writing in.

"My — uh—lesson plan," she said, a little flustered.

"The apple doesn't fall far from the tree," my father remarked, turning on the television.

"When you and your daughter," my mother began, glaring at my father, "take over the cooking and the cleaning, et cetera, et cetera, I will have my lesson plans done three months in advance. Anyway —" she closed the book with a satisfied snap—"*I'm* finished. What are you watching?"

"It's an interview with Charlotte Holland," he said.

My mother settled down on the couch next to him.

"Oh, the one who wrote *The Sins of Silver City*?"

"Right, that's her."

My mother glanced at my father, then looked over at me.

"Um, Vicky, don't you think you'd better work on that up in your room? You won't be able to concentrate with the TV on."

"Oh, that's okay," I said. "It doesn't bother me."

"But, Victory, I really don't see how —"

"What your mother means," explained my father gently, "is go to your room."

"Good grief," I muttered, gathering up my paper and pen.

I went upstairs and flopped down on my bed, with a book under my paper. I sort of forgot to close the door, so I could still hear the television.

A man was asking Charlotte Holland about this book she had written, which sold so many copies she was now rich and famous.

"You mean to tell me that this book isn't true?" he asked, sounding really surprised.

"Well, I grew up in a town very much like Silver City," the author replied. "But none of the things I wrote about in my book really happened. At least, not that I know of."

"Then you made the whole thing up?"

"Most of it."

I stared at the blank piece of loose-leaf paper in front of me. Sure, I thought, authors don't have this kind of trouble. They just sit down and make things up out of their heads, and before you know it, they've written a whole book, and they sell a million copies and get rich and famous. Now, if I were a writer, one dumb composition would be child's play to me. If I were a writer, I'd . . .

"Okay, Miss Benneker, you're on next." The producer of "The Jerry Griffith Show" patted her shoulder, and pointed toward the opening in the curtain.

"When you're announced, just walk right out and sit down next to Jerry. You're not nervous, are you?"

"Oh, no," she said nervously.

". . . Our next guest, give her a big welcome, Miss Victory Benneker!"

She walked out on stage, and the bright lights in the television studio nearly blinded her.

Victory made her way over to the table where Jerry Griffith sat and slid into the seat next to him.

"Well, Miss Benneker," he smiled, holding up a copy of her book, "so you're the author of this fascinating novel."

"Yes," she said modestly.

"Can I ask you a personal question? How much money have you made from the sales of The Shame of Oakvale?"

"Oh, about a million dollars."

"A million dollars! *Isn't that* fantastic?"

The audience gasped and applauded.

"*Tell me something,*" *he asked confidentially.* "*Is this a true story?*"

"*Well, no, not really,*" *she said, beginning to feel less nervous.* "*Most of it I made up.*"

"*You made it up?*" *he asked incredulously.* "*You made up a million-dollar best seller out of your own head?*"

Victory nodded.

"*What about this character—Beatrice Hive. Bee Hive, you call her.*" *The audience laughed.*

"*Well, she's based on a real person,*" *she admitted.* "*But the rest is all my own ideas.*"

"*All these incredible things that go on in Oakvale, all those fantastic people in your book, I can hardly believe one person could have thought up such a—a fantastic novel. You must have* some *imagination!*"

"*I suppose I do,*" *she said simply.*

"*Fantastic,*" *said Jerry Griffith.* "*Fantastic . . .*"

Sure, if I were a famous writer, this composition would be a cinch. A little imagination, that's all it takes.

I sat up on my bed.

But I *do* have imagination. I must have. How else could I imagine that I was a famous writer? I must have a *lot* of imagination. Why, I could even feel the heat of the television lights, and how nervous I would be—I could hear the applause. Now, if *that* isn't imagination . . .

I turned over onto my stomach and began to write.

Imagination
by Victory Benniker

"All right, class, I've marked your compositions. Some of you did very well. Others—well, I'm afraid some people just didn't seem to understand what this assignment was all about."

Mrs. Friedman started handing back our papers.

"Aww—she gave me a D," Kenny Clark grumbled.

Mrs. Friedman stopped next to his desk.

"No, Kenneth," she said cheerfully. "She didn't give you a D—*you earned* a D."

She finished handing out the papers. Everybody got their paper back—except me. She was holding one paper in her hand—it must be mine!

Oh, no, I thought. I got an F and she's going to tell everybody what a lousy composition it was, and she'll read it, and then she'll hand it back to me, and everyone will know how rotten I did.

I tried to sort of hunch up in my seat, making myself as small and unnoticeable as possible. But Judy Olivera and Jane, who sat near me, could see that I didn't have anything on my desk, so they knew I hadn't gotten my composition back. Jane looked at me questioningly.

"I want you to hear one paper," Mrs. Friedman said, "that really stood out from the rest."

I looked up in surprise. She couldn't mean it stood out because it was so lousy. Could she?

"When I gave you this assignment, this composition," she waved my paper in the air, "is really what I had in mind."

I began to sit up straighter in my chair.

"Victory, will you read this out loud, please?" She held the paper out toward me as I slowly walked to the front of the room.

She handed me my composition, and I smiled with relief as I saw the big red A+ on the top.

I turned to face the class and nervously cleared my throat.

"Imagination. By Victory Benneker. Imagination is one thing that makes man different from animals. A mouse can't imagine he's a lion, but a person can imagine he's anything he wants to be. If you have a bad day, you can imagine what it will be like when you have a good day. If you're afraid to do something, you can imagine what it's like to be brave enough to do *anything*."

Kenny Clark snickered. "Chicken Vicky," he hissed.

"Kenneth—any more of that and we'll have you read *your* composition so the class can hear what a D paper sounds like."

Kenny slumped down in his seat.

"Whatever you want in life," I continued reading, "is right there in your head. You can be rich, famous,

anything you ever dreamed of, just by using a little imagination.

"Imagination is important, and not just for dreaming things up in your head. All the great books that were ever written were thought up in somebody's imagination. Somebody had to imagine the airplane before it was invented. Somebody had to imagine the telephone before Alexander Graham Bell actually made one. Everything that was ever invented or created by man had to be dreamed up in someone's imagination.

"So no matter what you want to be, or what you want to have, you have to imagine it first. Because imagination isn't only fun. It's something you need all through your life.

"As a matter of fact, if it weren't for imagination, I never could have written this composition. The End."

"Thank you, Victory," Mrs. Friedman said.

I walked back to my desk. Judy Olivera was staring at

me like she didn't recognize me. Jane looked at me like I was suddenly an entirely different person. Mark Vogel was frowning and nodding his head. Kenny Clark was balancing a pencil on the toe of his shoe.

"You see," Mrs. Friedman said, "what Victory did was to describe a quality, and explain what the quality was, how it worked, and what makes it important to people. And she wrote about it well — and with imagination! That was exactly what I had in mind when I gave you this assignment. Anybody want to make any comments about this?"

Everybody started buzzing at once.

"Yes, Mark?"

"It's true, what she said. I mean, a man, he can think about being something different, and if he can't be different, no matter how hard he tries, he can always pretend in his mind that he is. I mean — and then maybe, someday, he will be. Different, I mean."

"And you can sort of — daydream," Jimmy Fallon broke in. "I mean, like little kids do, you know — pretend." He sounded sort of embarrassed.

"Not only little kids daydream, Jimmy. Everybody does, sometimes. As Victory said, it's part of being a human being."

I sat straight up in my seat, listening to everyone talking about my composition. A lot of kids were waving their hands in the air, anxious for Mrs. Friedman to call on them. And they were all saying how I was right, and my composition was true, and they knew exactly what I meant.

I didn't say anything. I just sat there. I felt myself smiling and smiling, and I couldn't stop.

The bell rang, and Jane and Judy collected their books and came up to my desk.

"Wow," Janey said, "I've known you almost my whole life, and I didn't know you could write that well."

"Yeah," Judy said. "You must have lots of it — I mean, imagination."

"I guess so," I said.

"You ought to be a writer," Judy said. "I'll bet you'd be famous some day."

". . . And they tell me, Victory, that your book has sold a million copies already. Isn't that fantastic?"

"Yeah," Jane was agreeing, "and we can say we knew you before you were famous, when you were struggling over compositions in the sixth grade!"

". . . fantastic!"

1. How did serendipity help Victory do her homework assignment?
2. Why did Victory's attitude toward herself and her writing abilities change?
3. How did you feel about the ideas in Victory's composition?
4. How did a fantasy solve a realistic problem for Victory?
5. When did you first begin to believe that Victory might have done well on her homework assignment? Find that part of the story.

A story that has made-up characters and events that seem real is called realistic fiction. The characters in a realistic fiction story are like the people you know in real life.

1. Explain what makes "Dreams of Victory" realistic fiction.
2. What part of the story is fantasy?
3. How did the author of this story make Victory Benneker seem like a real person?

Prewrite

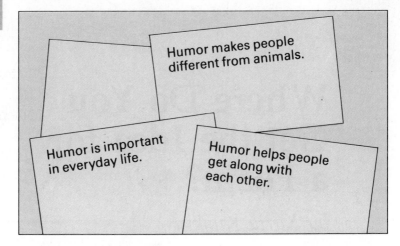

Humor makes people different from animals.

Humor is important in everyday life.

Humor helps people get along with each other.

Before you write a composition, it is important to organize your ideas. Making notes about what you want to say is one way to organize your ideas. The note cards above list some of the important ideas that Victory Benneker might have included in a composition titled "Humor." Make a note card about one other important idea that could be included in a composition about humor.

Compose

Refer to all the note cards to write a composition about humor. Use the sentence on each note card as the topic sentence of a new paragraph. Follow each topic sentence with supporting sentences that explain or give examples of your opinion.

Revise

Read your composition. Make sure that each supporting sentence explains or gives an example for that paragraph's topic sentence. If not, revise your work.

Where Do You Get the Idea for a Poem?

by Karla Kuskin

Where do you get the idea for a poem? . . .
Does it shake you awake?
Do you dream it asleep?
. . . [Does it] pop from your pen
When you are not aware
Or leap from your pocket
Or fall from your hair
Or is it just silently
Suddenly
There?

21

There has probably never been a more unusual dinner party than the one held by Chester Cricket and his friends. Find out how an unexpected accident causes their celebration to become an adventure.

As you read, think about why this story is not realistic fiction.

The Cricket in Times Square

by George Selden

To his great surprise, and quite by accident, Chester, a cricket, has been carried in a picnic basket from the beautiful fields of Connecticut to New York City. Tired, hungry, and lost, he hops into a newsstand in the Times Square subway station. There he is lucky enough to make three wonderful friends. He meets Mario, the boy whose parents own the newsstand. He also makes two other friends, Harry the cat and Tucker the mouse.

Mario has taken Chester to Chinatown and found a beautiful Oriental cricket cage for him. Now Mario has gone home, and it is night. The cricket, the mouse, and the cat are getting ready to have a party. It will be a celebration for Chester, who has been with them for two months in the city.

Late one night Chester Cricket was very busy inside the newsstand. As soon as the Bellinis went home, he hopped out of the matchbox and began to clean up. First he pushed in the box so its sides were even and then slid it over beside the alarm clock. Next he pulled a piece of tissue out of the box and dragged it back and forth across the shelf. When the shelf was dusted, he picked up the tissue paper in his two front legs and polished the cricket cage so its bars shone. He wiped off the glass in the front of the alarm clock and the radio too until he could see his own reflection. The dial of the clock was luminous and it shed a very soft green light. Chester wanted everything to be perfect on this particular evening. There was going to be a party.

It was exactly two months since Chester had arrived in New York, and he and his friends, Tucker Mouse and Harry Cat, wanted to celebrate the anniversary. Nothing too formal, you understand — just a little dinner for everyone. Tucker Mouse had volunteered to let them use the drain pipe, but Chester didn't want to eat amidst all the waste paper and rubbish his friend had collected. So after many conferences, they resolved on the newsstand. It was sheltered, and quite big enough, and the radio could provide nice background music.

Tucker Mouse jumped up beside Chester. "How is the food coming, Tucker?" asked the cricket. Tucker had been put in charge of refreshments.

"Hic hic hic," laughed Tucker Mouse, rubbing his front feet together, "wait till I tell you." He lifted up one foot. "I have: two chunks of liverwurst, one slice of ham, three pieces of bacon — from a bacon, lettuce, and tomato sandwich — some lettuce and tomato — from said sandwich — whole-wheat, rye, and white crusts, a big gob of coleslaw, four squares from a chocolate bar—with nuts!—and now comes the climax." Tucker paused. "Iced soft drinks!"

"How did you get the ice?" asked Chester.

"Wait, I'll tell you," said Tucker. "All day I've been hiding by the lunch counter. When the soda jerks made a drink I grabbed the ice they spilled, which I then took to the drain pipe. There," he went on with special pride, "it happens I have a heat-proof, insulated bag saved up for just such an occasion. I put in the ice, shut up the opening—we have ice! Nice, eh?"

He sat back on his haunches and grinned at Chester.

"Very nice," said Chester. "Where are the drinks?"

"In paper cups," said Tucker. "And no mixing of drinks either. For each kind of soft drink—another cup."

"That's wonderful," said the cricket with admiration.

"Oh, it's nothing really," said Tucker, waving a foot. "I mean, it's something — but nothing too much." He looked around at the shelf and clock and everything. "You are to be congratulated on the cleanliness. Of course it isn't as important as food-getting, but to be clean is very nice too."

While they were talking, Harry Cat came in through the opening at the side of the newsstand. Chester hopped down, like a good host, to greet his new guest.

"How was the concert?" he asked. Harry had been down to Washington Square to hear an open air concert of chamber music.

"Very good," answered Harry. "But I don't think the violinist played nearly as well as you do."

It made Chester very happy to hear that, but he had to turn away so Harry wouldn't see him blush.

"Harry, help me with the food," said Tucker. He jumped down to the floor and hurried over to the drain pipe.

The mouse and the cat put all the different courses over to one side with the soft drinks so everyone could just go up and help himself. It was buffet style. Tucker and Chester sat on the shelf and Harry, who was taller, sat on the stool. But his head was on a level with theirs.

Tucker Mouse took great pride in cooling the soft drinks. There were four cups, one with grape soda, one with cola, one root beer, and the last orange pop. Tucker put a big piece of ice in each and then made a show of stirring them up with a straw he had found that afternoon.

"Ah," he sighed. "Where but New York could a mouse have ice in his soda?"

"We should have music," said Harry. He reached over and turned on the radio.

First they got a news report. But that wouldn't do for a party. Harry twisted the dial and went through a quiz show, an amateur hour, and a play about the deep South before he got what he wanted. Music is very nice for a party because it gives you time to eat your fill without having to make conversation.

Harry Cat was working on his second piece of chocolate when he suddenly stopped chewing and listened to the tune the radio was playing. His head began to sway from side to side.

"That's my favorite song," he said, beginning to hum along with it.

"Sing it, Harry," said Chester Cricket.

"You don't know what you're letting yourself in for," blurted out Tucker Mouse through a mouthful of bacon, lettuce, and tomato sandwich.

But Harry was in a party mood, so he cleared his throat and began:

"When I'm calling youuuuuuuu
Ooooo-ooooooo-oooooo
Ooooo-ooooooo-oooooo —"
Harry had a delightful howl that went very well with the
lyrics of the song.
"You see what I told you?" groaned Tucker.

Harry went right on, however:

"Will you answer truuuuuu

Oooo-oooo-oooo

Oooo-oooo-oooo?"

"Maybe we should turn back to the amateur hour," said Tucker Mouse, helping himself to some chocolate.

"I think Harry sings beautifully," said Chester.

"You sing now, Chester," said Harry Cat.

Secretly the cricket was very anxious to perform for them, but he had to have some encouragement first. He limbered his wings and said, "It's not really singing, you know —"

"Singing, playing — who cares, as long as it doesn't sound like Harry," said Tucker Mouse. He slurped up the last of the orange soda and they all fell silent.

It was well along in August by now, and just the time of the year that crickets all over the world like most. Chester hadn't done nearly as much chirping as usual this summer because he was living in New York, but tonight he played to his heart's content. He thought of his favorite spots back when he had lived in the country — his meadow and the stump, the brook and the old willow tree. The song swelled up from his wings as he rubbed them together rapidly.

When it was over, Tucker and Harry applauded and congratulated Chester. "Now play us something we know," suggested Harry Cat.

"Well, I don't know if I can," said Chester. "All my songs are my own compositions."

"Listen to the radio and play what it does," said Harry. He turned up the music.

Chester cocked his head on one side. The radio was playing the "Blue Danube Waltz." When he had heard enough to memorize the melody, Chester joined in. And he played it perfectly! The cricket was such a natural musician that he not only chirped the tune—in a few minutes he was making up variations and spinning them out without ever losing the rhythm of the waltz. He found that by tilting his wings he could make the notes go higher or lower, just as he wanted.

Chester got an ovation from his friends. Harry Cat, who had crept into the Metropolitan Opera House a few times and knew how people acted there, shouted, "Bravo, Chester! Bravo!" Of course after such a sample of his talent for imitating songs, his friends insisted that he keep on. And Chester was happy to oblige. There's nothing like a good audience to encourage a performer.

The next selection from the radio was a group of Italian folk songs. Chester picked out the different melodies and chirped them along with the orchestra. After the folk songs came a group of operatic arias. It was easier for Chester to play the ones written for tenors than the ones for sopranos, contraltos and basses, but he did them all beautifully.

Each time he stopped after singing a new piece, his friends shouted, "More! More! More!" So Chester went right on. Now came a South American rhumba. The rhythm was very tricky and it took the cricket a few minutes to catch on to it, but once he had it, he never lost the beat. Chirping away, he sounded like a pair of lively castanets.

"Imagine!" exclaimed Tucker Mouse. "He plays pop as well as classical."

Tucker was feeling very lively himself because of all the soda water he had swallowed. The South American tempo began to excite him. He jumped up and started to dance around the shelf.

Harry Cat burst out laughing, but that didn't bother Tucker. He was a carefree soul. "Chester can play—I can dance," he panted. "We should go into vaudeville."

"If you danced as well as he played, you could," said Harry.

"So I'm just learning," said Tucker and threw himself into a wild twirl next to Papa Bellini's pipe.

He couldn't see where he was going and he toppled over into the box of kitchen matches. The box flipped over. A shower of matches fell around the shelf and onto the cement floor. There were several yellow bursts and the sharp scratch that a match makes when it's lit. Most of them fell far enough away from the wooden walls so they could burn themselves out without danger. But one match, unluckily, struck right next to a pile of that morning's newspapers. The spurt of flames it sent up lit the frayed edge of the papers and quickly spread over the whole bundle.

"Watch out!" shouted Chester. Harry Cat leaped up to the shelf just in time to keep his tail from being burned. The cricket was the first to realize what had happened— and what was likely to happen if they didn't put the fire out. "Get the soda," he said. "Pour it over."

"I drank it all," shouted Tucker.

"You would!" said Chester. "Is there any ice?"

Harry and Tucker dumped what was left in the insulated bag down on the flames. But it wasn't enough. The fire sputtered, died down and then flared up again, larger than ever.

"Maybe we can smother it," said Harry.

There was a pile of magazines on the very edge of the shelf, just above the fire. Harry strained and pushed and

succeeded in toppling them over. They all peered over the edge to see if the fire was out.

"Oh fine!" said Tucker. "It's still burning and you blocked the hole to get out!"

They were trapped. Harry and Tucker jumped down and started pulling away the magazines furiously. But the fire crept closer and they had to back away. "What a way to go," said Tucker. "I should have stayed on Tenth Avenue."

For a moment Chester got panicky. But he forced his thoughts back into order and took stock of the situation. And an idea struck him. In one leap he jumped onto the alarm clock, landing right on the button that set off the alarm. The old clock began ringing so wildly it shook itself around the shelf in a mad dance. Chester hopped back to his friends.

"Any alarm in a fire," he said.

They waited, crouched against the wall. On the opposite side of the stand the flames were lapping against the wood. Already the paint on it had begun to blister.

Chester could hear voices outside the newsstand. Even at this hour there were always a few people in the station. Somebody said, "What's that?"

"I smell smoke," said another. Chester recognized the voice. It was Paul, the conductor on the shuttle train. There was a sound of footsteps running away, then running back again, and a hammering began. The newsstand shook all over.

"Somebody get the other side," said Paul.

The cover was wrenched off. Clouds of smoke billowed up. The people standing around were astonished to see, through the fumes and glare of the fire, a cat, a mouse, and a cricket, running, jumping, to safety.

1. How did an unexpected accident cause the dinner celebration to become an adventure?
2. Suppose that Paul, the shuttle train conductor, had caught Chester Cricket and demanded to know what had been going on all evening. What answer might Chester Cricket have given?
3. What do you think of the way the animals behaved when the fire started?
4. How did the animals solve the problems created by the burning newsstand?
5. When did you first know that there would be trouble at the party? Find that part of the story and tell about it.

Apply
the
Skills

In a realistic fiction story, characters and events seem real. In a fantasy story, characters and events are clearly imaginary.

1. Why isn't "The Cricket in Times Square" realistic fiction?
2. What type of story is this? Explain the reasons for your answer.

Prewrite

1. To celebrate his two-month anniversary in New York, <u>Chester decided to give a party.</u>

2. When Harry heard his favorite song on the radio _____

3. Tucker began to dance because _____

_____

4. A fire started when _____

_____

5. When Paul uncovered the newsstand _____

_____

A *cause* is the reason why something happens. An *effect* is what happens. The box above contains incomplete sentences that state causes and effects. The first sentence has been finished for you. Copy and complete the rest of the sentences with either a cause or an effect. You may refer to the story.

Compose

Using the sentences from the box as a guide, write a summary of "The Cricket in Times Square." Include at least two more sentences that contain causes and effects.

Revise

Read your summary to make sure that each sentence contains a cause and an effect. Revise any sentences that do not summarize the story.

Context Clues

A **clue** is a hint or piece of evidence that helps to solve a problem or mystery. When we hear the word *clue*, we think of a detective solving a mystery.

When you find a word that is not known to you, you can become a detective. You can use clues to solve a word mystery. These clues are called **context clues**. Context clues are the words and phrases around a word that give a hint to its meaning.

Practice using context clues in the following story. Read the story, paying special attention to the underlined words. Look for context clues around each underlined word to help you figure out its meaning.

"Hi, Annie," Mrs. Morris called over the backyard fence. "Come and sample a peach."

Mrs. Morris was standing next to her peach tree, holding a basket of peaches. "I just picked these. I can tell they're ready to eat. Feel how <u>succulent</u>, or full of juice, they are. Here, try this one. But be careful, don't drip peach juice on your clothes."

"Oh, I'll be careful," Annie said as she took her first bite. "This is delicious! You know, Mrs. Morris, peaches are my favorite fruit. When I grow up I think I'll plant a large group of peach trees all around my house. I would enjoy living in an <u>orchard</u>. Thanks for the peach, Mrs. Morris. I'd better get back to my gardening."

"It was nice <u>conversing</u> with you, Annie."

"It was nice talking to you, too, Mrs. Morris."

Look back at the first underlined word in the story, *succulent*. The word *succulent* means "full of juice." The author gave you the meaning of the word in a context clue right in the same sentence.

Sometimes the author of a story gives a word's meaning elsewhere in the selection. Then you have to look for context clues in sentences before or after the unknown word to find its meaning. Reread the sentences around the word *orchard* to find its meaning. Did you guess that *orchard* means "a large group of trees"?

Find the underlined word *conversing* in the story. Use context clues to figure out the word's meaning.

For more practice in using context clues, read the paragraph below. Then use context clues to help you choose the correct meaning of the underlined word.

My grandmother does daily <u>calisthenics</u> at home. She knows that the exercises help to keep her body healthy, graceful, and strong. She is sure that this activity is part of what has kept her physically fit.

a. old-fashioned home cooking
b. exercises that promote health, grace, and strength
c. activities for people who are physically fit

In 1869, a fifteen-year-old black boy headed west to begin a cowboy career. Was he headed for a life of adventure?

As you read, remember to use context clues to help you figure out the meaning of unfamiliar words.

Deadwood Dick

by La Vere Anderson

Although we do not often read of them in the stories of our country, many black men and women helped settle the old West. Some were farmers and hunters. Others mined for gold. Some helped lay thousands of miles of railroad track across the country. Others guarded wagon trains going West. Many black men were expert horsemen, cavalrymen, lawmen, and cowboys. Unfortunately, no one wrote about these men when they were living. Much of what they did has been forgotten.

We know about one black cowboy because he wrote his autobiography. His name was Nat Love. From the time he was a small boy, he loved horses. His skill and bravery in riding bucking broncos brought him fame. In the cattle country he was known as "Deadwood Dick."

The small boy stared at the big black horse. The horse was Highwayman. He had never been ridden, and there was a wicked gleam in his eyes. The boy was Nat Love, born a slave in a log cabin near Nashville, Tennessee. He'd been seven years old when the Civil War began. Now the war was over, the slaves were free, and Nat was twelve. He was undersized for his age, but he was a wiry boy.

To help support his mother, Nat worked on the big Williams Horse Ranch a few miles from his home. He earned his money by breaking colts—taming them so they could be ridden.

The young horses did not like to be broken. They ran, jumped, kicked, and tossed. Even mounting such a colt was a problem. He had to be backed into a stall and held until the rider could get a firm seat on his back. Then somebody opened the stall gate, and out into the corral the colt went like a shot.

Rancher Williams's corral had seen some fiery young animals, but Nat always managed to stick to their bare backs. When he had ridden a bucking colt until it could buck no more, the colt was considered broken and Nat collected ten cents for his work. Then he wiped his sweating face, drove a fresh colt into a stall, and managed to get onto its back. He stayed there until he had earned another dime.

Rancher Williams had two sons about Nat's age. On a summer day in 1866, when their father was away, they challenged Nat. "Bet you can't ride Highwayman," one said.

"Bet I can," Nat answered.

"Bet you can't."

Nat took a hard look at the big rough horse. Highwayman was no colt. And he was guaranteed mean.

"Bet I can," Nat said.

It took the efforts of all three boys to get the horse into a stall. As soon as Nat scrambled on his back, Highwayman began to jump. The Williams boys opened the stall gate and sprang aside. Out into the corral shot the furious horse in a leap that almost toppled Nat.

Around the corral Highwayman plunged. Then he jumped the rail fence and galloped off across the green fields. Nat yelled. The Williams boys shouted. Every dog within hearing began to bark and run after the horse. Highwayman galloped across an open pasture where mares grazed with their colts. Mothers and babies promptly joined the race.

The noisy parade attracted the attention of some ranchers. "It looks like a runaway!" they said.

Hurriedly they mounted their horses and started in pursuit, but nobody could catch Highwayman. Nat, all hunched up like a toad, clung to the horse's mane. He couldn't stop the horse and he couldn't get off without falling off and perhaps breaking his neck.

Highwayman easily outran his followers. He covered miles. He jumped fences as if they were anthills. His black hide glistened with sweat, and his breath came hard. At last he began to tire. His pace slowed. He came to another fence, but he had no heart to jump it. He stopped.

Cautiously Nat sat up. He smiled with relief and stroked the horse's steaming shoulder. "Good boy," he said. "Good old Highwayman."

"You're the best rider in Tennessee!" the Williams boys shouted when Nat rode into the corral on his well-broken mount.

"Thanks," said Nat, at the moment feeling that he never wanted to see a horse again. Yet soon he was breaking another colt. He kept his job for three years.

By then, Nat had heard that there were large cattle
ranches in the western part of the United States where
good horsemen were needed to handle the herds. And
he had saved a little money.

"I'm good with horses," he thought. "If I go out there
I can get a real job with real pay."

He told his mother, "Mama, here is half of my money.
It should last until I can send you some more. I'm going
out West and get a ranch job."

Quick tears came to his mother's eyes, but she nodded her head. "It will be hard to see you go, son, but I'll
not try to stop you," she said. "There are too many poor
boys in Tennessee and hardly any work for them. You'll
have a better chance to make something of yourself out
West."

On a February morning in 1869, fifteen-year-old Nat
Love left Tennessee. Over his shoulder he carried a

cloth sack. It held some cornbread and bacon and an extra pair of socks.

It was a long way from Tennessee to the West. Nat tramped down icy roads and across frozen fields. Sometimes he got a ride on a farm wagon. Sometimes, in return for some wood chopping, a farmer's wife gave him a hot meal. Spring had come before he reached a little frontier town in Kansas where cattle from western ranches were shipped by railroad to markets in the East.

When Nat arrived in town he found the streets alive with cowpunchers. He watched in amazement as the punchers, whooping and firing their guns, galloped by on their tough range ponies. He soon learned that these men had just collected their pay for driving a herd of longhorn cattle up from Texas, and they wanted to celebrate. He saw that there were some black cowboys among them.

"I'm not the first man born in a slave cabin to get the idea of coming West," he thought.

The next morning Nat went to the herders' camp outside of town and asked the boss if he needed help.

"Can you ride a wild horse?" the boss asked.

"Yes, sir."

The boss turned to a cowboy. "Bronco Jim, go out and rope old Good Eye. We'll see if this fellow can ride."

As Bronco Jim saddled Good Eye, he whispered to Nat, "Watch out for this critter. He's a bad one — mean as they come."

Confidently, Nat swung onto the horse while the grinning Texans watched. Whee! Years later Nat would tell how Good Eye was the worst horse he had ever ridden. But as with Highwayman, Nat rode because he couldn't get off without falling off. And how the Texans cheered! They had been ready to make a fool of Nat when they thought he was a tenderfoot, but they had respect for a good rider.

"I'll pay you thirty dollars a month," the surprised camp boss told Nat when the ride was over. "We leave at sunup tomorrow for the Red River and Texas. What's your name?"

"Nat Love."

"We already have a Nat in this outfit. We'll call you Dick." The boss paused. "That's hardly enough name. Let's make it Red River Dick."

So Nat Love of Tennessee became Red River Dick of Texas.

They gave him a horse, a saddle, a bridle, and spurs. They gave him tough leather chaps to wear over his patched trousers, boots, a pair of warm blankets, and a .45 Colt revolver. Proudly Nat put on his new outfit and paraded around camp. He wished that his mother could see him now.

A cowboy's life—Nat Love in Tennessee could never have imagined what the real thing was like. But Red River Dick took to "cowboying" as though he had been born on the range.

Nat soon felt a genuine love for the wild free life of the plains and for the cowboys who were his comrades. He thought a braver, truer set of men never lived. They were always ready to share their blankets or their last bit of food with a needy companion. When trouble struck—and it struck often—many a cowboy risked his life to save another.

The work on a cattle ranch was hard. Nat learned to rope and brand wild cattle, and to spend long hours in the saddle driving the slow herds up the dusty cow trails to northern markets. He learned to brave lightning and hailstorms and stampedes.

After three years in Texas, Nat moved to Arizona to work for a larger outfit. For years he rode the ranges and covered all the trails south to Mexico and north to the Dakotas.

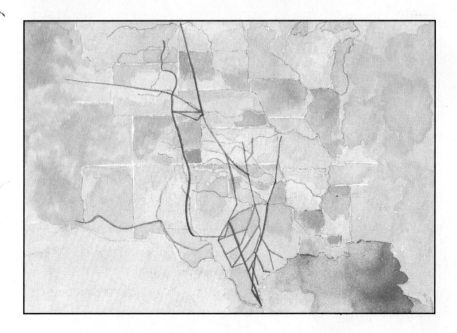

He learned to speak Spanish and to read and write. He became known as a "top hand" and the hero of many a fight on the trail. Nat had been wise to travel to the West and to learn a trade well in a land where few good men were to be found. On western ranches a man was respected for the job he could do. Blacks and whites worked together and shared the same dangers and the same campfires.

Nat had dozens of stories to tell about his feats. But if anyone still doubted that Nat was a great all-round cowboy, they lost those doubts on July 4, 1876, in Deadwood City in the Dakota Territory.

That spring Nat's Arizona outfit had an order for 3,000 head of steers to be delivered near Deadwood. It was a large order, but they filled it and arrived in Dakota on July third with their herd in good shape.

Deadwood at holiday time was a lively place. Every puncher from miles around had come to town to celebrate the Fourth.

Some of the men arranged a roping contest. Twelve mustangs—the most vicious dozen of the lot—were cut

from a herd of wild horses just off the range. The idea was that the dozen competing cowboys were each to rope, throw, tie, bridle, saddle, and mount a particular mustang in the shortest possible time. The fastest time would win.

When all was ready, the starting gun cracked. Out sprang the twelve cowboys together, each making for his mount. Nat's trail boss had picked the mustangs, and the one Nat got was the worst of the bunch. The horse had no name, but before Nat could rope and tie it, he had his own name for the animal—Red Hot Mustard!

When Nat finally mounted the furious horse, there was nothing to be seen for a moment but dust and hoofs. The mustang bucked and kicked. It reared on its hind legs. It doubled up like a jackknife. It did everything but lie down and roll over on its rider. All the while a whooping Nat kept "sticking in" with his spurs, and using his whip on the horse's flanks. Riding the mustang was not part of the contest, but Nat was having fun.

His time in mounting had been exactly 9 minutes. The next best was 12½ minutes. That made Nat the winner.

"Red River Dick! The Champion!" a boy shouted.

Then a man's louder voice yelled, *Deadwood Dick! Champion Deadwood Dick!*"

The crowd took it up. Soon everybody was chanting, "Deadwood Dick!"

And was he proud—Nat Love, the boy from Tennessee!

Years later, Nat Love wrote a book. He called it *The Life and Adventures of Nat Love—Better Known in the Cattle Country as Deadwood Dick.* In it he said his chest swelled with pride because he was an American and had lived in the West and known the men of that frontier— "men whose minds were as broad as the plains they roamed, and whose creed was every man for himself and every friend for each other. . . ."

1. How was Nat Love's life full of adventure?
2. In what ways was Deadwood Dick a top hand?
3. Do you think Nat's mother's decision to allow him to go West was a good decision? Explain.
4. Why did Nat feel proud to have been a cowboy?
5. When did you first begin to think that Nat Love would become a champion rider? Find that part of the story.

Apply

the

Skills

Context clues are the words or phrases surrounding a word that hint at the word's meaning. Context clues can help you to figure out the meaning of unfamiliar words. Use context clues to figure out the meaning of each underlined word below.

1. Nat Love earned money by breaking colts—taming them so they could be ridden.
2. The cowboys all mounted their horses and sped off in pursuit, but nobody could catch the runaway horse.
3. Twelve vicious mustangs were cut from a herd of wild horses captured on the range.
4. Nat and his cowboy friends lived by the creed "every man for himself and every friend for each other. . . ."

Prewrite

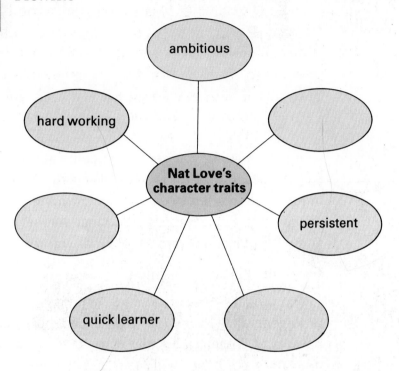

This diagram might be called an "ideaburst." The words in the center, *Nat Love's character traits*, are a central idea. The surrounding words name some of Nat's character traits. Copy the ideaburst and complete it by adding three additional character traits.

Compose

Write a description of Nat Love's character using the ideas in the ideaburst. Give examples of Nat Love's character traits.

Revise

Reread your character description. Make sure that you have included sentences that give examples of each of Nat Love's character traits.

Make Generalizations

In your reading you very often come across a series of facts. A **generalization** is a broad statement that shows how the facts are related to each other. Forming your own generalizations and recognizing those that authors make will help you understand and remember what you read.

Forming Generalizations

You probably already know how to make generalizations, or to **generalize**, from your own experience. Perhaps you have a cat. You observe that your cat jumps well. Your neighbor's cat jumps well, too. In fact, every cat you have ever seen jumps well. From these facts you might generalize that all cats jump well.

You can use the same method when you read. Notice the facts, figure out how they are related, and make a broad general statement that ties all the facts together.

Try it as you read the following facts. Ask yourself these questions: "How are these facts related?" and "What broad, general statement can I make to tie the facts together?"

Scotties were originally bred to catch rats. Cairns were originally bred to catch rats. Westies were originally bred to catch rats. Scotties, Cairns, and Westies are types of dogs called terriers.

What relationships did you find in the facts? The statements tell you that Scotties, Cairns, and Westies were all bred to catch rats. The statements also tell you that these dogs are all terriers. What broad, general statement would tie these facts together? One generalization might be: *Terriers were originally bred to catch rats.*

Recognizing Generalizations

Now that you know what generalizations are, you can try to find them as you read. Just ask yourself these questions: "What are the facts?" and "What broad, general statement has the author made about the facts?"

The following paragraph contains some facts about dogs. What generalization do the authors make from the facts?

> Collies can be trained to herd sheep. Setters are good hunting dogs. German shepherds are often used as guide dogs for the blind. Many dogs perform useful work.

Did you find the author's generalization? It is the last sentence: *Many dogs perform useful work.* Why is that a generalization? It is a broad, general statement that shows how all the facts in the selection are related.

Considering the Facts

True, valid generalizations are based on several facts. A generalization based on only one or two particular cases is unreliable.

See if you can tell what is wrong with the generalization in the last sentence of the following paragraph.

> I like books about horses. My friend Zeke also likes books about horses. Everybody likes to read books about horses.

Did you find the error? The generalization is based on too few facts. The two cases reported in the paragraph are not enough evidence to prove that *everybody* enjoys reading books about horses.

When you make a generalization, be sure that it does not go beyond the facts you have.

When you come across a generalization in your reading, ask yourself, "Is this a valid generalization, based on the facts?" "Or does it go beyond the facts the author has given?"

Qualifying Words in Generalizations

As you read the following paragraph, think about how the facts in it are related to each other.

Dogs can hear sounds that are pitched too high for the human ear. They can also detect smells that are imperceptible to the human nose. Owls can see in near-total darkness. Bats' hearing is so acute that they can judge distance from the echoes made by their own voices.

Read the following generalizations. Which one is the best generalization about the facts in the paragraph?

1. All animals have senses that are better than human senses.
2. Some animals have senses that are better than human senses.
3. Most animals have senses that are better than human senses.

Look at the example paragraph again. Does it tell you about the senses of all animals? No. Does it tell you about the senses of most animals? No. Therefore, sentences 1 and 3 are not valid generalizations.

Does the example paragraph tell you about some animals' senses? Yes, it does. Sentence 2 is a valid generalization.

Generalizations often contain qualifying words, such as *some, all, most, many, several, none, a few, always, often, sometimes,* or *never.* When you read, watch for these words. They may give you the clue that a generalization is being made.

When you write, use qualifying words to help make your generalizations valid. Choose the qualifying words carefully. Use words, such as *all, every,* and *always* only when your facts cover all cases. Otherwise, use words such as *some, several,* and *sometimes.*

Textbook Application: Generalizing in Science

Textbooks contain facts. They also contain generalizations. A generalization is a broad statement that shows how the facts are related to each other. Recognizing generalizations from the facts that are given will help you understand and remember what you read.

To find a generalization in a textbook, ask yourself, "What broad, general statement has the author made about the facts?" Qualifying words such as *all, some, many, most, several, none, a few, always, often, sometimes,* and *never* are clues that a generalization is being made. Check the accuracy of the generalizations by asking yourself, "Is this a valid generalization that is based on facts and does not go beyond them?"

To form your own generalization, first decide how the facts are related. Then make a broad, general statement that ties the facts together. Be careful not to go beyond the facts. Use an appropriate qualifying word.

Here is a selection from a science book. Read it to yourself. The sidenotes will help you find the generalizations and decide whether they are valid.

First the authors give some facts. Then they generalize. What is their generalization?

It takes less force to pull a block over a waxed surface than over an unwaxed surface. Wax reduces friction. Oil also reduces friction. Wax and oil are two lubricants. A **lubricant** is a material used to make a surface slippery. By using a lubricant such as wax or oil, you can reduce friction.

You can reduce friction in another way. You know that it is much easier to roll a ball along a floor than to slide it. If you think about what causes friction, you can see why this is so. *Sliding friction* is caused when two surfaces rub as one moves over the other. When an object rolls on a surface, however, only a small part of the object touches the surface at a time.

Some friction is produced when a wheel rolls over a surface. Yet this friction is much less than the friction produced when an object slides over the surface. Rolling something rather than sliding it produces less friction.

Do you always want less friction? Imagine the soles of your shoes without friction. What would happen if you tried to walk? Reducing friction is not always helpful. Sometimes it is harmful. Why is it a good idea to wipe up any spills from the floor? Friction is sometimes a good thing.

— *HBJ Science*
Harcourt Brace Jovanovich

> Where is the generalization here? Is it justified by all the facts presented so far?

> Here are facts about two kinds of friction. What general statement would show how they are related?

> This paragraph contains three generalizations. What qualifying words are used in them?

Remember to watch for generalizations when you read a selection in a textbook. Finding these broad, general statements and deciding whether they fit the facts will help you understand and remember what you read.

Qualifying for the Olympics is an exciting adventure for anyone. But to Donna deVarona, there was a goal even more important than the Olympics. Did she achieve it?

As you read, remember to use the facts to make your own generalizations.

Donna deVarona, Gold Medal Swimmer

by Bob Thomas

When people are at the top, it seems as though they have everything going for them. Was this true about Donna deVarona?

Donna grew up at a time when girls were not encouraged in athletics. She wasn't allowed to participate in Little League games, even though she could hit and catch as well or better than most of the boys.

Donna wasn't strong. To help build her strength, her father took her for diving lessons. She did well, but it frightened her.

Swimming turned out to be right for her. Yet there were still problems. She was short—five feet two inches—and in swimming, height is important. But Donna was a natural, and soon she began winning. In this selection, she is entering an important race.

"Gee, I'd give anything to win this race," Donna said to Debbie Lee as she pulled on a dry swimsuit. They were sitting in the locker room of the stadium in Indianapolis, where the outdoor nationals were being held. The place was filled with other girls who were waiting to swim in the afternoon events on the first day.

"You've done all right so far," Debbie pointed out. Donna had already raced in three events that day. In the morning she had swum the 100-meter freestyle and the 400-meter individual, and her times were good enough to place her in the finals. That afternoon she had placed third in the 100-meter finals, which indicated she would have a good chance of being a member of the Olympic team when the trials were held in Detroit.

"But it is the 400 that means the most to me," Donna said.

"Why?" Debbie asked. "The race isn't one of the Olympic events."

"I know, but it is still my favorite race. It shows I can be good in every stroke."

Debbie smiled. "I don't suppose the fact that Carol Swenson is also swimming the 400 has anything to do with it?"

"Well, I wouldn't mind beating her," Donna admitted. "But that isn't the entire story. I just want to win that race."

The loudspeaker in the corner of the locker room announced: "Next event — women's 400-meter individual."

"Oh, boy, here it is!" Donna said.

She hurried out into the sunlight and walked briskly toward the starting area. Suddenly she came face to face with Coach Swenson. Donna hadn't seen him since she defeated his daughter Jan at the indoor finals at Bartlesville. She was afraid he might be angry with her, and she didn't want him to be. She had valued his coaching, particularly his insisting on long workouts in every stroke, and she hoped they could remain friends.

She greeted him with a casual, "Hi, Coach."

"Oh, it's you," the coach said. "How do you feel?"

"I'm really nervous," Donna answered honestly.

"Afraid you might lose this time?"

Donna went on to the starting line. Her heart was pounding, and suddenly she realized how nervous she was. When she sat down on the starting blocks, she was trembling and crying. All at once the pressure seemed too great.

"Swimmers, take your marks!"

The familiar words brought Donna back to reality, and she mounted slowly to the starting block. She gazed to the left and saw Coach Swenson's other daughter, Carol Swenson, in position for the start. Now the race seemed impossible. Carol was a perfectly formed five feet eleven inches, a full nine inches taller than Donna. Carol was nineteen years old, six years older than Donna. She had been started in swimming by her father at a much earlier age than Donna and was the world record holder in this event.

She looked to her right and saw Becky Collins, the seventeen-year-old holder of the world's record for the 200-meter butterfly. The race included other previous meet winners and record holders. But Donna had no time left to think about her competition. The race was scheduled to begin in a few seconds.

"One, two, three, four," she counted to herself, and the starting pistol shot rang out.

The start was clean. All eight girls hit the water at the same moment. Immediately the pool was splashing white from the windmill strokes of the butterfly.

Becky Collins took the lead, as expected. At the first turn she was half a length ahead of Carol and Donna. By the end of the butterfly she was a length ahead. Then came the backstroke.

Now Becky was left behind as Donna and Carol pulled ahead of her, almost neck-and-neck. Donna was surprised to find her backstroke working so easily. It had never been a good stroke for her, but by the end of the first 200 meters she had overtaken Carol and was ahead by a length and a half.

The breast stroke lost Donna's lead. Carol's steady stroke brought her into the lead by three-quarters of a length, and now Becky Collins was gaining on Donna for second place. Donna found the breast stroke the most tiring of all. Her entire body began to ache.

She took a flat-handed turn against the end of the pool — pushing off the pool edge with the palm of her hand as she turned — and began the final two laps in the free style.

Becky had used up her reserve strength. Now it became a two-girl race — Carol Swenson and Donna deVarona. The crowd roared at the fury of the competition.

Donna whipped her arms through the water and began gaining on Carol. The lead had been cut to half a length as they approached the final turn.

"I've got to flip this last turn," Donna told herself. "With Carol's height, she's bound to get a better turn if she pushes off. But I could get a faster turn if I flip. Do I have enough reserve strength left?"

She did. She flipped under water — a sort of underwater somersault — and came up to discover she was even with Carol. The finish wall was getting closer and closer, and neither of them gave an inch.

"Can I do it?" Donna wondered. "I don't know, but here goes!"

She took a gulp of air, put her head down and raced through the water until she touched the wall with her fingertips.

Donna didn't have the strength to get out of the pool. She ached in every bone, every muscle. She felt as though she would sink to the bottom of the pool if she didn't grab onto the rope separating the lanes. She was so totally exhausted she couldn't hear the cheers of the crowd in the stadium.

"You won!" shouted Debbie Lee as she leaned over the side and offered a welcome helping hand to lift Donna out of the pool.

"You not only won," added George Haines, who was bending to help on the other side, "you broke the previous world's record by fifteen seconds!"

"I did what?"

"It is official," George Haines said, as other members of the Santa Clara team gathered around Donna. "You won in five minutes thirty-six and five-tenths seconds. You broke Carol Swenson's record."

Donna still couldn't completely believe her victory even after she heard her name over the loudspeaker, even after she was awarded her medal. Only when she returned to her hotel did she realize what had happened. Her first clear thought was that she had to call her parents, back in Lafayette.

It seemed like an eternity before she heard her father's voice on the other end of the phone.

"Dad—guess what happened!"

"You won the 400 individual and set a new world's record," he said at once.

"Oh." Donna was disappointed. "You know already."

"Yes, we know, and so does everyone else in Lafayette. It's being broadcast all over the radio and TV."

"Is it really?"

"Of course! And the local paper has a headline story about Donna deVarona setting a world's record."

"Honest to goodness?"

"I wouldn't kid you. And Donna . . ."

"Yes, Dad?"

"Your mother and I are very proud."

At last she had achieved what she had worked for all those long cold nights at the pool. She had been able to swim one of the toughest of all races faster than any woman ever had done before. And in so doing, she had defeated Carol Swenson and had taken the world's record away from her.

She thought for a moment about Coach Swenson. He had trained her well and had given her the will to succeed. Her father had once told her to concentrate on getting all the benefit she could out of Karl Swenson as a coach. It had worked.

Completely weary, Donna drifted into a deep sleep.

1. What important goal did Donna deVarona have? Did she achieve it?
2. Why did winning the race mean so much to Donna?
3. What part of the story was the most exciting to you? Why?
4. What is one thing Donna did near the end of the race that helped her to win?
5. When did you first realize that Donna appreciated Coach Swenson? Find that part of the story.

In your reading you often come across related facts. Generalizations are broad statements that tie facts together.

Choose one of the following generalizations. Find facts from the story that support that generalization.

1. Donna deVarona was a very determined person.
2. Donna deVarona was proud of her swimming skills and achievements.
3. Donna faced tough competition in the race.

Prewrite

I. Before the race
A. Donna's pre-race feelings
1.
2.
B. Meeting Coach Swenson

II. During the race
A. The first three laps
B. The flip and final lap

III. After the race
A. Tiredness
B. The results
1.
2.

Imagine that you are Donna deVarona. You are preparing to write a personal letter about your record-setting race to your best friend at home in Lafayette. A good way to organize your thoughts is to make an outline. The outline above contains topics and subtopics about the race. Copy and complete the outline by referring to the story.

Compose
Using the outline, write a personal letter that tells about the day of the race. Be sure to include the date, a greeting, and a closing.

Revise
Reread your letter to be sure that it includes all of the topics on the outline as well as the date, a greeting, and a closing.

Food Labels

Every package, whether it is a can, a box, a bottle, or a bag, has a **label.** Many labels are designed to catch your eye as you walk through the supermarket. They have pictures and bright colors. But most labels do much more than catch your eye. They give you important information about what you are getting for your money—if you know how to read them.

Labels on Fresh Foods

Are there labels on all of the fresh foods in your supermarket? Only a very few fresh foods, such as meats and bananas, have labels. Labels are not needed on most fresh fruits and vegetables. Why? Shoppers know, without reading a label, what is inside a tomato or an apple. Nothing has been added to fresh foods. Signs near these foods explain what is being sold and what the cost is. These signs take the place of labels.

Labels on Packaged Foods

Years ago, companies that packaged foods did not have to list all of the food's ingredients on the label. But people who bought these foods wanted to know exactly what was in the foods they were buying and eating. The government listened to these people. Congress passed a law that certain information must be listed on a food label.

By carefully reading a food label, you can discover the following required information:

1. **The usual name of the food**. The common name of the food must be somewhere on the label. Why? If the product name, such as "Fruit Delight," does not give a clear idea of what the food is, the label must state the usual name, mixed fruit juice.

   The name of a product may be especially important for names such as "Turkey with Gravy" or "Gravy with Turkey." Which product would you expect to have more turkey? Which product do you think might cost more?

2. **The weight of the food in the package**. This part of the label tells shoppers how much of the product they are buying.

   The weight of a product is helpful when a shopper is trying to decide which size or brand is a better buy. A 6-ounce can of "Fruit Delight" for 49¢ is not as good a bargain as a 12-ounce can for 89¢.

3. **The ingredients in the food**. One important part of the label tells shoppers exactly what is in the food. It tells what has been added to it, and what ingredients make up the most and least in weight.

   Some foods are canned, frozen, or dried before they are sold. These foods are called **processed foods** because a process was used to make them. In processing, things are sometimes added to foods. These things, such as spices, coloring, or chemicals, are called **additives**.

Additives can be put into foods for several reasons. A chemical additive might be put into a can of peas to keep the peas green. Another additive might be used to keep the peas fresh. A shopper would not know that anything had been added to the peas if that information were not on the label. Each additive must be included in the list of ingredients.

The ingredients in the food must be listed in the order of weight. The ingredient that makes up the most weight will be listed first. The ingredient listed last makes up the least weight. If a can of mixed nuts lists peanuts ahead of cashews, what does that mean?

4. **The name and address of the food distributor**. This part of the label may list the company that processed the food, the company that packaged the food, or the company that sold the food to the store.

   This information is given in case shoppers have questions or complaints about the product.

Labels on cans of vegetables and fruits often also have the following information:

1. **Information for people on special diets.** Words such as *artificially sweetened, low in salt,* or *enriched* may be used. Vitamin and mineral information about the food is given on some packages.

2. **Information about style and medium**. Label information about style might tell whether whole or creamed corn is in a can. Information about medium might tell whether peaches are packed in water or in syrup.

Some states also require food packages to list the date of processing or packaging and the last date of sale. This is important if a shopper wants to buy only the freshest foods.

Comparison Shopping Using Labels

The labels on food packages make it possible to **comparison shop**. A shopper can compare brands to get the most value.

Suppose you were looking for a can of tomato paste and you found three different brands on the store shelf. You might begin your comparison shopping by looking at the prices. Before deciding if you could save money by buying one brand, you would compare the weights listed on the labels. You would then read the ingredients. One brand might list tomatoes, onions, salt, spices, and two chemicals. Another might not have any chemicals. One brand might contain an ingredient, such as garlic, that you don't like. You could use the labels to find the best brand for you at the price you want to pay.

Be a careful shopper. Before buying a package of food, read the label. Look for the information required by law. Does the package contain exactly what you want? Does it contain additives? Reading labels can help you to become a wise shopper.

Few people have seen the ghost of the lagoon. Those who have say it is huge and terrible. Why then does Mako long for the adventure of meeting the ghost?

Read to find out how this story about a ghost can be realistic fiction.

Ghost of the Lagoon

by Armstrong Sperry

The island of Bora Bora, where Mako lived, is far away in the South Pacific. It is not a large island—you can paddle around it in a single day—but the main body of it rises straight out of the sea, very high into the air like a castle. Waterfalls trail down the faces of the cliffs. As you look upward you see wild goats leaping from crag to crag.

Mako had been born on the very edge of the sea, and most of his waking hours were spent in the waters of the lagoon, which was nearly enclosed by the two outstretched arms of the island. He was very clever with his hands; he had made a harpoon that was as straight as an arrow and tipped with five-pointed iron spears. He had made a canoe, hollowing it out of a tree. It wasn't a very big canoe—only a little longer than his own height. It had an outrigger, a sort of balancing pole, fastened to one side to keep the boat from tipping over. The canoe was just large enough to hold Mako and his little dog, Afa. They were great friends, these two.

One evening Mako lay stretched at full length on a mat, listening to Grandfather's voice. Overhead, stars shone in the dark sky. From far off came the thunder of the surf on the reef.

The old man was speaking of Tupa, the ghost of the lagoon. Ever since the boy could remember, he had heard tales of this terrible monster. Frightened fishermen, returning from the reef at midnight, spoke of the ghost. Over the evening fires old men told endless tales about the monster.

Tupa seemed to think the lagoon of Bora Bora belonged to him. The people left presents of food for him out on the reef: a dead goat, a chicken, or a pig. The presents always disappeared mysteriously, but everyone felt sure that it was Tupa who carried them away. Still, in spite of all this food, the nets of the fishermen were torn during the night, the fish stolen. What an appetite Tupa seemed to have!

Not many people had ever seen the ghost of the lagoon. Grandfather was one of the few who had.

"What does he really look like, Grandfather?" the boy asked for the hundredth time.

The old man shook his head. The light from the cook fire glistened on his white hair. "Tupa lives in the great caves of the reef. He is longer than this house. There is a sail on his back, not large but terrible to see, for it burns with a white fire. Once when I was fishing beyond the reef at night I saw him come up right under another canoe—"

"What happened then?" Mako asked. He half rose on one elbow. This was a story he had not heard before.

The old man's voice dropped to a whisper. "Tupa dragged the canoe right under the water—and the water boiled with white flame. The three fishermen in it were never seen again. Fine swimmers they were, too."

Grandfather shook his head. "It is bad fortune even to speak of Tupa. There is evil in his very name."

"But King Opu Nui has offered a reward for him," the boy pointed out.

"Thirty acres of fine coconut land and a sailing canoe, as well," said the old man. "But who ever heard of killing a ghost?"

Mako's eyes glistened. "Thirty acres of land and a sailing canoe. How I should love to win that reward!"

Grandfather nodded, but Mako's mother scolded her son for such foolish talk. "Be quiet now, son, and go to sleep. Grandfather has told you that it is bad fortune to speak of Tupa. Alas, how well we have learned that lesson! Your father—" She stopped herself.

"What of my father?" the boy asked quickly. And now he sat up straight on the mats.

"Tell him, Grandfather," his mother whispered.

The old man cleared his throat and poked at the fire. A little shower of sparks whirled up into the darkness.

"Your father," he explained gently, "was one of the three fishermen in the canoe that Tupa destroyed." His words fell upon the air like stones dropped into a deep well.

Mako shivered. He brushed back the hair from his damp forehead. Then he squared his shoulders and cried fiercely, "I shall kill Tupa and win the king's reward!" He rose to his knees, his slim body tense, his eyes flashing in the firelight.

"Hush!" his mother said. "Go to sleep now. Enough of such foolish talk. Would you bring trouble upon us all?"

Mako lay down again upon the mat. He rolled over on his side and closed his eyes, but sleep was long in coming.

The palm trees whispered above the dark lagoon, and far out on the reef the sea thundered.

The boy was slow to wake up the next morning. The ghost of Tupa had played through his dreams, making him restless. And so it was almost noon before Mako sat up on the mat and stretched himself. He called Afa. Then the boy and his dog ran down to the lagoon for their morning swim.

When they returned to the house, wide-awake and hungry, Mako's mother had food ready and waiting.

"These are the last of our bananas," she told him. "I wish you would paddle out to the reef this afternoon and bring back a new bunch."

The boy agreed eagerly. Nothing pleased him more than such an errand, which would take him to a little island on the outer reef half a mile from shore. It was one of Mako's favorite playgrounds, and there bananas and oranges grew in great plenty.

"Come, Afa," he called, gulping the last mouthful. "We're going on an expedition." He picked up his long-bladed knife and his spear and dashed across the white sand where his canoe was drawn up beyond the water's reach.

Afa barked at his heels. The dog was all white except for a black spot over each eye. Wherever Mako went, there went Afa also. Now the little dog leaped into the bow of the canoe, his tail wagging with delight. The boy shoved the canoe into the water and climbed aboard. Then, picking up his paddle, he thrust it into the water. The canoe shot ahead. Its sharp bow cut through the green water of the lagoon like a knife through cheese. And so clear was the water that Mako could see the coral gardens, forty feet below him, growing in the sand. The shadow of the canoe moved over them.

A school of fish swept by like silver arrows. He saw scarlet rock cod with ruby eyes, and the head of an eel peering out from a cave in the coral. The boy thought suddenly of Tupa, ghost of the lagoon. On such a bright day it was hard to believe in ghosts of any sort. The fierce sunlight drove away all thought of them. Perhaps ghosts were only old men's stories, anyway!

Mako's eyes came to rest upon his spear—the spear that he had made with his own hands—the spear that was as straight and true as an arrow. He remembered his vow of the night before. Could a ghost be killed with a spear? Some night when all the village was sleeping, Mako swore to himself, he would find out! He would paddle out to the reef and challenge Tupa! Perhaps tonight. Why not? He caught his breath at the thought. A shiver ran down his back. His hands were tense on the paddle.

As the canoe drew away from shore, the boy saw the coral reef that above all others had always interested him. It was of white coral—a long, slim shape that rose slightly above the surface of the water. It looked very much like a shark. There was a ridge on the back that the boy could pretend was a dorsal fin, while up near one end were two dark holes that looked like eyes!

Times without number the boy had practiced spearing this make-believe shark, aiming always for the eyes, the most vulnerable spot. So true and straight had his aim become that the spear would pass right into the eyeholes without even touching the sides of the coral. Mako had named the coral reef "Tupa."

This morning as he paddled past it, he shook his fist and called, "Ho, Mister Tupa! Just wait till I get my bananas. When I come back, I'll make short work of you!"

Afa followed his master's words with a sharp bark. He knew Mako was excited about something.

The bow of the canoe touched the sand of the little island where the bananas grew. Afa leaped ashore and ran barking into the jungle, now on this trail, now on that. Clouds of seabirds rose from their nests into the air with angry cries.

Mako climbed into the shallow water, waded ashore, and pulled his canoe up on the beach. Then, picking up his banana knife, he followed Afa. In the jungle the light was so dense and green that the boy felt as if he were moving underwater. Ferns grew higher than his head. The branches of the trees formed a green roof over him. A flock of parakeets fled on swift wings. Somewhere a wild pig crashed through the undergrowth while Afa dashed away in pursuit. Mako paused anxiously. Armed only with his banana knife, he had no desire to meet the wild pig. The pig, it seemed, had no desire to meet him, either.

Then ahead of him the boy saw the broad green leaves of a banana tree. A bunch of bananas, golden ripe, was growing out of the top.

At the foot of the tree he made a nest of soft leaves for the bunch to fall upon. In this way the fruit wouldn't be crushed. Then with a swift slash of his blade he cut the stem. The bananas fell to the earth with a dull thud. He found two more bunches.

Then he thought, *I might as well get some oranges while I'm here. Those little rusty ones are sweeter than any that grow on Bora Bora.*

So he set about making a net of palm leaves in which to carry the oranges. As he worked, his swift fingers moving in and out among the strong green leaves, he could hear Afa's excited barks off in the jungle. That was just like Afa,

always barking at something: a bird, a fish, a wild pig. He never caught anything, either. Still, no boy ever had a finer companion.

The palm net took longer to make than Mako had thought. By the time it was finished and filled with oranges, the jungle was dark and gloomy. Night comes quickly and without warning in the islands of the Tropics.

Mako carried the fruit down to the shore and loaded it into the canoe. Then he whistled to Afa. The dog came bounding out of the bush, wagging his tail.

"Hurry!" Mako scolded. "We won't be home by dark."

The little dog leaped into the bow of the canoe, and Mako came aboard. Night seemed to rise up from the surface of the water and swallow them. On the distant shore of Bora Bora, cook fires were being lighted. The first star twinkled just over the dark mountains. Mako dug his paddle into the water, and the canoe leaped ahead.

The dark water was bright with phosphorus. The bow of the canoe seemed to cut through a pale, liquid fire. Each dip of the paddle trailed streamers of light. As the canoe approached the coral reef the boy called, "Ho, Tupa! It's too late tonight to teach you your lesson. But I'll come back tomorrow." The coral shark glistened in the darkness.

And then suddenly Mako's breath caught in his throat. His hands felt weak. Just beyond the fin of the coral Tupa there was another fin—a huge one. It had never been there before. And—could he believe his eyes? It was moving.

The boy stopped paddling. He dashed his hand across his eyes. Afa began to bark furiously. The great white fin, shaped like a small sail, glowed with phosphorescent light. Then Mako knew. Here was Tupa—the real Tupa—ghost of the lagoon!

His knees felt weak. He tried to cry out, but his voice died in his throat. The great shark was circling slowly around the canoe. With each circle it moved closer and closer. Now the boy could see the phosphorescent glow of the great shark's sides. As it moved in closer he saw the yellow eyes, the gill slits in its throat.

Afa leaped from one side of the canoe to the other. In sudden anger Mako leaned forward to grab the dog and shake him soundly. Afa wriggled out of his grasp as Mako tried to catch him, and the shift in weight tipped the canoe on one side. The outrigger rose from the water. In another second they would be overboard. The boy threw his weight over quickly to balance the canoe, but with a loud splash Afa fell over into the dark water.

Mako stared after him in dismay. The little dog, instead of swimming back to the canoe, had headed for the distant shore. And there was the great white shark — very near.

"Afa! Afa! Come back! Come quickly!" Mako shouted.

The little dog turned back toward the canoe. He was swimming with all his strength. Mako leaned forward. Could Afa make it? Swiftly the boy seized his spear. Bracing himself, he stood. There was no weakness in him now. His dog, his friend, was in danger of instant death.

Afa was swimming desperately to reach the canoe. The white shark had paused in his circling to gather speed for the attack. Mako raised his arm, took aim. In that instant the shark charged. Mako's arm flashed forward. All his strength was behind that thrust. The spear drove right into the great shark's eye. Mad with pain and rage, Tupa whipped about, lashing the water in fury. The canoe rocked back and forth. Mako struggled to keep his balance as he drew back the spear by the cord fastened to his wrist.

He bent over to grab Afa and drag him aboard. Then he stood up, not a moment too soon. Once again the shark charged. Once again Mako threw his spear, this time at the other eye. The spear found its mark. Blinded and weak from loss of blood, Tupa rolled to the surface, turned slightly on his side. Was he dead?

Mako knew how clever sharks could be, and he was taking no chances. Hardly daring to breathe, he paddled toward the still body. He saw the faintest motion of the great tail. The shark was still alive. The boy knew that one flip of that tail could overturn the canoe and send him and Afa into the water, where Tupa could destroy them.

Swiftly, yet calmly, Mako stood upright and braced himself firmly. Then, murmuring a prayer to the Shark God, he threw his spear for the last time. Swift as sound, the spear plunged into a white shoulder.

Peering over the side of the canoe, Mako could see the great fish turn over far below the surface. Then slowly, slowly, the great shark rose to the surface of the lagoon. There he floated, half on one side.

Tupa was dead.

Mako flung back his head and shouted for joy. Hitching a strong line about the shark's tail, the boy began to paddle toward the shore of Bora Bora. The dorsal fin, burning with the white fire of phosphorus, trailed after the canoe.

Men were running down the beaches of Bora Bora, shouting as they leaped into their canoes and put out across

the lagoon. Their cries reached the boy's ears across the water.

"It is Tupa—ghost of the lagoon," he heard their voices shouting.

"Mako has killed him!"

That night as the tired boy lay on his mat listening to the distant thunder of the sea, he heard Grandfather singing a new song. It was the song that would be sung the next day at the feast that King Opu Nui would give in Mako's honor. The boy saw his mother bending over the cook fire. The stars leaned close, winking like friendly eyes. Grandfather's voice reached him now from a great distance, "Thirty acres of land and a sailing canoe. . . ."

1. Why did Mako long for the adventure of meeting the ghost of the lagoon?

2. Why was Grandfather singing a new song at the end of the story? What did his new song seem to be about?

3. What part of the story did you think was the most exciting?

4. How did the words of the king lead to solving the problem of the island?

5. When did you first know that Mako was skilled with a spear? Find that part of the story.

A realistic fiction story contains events and characters that seem real. In this kind of story, the characters are like the people you know in real life.

In "Ghost of the Lagoon," the villagers fear a deadly ghost. Explain how a story that seems to be about a fantastic character — a ghost — can be realistic fiction.

Prewrite

This photograph shows the island of Bora Bora. Look carefully at the photo. What words can you think of to describe the island? Make a list of your descriptive words and phrases. Then underline the ones you think are most colorful or especially clear.

Compose

Imagine that you are a travel agent. Write a paragraph that will persuade people to visit the island of Bora Bora. Tell about the island. You might describe what it looks like, its climate, and what visitors can do there. Use some of the descriptive words and phrases you have listed.

Revise

Reread your paragraph. Ask yourself how you could improve it to make Bora Bora sound even more inviting. As you revise, try to use some of the words and phrases that you listed but did not use before.

Main Idea

The stories and textbook articles that you read are made up of many paragraphs. A paragraph is a group of sentences that have something in common. The thing that they have in common is called the **topic** of the paragraph. The most important information the paragraph gives about the topic is called the **main idea**.

Recognizing the topic and the main idea of a paragraph will help you understand and remember what you read.

Finding the Topic

The topic is what all or most of the sentences in a paragraph are about. As you read the following paragraph, try to decide what the topic is by asking yourself this question: "What does every sentence tell about?"

Sharks' bodies are different from those of other kinds of fish in several ways. For example, a shark does not have bones. Its skeleton is made of cartilage, a tough, elastic material. A shark has several rows of teeth in its mouth. If one tooth is lost, a new one can move forward to take its place. A shark's body is covered with small, toothlike scales. This makes a shark's skin very rough. Sharkskin was once used as sandpaper.

Did you find the topic? What would you say if someone asked you what the paragraph is about? It is about sharks. That is the topic. Every sentence in the paragraph gives some information about this topic.

Finding the Main Idea

Look back at the example paragraph. You can see that it says several things about its topic. The next step is to decide which thing is most important. The most important thing a paragraph says about its topic is the **main idea**. The main idea gives general information about the topic.

Read the paragraph again. This time try to find the sentence with the main idea. Ask yourself this question: "Which sentence gives the most important, most general information about the topic?"

Did you find the main idea? It is stated in the first sentence: *Sharks' bodies are different from those of other kinds of fish in several ways.* That is the sentence that gives the most information about the topic. Each of the other sentences in the paragraph tells only one thing about a shark's body.

The main idea may not always be in the first sentence of the paragraph. It may be given in the last sentence or in one of the middle sentences. See if you can find the topic and the main idea in the following paragraph. First look for the one thing that most sentences say something about. Then find the sentence that gives the most important information about this thing.

> Most sharks eat live fish, including other sharks. Sharks have senses that are well suited for hunting. Their sense of smell is particularly strong. Sharks can smell some odors, such as blood, as far as ¼ mile away. Sharks have excellent hearing. They can hear a fish struggling as far as ½ mile away.

What is the topic of the paragraph? It is *sharks' senses.* Why is this the topic? Most of the sentences tell something about it.

What is the main idea? It is given in the second sentence: *Sharks have senses that are well suited for hunting.* That sentence gives the most information about the topic.

Why isn't the first sentence the main idea sentence? The first sentence does not give important information about sharks' senses. Why aren't the third, fourth, or fifth sentences main idea sentences? Those sentences just give details about the topic.

Stating the Main Idea Yourself

In some paragraphs, the main idea is not stated in a sentence. But you can state the main idea yourself if you figure out the topic and understand what all the sentences are telling you about the topic. Add up all the clues and you will be able to make up a good main idea sentence.

The main idea of the following paragraph is not stated. Use the sentences to figure out the paragraph's main idea. Remember, the main idea is the most important idea about the topic of a paragraph.

Shark hide makes a long-lasting leather after the scales are removed. People in many parts of the world eat shark meat. The Chinese use shark fins in making soup. Today, sharks are used in scientific studies. Scientists are trying to find out how sharks are protected from disease.

All the sentences in the paragraph say something about *how sharks are used.* This is the topic of the paragraph. Each sentence states a fact that contributes to the main idea. Which of the following sentences states the main idea best?

1. Some people eat shark meat.
2. Sharks are studied by scientists.
3. Sharks are used by people in several ways.

Read sentence 1 again. Does this sentence tell you several ways sharks are used? No, it tells you only one way. It does not give the whole main idea. Does sentence 2 give the whole main idea? No, it tells you only one way sharks are used. This is not important enough to be the main idea.

Look at sentence 3 again. Does sentence 3 state an important fact about the topic? Yes, it does. Does the information in sentence 3 include all the information in the paragraph? Yes, it does. Therefore, sentence 3 best states the main idea.

Textbook Application: Main Idea in Social Studies

Each paragraph in a textbook has a topic and a main idea. You will be able to better understand and remember the information in a textbook if you can recognize these parts of a paragraph.

The topic of a paragraph is the one thing that all or most of the sentences are about. The main idea in the paragraph is the most important. The main idea gives the most general information about the topic.

Authors may state the main idea in a sentence at the beginning, in the middle, or at the end of a paragraph. When the main idea is not stated, you can state it yourself by figuring out what all the sentences are telling you about the topic.

Read the following selection from a social studies book. It is about drilling wells in the ocean. The sidenotes will help you find the topic and the main idea of each paragraph.

Some sentences tell how hard it is to drill an oil well in the ocean. Other sentences tell how it is done. What do all the sentences have in common? Which sentence gives the most important idea of what the paragraph is about?

How do you drill a well when the ocean floor is 100 feet (30 m) or more below the surface of the water? And that is just the beginning! A well may have to be drilled another 20,000 feet (6,100 m) before oil or gas is found. Drilling platforms have been designed that float on the ocean surface. The derrick, or tall steel frame, is anchored to the ocean floor. The platforms and derricks are built to hold up in the strong winds and high waves of a storm.

Workers are taken to and from the drilling platform by boat or helicopter. They live on the platform. They can sleep, eat, bathe, and watch TV or movies, as well as work on the platform. The workers stay on the platform for two or three weeks at a time.

A well that is 20,000 feet (6,100 m) deep may take more than a year to drill. The drilling goes on every day, 24 hours a day. The drill goes through the soil and into the rock layers of the earth. The drill must be hard and sharp to break through the rock layers. The cutting edges on the drill are made of diamonds. Diamonds are hard enough to cut away the rock.

—*The United States and Its Neighbors,*
Silver Burdett

In this paragraph, what one thing are all the sentences talking about? How would you state the most important information in a sentence?

When the topic changes, the author starts a new paragraph. What is the topic of this paragraph? Is there a main idea sentence? If so, which is it?

Look for topics and main ideas when you read paragraphs in a textbook. This will help you understand and remember what you read.

*Link had a goal in mind when he set out
on this day's adventure. How did he manage
to meet his goal?*

*As you read, think about what aspects of
this realistic fiction story make it appear to
be nonfiction.*

In Search of a Sandhill Crane

by Keith Robertson

Link, a city boy, is spending the summer with his aunt in a wilderness camp in Michigan. He has promised his uncle back East that he will take pictures of a certain kind of crane. Link has found that this is easier said than done.

In trying to photograph the cranes, Link was bitten, stranded on an island when his boat drifted off, and had his back stuck full of porcupine quills. His aunt had to pull them out one by one, with pliers. Another time, he saw the birds he wished to photograph do a wonderful strange dance. But he missed the shot because he had forgotten to load his camera. As the selection opens, he is waiting for Dan Olson, a bird expert who is studying the cranes.

Link cooked an early dinner at his campsite and then, with his sleeping bag and enough food for breakfast, he hiked back through the woods to a spot not far from the "blind" he had made—a hiding place of cut bushes from which he could watch the birds without being seen. He slept well and got up a short while before dawn and ate a cold breakfast of a banana, two pieces of bread, and a slice of cold ham. He would have liked a cup of hot coffee and an egg, but he did not want any smoke rising from a campfire to alarm the cranes. When he had finished he carried his sleeping bag out to his blind and made a comfortable spot where he could sit or lie while he waited. He had scarcely settled himself when Olson appeared. The wildlife expert had come up quietly and Link had no idea he was around until he was within a few feet of the blind.

"You've got yourself set quite comfortably," Olson said as he sat down beside Link. "What did you do, sleep here?"

"No, over there a ways, back in the trees," Link said. "There's a tiny little stream with some water."

"Have any breakfast?"

"Not much of a one," Link said.

"I brought along a big hunk of coffee cake," Olson said. He reached into a small knapsack he was carrying and took out a package and a thermos of hot coffee. "Thought you might like some."

Olson inspected and loaded his gun—not with bullets, but with tranquilizing darts. Link checked his camera as the field grew lighter.

"Cranes eat seeds, berries, roots, worms, bugs, almost anything," Olson said. "My guess is that at this time of the year it's grasshoppers and bugs that they're after in a place like this. You'll want to wait until the sun gets up a ways so you will have good light for your pictures. They'll hang around for several hours if they come, so there's plenty of time."

"I hope they land near enough to our blind," Link said. "If they don't show up this morning, I'm going to wait here until this afternoon."

"You're determined, aren't you?" Olson said. "That's the only way to accomplish anything in this wildlife field. It took years before they could discover where the whooping crane nested. By the way, did you know they used sandhill cranes as sort of test birds for the whooping cranes?"

"No, I didn't," Link said. "How?"

"The whooping crane was practically extinct," Olson said. "There was a lot of publicity on whooping cranes so you probably know that they are on the increase now. I think that everyone is pretty well agreed that the best way to save an endangered species, bird or animal, is to protect it from hunters, provide it with its natural habitat, and let nature take its course. But when a species gets as low as the whooping crane did, twelve or fifteen pair, one single disaster — for example, an oil slick in a nesting marsh — could wipe it out. So the Bureau of Sport Fisheries and Wildlife has a sort of backstop operation. It's at the Patuxent Wildlife Research Center in Laurel, Maryland. They're doing work on a number of scarce species — the whooping crane, the Florida kite, the California condor, the masked quail, just to name a few."

"What sort of work?" Link asked.

"Oh, they study a bird's nesting habits, what it eats,

how many young it usually hatches, what conditions it likes best. The sandhill crane isn't exactly plentiful, but there are lots of them compared to whooping cranes. The two are much alike — sort of cousins. At Patuxent they study the sandhill crane to know how to best help the whooping crane."

They heard a distant "*garoooa*" and fell silent. A few minutes later the cranes appeared. Two times the big birds circled over the larger field. Then they started downward. They were flying in a formation of three, two, and three. Suddenly the rear three swooped down under the others and took the lead. Then all of them made a quick turn to the right, then to the left again.

The middle two passed through the space between the three in the lead, who dropped back. Finally they seemed to tire of the game. They dived downward sharply and landed at a good speed, taking several bouncing steps and beating the air with their wings.

There were eight of the big gangly birds. They scattered and looked around cautiously. Then they began to feed, stabbing at the ground with their long sharp beaks. Link and Olson sat watching quietly as the light grew stronger. The largest of the birds was more than four feet tall when its head was raised. It had an almost black beak and legs, light gray back and wings, light gray breast and stomach, a featherless forehead, and a crown that was bright red.

The cranes stalked around, making darting stabs for insects, but always raising their heads high every few minutes to look around carefully. After almost an hour one started in the direction of the blind, feeding as it came. Link had been ready for some time, keeping his camera focused and changing the exposure as the light grew stronger. Using his telescopic lens, he began snapping pictures. He took almost half a roll of the feeding bird, some with its head raised high and some with its long beak almost touching the ground. He put down his camera and picked up the movie camera. Olson tapped him on the arm.

"Wait," he said soundlessly. His lips formed the word rather than saying it. He pointed to the other birds. They were all moving in the direction of the blind.

A few minutes later the cranes had formed a circle about ten feet in diameter only a short distance from where Link and Olson were hiding. They faced inward

and for a minute or two did nothing. Then one leaped into the air, hopping upward and slightly backward. It flapped its wings and landed a foot or so from where it had been. Then it solemnly bowed to the circle of cranes, facing first right and then left. Link raised his movie camera and began recording the dance on film.

A second bird dropped one wing, another raised a wing. Then one crane reached down and picked up a stick in its long, sharp beak and tossed it high in the air.

As the stick fell, the crane gave a leap into the air, whirling a bit as it rose. It landed gracefully, bowed to all the others and then repeated the performance. One by one, they all joined in the strange dance. They did not leap into the air or bow together but moved as the mood seemed to strike them. First one and then the other would leap and bow or toss sticks and bits of weeds into the air. Sometimes there would be two or three in the air at once. Some would dance a moment and then stand and watch the others. The whole performance lasted not quite five minutes. Then as suddenly as it had started, it stopped.

Olson looked at Link and raised his eyebrows. Link put down his camera and nodded. He had been afraid that the sound of the camera might reach the dancing birds, but it seemed they had been too excited to notice. Olson raised his rifle, fired three times in quick succession. At the first crack, the birds sounded a wild alarm and all started to take off. Two did not get off the ground, and the third flew only a few feet before it dropped.

Olson raced out of the blind with Link close behind. Olson stopped at the first two birds, while Link ran on to the one that had fallen a short distance away. Olson had given him some broad canvas straps. He fastened a long one around the body of the crane, pinioning its wings, and put a shorter one around its legs just above the feet.

Olson quickly banded his two cranes. "If it starts to move, get back," he said. "That beak is dangerous. It can put an eye out."

He banded all three birds and made a quick inspection

of each one. The birds were still limp when they took off
the straps. Link changed lenses and snapped some pictures of the unconscious cranes, lying stretched out on
the ground. He took several close-ups of their heads, and
then he and Olson returned to the blind.

They did not have to wait long. The three birds began
to stir. First they got groggily to their feet and staggered a few steps. Then one sounded a call of alarm.
They all ran a short distance and took off. As they
climbed they seemed to fly faster. When Link and Olson
last saw the big birds they were tiny dots in the sky,
heading back toward the lake.

"A very successful morning, I'd call that," Olson said.

"I can't believe it! I finally got my pictures!" Link
said. "And some good ones, I think."

There were only two shots left in the camera, so he
took one picture of Olson and one of the blind. Then he
rewound the film. Uncle Albert ought to be happy with
some of those shots, he thought. He put the roll of film
carefully inside its little aluminum container and then in
his knapsack. He'd slept any number of nights on the
hard ground, got up at four in the morning, and been
marooned on an island. But he'd got the slides for Uncle
Albert's collection. Visitors would drop in and Albert
would proudly show his slides. And when he came to the
sandhill cranes, one or two people might ask what that·
odd-looking bird was and that would be all. Link
grinned. It didn't matter that none of them would know
what a triumph that slide or two was. He knew. He'd set
out to do something and he'd succeeded. He'd found his
sandhill cranes.

Sandhill Cranes

Each year, sandhill cranes migrate from their nesting grounds in the North to wintering grounds in the Southwest. They sometimes fly at altitudes of 10,000 feet or more.

The crane chick can walk and swim when it is a few hours old.

After the eggs — usually two — are laid, the mother and father crane take turns sitting on the nest. The eggs, three to four inches long, hatch in about 32 days.

The crane's long toes keep it from sinking into mud at the bottom of the marsh.

Its long legs, long neck and long bill help it to walk about in marshlands and catch fish. Cranes eat a great variety of foods, including worms, frogs, small snakes, and grasshoppers, as well as grain and other vegetation. A sandhill crane will sometimes eat 500 grasshoppers and worms a day.

Both males and females take part in the bowing, swinging dance, usually done before the breeding season. They utter loud, bugle-like calls as they dance. Sometimes a large group dances; other times a pair or even a single crane dances.

The whooping crane, at 4 to 5 feet, is the tallest of the cranes.

A rare whooping crane (the white one) is seen here with a group of sandhills. In 1941, the total number of whooping cranes was down to 15. By 1977, with protection, their number had increased to about 70. This is still very low, and this beautiful bird remains in danger of becoming extinct.

1. What was Link's goal for the day? How did he meet it?
2. How was the cranes' behavior special for Link and Olson?
3. How did you feel when Olson first aimed his gun at the birds?
4. Why didn't Link seem to mind that his uncle's visitors would never know the real story behind the slides of the sandhill cranes?
5. What did you read that made you realize that endangered species can be saved? Find that part of the story.

Apply

the

Skills

Realistic fiction stories are stories that seem real. The characters readers meet and the things that happen are much like real-life characters and events.

What aspects of "In Search of a Sandhill Crane" make it appear to be nonfiction, a story about real characters and events?

Prewrite

Appearance	Diet	Social Habits
1. bright red crown	seeds	travel in groups
2. gray feathers	roots	dance
3. large	worms	playful
4.		
5.		

The author of "In Search of a Sandhill Crane" describes many of the attributes of this unusual bird. The chart above includes information about the bird's appearance, its diet, and its social habits. Refer to the story to complete the chart. Add two more attributes to each category.

Compose

Choose one category from the chart. Write a descriptive paragraph about the sandhill crane using the information in that category. Use the category heading as part of the main idea in your topic sentence.

Revise

Reread your paragraph. Check to be sure that your topic sentence states the main idea of all of the sentences in the paragraph. If not, revise your work.

When I Read

by Lillian Morrison

I'm a runner, a racer,
I've got a lot of speed.
I can sprint
from here to there
with time to spare.
But when I read
then I'm a diver!
I plunge
    right
        in
and until the story's over
I don't come up for air.
Then too I'm an explorer,
a tracker and a rover
and I always
find something
I didn't know was there.

Story Elements

When you read a story or a book that you like, you sometimes want to tell a friend what happened in the story. You tell your friend the plot. The **plot** is the series of related events that happen in a story.

Most plots involve characters facing and trying to solve **problems**. The way these problems are solved is the **solution**. Read the following plot summary. Look for the problem and the solution.

Three scouts become separated from the troop on a hike. They become lost. They try to find their way back but they have a hard time. Finally, they are rescued.

What is the problem? Three scouts are lost. What is the solution? They are rescued. The rest of the plot tells what the scouts do to try to find their way back.

Authors don't always tell the events of a story in chronological order. When an author goes back in time and tells you what happened earlier, it is called **flashback**. Look for flashback as you read the following example:

Thirteen-year-old Lee looked at little Andy's frightened face and trembling chin. Suddenly Lee was a six-year-old again, separated from his parents in a huge amusement park. He felt the panic of not knowing what to do to save himself.

Every story, in addition to a plot, has a setting. The **setting** is when and where the story takes place. The author of the story about the lost scouts might choose to set the story in a state park in 1987 or on another planet in the year 2080. What is the setting in this paragraph?

> Shivering even in the bright sunshine, the boys decided to search for firewood. There were plenty of branches in the thick forest nearby. If they built a fire in the clearing, a rescue plane might be able to see the smoke.

Mood is a general feeling you get from reading a story. For example, the mood in a good ghost story is often one of suspense and mystery.

When thinking about the mood of a story, look at the descriptions of setting and characters as well as what the characters think, say, and do. Read the next example and look for words that create a mood.

> The day was bright with sunshine and promise. Julie woke up and heard her mother's happy singing. Her mother hadn't sung in a long time, ever since the family's money trouble had begun. But now, Julie thought to herself as she jumped eagerly out of bed, things might be better. Today was the first day of her mother's new job.

Notice the words describing the setting: *bright, sunshine, promise*. Other clues to the mood are found in the descriptions of the characters' actions: *happy, singing, jumped eagerly out of bed*. These descriptions, combined with Julie's thoughts, create a feeling of hope and happiness.

An awareness of the elements of a story—plot, flashback, setting, and mood—will help you better understand and enjoy what you read.

Margaretha Shemin

Sometimes, a bad experience can have a very good result. This was certainly true for Margaretha Shemin. As a young girl, Margaretha lived in a war-torn country. But many years later, she was able to turn that time of fear and danger into two wonderful books. One book, *The Little Riders*, was closely based on her own memories.

Margaretha A. Shemin was born Margaretha Hoeneveld, in 1928, in Alkmaar, the Netherlands. She lived in this city through her teenage years. When Margaretha was twelve, Nazi troops overran her country. She later called this time "one of the darkest periods in the history of my people."

During the war, Margaretha's parents worked with the Underground. The Underground was made up of people who worked secretly against the Nazi occupying forces. Margaretha's father was put in prison twice for his work in hiding Jewish people. Her mother worked to help downed Allied airmen on their way to freedom.

Margaretha Shemin wrote only three books. Each one takes place in the Netherlands. One of her aims as an author was to tell American readers what Holland was *really* like. She didn't like the way people outside her country viewed her homeland. "In American children's books, Holland is often pictured as a quaint country below sea level, where people wear wooden shoes and grow tulips," she said. "It is out of this desire to break away from this stereotyped version of the Netherlands that I decided to write my books."

Margaretha felt that America and Holland are the same in many ways. Both countries have fought for their freedom. When you have to fight for something, you understand how much it matters to you.

Margaretha Shemin went to the University of Leiden. She left with a degree in law. After marrying an American doctor and moving to the United States, she had three children. By this time, she had learned to speak and read English, German, and French. After earning a degree in library science from Columbia University, she became a children's librarian. She died in 1976.

The little riders, statues of people on horseback, are in danger of being destroyed. Read to find out why these figures are so important and how help comes from an unexpected source.

The elements of plot are very important in this story. What effect does the setting have on the problems that Johanna and her grandparents must face?

The Little Riders

by Margaretha Shemin

In 1939 World War II began, and one year later the German Army invaded Holland. This story is about a fictional character named Johanna. In the story, Johanna could not return to her parents in America because of the war. She had to stay in Holland with her grandparents.

From the window of her room in Holland, Johanna could see the special clock under the church steeple. In the old clock were twelve statues of people on horseback. For hundreds of years, these little riders had ridden around the clock every hour when it chimed. Johanna's grandfather took care of the clock and the little riders. But then German soldiers came, and the little riders and the entire town were in danger.

One day at dinner, Grandfather looked straight at Johanna, and his eyes were filled with pride and love. "There is bad news today, but nothing so bad that we can't bear it. A German soldier came to requisition a room in our house for a German officer, a certain Captain Braun. I explained to him that we used all the rooms and didn't have one room to spare. He never listened to me. He took your room," Grandfather continued. "There was nothing I could do about it, although I tried very hard for you."

It would be extremely dangerous, Johanna realized, to have a German soldier in the house. Johanna knew about the radio hidden in Grandfather's den and the weekly meetings Grandfather held upstairs. She knew there were many other dangerous secrets that Grandfather and Grandmother had never told her. All these secrets the house had kept within its walls, and the house had been the only safe place in a world full of enemies and danger. Now the house had been invaded too.

All afternoon, Johanna helped Grandmother. She took all her clothes out of the attic closet. Now that the closet was empty she could almost see the cubbyhole hiding all the way at the back of the closet. It had always been Johanna's secret hiding place. She opened the small door that was only big enough for her to crawl through. In the cubbyhole were some of her old toys, her teddy bear, which had traveled with her all the way from America to Holland, and some seashells her father had once brought back for her from a far country. She never played with them anymore, but she didn't want to leave them with Captain Braun.

When Captain Braun arrived, he clicked his heels and made a little bow in the direction of Grandmother and Johanna. Johanna turned her head away.

"I apologize to you," he said in broken Dutch. "I will try to cause no trouble to you. I wish you a good evening." Then he turned directly to Grandfather. "Would you be kind, sir, and show me the room?"

Grandfather didn't speak but led Captain Braun to the stairs and mounted them quickly. Captain Braun picked up his heavy sack and followed slowly. Johanna could hear the sack bump heavily on every step till it was carried all the way high up to her attic room. Then she heard the door close and Grandfather's footsteps coming downstairs.

Johanna went to bed early that night. She had felt tired, but now she couldn't fall asleep. She kept tossing in her new bed. There were strange, unfamiliar shadows on the wall. The big gray wall of the church seemed so near, ready to fall on top of the room. Faintly she heard the clock strike ten times. Then the door was opened very softly, and Grandfather came into the room. He sat down in the chair next to Johanna's bed and took her hand in his own.

"Why don't you sleep, Johanna?" he asked. "You should try to sleep now. We have all had a hard day and so much has happened."

"I hate him," Johanna said, "and I hate this room, too. From here I can see only the gray wall of the church. I can't see the riders, I can't even hear the carillon very clearly. How can I ever fall asleep without the little riders? I have always watched them just before I went to sleep. In the morning the carillon woke me up. Now a German soldier has my room that once was Father's room. He has no right to sit there and watch the riders and listen to the carillon."

Grandfather got up from the chair and walked over to the window. He looked up at the gray wall of the church.

"Captain Braun," he said, "will never see the little riders ride out on their horses and he will never hear the carillon. Today an ordinance came from the town commander. The riders are not allowed to ride anymore and the carillon may not play again. I just went to the church tower."

Grandfather turned away from the window and paced up and down the small room.

"All these years I have taken care of the riders so that they could ride when the clock struck the hour. But tonight I closed the little doors."

Johanna sat up in her bed, her arms around her thin knees. Her face looked small and white, her eyes big and dark.

"Why?" she asked Grandfather. "Why may the little riders not ride out anymore?"

"They didn't give us any reasons," Grandfather answered, "but we have seen this coming for a long time. This ordinance is only the beginning. The little riders are made of lead. The Germans need metal, and they may throw them into a melting pot to make munitions out of them for their armies. Everywhere the occupied countries are being plundered, their treasures taken away, and the bells of their churches melted down to be made into weapons. Grandmother and I have often talked of what to do if this ever threatened to happen to the little riders."

Grandfather patted Johanna's hand gently. "We will have to hide the riders, Johanna, if we want to keep them for the town. Go to sleep now, there is much to be done tomorrow."

Grandfather tucked the blanket around Johanna and left the room, but Johanna didn't want to sleep. She wanted to think about everything Grandfather had told her. The night was cool and quiet. From somewhere she heard the sound of a flute. She walked across the room and opened the door to the hall. The sound came from the top of the house. Barefoot, Johanna climbed silently up the attic stairs. Halfway up she could see her room.

Captain Braun had left the door open so that the cool night wind could blow through the warm room. He was sitting on Johanna's windowsill. His back was turned to the door, his long legs dangling out of the window. And he played his flute over the silent marketplace.

Johanna didn't watch him for long. She went downstairs without making a noise. She didn't close her door with a bang, but she closed it very firmly. When she was back in bed, she pulled the cover over her ears so that she couldn't hear a sound that could keep her awake. But it was a long time before she fell asleep.

The next day, everybody looked up at the church steeple, wondering what had happened. It was the first time in many hundreds of years that the little riders had not ridden out and the carillon had not played. Soon the town buzzed with the news of the ordinance from the town commander.

After a few days something happened—something of such tremendous importance that the Germans had suddenly much more urgent and grave matters on their minds than the twelve little riders high up on the church tower. Grandfather didn't think anymore about hiding them.

Johanna was sitting with Grandfather and Grandmother in the den, listening to the radio hidden behind the books in the bookcase. Then the big news came crackling and almost inaudible, and none of them dared to believe it was true. Allied armies had landed in France. All morning long, Johanna and her grandparents kept the radio on. They had to hear over and over again the crackling voice that kept repeating the same bulletin.

Grandfather and Grandmother and Johanna spent much time upstairs in the den, listening to the radio. At first the liberating armies advanced fast. The south of Holland was free. Then the days became weeks and the weeks became months. The liberation of the north still seemed sure, but not so near anymore. Johanna still dreamed about her father, but she was afraid he would not come soon.

Life went on as it had in the four years before. Grandfather started to think again about a safe hiding place for the little riders, because now more than ever the Germans needed every scrap of metal for ammunition.

Now Johanna was almost used to the presence of Captain Braun in the house, but still she had never seen his face. In the morning she met him on the stairs, she going down for breakfast, he going up to his room after morning drill. In the evening she met him again, she going up to the den, he going down on his way out for dinner. He always said "Good morning" and "Good evening." Johanna always turned her head away from him and never answered. He walked softly in his heavy boots except when he had to ask Grandfather or Grandmother something. Then he stamped noisily with his boots so that they could hear him long before he knocked on the door. There was always time to hide the radio behind the books in the bookcase.

At night now Johanna sometimes forgot to close the door of her room, and she could hear the music of the flute. When the summer nights were quiet, Captain Braun always played. But often now the air outside was filled with the droning sounds of heavy airplanes flying over. On such nights Johanna climbed out of her bed and leaned far out the window to see their lights high against the dark sky. She knew that many of them were American planes, and she imagined that her father might be in one of them. They were airplanes flying over Germany. On those nights, Captain Braun did not play his flute.

One day when Captain Braun had gone out, Johanna went upstairs and looked at her old room. Her closet was full of coats and army caps with the German eagle on them.

On the wall, where once her pictures had hung, were now the pictures of Captain Braun's family. In one, an older lady and an older man were standing arm in arm in a garden full of flowers. In another, a young woman and a laughing boy were standing on skis in dazzling white snow. It was strange to see real Germans in a garden full of flowers and with skis on a sunny mountain slope.

Before Johanna left the room she sat down on her windowsill and looked at the church steeple. The little doors were closed now and the steeple looked old and gray, like any other church steeple.

"Don't worry, little riders," Johanna whispered to the closed doors. "It will be all right, the Germans will not get you." Tonight, Grandfather had told her, they would hide the little riders.

The night was loud with the sounds of the wind and the rain, but there were no overflying airplanes. Grandfather crossed the street first to open the door. Then came Grandmother and last Johanna.

Inside the tower it was completely dark. Grandfather had climbed the steps so often that he led the way. No one talked, and Johanna could not remember when the steps had ever seemed so long and steep. As they climbed higher, the sound of the wind and rain came louder and louder. Grandfather had already reached the top of the stairs, and now he handed the riders and the horses to Grandmother and Johanna.

The staircase was so narrow and steep they could take only one rider at a time. It was too dark for Johanna to see the little rider that she carried. She could only feel the cool metal against her hands. The rider was bigger than she had expected, reaching up almost to her waist. She started to carry him down. The rider, although made of lead, was hollow inside and not too heavy, but was clumsy to carry on the narrow, steep staircase. Each trip across the street and back up the church tower was harder than the one before. The last little rider seemed heaviest of all. Grandfather made one more trip to lock the door of the church tower.

In their own house they must be careful to make no noise that could waken Captain Braun, but here the stairs were wider and Grandfather and Grandmother could carry two riders at a time. Johanna felt weak and shaky when the last rider with his horse was finally carried safely into Grandfather's den.

The next morning after breakfast, Grandfather went to a nearby village where he had a friend who was a farmer. Dirk was one of the few farmers who had been allowed to keep his horse and wagon. Because he delivered eggs and fresh milk several times a week at the house of the German town commander, the German sentries who stood guard at the entrances of the town never searched his wagon. Many times young men who were hiding from the Germans had

left town in Dirk's wagon, hidden underneath the tarpaulin between the empty egg boxes and the rattling milk containers. Grandfather and Dirk had often worked together to take such young men to safer places in the country, and Grandfather was sure Dirk would help hide the little riders. He knew they would stay hidden on Dirk's farm until they could return to the church steeple.

When Grandfather returned, it was still a few hours before dark. He and Johanna went upstairs to put the riders and their horses in the burlap sacks so that they could be taken away without delay when Dirk came. Johanna looked for the last time at the riders' faces. With her hands she covered their small hands that so many times had lifted the swords in proud salute to each other. The Germans will not get them, she thought. They will always ride over the town. Even a hundred years from now.

It was still light when Johanna and Grandfather finished and went downstairs. Except for the bark of a dog and the cooing of the doves that nested under the eaves of the church tower, it was quiet outside. Then, from the side street that led to the marketplace, came the sound of marching soldiers. It was unusual for a group of soldiers to be exercising at this late hour.

The doorbell rang loudly and insistently, and Grandfather went to open the door. Grandmother and Johanna followed him into the hall. Nine soldiers were standing on the doorstep, and one of them was the spokesman.

"We were sent by the town commander to requisition from you the key to the church tower." As he spoke he looked around with his shiny little eyes. "We will take the statues of the riders with us tonight, and you can get the key back afterward at Headquarters. Hurry, we don't have all night," he concluded.

Grandfather reached up slowly for the big iron key that always hung on a peg near the stairs. He handed the key to the soldier. When they had gone, he closed the door and for a moment leaned heavily against it. Johanna saw small drops of perspiration under his nose and on his forehead.

"They will be back as soon as they have seen the riders are gone," Grandmother said. "We will have to hide them better."

"There is no time," Grandfather said. "They will be back in a few minutes, and where can we hide the riders? No, our only chance is somehow to keep them from going upstairs. If we can tell them something that will make them go away, even if it's only for a short time . . . ."

Grandmother looked doubtful, Johanna thought, but Grandfather couldn't talk about it further. The soldiers were

back. This time they didn't ring the doorbell. Instead they pounded the stocks of their rifles on the door. The spokesman was hot and red and angry.

"The old man and the old woman will come with us to Headquarters. The town commander can conduct the hearing himself. If he orders so, we will search the house later. We will not leave a thing unturned, and if those riders are hidden here," he said, shrugging his shoulders in disgust, "we will find them. And these people will learn what happens to those who dare defy an order given by a German officer." He looked at Johanna. "The child can stay," he said.

When the last soldier slammed the door behind him, Johanna found that her knees were shaking. She had to sit down on the bottom step of the staircase. The clock in the hall ticked, and the minutes passed by.

"If those riders are hidden here, these people will learn what happens to those who dare defy an order given by a German officer," the soldier had said.

They must be hidden more safely, Johanna knew, and she would have to do it. Dirk would certainly not come now. The neighbors must have seen what happened and they would have warned Dirk to stay far away from the house. Johanna looked out of the peephole in the door. One soldier was left standing on guard.

"We will not leave a thing unturned, and if those riders are hidden here, we will find them," the German had said.

The riders were big and there were twelve of them and the horses, too. What hiding place would be big enough? Sitting on the bottom step of the stairs, Johanna's mind wandered through the whole house, thinking of all the different closets, but not one was big enough to hide the riders safely. At last she thought of her attic room. Of course, her own secret hiding place was there. It was certainly big enough, but it was right in Captain Braun's room. But the more she thought about it now, the more she became convinced that it would also be the safest place to hide the riders. The Germans would certainly not think that the riders might be hidden in the room of a German officer, and they would probably not search his room. Captain Braun probably had not discovered the cubbyhole. Anyhow, it was the only place in the house where she could hide the riders. She would leave them in the burlap sacks and push them all the way deep in.

Tonight was Friday night and Captain Braun was not home. If she worked fast, the riders would be hidden before he came back. Johanna ran upstairs and started to carry the sacks to the attic room. She didn't put on the light for fear the soldiers on guard would see it and come to investigate; instead, she took Grandfather's flashlight. She decided to do the heavy work fast and carry everything upstairs. Putting the riders in the cubbyhole would be easier. She decided also to take the radio from behind the books and put it in the cubbyhole, too.

It wasn't easy. By the time the last horse and rider were in the attic room, Johanna was out of breath. Her hair was mussed and her skirt was torn in several places. It had also taken her much longer than she had expected, but if she worked fast there was still time enough before Captain Braun came home. In the closet, she pushed Captain Braun's uniforms aside and reached to open the bolt of the little door, but it had become stiff and rusty. She got down on her knees and tried again. The bolt didn't yield. Johanna felt warm and her hands started to tremble. Surely she would be able to open the bolt, it had never given her trouble before. But no matter how hard she tried, she could not open the bolt on the little door. She forgot everything around her, even the riders and Grandfather and Grandmother and the danger they were in at this moment. She thought only of one thing. The door must open. It must.

She was so busy she didn't hear the footseps on the stairs nor the door of the attic room opening. She first saw Captain Braun when he was standing in the door of the big closet. He had to bend down a little not to hit his head against the low ceiling.

"What are you doing in the dark in my closet?" he asked.

He switched the light on so that Johanna's eyes were blinded by it, and she turned her head away. Around her on the floor were the sacks with the riders. The radio was right beside her and Johanna pushed it behind her back, but she couldn't hide the riders. Captain Braun kneeled down and opened one of the bags. There was nothing Johanna could do or say. He took out a white horse with gentle black eyes and a fierce curly mane. Then he opened the other bags. The little riders and their horses were laying helpless on their backs on the floor of the closet. The legs of the horses were bent as if they wanted to get up and gallop away. The riders looked more brave and proud than ever, but Johanna knew that no matter how brave and proud they looked, they were forever lost and she could not save them anymore. Everything she had ever felt against the Germans welled up suddenly in her.

"I hate and I despise you," she burst out, "and so does every decent person and you'll never win the war. Grandfather says that you have already lost it." She talked so fast that she had to take a deep breath.

129

Then Johanna raised her eyes and looked at Captain Braun's face for the first time. He did not have a soldier's face. He had the face of a flute player.

"So these are the famous little riders," he said quietly. "I would like to look at them much longer, but it would be safer for them and for you to put them back in the sacks and hide them where they will not be found."

"But I can't," Johanna said. She wasn't feeling angry anymore, only very frightened. "The bolt of the door is rusty. I can't open it." She was surprised to hear that she was crying. "And they took Grandfather and Grandmother. They said, 'If we find the riders in this house, you will see what happens to people who disobey an order given by a German officer.'"

Captain Braun kneeled beside Johanna. His hands were strong and quick as he slipped aside the stiff bolt. He took the sacks and started to put the riders back in.

"What will you do to them?" Johanna asked.

"The little riders will be my guests for as long as they want to be," Captain Braun said. "I owe that to them. They are the first Dutchmen who looked at me in a friendly way and did not turn their faces away when I spoke to them."

Johanna felt her face grow hot and red as he spoke. She bent down and started to help him put the riders and the horses back into the sacks.

In a few minutes the riders were hidden and the radio, too. At a moment when Captain Braun had his back turned, Johanna pushed it deep into the closet. One day when he was out she would come back and get it. Grandfather couldn't be without his radio.

"Go down now," Captain Braun said. "It's better for all of us if no one sees us together."

Johanna went downstairs and alone she waited in the dark living room. Outside, the soldier was still standing guard. She pushed Grandfather's big chair near the window and sat down, her tired arms leaning on the windowsill. From there, she saw them come across the marketplace.

Grandfather had his arm around Grandmother's shoulders as if to protect her from the soldiers who were all around them. This time, there were more than nine. As soon as Grandfather opened the door with his key, the soldiers swarmed over the room. The big, red-faced soldier was again in charge. At his command the others pushed aside the furniture and looked behind it. They ripped open the upholstery, although Johanna couldn't understand why. The riders and the horses were much too big to be hidden in the upholstery of a chair. When they left to search the upstairs, the room looked as if a tornado had passed through.

Grandfather and Grandmother went upstairs, too, but they were always surrounded by soldiers, so that Johanna could not speak one word to them.

The soldiers began with the desk in the den, taking out the drawers and dumping the contents in a heap on the floor. Then they got down on their knees and looked under the bed and knocked on the wooden floor.

The soldiers finally gave up. They had realized that there was nothing hidden in these rooms. Only the attic room was left. They climbed the last stairs. Johanna felt weak and shaky again. Even when they found Captain Braun, they

might still decide to search the room. She was glad that Grandfather and Grandmother had no idea where the riders were hidden. They walked confidently up the stairs, Grandmother winking again at Johanna behind the soldiers' backs.

The soldiers must not have known that the room was occupied by one of their own officers, because they were taken aback when they found Captain Braun with his legs on the table, writing in his music book. He rose from his chair. The soldiers apologized profusely, and the red-faced man especially seemed extremely upset at having intruded so unceremoniously on the room of a German officer.

Captain Braun put all of them at ease with a few friendly words, and he must have made a joke, for they laughed. For one terrible moment, Johanna thought that, after all, Captain Braun's face looked no different from all the other soldiers. What he had done tonight could be a trap and he could betray them. But the soldiers now made ready to go, and they went without searching the room. Captain Braun took up his pencil and music book.

The attitude of the soldiers changed during their walk downstairs. When they came they had been sure they would find the riders. Now they seemed uncertain. The big red-faced soldier seemed to take it very much to heart that he had failed to find the riders. He and the other soldiers seemed suddenly to be in a terrible hurry and left the house without saying a word.

Grandfather picked up Johanna and swung her high in the air, as he had done when she had still been a little girl.

"Oh, Johanna, we are so proud of you, but where in this house did you hide the little riders?"

Grandmother hugged Johanna, but she wouldn't let her tell the secret until they were all sitting quietly with a warm drink.

"Will they ever come back?" Johanna asked.

"I don't think so," Grandfather said. "They are convinced that the riders are not hidden here, and they can't prove that we ever had anything to do with their disappearance.

Johanna lay in bed that night, thinking about everything that had happened during the long day. She could hear the airplanes flying over the house. Every night it sounded as if there were more planes than the night before. This time, Johanna didn't think of her father; instead she thought of

135

Captain Braun. She put on her slippers and walked upstairs. The door of the room stood ajar. Johanna pushed it open. Captain Braun was sitting at the table with his face buried in his hands. He looked up when he heard Johanna.

"I cannot sleep," Johanna said. "If I leave my door open, would you, please, play the flute for me?"

1. How did Johanna receive unexpected help in saving the little riders?

2. Why were the little riders in danger of being destroyed?

3. How did you feel when Captain Braun caught Johanna trying to hide the statues?

4. Why was saving the little riders so important to Johanna, her grandparents, and others in their town?

5. Throughout the story, Captain Braun is shown to be a more caring and thoughtful man than the other German soldiers. Find and read those parts.

Although this story is fiction, it is set in a true historical time period — during World War II in a small town in Holland which has been occupied by the German Army. Explain how the presence of the German Army created problems for Johanna, her grandparents, and the other townspeople.

Thinking About "Serendipity"

This has been a unit of adventures and serendipitous discoveries. Vicky's discovery, in "Dreams of Victory," was quiet and personal. She discovered that her imagination was an important strength.

Often we think that having an adventure means going away to some far-off place. But many of this unit's story characters had adventures right in their own backyards. Chester Cricket's adventure took place in his new home. The familiar waters of the lagoon were the setting for Mako's struggle with the ghost shark.

People learn many kinds of things from their adventures and serendipitous discoveries. Nat Love learned that a person can achieve whatever he or she wants. Donna deVarona discovered that she had an inner strength that helped her become a champion. Link found that patience can pay off; and Johanna found that not all people are what they seem to be.

Adventures and serendipitous discoveries don't just happen in the world of make-believe. They happen in ordinary lives, too. Maybe someday soon you'll have a serendipitous discovery yourself.

1. Both Donna deVarona and Victory learned something about themselves. What did they learn?

2. If, like Victory, you had to write an essay about an important quality, which would you choose? Explain your answer.

3. People sometimes panic when the unexpected happens to them. How were the adventures of Mako, Johanna, and Chester Cricket unexpected? How did they react? Did they panic?

4. Johanna risked her life and the lives of her grandparents to save the little riders. What do you think makes a person take such a chance?

5. What do you think might have happened to Mako and Johanna after their stories ended? Choose one character and explain what might have happened.

6. Nat Love's life story seems like an exciting adventure to us. Why might it not have seemed that way in real life to Nat?

7. Which story character's adventure did you find the most exciting? Explain your answer.

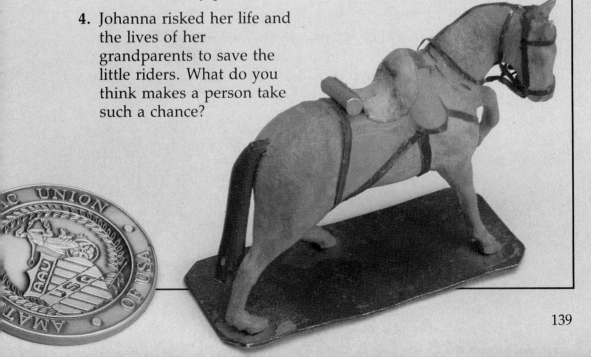

Read on Your Own

Have You Ever Heard of a Kangaroo Bird? by Barbara Brenner. Coward-McCann. In these short chapters you can learn about some of the most unusual birds in the world, including the puffin, the snakebird, and the oilbird.

Dreams of Victory by Ellen Conford. Little, Brown. Victory Benneker discovers that daydreams can be a big help in real life.

Bears in the Wild by Ada and Frank Graham. Delacorte. Many interesting facts and stories about bears, especially black bears and grizzlies, are to be found in this book.

Boris by Jaap ter Haar. Delacorte. Boris's story reflects the true hardships that World War II meant for many European children.

Near the Window Tree by Karla Kuskin. Harper & Row. In this book of poems, you can learn how to write poems about almost anything, including a radish, a bug, a gray day, and multiplication.

The Toothpaste Millionaire by Jean Merrill. Houghton Mifflin. Kate and Rufus work a simple idea into a million-dollar business.

Impossible Charlie by Barbara Morgenroth. Atheneum. Jackie keeps wishing for a horse of her own. But when somebody gives her Charlie, her troubles begin!

In Search of a Sandhill Crane by Keith Robertson. Viking. In the Michigan wilderness, Link finds out a lot about wildlife, about friendship, and about himself.

The Cricket in Times Square by George Selden. Farrar, Straus and Giroux. Chester, a country cricket who has arrived in New York City by accident, makes friends with Harry Cat and Tucker Mouse.

Chester Cricket's New Home and **Chester Cricket's Pigeon Ride** by George Selden. Farrar, Straus and Giroux. The adventures of Chester Cricket and his friends are featured in these two books.

Magdalena by Louisa Shotwell. Viking. When she goes into the IGC (Intellectually Gifted Child) class, Magdalena finds that people are often quite different from the way they seem at first.

Donna deVarona, Gold Medal Swimmer by Bob Thomas. Doubleday. Not allowed in Little League because she is a girl, Donna makes her way to the top as a gold medal swimmer in the Olympics.

Unit 2
Turning Points

A turning point is an event that causes a change. Everyone's life has sudden shifts and changes, after which things are different. Some turning points are big, dramatic changes. Moving to another country, for example, is such a tremendous change that people who do it sometimes say they are beginning a new life. Of course, they don't really have a new life, but they do have so many new experiences that their whole way of life has changed.

There are small turning points, too. For example, you might be struggling to learn something new. Then suddenly, you understand. Something clicks. You get it! That's a turning point.

You might be playing baseball and find that it's just not a good day for you. Nothing's working out. Then suddenly, there's a turnabout. You begin to get hits and to do things right — that's another kind of turning point.

The characters in the stories and plays you are going to read experience turning points. Sometimes the characters are waiting and hoping for a turning point to happen. But often, as you will see, a turning point is an unexpected event.

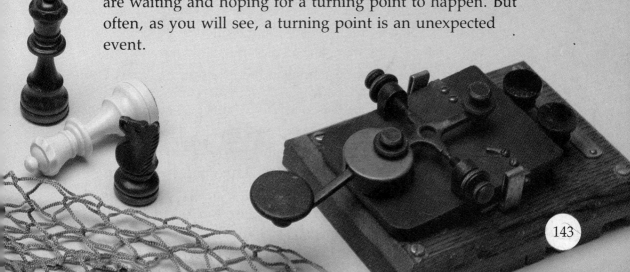

Plays

Reading a Play

A **play** is a story that was written to be acted out. At the beginning of a play you will find a list of the characters with a short description of each character. You will also find a note about when and where the play takes place. This is called the **setting.**

The action of the story is shown through the words spoken by the performers. These words are called **dialogue.** The dialogue of a play is written in a special way. No quotation marks are used. The character's name is written first, followed by the words the character is to say. For example:

> **Jim:** I'm sorry. I can't play baseball today. I have too much homework to do.

This makes it easy for the performers to find their parts.

Stage directions tell the performers what to do or how to speak. Stage directions are often written in parentheses after the character's name. The stage directions are not spoken. Notice the stage directions in this example:

> **Paul** (*Disappointedly*)**:** Aww, the team was counting on you. You are our best pitcher. (*Walks away.*)
> **Jim** (*Excitedly*)**:** Maybe if I go home and start my homework right away, I can finish in time to play for half the game!

Many people enjoy going to the theater to see live actors perform. The performers act out the play from beginning to end. The audience laughs or applauds throughout the play. There is communication between the actors and the audience.

Television Plays and Movies

Some plays are written for television or for the movies. Instead of having to use stage scenery to show a place, a television play or a movie can film on location. **On location** means to use the actual location that is the setting of the play. Special effects can be used to make things appear to happen. These include airplanes flying, explosions, even earthquakes. The most elaborate special effects can simulate space travel or monsters coming to life.

Each scene of a television play or movie can be filmed several times. The best versions are then put together to make the final show. On stage, if actors make a mistake, they have to continue the play. On television or in the movies, the mistakes can be taken out so the audience does not see them.

Radio Plays

Plays are also presented on radio. The audience of a radio play cannot see what is happening. The audience must imagine what is happening. Radio plays use sound effects to make the play more exciting. Sound effects create the sounds of events in the play. If it is raining, you'll hear the sound of rain. If a character drops a glass, you'll hear the sound of breaking glass.

When you read a play, try to picture the action in your mind. Imagine each character speaking as you read the dialogue. The setting and the stage directions will help you understand the play.

The Stranger and the Widow meet twice. How is each meeting a turning point?

Stage directions in a play tell the actors how to behave and what emotions to express. As you read, notice the stage directions for the Widow.

The Price of Eggs

by Mary Ann Nicholson

Characters

Widow
Neighbor } French peasants
Stranger   a young peasant
Village Magistrate   an older man

Time: *A summer morning.*
Setting: *A French village street.*
At Rise: *Widow is sweeping the doorstep in front of her house and stops to greet her Neighbor who is passing on her way to market.*

Widow: Good day to you, Neighbor. I see you are off to market.

Neighbor: And good day to you, Widow. I have not seen you for a long while, not since your late husband's funeral.

Widow *(Sadly)*: May heaven keep him.

Neighbor: How do you get along these days, Widow?

Widow *(Sighing)*: I manage, though I do have to work hard. I have my goats and my chickens. With the money I get from selling the eggs, I buy more chickens. I'm not starving.

Neighbor: Indeed, you are a lucky woman to be able to say that. My husband has gone away to the iron ore mines. He sends home his week's pay for me to buy food and shoes for our children, but it is never as much as we need.

Widow: Alas, times are hard for everyone. Every day one sees a stream of men going past the door on their way to work in the iron ore mines. Look, here comes one now.

(Ragged Stranger enters from right, walking wearily. As he approaches the two women, he stumbles and slumps onto doorstep.)

Stranger: I beg your pardon, my good woman, but I must sit down. I am too weary to walk another step without rest.

Neighbor: You must have come a great distance. I suppose you are on your way to find work in the iron ore mines like all the others.

Stranger: Yes, I am on my way to the mines. I have walked from a province beyond this one and still have many miles to travel.

Widow: Rest awhile on my doorstep if you wish.

Stranger: Thank you, madam. If I had some food, I might have more strength to continue my journey. Could you spare a crust of bread, kind woman? I have had nothing to eat all day.

Widow *(Coldly)*: I have little enough to eat myself. I am a poor widow alone in the world. I cannot help every stranger who passes by.

Neighbor *(Whispering to her)*: You could sell him some

of your eggs, Widow. Take pity on him, he is so tired and hungry. Surely, you can't refuse him a little kindness. Remember, we, too, know what it is to be hungry. Help him.

Widow (*Reluctantly, to Stranger*): I could sell you a dozen eggs. They were fresh from under the hens this morning. You could eat them on your way.

Stranger: How wonderful they would taste, but I have no money to pay you for them. I cannot give you anything but a promise to pay at some later date.

Widow: I would be a fool to do business that way.

Neighbor: Good Widow, how can you be so mercenary? He is starving and you do nothing. Give him some eggs.

Widow: Give him eggs? Certainly not. How you talk! No wonder you are always poor.

Neighbor: Then accept his promise to pay. He has an honest face. I'm sure you can trust him.

Widow (*Giving in*): All right, but he will have to take yesterday's eggs which I cooked this morning. I shall get a good price for my best fresh eggs in the market.

Stranger: Cooked eggs will be very welcome, and I won't have to worry about breaking them. Thank you, kind and generous Widow. You have my word of honor that I will pay for the eggs when I come back this way again, no matter how long it takes me to make my fortune at the iron mines. (*Widow goes into house and returns with a dozen hard-boiled eggs in a kerchief which she hands to Stranger.*)

Neighbor: Heaven preserve you, Stranger. (*Stranger exits down left.*) Don't you feel lighter in your heart for having helped a stranger, Widow?

Widow: No, I only feel lighter in my larder. I will never see him again, thanks to you. It's the last time I'll listen to you.

Neighbor: Heaven will bless you many times for your kindness today, wait and see. (*Widow turns and shuts door in anger. Curtain.*)

SCENE 2

Time: *Ten years later.*

Setting: *Same as Scene 1.*

At Rise: *Stranger enters, dressed in fine clothes. He is accompanied by the Neighbor.*

Neighbor: When I saw you in the marketplace, I didn't recognize you at first. Ten years can make a lot of difference in people. When you were here before, you were in rags.

Stranger: I have been blessed with prosperity from my work in the iron ore mines. Now I am part owner of those mines. I can repay my debt to the Widow who gave me a dozen eggs when I needed food. Does she still live here?

Neighbor: Yes, she does, but I rarely see her. She has become a miser and is so bitter with the world that she can't say a kind word about anybody. Your paying the debt will please her very much.

Stranger (*Knocking on door*): I hope it will be a happy surprise.

Widow (*Now older and very cranky*): Who's there? Who's knocking? (*She opens door a crack and peeks out.*)

Stranger: It is I, good Widow. I have come to pay you for the dozen eggs you gave me ten years ago. (*She* *comes out eagerly.*) You see, I have never forgotten your great kindness to me. I want to keep my promise to pay. Here are two bags of gold for you. (*Holds out bags.*)

Widow: Only two bags of gold? It will take all you possess to pay me after ten years.

Stranger: How can that be?

Neighbor: I see trouble brewing for you, Stranger. I warned you she had become greedy. I'll run and fetch the Village Magistrate. He is wise in handling such matters. (*Hurriedly, she exits right.*)

Stranger: Just a moment, old Widow. Your neighbor is fetching a Magistrate. Perhaps he can solve this difficulty. I don't understand why a dozen eggs should be worth more than two bags of gold, even with interest on the debt for ten years.

Widow: The Magistrate will understand and protect a poor old widow's rights. (*Neighbor enters, breathless, with an aged Magistrate.*)

Neighbor: Here is the Magistrate. Now you can tell him your story, Widow.

Widow: Well, Your Honor, if I had not given this man a dozen eggs, I would have hatched a dozen chickens from them. And, from those dozen chickens I would have had more eggs and more chickens. In these ten years I would have had thousands of chickens, and I, too, would be rich.

Magistrate: What you say sounds logical enough. (*Turning to Stranger*) Has she left any point out, Stranger?

Stranger: Not that I can see, Your Honor.

Magistrate: Ahem, ahem, then I shall proceed with the verdict . . . .

152

Neighbor: Wait a minute, Your Honor. I have just remembered something. (*She whispers excitedly to Magistrate. He registers surprise, then nods.*)

Magistrate: Before I offer you my decision, I want to ask the Widow if she will do me one favor.

Widow (*Curious*)**:** What is that, Your Honor?

Magistrate: Will you cook me some ears of corn? I'm thinking of planting a garden.

Widow: You must be joking, Your Honor. Everyone knows you can't grow corn that has been cooked.

Magistrate: Aha, there you see. Then you have forgotten one very important thing. The eggs you gave this Stranger were hard-boiled. How did you think you were going to hatch chickens from cooked eggs?

Widow (*Eager to retreat*)**:** You are right, Your Honor. I have been very foolish. I will be satisfied with the two bags of gold the Stranger offered.

Magistrate: Not so fast, old Widow. You should be taught a lesson for your meanness. (*To Stranger*) Sir, pay her no more than the price of a dozen hard-boiled eggs.

Stranger: If it's all right with you, Your Honor, I would rather give her the two bags of gold to show my gratitude to her for the kindness she showed me ten years ago.

Magistrate: You are very generous and forgiving, Stranger. I hope that after today, the Widow will know better than to count her chickens before they are hatched. (*Curtain falls, as Stranger hands bags of gold to Widow.*)

THE END

1. How was each meeting of the Stranger and the Widow a turning point?

2. How did the Neighbor help the Stranger at the beginning and at the end of the play?

3. What did you think of the Stranger's willingness to give the Widow two bags of gold after she had been so ungrateful?

4. Why did the Magistrate tell the Widow he wanted some cooked corn to plant?

5. Find the place where the author lets you know that it had been ten years since the Widow and the Stranger met.

In a play, a character's words and actions are written as dialogue and stage directions.

Look at the stage directions for the Widow. Tell how her attitude changes throughout the play.

154

Prewrite

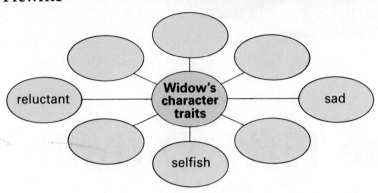

The words in the center of this "ideaburst," *Widow's character traits*, are the central idea. The surrounding words name some of the Widow's character traits. Think about the story. Then copy and complete the ideaburst by writing words that name other character traits of the Widow.

Compose

Pretend you are the Stranger. Write a paragraph that describes the Widow from the Stranger's point of view. Write in the first person, using the words *I, me, we,* and *us*. Tell what the Widow was like at the beginning of the story, when she gave the Stranger the eggs, or tell how she behaved when the Stranger returned to pay her. Use words from the ideaburst in your paragraph. Give examples of the Widow's behavior that support the Stranger's opinions.

Revise

Read your paragraph. Check to make sure it is written in the first person. Make sure that you gave examples of the Widow's behavior for each character trait you described. If not, revise your work.

A turning point occurs in Ramona's life that helps her see herself differently. What does she learn?

What parts of this story could be made into a play?

The Fifth Quimby

by Beverly Cleary

Ramona Quimby is growing up and everything seems to be changing. For one thing, she doesn't go to a sitter's house after school anymore. For another, her wonderful Aunt Bea—always so great when there were doubts and questions, and always so much fun—is not around anymore. She has married and gone far away to Alaska with her new husband, Hobart.

The biggest change in Ramona's life, however, is still to come. It is a change that will cause her much upset.

For as long as Ramona can remember, there have been four Quimbys—Ramona, her mom and dad, and her sister, Beezus. But soon, there will be a fifth Quimby—a new baby. The family has gotten into the habit of calling him "Algie." Even Algie turns out to be quite a surprise.

After the wedding, everyone felt let down, the way they always felt the day after Christmas, only worse. Nothing seemed interesting after so much excitement. Grandpa Day had flown back home. Mr. Quimby was at work all day. Friends had gone off to camp, to the mountains, or to the beach. Howie and Willa Jean had gone to visit their other grandmother.

"Girls, please stop moping around," said Mrs. Quimby.

"We can't find anything to do," said Beezus.

Ramona was silent. If she complained, her mother would tell her to clean out her closet.

"Read a book," said Mrs. Quimby. "Both of you, read a book."

"I've read all my books a million times," said Ramona, who usually enjoyed rereading her favorites.

"Then go to the library." Mrs. Quimby was beginning to sound irritable.

"It's too hot," complained Ramona.

Mrs. Quimby glanced at her watch.

"Mother, are you expecting someone?" asked Ramona. "You keep looking at your watch."

"I certainly am," said her mother. "A stranger." With a big sigh, Mrs. Quimby sank heavily to the couch, glanced at her watch again and closed her eyes. The girls exchanged guilty looks.

"Mother, are you all right?" Beezus sounded worried.

"I'm fine," snapped Mrs. Quimby, which surprised the girls into behaving.

That evening, the sisters helped their mother put together a cold supper of tuna fish salad and sliced tomatoes. While the family was eating, Mr. Quimby told them that now that the "Hawaiian Holidays" sale with bargains in fresh pineapple and papaya had come to an end, all the markets were preparing for "Western Bar-b-q Week" with specials on steak, baked beans, tomato sauce, and chili. He planned to paint bucking broncos on the front windows.

Mrs. Quimby nibbled at her salad and glanced at her watch.

"And everybody will see your paintings," said Ramona, happy that her father was now an artist as well as a market manager.

"Not quite the same as an exhibit in a museum," said Mr. Quimby, who did not sound as happy as Ramona expected.

Mrs. Quimby pushed her chair farther from the table and glanced at her watch. All eyes were on her.

"Shall I call the doctor?" asked Mr. Quimby.

"Please," said Mrs. Quimby as she rose from the table.

Ramona and Beezus, excited and frightened, looked at one another. At last! The fifth Quimby would soon be here. Nothing would be the same again, ever. Mr. Quimby reported that the doctor would meet them at the hospital. Without being asked, Beezus ran for the bag her mother had packed several weeks ago.

Mrs. Quimby kissed her daughters. "Don't look so frightened," she said. "Everything is going to be all right. Be good girls, and Daddy will be home as soon as he can."

The house suddenly seemed empty. The girls listened to the car back out of the driveway. The sound of the motor became lost in traffic.

"Well," said Beezus, "I suppose we might as well do the dishes."

"I suppose so." Ramona tested all the doors, including the door to the basement, to make sure they were locked.

"Too bad Picky-picky isn't here to eat all this tuna salad no one felt like eating." Beezus scraped the plates into the garbage.

To her own surprise, Ramona then burst into tears and buried her face in a dish towel. "I just want Mother to come home," she wept.

Beezus wiped her soapy hands on the seat of her cutoff jeans. Then she put her arms around Ramona, something she had never done before. "Don't worry, Ramona. Everything will be all right. Mother said so, and I remember when you came."

Ramona felt better. A big sister could be a comfort if she wanted to.

"You got born and Mother was fine." Beezus handed Ramona a clean dish towel.

Minutes crawled by. The long Oregon dusk turned into night. The girls turned on the television set to a program about people in a hospital, running, shouting, giving orders. Quickly they turned it off. "I hope Aunt Bea and Uncle Hobart are all right," said Ramona. The girls longed for their loving aunt, who was cheerful in times of trouble and who was always there when the family needed her. Now she was in a truck, riding along the Canadian Highway to Alaska. Ramona thought about bears, mean bears.

The ring of the telephone made Ramona feel as if arrows of electricity had shot through her stomach as Beezus ran to answer.

"Oh." There was disappointment in Beezus's voice. "All right, Daddy. No. No, we don't mind." When the conversation ended, she turned to Ramona, who was wild for news, and said, "Algie is taking his time." (They had several months ago, begun calling the baby-to-come "Algie.") "Daddy wants to stay with Mom and wanted to be sure we didn't mind staying alone. I said we didn't, and he said we were brave girls."

"Oh," said Ramona, who longed for her father's return. "Well, I'm brave, I guess." Even though the evening was unusually warm, she closed all the windows.

"I suppose we should go to bed," said Beezus. "If you want, you can get in bed with me."

"We better leave the lights on for Daddy." Ramona turned on the porch light, as well as all the lights in the living room and hall, before she climbed into her sister's bed. "So Daddy won't fall over anything," she explained.

"Good idea," agreed Beezus. Each sister knew the other felt safer with the lights on.

"I hope Algie will hurry," said Ramona.

"So do I," agreed Beezus.

The girls slept lightly until the sound of a key in the door awoke them. "Daddy?" Beezus called out.

"Yes." Mr. Quimby came down the hall to the door of Beezus's room. "Great news. Roberta Day Quimby, six pounds, four ounces, arrived safe and sound. Your mother is fine."

Barely awake, Ramona asked, "Who's Roberta?"

"Your new sister," answered her father, "and my namesake."

"Sister." Now Ramona was wide-awake. The family had referred to the baby as Algie so long she had assumed that of course she would have a brother.

"Yes, a beautiful little sister," said her father. "Now, go back to sleep. It's four o'clock in the morning, and I've got to get up at seven-thirty."

The next morning, Mr. Quimby overslept and ate his breakfast standing up. He was half-way out the door when he called back, "When I get off work, we'll have dinner at the Whopperburger, and then we'll all go see Roberta and your mother."

The day was long and lonely. Even a swimming lesson at the park and a trip to the library did little to make time pass. "I wonder what Roberta looks like?" said Beezus.

"And whose room she will share when she outgrows the bassinet?" worried Ramona.

The one happy moment in the day for the girls was a telephone call from their mother, who reported that Roberta was a beautiful, healthy little sister. She couldn't wait to bring her home, and she was proud of her daughters for being so good about staying home alone. This pleased Beezus and Ramona so much they ran the vacuum cleaner and dusted, which made time pass faster until their father, looking exhausted, came home to take them out for hamburgers and a visit to the fifth Quimby.

Ramona could feel her heart pounding as she finally climbed the steps to the hospital. Visitors, some carrying flowers and others looking careworn, walked toward the elevators. Nurses hurried, a doctor was paged over the loudspeaker. Ramona could scarcely bear her own excitement. The rising of the elevator made her stomach feel as if it had stayed behind on the first floor. When the elevator stopped, Mr. Quimby led the way down the hall.

"Excuse me," called a nurse.

Surprised, the family stopped and turned.

"Children under twelve are not allowed to visit the maternity ward," said the nurse. "Little girl, you will have to go down and wait in the lobby."

"Why is that?" asked Mr. Quimby.

"Children under twelve might have contagious diseases," explained the nurse. "We have to protect the babies."

"I'm sorry, Ramona," said Mr. Quimby. "I didn't know. I am afraid you will have to do as the nurse says."

"Does she mean I'm germy?" Ramona was humiliated. "I took a shower this morning and washed my hands at the Whopperburger so I would be extra clean."

"Sometimes children are coming down with something and don't know it," explained Mr. Quimby. "Now, be a big girl and go downstairs and wait for us."

Ramona's eyes filled with tears of disappointment, but she found some pleasure in riding in the elevator alone. By the time she reached the lobby, she felt worse. The nurse called her a little girl. Her father called her a big girl. What was she? A germy girl.

Ramona sat gingerly on the edge of a couch. If she leaned back, she might get germs on it, or it might get germs on her. She swallowed hard. Was her throat a little bit sore? She thought maybe it was, way down in back. She put her hand to her forehead the way her mother did when she thought Ramona might have a fever. Her forehead was warm, maybe too warm.

As Ramona waited, she began to itch the way she itched when she had chicken pox. Her head itched, her back itched, her legs itched. Ramona scratched. A woman sat down on the couch, looked at Ramona, got up, and moved to another couch.

Ramona felt worse. She itched more and scratched harder. She swallowed often to see how her sore throat was coming along. She sniffed from time to time to see if she had a runny nose.

Now Ramona was angry. It would serve everybody right if she came down with some horrible disease, right there in their old hospital. That would show everybody how germfree the place was. Ramona squirmed and gave that hard-to-reach place between her shoulder blades a good hard scratch. Then she scratched her head with both hands. People stopped to stare.

164

A man in a white coat, with a stethoscope hanging out of his pocket, came hurrying through the lobby, glanced at Ramona, stopped, and took a good look at her. "How do you feel?" he asked.

"Awful," she admitted. "A nurse said I was too germy to go see my mother and new sister, but I think I caught some disease right here."

"I see," said the doctor. "Open your mouth and say 'ah.'"
Ramona *ah-ed* until she gagged.

"Mh-hm," murmured the doctor. He looked so serious Ramona was alarmed. Then he pulled out his stethoscope and listened to her front and back, thumping as he did so. What was he hearing? Was there something wrong with her insides? Why didn't her father come?

The doctor nodded as if his worst suspicions had been confirmed. "Just as I thought," he said, pulling out his prescription pad.

Medicine, ugh. Ramona's twitching stopped. Her nose and throat felt fine. "I feel much better," she assured the doctor as she eyed that prescription pad with distrust.

"An acute case of siblingitis. Not at all unusual around here, but it shouldn't last long." He tore off the prescription he had written, instructed Ramona to give it to her father, and hurried on down the hall.

Ramona could not remember the name of her illness. She tried to read the doctor's scribbly cursive writing, but she could not.

Itching again, she was still staring at the slip of paper when Mr. Quimby and Beezus stepped out of the elevator. "Roberta is so tiny." Beezus was radiant with joy. "And she is perfectly darling. She has a little round nose and — oh, when you see her, you'll love her."

"I'm sick." Ramona tried to sound pitiful. "I've got something awful. A doctor said so."

Beezus paid no attention. "And Roberta has brown hair —"

Mr. Quimby interrupted. "What's this all about, Ramona?"

"A doctor said I had something, some kind of *itis*, and I have to have this right away." She handed her father her prescription and scratched one shoulder. "If I don't, I might get sicker."

Mr. Quimby read the scribbly cursive, and then he did a strange thing. He lifted Ramona and gave her a big hug and a kiss, right there in the lobby. The itching stopped. Ramona felt much better. "You have acute siblingitis," explained her father. "*Itis* means inflammation."

Ramona already knew the meaning of *sibling*. Since her father had studied to be a teacher, brothers and sisters had become siblings to him.

"He understood you were worried and angry because you weren't allowed to see your new sibling, and pre-scribed attention," explained Mr. Quimby. "Now let's all go buy ice-cream cones before I fall asleep standing up."

Beezus said Roberta was too darling to be called a dumb word like *sibling*. Ramona felt silly, but she also felt better.

For the next three nights, Ramona took a book to the hospital and sat in the lobby, not reading, but sulking about the injustice of having to wait to see the strange new Roberta.

On the fourth day, Mr. Quimby took an hour off from the market, picked up Beezus and Ramona, who were waiting in clean clothes, and drove to the hospital to bring home his wife and new daughter.

Ramona moved closer to Beezus when she saw her mother, holding a pink bundle, emerge from the elevator in a wheelchair pushed by a nurse and followed by Mr. Quimby carrying her bag. "Can't Mother walk?" she whispered.

"Of course she can walk," answered Beezus. "The hospital wants to make sure people get out without falling down and suing for a million dollars."

Mrs. Quimby waved to the girls. Roberta's face was hidden by a corner of a pink blanket, but the nurse had no time for a little girl eager to see a new baby. She pushed the wheelchair through the automatic door to the waiting car.

"Now can I see her?" begged Ramona when her mother and Roberta were settled in the front, and the girls had climbed into the back seat.

"Dear Heart, of course you may." Mrs. Quimby then spoke the most beautiful words Ramona had ever heard, "Oh, Ramona, how I've missed you," as she turned back the blanket.

Ramona, leaning over the front seat for her first glimpse of the new baby sister, tried to hold her breath so she wouldn't breathe germs on Roberta, who did not look at all like the picture on the cover of *A Name for Your Baby*. Her face was bright pink, almost red, and her hair, unlike the smooth pale hair of the baby on the cover of the pamphlet, was dark and wild. Ramona did not know what to say. She did not feel that words like darling or adorable fitted this baby.

"She looks exactly like you looked when you were born," Mrs. Quimby told Ramona.

"She does?" Ramona found this hard to believe. She could not imagine that she had once looked like this red, frowning little creature.

"Well, what do you think of your new sister?" asked Mr. Quimby.

"She's so — so little," Ramona answered truthfully.

Roberta opened her blue-gray eyes.

"Mother!" cried Ramona. "She's cross-eyed."

Mrs. Quimby laughed. "All babies look cross-eyed sometimes. They outgrow it when they learn to focus." Sure enough, Roberta's eyes straightened out for a moment and then crossed again. She worked her mouth as if she didn't know what to do with it. She made little snuffling noises and lifted one arm as if she didn't know what it was for.

Ramona sat back and buckled her seat belt. She had once looked like Roberta. Amazing! She had once been that tiny, but she had grown, her hair had calmed down when she remembered to comb it, and she had learned to use her eyes and hands. "You know what I think?" she asked and did not wait for an answer. "I think it is hard work to be a baby." Ramona spoke as if she had discovered something unknown to the rest of the world. With her words came unexpected love and sympathy for the tiny person in her mother's arms.

"I hadn't thought of it that way," said Mrs. Quimby, "but I think you're right."

"Growing up is hard work," said Mr. Quimby as he drove away from the hospital. "Sometimes being grown-up is hard work."

"I know," said Ramona and thought some more. She thought about loose teeth, real sore throats, quarrels, misunderstandings with her teachers, longing for a bicycle her family could not afford, worrying when her parents bickered and how terrible she had felt when she hurt Beezus's feelings without meaning to. She had survived it all. "Isn't it funny?" she remarked as her father steered the car into their driveway.

"Isn't what funny?" asked her mother.

"That I used to be little and funny-looking and cross-eyed like Roberta," said Ramona. "And now look at me. I'm wonderful me!"

"Except when you're blunderful you," said Beezus.

Ramona did not mind when her family, except Roberta, who was too little, laughed. "Yup, wonderful, blunderful me," she said and was happy. She was winning at growing up.

1. The arrival of her baby sister was a turning point for Ramona. What did Ramona learn about herself?

2. Mrs. Quimby said to Ramona, after they were settled in the car, "Oh, Ramona, how I've missed you." Why were these "the most beautiful words Ramona had ever heard"?

3. How did you feel when Ramona was not allowed to see the baby and was sent to the lobby?

4. What was the cure for Ramona's "siblingitis"?

5. When Ramona thought she was "germy," she came down with a "disease." Find the part of the story that describes how she got the disease and tell how she got over it.

The action of a play is shown mostly through the dialogue of the characters. Stage directions tell actors what to do and how to speak.

Ask a friend to help you read, as if it were a play, the part of the story in which the nurse sends Ramona to the lobby.

Prewrite

Characters

Ramona a young girl
Beezus Ramona's older sister

Time: After dinner. Mr. and Mrs. Quimby
are just leaving for the hospital.

Setting: The Quimby house

Beezus (   ):
Ramona (   ):

"The Fifth Quimby" could be made into a play. Here is the beginning of the script for one part of the story. Find the part of the story that is in the script.

Compose

Copy the script and complete it by writing the dialogue for Ramona and Beezus. Put stage directions for each character in parentheses. You may want to end the scene when the girls go to bed.

Revise

Read through your script. Does the dialogue tell everything that happens? Did you include enough information in the stage directions to tell the performers how to speak and what to do? Revise your script to include any missing information.

Compound Words

Take a careful look at a word that seems to be unfamiliar. You may see that it is made up of two words that you know. A word that is made up of two or more words is called a **compound word**.

Closed Compound Words

Houseboat, underwater, daydream, and *playground* are compound words. They are called **closed compound words** because the space between two words has been closed up to make one word. Often you can figure out the meaning of a compound word by thinking about the meaning of the words that make up the compound word. Look at *houseboat*. You know that a house is a building you live in. You know that a boat is used for traveling on water. What is a houseboat? A boat you can live in on water. What is the meaning of *underwater?* of *daydream?* of *playground?*

Hyphenated Compound Words

Part-time, old-fashioned, brand-new, out-of-date, far-off, and *double-decker* are also compound words. These words are called **hyphenated compound words** because two or more words have been joined together with a punctuation mark called a hyphen. Hyphenated compound words often describe something:

I rode on a double-decker bus.

Look at the hyphenated compound words above. Tell what each hyphenated compound word could describe.

Open Compound Words

Living room, fire engine, high school, seat belts, and *sleeping bag* may not look like compound words, but they are. Each pair of words is thought of as one word, and is called an **open compound word**. The two words are dependent upon each other for their meaning. Say each of the words in the open compounds above to yourself. Think of the meaning each word has alone. See how the meaning changes when the words are put together.

Read the sentences below. What is the open compound word in each sentence? What does each open compound word mean?

1. My uncle cut down the tree with a chain saw.
2. That rocking horse was my favorite toy.
3. My brother loves sweet potatoes.
4. She learned to swim at a swimming pool.
5. How many planets are in our solar system?
6. The post office is always busy around Christmas.

Look at the words in the columns below. How could you combine words from each column to make compound words? Tell what each compound word means.

Column A	Column B
1. flash	boat
2. day	board
3. house	light
4. sail	coat
5. over	time

Remember to look at a word that seems unfamiliar to see if it might be a compound word. You may discover that you know the words that have been put together and that you can figure out the meaning of the compound word.

Kino and Jiya experience a turning point that is emotional and intense. How will their lives change?

As you read, notice the kinds of compound words in the story.

The Big Wave

by Pearl S. Buck

This story of Japan grew out of my own memories. Once I lived in a little Japanese house on a hillside above the sea, and in the summer a big wave came up and washed away the fishing village on the beach. So the story of Kino and Jiya may be said to be a true one.

When I thought about pictures for the book, it seemed to me that they should express the spirit of Japan and her people. It is a beautiful country, this Japan, and so they must be beautiful pictures. Where could I find them? Why, in the pictures made by great Japanese artists. So I went to my books of Japanese prints and there I found just what I wanted, the mountain, the beach, the cave, the village, the hillside, the little island, the great wave. Of course these are not pictures of Kino and Jiya, but of the land where they live and the sea around it and how that land and that sea have made them what they are, brave boys, not afraid of danger and death, able to live simply and do much.

These pictures were made long ago by two famous artists, Hokusai, who lived between 1760 and 1849, and Hiroshige, who lived between 1797 and 1858.

They, more than any other, loved to paint their country just as it was, and Hokusai especially liked to

paint fishermen and farmers and their children. He loved
people at work and at play, and his pictures are full
of them. Hiroshige liked to paint landscapes and birds,
especially wild geese against the moon, or an eagle on a
snow-covered pine.

Both of these men were able to put into their pictures
the feeling of Japan and her people, and that is why I
have chosen their pictures to go with my story. If you
look long and deeply into the pictures while you read
the story, you will know how it seems to be in Japan,
and you will understand Kino and Jiya and when you
understand them, you will like them.

Pearl S. Buck

A snow-covered landscape — Hiroshige

Kino lived on a farm. The farm lay on the side of a mountain in Japan. The fields were terraced by walls of stone, each one of them like a broad step up the mountain.

Above all the fields stood the farmhouse that was Kino's home. Sometimes he felt the climb was a hard one, especially when he had been working in the lowest field and he wanted his supper. But after he had eaten at night and in the morning, he was glad that he lived so high up because he could look down on the broad blue ocean at the foot of the mountain.

The mountain rose so steeply out of the ocean that there was only a strip of sandy shore at its foot. Upon this strip was the small fishing village where Kino's good friend Jiya lived.

On days when the sky was bright and the winds mild the ocean lay so calm and blue that it was hard to believe that it could ever be cruel and angry. Yet even Kino never quite forgot that when he dived down under the warm blue surface, the water was cold and green. When the sun shone the deep water was still. But when the deep water moved and heaved and stirred, ah, then Kino was glad that his father was a farmer and not a fisherman.

And yet, one day, it was the earth that brought the big wave. Deep under the deepest part of the ocean, miles under the still green waters, fires raged in the heart of the earth. The icy cold of the water could not chill those fires. Rocks were melted and boiled under the crust of the ocean's bed, under the weight of the water, but they could not break through. At last the steam grew so strong that it forced its way through to the mouth of the far-off volcano. That day, as he helped his father plant turnips,

Kino saw the sky overcast halfway to the zenith.

"Look, Father!" he cried. "The volcano is burning again!"

His father stopped and gazed anxiously at the sky. "It looks very angry," he said. "I shall not sleep tonight."

All night while the others slept, Kino's father kept watch. When it was dark, the sky was lit with red and the earth trembled under the farmhouses. Down at the fishing village, lights in the little houses showed that other fathers watched, too. For generations fathers had watched earth and sea.

Morning came, a strange fiery dawn. The sky was red and gray, and even here upon the farms, cinders and ash fell from the volcano. Kino had a strange feeling, when he stepped barefoot upon the earth, that it was hot under his feet. In the house his mother had taken down everything from the walls that could fall or be broken, and her few good dishes she had packed into straw in a basket and set outside.

"Shall we have an earthquake, Father?" Kino asked as they ate breakfast.

"I cannot tell, my son," his father replied. "Earth and sea are struggling together against the fires inside the earth."

No fishing boats set sail that hot summer morning. There was no wind. The sea lay dead and calm, as though oil had been poured upon the waters. It was a purple gray, suave and beautiful, but when Kino looked at it he felt afraid.

No one stirred from home that day. Kino's father sat at the door, watching the sky and the oily sea, and Kino stayed near him. He did not know what Jiya was doing,

Dragging a net up a mountain stream — Hokusai

but he imagined that Jiya, too, stayed by his father. So the hours passed until noon.

At noon his father pointed down the mountainside. "Look at Old Gentleman's castle," he said.

Halfway down the mountainside on the knoll where the castle stood, Kino now saw a red flag rise slowly to the top of a tall pole and hang limp against the gray sky.

"Old Gentleman is telling everyone to be ready," Kino's father went on. "Twice have I seen that flag go up, both times before you were born."

"Be ready for what?" Kino asked in a frightened voice.

"For whatever happens," Kino's father replied.

At two o'clock the sky began to grow black. The air was as hot as though a forest fire was burning, but there was no sign of such a fire. The glow of the volcano glared over the mountaintop, blood-red against the black. A deep-toned bell tolled over the hills.

"What is that bell?" Kino asked his father. "I never heard it before."

"It rang twice before you were born," his father replied. "It is the bell in the temple inside the walls of Old Gentleman's castle. He is calling the people to come up out of the village and shelter within his walls."

"Will they come?" Kino asked.

"Not all of them," his father replied. "Parents will try to make their children go, but the children will not want to leave their parents. Mothers will not want to leave fathers, and the fathers will stay by their boats. But some will want to be sure of life."

The bell kept on ringing urgently, and soon out of the village a trickling stream of people, nearly all of them children, began to climb toward the knoll.

"I wish Jiya would come," Kino said. "Do you think he will see me if I stand on the edge of the terrace and wave my white girdle cloth?"

"Try it," his father said.

"Come with me," Kino begged.

So Kino and his father stood on the edge of the terrace and waved. Kino took off the strip of white cloth from about his waist that he wore instead of a belt, and he waved it, holding it in both hands, high above his head.

Far down the hill Jiya saw the two figures and the waving strip of white against the day sky. He was crying as he climbed, and trying not to cry. He had not wanted to leave his father, but because he was the youngest one, his older brother and his father and mother had all told him that he must go up the mountain. "We must divide ourselves," Jiya's father said. "If the ocean yields to the fires you must live after us."

179

"I don't want to live alone," Jiya said.

"It is your duty to obey me, as a good Japanese son," his father told him.

Jiya had run out of the house, crying. Now when he saw Kino, he decided that he would go there instead of to the castle, and he began to hurry up the hill to the farm. Next to his own family he loved Kino's strong father and kind mother. He had no sister of his own and he thought Kino's sister Setsu was the prettiest girl he had ever seen.

Kino's father put out his hand to help Jiya up the stone wall and Kino was just about to shout out his welcome when suddenly a hurricane wind broke out of the ocean. Kino and Jiya clung together and wrapped their arms about the father's waist.

"Look—look—what is that?" Kino screamed.

The purple rim of the ocean seemed to lift and rise against the clouds. A silver-green band of bright sky appeared like a low dawn above the sea.

"May the gods save us," Kino heard his father mutter. The castle bell began to toll again, deep and pleading. Ah, but would the people hear it in the roaring wind? Their houses had no windows toward the sea. Did they know what was about to happen?

Under the deep waters of the ocean, miles down under the cold, the earth had yielded at last to the fire. It groaned and split open and the cold water fell into the middle of the boiling rocks. Steam burst out and lifted the ocean high into the sky in a big wave. It rushed toward the shore, green and solid, frothing into white at its edges. It rose, higher and higher, lifting up hands and claws.

"I must tell my father!" Jiya screamed.

A great wave covers the land — Hokusai

But Kino's father held him fast with both arms. "It is too late," he said sternly.

And he would not let Jiya go.

In a few seconds, before their eyes the wave had grown and come nearer and nearer, higher and higher. The air was filled with its roar and shout. It rushed over the flat still waters of the ocean and before Jiya could scream again it reached the village and covered it fathoms deep in swirling wild water, green laced with fierce white foam. The wave ran up the mountainside, until the knoll where the castle stood was an island. All who were still climbing the path were swept away—black, tossing scraps in the wicked waters. The wave ran up the mountain until Kino and Jiya saw the wavelets curl at the terrace wall upon which they stood. Then with a great sucking sigh, the wave swept back again, ebbing into the ocean, dragging everything with it, trees and stones and houses. They stood, the man and the two boys, utterly silent, clinging together, facing the wave as it went away. It swept back over the village and returned slowly again to the ocean, subsiding, sinking into a great stillness.

Upon the beach where the village stood not a house remained, no wreckage of wood or fallen stone wall, no little street of shops, no docks, not a single boat. The beach was as clean of houses as if no human beings had ever lived there. All that had been was now no more.

Jiya gave a wild cry and Kino felt him slip to the ground. He was unconscious. What he had seen was too much for him. What he knew, he could not bear. His family and his home were gone.

Kino began to cry and Kino's father did not stop him. He stooped and gathered Jiya into his arms and carried him into the house, and Kino's mother ran out of the kitchen and put down a mattress and Kino's father laid Jiya upon it.

"It is better that he is unconscious," he said gently. "Let him remain so until his own will wakes him. I will sit by him."

"I will rub his hands and feet," Kino's mother said sadly.

Kino could say nothing. He was still crying and his father let him cry for a while. Then he said to his wife, "Heat a little rice soup for Kino and put some ginger in it. He feels cold."

Now Kino did not know until his father spoke that he did feel cold. He was shivering and he could not stop crying. Setsu came in. She had not seen the big wave, for her mother had closed the windows and drawn the curtains against the sea. But now she saw Jiya lying white-pale and still.

"Is Jiya dead?" she asked.

"No, Jiya is living," her father replied.

"Why doesn't he open his eyes?" she asked again.

"Soon he will open his eyes," the father replied.

"If Jiya is not dead, why does Kino cry?" Setsu asked.

"You are asking too many questions," her father told her. "Go back to the kitchen and help your mother."

So Setsu went back again, sucking her forefinger, and staring at Jiya and Kino as she went, and soon the mother came in with the hot rice soup and Kino drank it. He felt warm now and he could stop crying. But he was still frightened and sad.

"What will we say to Jiya when he wakes?" he asked his father.

"We will not talk," his father replied. "We will give him warm food and let him rest. We will help him to feel he still has a home."

"Here?" Kino asked.

"Yes," his father replied. "I have always wanted another son, and Jiya will be that son. As soon as he knows that this is his home, then we must help him to understand what has happened."

So they waited for Jiya to wake.

"I don't think Jiya can ever be happy again," Kino said sorrowfully.

"Yes, he will be happy someday," his father said, "for life is always stronger than death. Jiya will feel when he wakes that he can never be happy again. He will cry and cry and we must let him cry. But he cannot always cry.

After a few days he will stop crying all the time. He will cry only part of the time. He will sit sad and quiet. We must allow him to be sad and we must not make him speak. But we will do our work and live as always we do. Then one day he will be hungry and he will eat something that our mother cooks, something special, and he will begin to feel better. He will not cry anymore in the daytime but only at night. We must let him cry at night. But all the time his body will be renewing itself. His blood flowing in his veins, his growing bones, his mind beginning to think again, will make him live."

"He cannot forget his father and mother and his brother!" Kino exclaimed.

"He cannot and he should not forget them," Kino's father said. "Just as he lived with them alive, he will live with them dead. Someday he will accept their death as part of his life. He will weep no more. He will carry them in his memory and his thoughts. His flesh and blood are part of them. So long as he is alive, they, too, will live in him. The big wave came, but it went away. The sun shines again, birds sing, and earth flowers. Look out over the sea now!"

Kino looked out the open door, and he saw the ocean sparkling and smooth. The sky was blue again, a few clouds on the horizon were the only sign of what had passed—except for the empty beach.

"How cruel it seems for the sky to be so clear and the ocean so calm!" Kino said.

But his father shook his head. "No, it is wonderful that after the storm the ocean grows calm, and the sky is blue once more. It was not the ocean or the sky that made the evil storm."

"Who made it?" Kino asked. He let tears roll down his cheeks, because there was so much he could not understand. But only his father saw them and his father understood.

"Ah, no one knows who makes evil storms," his father replied. "We only know that they come. When they come we must live through them as bravely as we can, and after they are gone, we must feel again how wonderful is life. Every day of life is more valuable now than it was before the storm."

A fisherman at work — Hokusai

1. How was the big wave a turning point in the lives of Jiya and Kino?
2. How did Jiya's father save Jiya's life? In what way did Kino's father also save Jiya's life?
3. The fishermen thought the sea was their enemy. Do you agree? Why?
4. How did Kino's father say the family should handle Jiya's crying?
5. When did the author make you feel that the situation was getting worse and would end in disaster? Find that part of the story.

Compound words may be closed, open, or hyphenated. Taking a careful look at a compound word's parts will often help you to understand the word's meaning.

Find the compound word or words in each of the sentences below. Tell what kind of compound word each one is.

1. The glow of the volcano glared over the mountaintop, blood-red against the black.
2. When it was dark, the sky was lit with red and the earth trembled under the farmhouses.
3. No fishing boats set sail that hot summer morning.
4. But now she saw Jiya lying white-pale and still.

Prewrite

The Big Wave	
The sea before the wave	**At the time of the big wave**
blue	solid green
beautiful	swirling wild water
quiet	roar

The author of "The Big Wave" paints vivid pictures of the sea by describing sights and sounds before, during, and after the big wave. Copy and complete the chart by adding at least two words or phrases to each category.

Compose

Use the information on your chart to write a paragraph that compares the sea under normal conditions with the sea during the great wave. Include sentences that tell about the sights and sounds of each. You might start with this topic sentence: *At the time of the great wave, the sea was very different from the way it usually was.* First write three sentences about the way the sea was before the wave, and then write three sentences about how it looked at the time of the great wave.

Revise

Read your paragraph. Did you include words that describe sights and sounds? If not, revise your work.

The tide rises, the tide falls

by Henry Wadsworth Longfellow

The tide rises, the tide falls,
The twilight darkens, the curlew calls;
Along the sea-sands damp and brown
The traveller hastens toward the town,
   And the tide rises, the tide falls.

Darkness settles on roofs and walls,
But the sea, the sea in the darkness calls;
The little waves, with their soft, white hands,
Efface the footprints in the sands,
   And the tide rises, the tide falls.

The morning breaks; the steeds in their stalls
Stamp and neigh, as the hostler calls;
The day returns, but nevermore
Returns the traveller to the shore,
   And the tide rises, the tide falls.

Details

Details are small bits of information that make an idea clearer. Details are often used to describe something. Here are two descriptions of a lost dog. Which one would help you find the dog?

Lost: Brown and white dog.

Lost: Small dog, part beagle. Brown with white face and paws. Friendly. Walks with a limp.

Of course the second description would be more helpful. It has bits of information that tell how the dog looks, how it behaves, and how it walks. These are details that give you a clearer idea of what kind of dog to look for. Details that describe something are called **descriptive details**. Read the following paragraph. How many descriptive details can you find?

David has a new ten-speed bicycle. It's blue with a tan seat. It has silver fenders to keep dirt from flying up from the wheels. David wrapped the handlebars with blue reflective tape.

There are other ways details can be used to help make an idea clearer. Sometimes an author uses details to support an idea. These details prove, or back up, the idea. Suppose it was a beautiful, sunny, summer day. A friend said, "Boy, this is a terrible day." You then wanted to know why your friend thought the day was terrible. You needed some details to support what your friend had said. Your friend then told you that she had lost the key to her bicycle lock and had to walk all the way home to get a spare. Losing the key and walking all the way home are reasons why she said it was a terrible day. These reasons are called **supporting details**.

Read this paragraph. Find the details that support the main idea, "Proper clothing can help keep a bicycle rider safe."

> Proper clothing can help keep a bicycle rider safe. Shoes should be rubber-soled to keep from slipping off the pedals. They should tie or fit snugly to stay on the rider's feet. Pants legs should be rolled up or tied to keep from tangling in the pedals and chain. Clothing should always be bright so that the rider can be seen by automobile drivers. It is a good idea for the rider to wear a safety helmet to protect the head in case of a fall.

In the paragraph you just read, the first sentence stated the main idea. The rest of the sentences gave details that supported the main idea.

Sometimes an author will not state the main idea in a single sentence. Then you will have to use the details in the paragraph to help you decide what the main idea is. The main idea of the following paragraph is not stated. Use all the details to figure out the main idea. Remember, the main idea is the most important idea of the paragraph.

Bicycle races have been an important event in the Olympics since 1896. Today, bicycle races are held in almost every country of the world. The most famous bicycle race is the *Tour de France*. It is held each year in the countryside of France. The *Tour de France* is over 2,500 miles long and lasts about 21 days. Bicycle racing has become so popular that special lightweight bicycles and special clothing have been developed for the sport.

Which of the statements on the next page best tells the main idea of the paragraph?

A bicycle race in New York City.

1. Bicycle races are held in the Olympics.
2. The *Tour de France* is a famous bicycle race.
3. Bicycle racing is a popular sport.

Do all the details in the paragraph have something to do with the Olympics? No, only the first sentence mentions the Olympics. Therefore, the first suggested main idea is not correct. Do all the details in the paragraph have something to do with the *Tour de France*? No, only three sentences mention the *Tour de France*. That means the second suggestion is not the main idea. Do all the details in the paragraph tell about bicycle racing and how popular it is? Yes. Therefore, the third sentence is the main idea of this paragraph.

Remember that a detail is a small bit of information. It may be a word, a phrase, or a whole sentence. When the main idea of a paragraph is stated, the rest of the sentences usually have details that support the main idea. When the main idea is not stated, you can use the details to figure out what the main idea is. Look for details as you read. Authors use details to make their ideas clearer to you.

Textbook Application: Details in Social Studies

Details give information about the main idea of a paragraph. Most paragraphs in your textbooks have details. You will understand and remember the information in a textbook better when you can spot details and use them to figure out the main idea.

The following selection is from a social studies textbook. Read it to yourself. Look for the main idea and the details in each paragraph. Ask yourself whether the details describe the main idea, or whether they support it.

The sidenotes will help you find the details and decide what they do.

Remember, the main idea isn't always stated in the first sentence. Which sentence in this paragraph states the main idea? Which sentences give details?	The first French explorers in North America had looked for gold and diamonds. Later explorers decided the most precious resource was the furry, funny-looking beaver. Probably 100 million beavers then lived in North America. Before long, trapping beavers and trading fur skins became the biggest business in northern America.
What do the detail sentences tell you about the beaver?	Beavers belong to the rodent family, as do squirrels, mice, and rats. The average beaver is about 3 feet (1 m) long and weighs about 50 pounds (23 kg). Beavers have sharp teeth. They eat the bark and young buds of trees.
Use these details to figure out the main idea of this paragraph.	Beavers are excellent swimmers. They have large, flat tails that they use to steer through the water. They also slap their tails

on the water to signal friends and warn of the presence of enemies. They live in groups and work together to build dams and shelters.

The early beaver trappers were interested in beavers for their fur. Beaver fur provides excellent protection against cold and moisture. It has been prized for centuries for hats and coats.

> How do the details support the first sentence?

Today, most states have laws protecting beavers. Beaver populations are higher than they were a century ago. Some trapping is still permitted, to keep the population from growing too large. In North America, most people now value beavers as much as they used to value beaver skins.

> Which detail describes the beaver population? Which detail supports the last sentence?

— *The United States: Its History and Neighbors,*
Harcourt Brace Jovanovich

Remember to look for descriptive and supporting details in the paragraphs you read in textbooks. Details will help you understand what you read by making ideas clearer.

Kari could not talk with her friends, her teacher, or her family. Read to find out about an important turning point in her life.

Much information is presented in this story. Look for sentences that provide important details.

The Story of Kari

by Elizabeth Helfman

Try to imagine what it would be like if you were never able to let anyone know what you were thinking or feeling. You could never tell a joke or let anyone know if you were happy or sad. You could never tell someone when something was hurting you.

That is what it was like for Kari, a Canadian girl, and for thousands of other children who suffer from severe cases of cerebral palsy. They could not speak or communicate by "signing" with their fingers the way the deaf do. Then a teacher found a special system of symbols described in a book. That system of symbols was just what Kari and others needed to make themselves understood. For the first time in their lives, they could reach out to others.

This story tells how the special system of symbols was brought to Kari and how it changed her life.

Seven-year-old Kari Harrington watched as her five-year-old sister, Linda, tried to get the last bit of catsup out of a narrow-necked bottle. Linda shook it and shook it, but nothing came out. The rest of the family were busy eating dinner, and no one else seemed to notice. Linda started to cry. Then Kari had an idea and began to wave her left arm. When Linda's attention was caught, Kari pointed at some designs on a board beside her plate.

Linda stopped crying. "What's Kari saying?"

Mrs. Harrington looked to see what Kari was pointing at. "She says, 'Put water in it.'"

The other Harringtons looked at one another in astonishment. Kari's brother was the first to speak. "Hey, good idea, Kari!" he said.

"Bravo, Kari!" her father added, as Linda ran to the kitchen to get some water.

Her mother gave Kari a big hug. Something incredible had just happened—much more than a bright little girl making a good suggestion. Kari had never before, in all her seven years, made any comment that anyone could understand. She could not talk.

Kari had been born with a serious form of cerebral palsy. She could

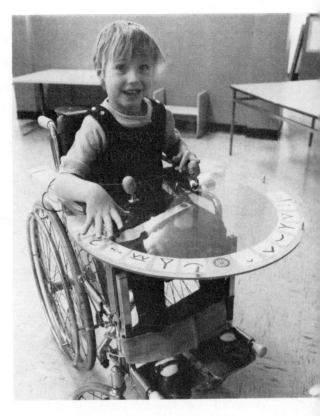

Kari uses her first symbol display.

not walk or speak or move any part of her body very well. She spent most of her waking hours in a wheelchair. Some things Kari could do. She could see, she could hear, she could move her left arm and hand enough to point. But she could not make signs with her fingers the way deaf people do.

A few months before, Kari had begun learning the meaning of some new special printed symbols she could use instead of spoken words. So when Linda asked, "What's Kari saying?" she meant, "What symbols is Kari pointing at?"

What were these symbols? And why was this the first time Kari had ever used them? To explain this, we have to go back in time a bit.

Kari attended a school called the Ontario Crippled Children's Centre in Toronto. For years the teachers there had been trying to find a way that young nonspeaking children like Kari could get their ideas across. Word boards and spelling boards and special electric typewriters could be used by older children, who could read and write to express themselves. But these methods did not help young children who could not yet read. To be sure, pictures helped. Some of the young children could point to a glass of water if they wanted a drink. They could point to a picture of their mother and father if they were lonely. But this method was very limited, for there are so many ideas and feelings you cannot make a picture of.

Several of the teachers at the school began to design special symbols that would stand for certain thoughts and feelings. One, for example, was a sort of abstract handshake, to represent a greeting. But it was hard to make up suitable symbols. Then one day Shirley McNaughton, a teacher, was looking at a book called *Signs and Symbols Around the World*. In it, she read about a special system of symbols, invented by a man named Charles Bliss. Some of the symbols were just what they needed. They expressed family relationships such as father, mother, child, and they expressed feelings such as happiness and sadness.

Ms. McNaughton wrote to the author of this book, a woman named Elizabeth Helfman, who sent her more of the special symbols designed by Charles Bliss.

The children began using them immediately. The teachers then wrote to Mr. Bliss himself, who was in Australia, asking for more symbols and permission to use them. To help explain their need, they sent him a picture of Kari.

Mr. Bliss had always hoped that his system of symbols would help humanity somehow. He had spent years devising it, but somehow nobody had had much interest in the symbols. Now, suddenly, there were people who needed them desperately. He wrote back to the school:

I cannot express the emotion that swept over me when I held your letter and the picture of Kari in my hand. It was the finest present I ever got in my long life—now in its seventy-fifth year.

For nearly thirty years, since I started my harebrained scheme of modern symbol-writing, I have thought of almost nothing else than applications for my symbols to help humanity. But never did it occur to me that they would help paralyzed children who cannot form words for thoughts or thoughts for words.

Of course he gave them permission to use his symbols.

Who are the children who needed these symbols so much? Like Kari, most are victims of cerebral palsy, in which lack of muscle control is often (though not always) a symptom. Cerebral palsy is caused by damage to the brain usually happening at birth. Certain kinds of illness or poisoning can also cause it. There is no cure for it.

Sometimes cerebral palsy can be so mild that the only symptom is a slight difficulty in speaking. In severe cases, like Kari's, victims do not have enough control of the muscles that make their bodies move. Some of these children can walk with difficulty. Others cannot walk at all. Most have limited control of head and hands. Their actions may appear jerky and uncertain. Often it is hard for them to hold on to anything with their hands or even to point with their fingers. As a result, most cannot write or draw or make the signs, with hands and fingers, that deaf people use to communicate.

Actually, most children with cerebral palsy can speak, though not always clearly. Some children's words come out in such a jumble that few people can understand them. Children with the most serious form of cerebral palsy cannot speak at all.

A few can only indicate *yes* or *no* by rolling their eyes to the left or to the right. Conversation, to them, was a one-way street. Their only possible response to anyone was a simple *yes* or a *no*—like a lifelong game of Twenty Questions. Try going through just one day saying nothing, just moving your head to answer *yes* or *no*, no matter what is said to you. You will see how frustrating this can be.

Until she was seven, Kari had not been able to get across to anyone her thoughts and ideas. She would try and try; there was so much she wanted to say. But instead of words, out came rough sounds. Her mother and father did their best to understand, but usually they could not. Finally, Kari would bang her wheelchair tray, put her head down, and cry with frustration. There seemed to be nothing anyone could do.

But now, the "Blissymbols" caused a dramatic breakthrough in the lives of Kari and others in the school.

When the project first started, about a dozen symbols were arranged in a semicircle on a tray that was fastened onto Kari's wheelchair above her lap. A pointer could be moved to indicate any symbol. Within a few weeks, the number of symbols used by Kari was increased to thirty, then to one hundred.

Today a child or an adult may have more than 500 symbols available, usually printed in squares on a board. The corresponding word is printed above each symbol. Symbols may also be placed on the wall, on a board that folds up for easy carrying, or on a handkerchief a child can carry in a pocket. There are even T-shirts with symbols printed on them.

Some important words:

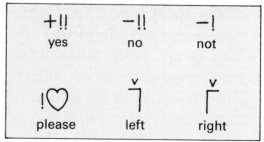

Arrows are used in intriguing ways:

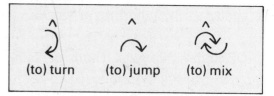

You can figure those out, as well as these:

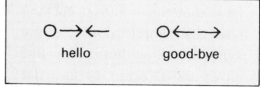

Numbers are sometimes used, as in the days of the week:

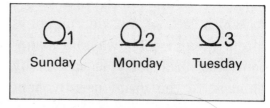

Letters may be needed to make the meaning more specific:

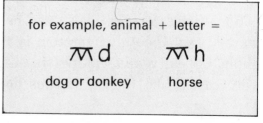

The children who are able point to symbols they want to express. Those who can't point can use "head sticks," attached to the head, or "joy sticks," which are electronic devices that can be operated by whatever part of the body the person can move, even a little. Some children are only able to "point" with their eyes by looking at a certain area of the board. Even with all these difficulties, they could now get their ideas and feelings across to others. This was a wonderful thing. Before, they were locked in silence and frustration. Now, at last, they could "speak."

Kari's parents were very proud of her. She could come home and tell them what had happened at school and on the ride to and from school. And she could tell them how she felt about things. It was an important day when she could first say, "I angry." Kari's mother put symbols on cards around the kitchen so she could communicate with Kari while she worked.

Not long after Kari learned to use the symbols, she had an operation

Kari communicates with a friend.

on her legs to keep them from crossing one over the other. She had been warned that the operation would not enable her to walk. But she could not help hoping. One night, after she got home from the hospital, Kari's mother heard crying from Kari's room. She rushed in and found Kari crumpled up on the floor. She comforted her and lifted her back into bed, but Kari was still upset. "What's wrong?" her mother asked. With the help of her symbol board, Kari answered. She had dreamed, she said, that she could walk, and so she had gotten up and tried. She had fallen down all in a heap.

Later her mother said "I cried along with her over that one." And she was grateful for Kari's symbols. How else would she have known what Kari was thinking and feeling?

For five more years, Kari flourished at the school. She learned to communicate with the symbols, and was able to whiz about in her new electric wheelchair. She could have stayed on there for several more years. But Kari had an ambition: to go to the same school—a regular school—that her brother and sister attended. Fortunately, there was a special education class there. There were no physical barriers or curbs. There was just one step, and when a ramp was built, Kari could get in with her wheelchair.

How did her parents feel about this? They were concerned.

"We were very aware of the feelings Kari might have," her mother wrote, "being the only one confined to a wheelchair in a school where there were hundreds of running, jumping, boisterous children. Already, we had had many occasions when she was dejected because of the unfairness of her lot, and, if anything, this new setting could only intensify those feelings. However, her wheelchair and her physical limitations are the facts of life which she must face and accept. Keeping her in a more protected setting wasn't going to change this. Knowing how much spunk she really has, we felt she could cope."

When Kari was thirteen, she began writing her autobiography. "I couldn't talk," she wrote, "so my Mom and Dad had to guess what I was saying." The chapter in which Kari tells about her early days at the Ontario Crippled Children's Centre is titled: "I Love You with All My Heart." On the title page of her book, Kari says: "Handicaps can be hard! This is a True Story. Please believe the handicaps."

We believe you, Kari. Good luck!

not	please	she, her	(to) teach	tree	who
on	present	sick	teacher	under	who, which, that, when, where
opposite meaning	rain	similar	teenager	up	why
or	(to) read	sister	telephone	upset	woman
paper, page	room	sky	television	(to) walk, go	wow
part (of)	sad	snow	thanks	(to) want	yes
pen, pencil	(to) say, tell	star	the	water, liquid	you
person	school	sun	thing	we, us	young
pet	secret	(to) surprise	time	wheelchair	yuck

1. How was learning Blissymbols a turning point for Kari?
2. What are three things that Kari did after she learned to use Blissymbols?
3. What do you admire about Kari?
4. Why did Kari's parents think it would be hard for Kari to go to a regular school?
5. Find the part of the story that explains how the children carry their symbols.

Details are small bits of information that help make a main idea clearer.

Find details in "The Story of Kari" that support each of these main ideas.

1. Kari's parents were grateful for Kari's symbols.
2. Kari has come a long way since she learned to use Blissymbols.

Prewrite

Story	Problem	Solution
The Big Wave	An unknown danger threatened to destroy Jiya's home.	Jiya climbed to safety in Kino's house.
The Story of Kari	Kari cannot communicate with speech or signs.	

All good stories present problems that must be solved. Look at the chart above. Read the problem and solution given for "The Big Wave." Then read the problem presented in "The Story of Kari." Think about the story. Then write a description of the solution to the problem.

Compose

Write two paragraphs about "The Story of Kari." In the first paragraph, state the problem as the topic sentence. Then write two or more sentences to provide details about the problem. In the second paragraph, state the solution as the topic sentence. Follow it with several sentences that give details about the solution.

Revise

Read your paragraphs. Make sure that each one begins with a topic sentence and is followed by two or more sentences that provide details. As you revise, take out any details that do not support your topic sentences.

Blast-Off!

A Symbol Poem by Kari Harrington

I'm pretending I'm going on the moon.

10   9   8   7   6   5   4   3   2   1

Blast-off!
(fire)

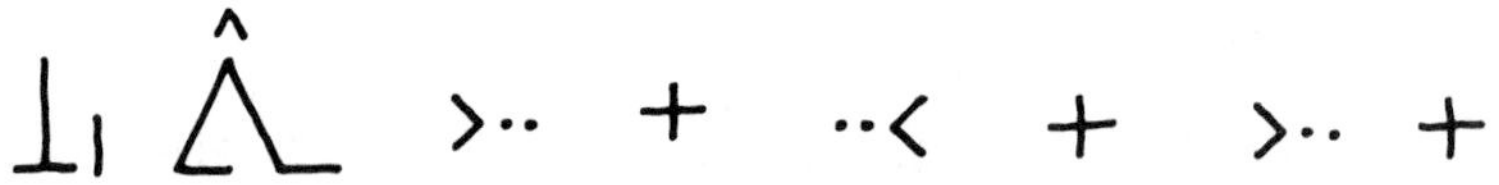

I'm going here and there and here and

there and here and there.

10   9   8   7   6   5   4   3   2   1

Blast-off!

206

I'm pretending I'm going home here and there.

I'm pretending I'm going in the cloud.

10   9   8   7   6   5   4   3   2   1

Blast-off!

I'm pretending I'm going in the weather.

10   9   8   7   6   5   4   3   2   1

Blast-off!

No more story.

Newspapers

A newspaper is very different from a book. The purpose of a newspaper is to tell people about the latest news. Most newspapers are printed every day. They tell what is happening in our town, our country, and the world.

News Stories

Local, national, and world news is reported in news stories. A **headline** tells you what a news story is about. For example, the headline "Martians Visit Chicago" tells you who the visitors are. You also learn that they are visiting Chicago. The **dateline** at the beginning of a story tells you three things. It tells where the news is from, the date when it was reported, and the name of the source. Some stories give the name of the reporter who wrote the story. This is called a **by-line**.

Read the following news story. Find the headline, the by-line, and the dateline.

COUNCIL VOTES TO REPAIR HIGHWAY

By Terri Lorenz

Parkersville, April 9 — The Parkersville town council decided late last night, in a 10–9 vote, to repair the highway that runs between Parkersville and Bilton. The decision came after three hours of discussion.

Said Marie Boudreau, town council member and owner of the Pine Tree Hotel, "I'm really glad that we're going to fix that highway at last. All those cracks and potholes are really killing my business."

People do not have time to read a newspaper from beginning to end, the way you read a book. This is why a news story is written in a special way. The most important information is in the first part of the story. That way a person can find out what is important without reading the whole story. The information in a news story answers six questions: Who? What? When? Where? Why? How? Find the parts that tell who, what, when, where, why, and how in the news story on the preceding page.

Feature Stories

Besides news stories, you'll find feature stories in a newspaper. Features are stories about people, places, or things that happen. Features are not news stories. Sometimes they give extra information about a news story. Suppose a baseball team wins the championship. The newspaper might print an interview with the coach. This feature story would make the news story more interesting.

Features that are often in the newspaper are called regular features. They give you information for daily living—about health, new products, or do-it-yourself advice.

One, Two, Buckle My Shoe —
Or Lace It, Or Slip It On, Or...

By MYRON JACKSON

Some people don't really care what kind of shoes they wear.

They think that shoes are just things we all have to put up with. If you didn't have shoes, you'd risk catching cold every time you stepped in a puddle. If you didn't have shoes, you'd have to worry about cutting your feet.

But then there are other people who think that shoes are very important. They think that shoes can reveal a part of your personality — that shoes are — well, fun!

Just think about all the different kinds of shoes there are. Take sneakers, for example. There are sneakers that go up over your ankles, and others that are cut low. There are sneakers that have laces, and others that don't. And as for colors — well, you can even get sneakers in bright pink, or sneakers with flowers painted on them, or sneakers with lace.

Opinions

Newspapers also print opinions. Opinions tell you how one person feels about something. An editorial tells you how someone from the newspaper feels about an issue. For example, there might be a news story about a child who was hit by a car while riding a bike. An editorial might say that the town should build a bike path where children can ride safely. The Letters to the Editor section gives people a chance to write in with their opinions. Reviews of movies, plays, and TV or radio programs are other kinds of opinions. They can help readers decide what they want to see or hear.

Newspaper Index

Newspapers are divided into sections. Often these sections are lettered. Each section has news and information about a certain subject. There are regular sections in every paper. Sections found in many newspapers are Sports, Local News, National News, World News, and Entertainment. Sometimes sections are added that cover special subjects, such as travel or winter sports.

A daily newspaper has something for everyone. But if you're like most people, you don't want to read everything in the paper. If you are looking for a certain story or subject, the index will tell you where to look.

The index in a newspaper is like the table of contents in a book. It lists, by subject, what is in the paper and gives the sections and page numbers. The index is often on the first or second page of the paper.

Inside

Radio and Television Listings

The daily listing of radio and TV programs is usually found in the Entertainment section. The TV schedule lists the programs by day, time, and channel. The radio schedule also lists programs. It gives the number on the AM or FM dial where you will find the program. Near each schedule you'll find a key to the information given. The TV key tells you the name of each station and the number of its channel. The radio key gives the call letters and the name of each station.

Sometimes radio and TV listings tell what a program is about. Part of a typical TV program listing is printed below.

1:30 (9) Movie:
"The Triumph of Sherlock Holmes."
Famous detective finds secret
society in America. Arthur Wonter
and Lyn Harding. 1935.

This listing tells you the program's time and channel. It tells you that the program is a movie, and gives the movie's name, a plot summary, the names of its stars, and the year it was made.

A newspaper has summaries of the news of the day. A newspaper can give you more information than you can learn from TV or radio news shows. A newspaper also has many stories that are both interesting and informative.

Raging flood waters have forced the Wielemaker family to climb to the roof of their house and to hope for rescue. Read to find out how the morning brings a turning point.

This story is based on an actual event. Imagine how the event would be reported in a newspaper article. What would the headline be?

The Tide in the Attic

by Aleid Van Rhijn

About two-thirds of the land in the Netherlands is below sea level. Some is more than twenty feet below sea level. To prevent the land from being flooded, there are wide sea walls called *dikes*. But sometimes, in terrible storms, the water breaks through the dikes, and the land is flooded.

Kees remembers his grandfather telling him about such a storm. Whole farms were underwater. Thousands of people and animals drowned. And now it is happening again.

To save themselves, Kees; his little sister Sjaantje; his mother and father, Mr. and Mrs. Wielemaker; Jacob, the farmhand; and Trui, his mother's helper; as well as the dog, Bob, and Miesje, the cat, have all climbed up on the roof. Now night is coming on. Will the house be swept away? Will they be rescued?

Slowly, the long hours ticked by.

Sjaantje was sitting in the top tier between her mother and Trui. Miesje, the cat, was still on her lap.

Just below them were Kees's father, Mr. Wielemaker, and his farmhand, Jacob, with Kees — his dog, Bob, on his lap — between them. Over to the right they could see a bit of the village, surrounded on all sides by the raging sea. They could see the roofs of some neighboring farmhouses and the tops of a few tall trees sticking up above the water.

To the left there was nothing at all. Now that the barn and the wash house had been swept away, it was a view of nothing but seething water. "We may have to spend the night here," said Father.

What would it be like up there when it got quite dark and you couldn't see your hand in front of your face? Wasn't there a danger of falling asleep and dropping off the roof?

The hours passed slowly.

Mr. Wielemaker checked the supplies in the box. "Well, we've got enough to eat anyway. That's something. We've got three loaves of bread, almost two whole hams, two smoked sausages, the best part of a cheese, a cake, and a bag of sugar; there are also a couple of quarts of milk. So, for the time being, we won't have to go hungry or thirsty."

Kees looked at his father. There were deep lines round his eyes. He suddenly looked much older.

Kees knew that his father was still thinking about the animals, about the horses, which he had so often yoked to his cart or plough and which knew him as well as he knew them. He had reared them himself from young long-legged foals. And the cows, which he and Jacob had gone out to milk every day. Then there were the pigs, healthy and fat.

All the animals had been led to a wide, flat, high dike-top, where they would be safe from the flood. But the water had risen higher and faster than anyone thought it would. Had the animals been swept away?

Kees felt a lump in his throat. Poor Father and poor Mother, disaster all round them! Suddenly he remembered Witje, the goat, and her big pathetic eyes as she was drowning. He tried to stop himself from thinking about her.

By now, it had got quite dark.

Now the six of them could see nothing but the dull gleam of the water. There were no stars in the sky. The wind died down a bit but the water was still rushing round the house. Kees felt as if he weren't on a house at all but in some extraordinary boat.

After a long silence, Jacob said, "The important thing is to get through the night. Tomorrow they're bound to come and fetch us."

Little Sjaantje had tired of sitting up all the time. She was lying down now, her head on Mother's lap. She held Miesje in her arms.

The dog, Bob, kept being handed from person to person. It was nice and warm when the furry dog was on your lap, but after a while his weight became too much for you. At Jacob's suggestion, they had tied themselves to each other with strips torn from a sheet. "If one of us should lose his grip, the rest of us can hold on to him."

"Try and sleep now, Kees," his father said. But it was easier said than done. After they had all been sitting in the dark for a few hours, the downpour started up again. Quite soon they were all drenched and shivering. Only Sjaantje slept on; the rain could not reach her because she was sheltered by the grown-ups' bodies. From time to time Bob howled.

Kees's teeth were chattering. He was aching all over and was terribly tired. In the end, he fell asleep.

"It's a good thing he's asleep," Mr. Wielemaker whispered to Jacob. Kees was leaning against his father's shoulder. His cheeks were ice cold. Carefully, his father drew the blanket over Kees's head.

Now Mr. Wielemaker had Bob on his lap. The dog was heavy but he kept him nicely warm.

After a long silence, Mr. Wielemaker asked Jacob, "What do you think has become of the animals?"

Jacob did not answer for a moment but then he said quite frankly, "I really don't think they have much chance up there."

The farmer nodded. He knew what Jacob was going to say. The water would be too high now, even on the dike. After an hour or so, Kees woke up.

"Did you sleep well, lad?" Jacob asked.

It took Kees a moment to realize where he was. His hands and feet were quite numb; he had a terrible backache and could hardly move. On top of that, he was exhausted. He tried to be brave but he hadn't the strength.

Jacob could see what state he was in. And rescue wasn't anywhere near—if ever it came at all.

"Take Bob on your lap," he said. "He'll act as a hot water bottle."

Bob growled a little at being disturbed, but then licked Kees's hands and shut his eyes again.

Jacob could see that Kees was losing courage. Nothing was left of the old Kees; he was miserable and despondent.

After awhile, Kees said, "My leg hurts so much. It seems to be on fire." No wonder; they had been sitting in the same position for hours.

"You'd better stand up," Father told Kees, "and stretch your legs. But be careful. I'll hold on to you."

He caught hold of Kees's hands, and Kees made a great effort to stand up.

"I can't," he said, his voice trembling. "I just can't stand up."

Jacob tried to coax him.

"Don't worry. Of course, it isn't easy. After all, your legs have been cramped and they've got to get used to being stretched out. Try again. Don't worry, I won't let go."

At last Kees was standing up. His back was bent like a tired old man's. He had terrible pins and needles all over his arms and legs. It was so bad that he wanted to scream out loud, and he just managed not to by biting his lower lip.

Would it never stop raining? Kees felt as if someone behind him was emptying buckets of water over his back. He felt cold right into his bones. But standing up like this, with Jacob holding on to him, he could feel blood gradually getting back into his feet. He looked around at Mother and Trui behind him. They're probably asleep, he decided.

"Are you all right, Kees?" It was his mother's voice. So she was awake after all. Suddenly he forgot his own misery. Hadn't Mother and Trui gone through the same thing? A big boy ought to be able to take as much as they could.

"Oh, I'm all right," he said as brightly as he could. "I'm just a bit stiff."

Then there was silence again. Now Kees noticed that the horizon looked a little brighter. That was the east. If only we can get through the night, his father had said. In an hour or two it would be daylight. Then someone was bound to come and take them off.

A new day dawned: Monday, February the 2nd, 1953.

The six of them looked at the dim outlines around them in the pale dawn. The first thing they saw was that the water had crept up further still. Now it was up to the gutter of the roof. The cowshed was completely under water.

Over on the right, a black object floated toward them. When it was quite close, they saw it was a dead horse, being sucked out to sea. Kees was reminded of seeing his goat Witje drown, and swallowed hard to get rid of the lump in his throat.

It was now twelve hours since they had moved up to their little refuge. They knew they ought to be grateful that nothing worse had happened to them. Kees tried hard to be brave about it all. He stroked Bob's head, while Bob looked at him sadly. He, too, was fed up with all of this.

Suddenly Trui called out, "Look, I can see rowboats over there." She pointed to the right, where two rowboats, full of people, were dancing on the waves. "It won't be long now before they come to fetch us, too," Trui said. "There's no need to be gloomy, now." She pressed her hand to her side where she had had a pain for hours.

"They must have seen the sheet we tied to the chimney," Jacob said. "They'll be here any time now."

"I wonder whether the sheet is still up," Mr. Wielemaker said.

"I'll go and have a look," Jacob replied at once.

But it was easier said than done. He had to climb right to the top of the roof so that he could look over the other side, and all the time he was so stiff that he could hardly lift his feet. And then he had to remove tile after tile in order to get a footing.

When he had finally got to the top, he saw that the sheet was gone.

"It's been blown away," he shouted down. "But there are a few airplanes flying low over the water," he said. "And over there, there's one of those . . . what d'you call them? . . . one of those helicopters."

Kees felt a little happier. Rowboats, airplanes, a helicopter—all these were signs of rescue close at hand. They were not alone and forgotten. Help would come soon.

With an effort, Kees sat up straight and looked across the water.

"Listen!" Trui said. "I can hear an airplane quite close."

Then the others heard it, as well. The roar of the engine became louder and louder.

Then, suddenly, they saw it, coming over from behind them. It was flying very low and they could see the pilot quite clearly. Jacob waved his handkerchief like a madman.

"He has seen us," Mr. Wielemaker called out. His voice sounded hoarse and Kees noticed his father wipe a tear away with the back of his hand.

Kees, himself, felt his heart pounding against his chest. He was still cold; all his limbs ached, and he was desperately tired. But now that they had been seen, he knew that it was only a matter of time before they were rescued . . . .

And then the miracle happened. It happened quite unexpectedly.

They hadn't seen it coming—but there it was now, a huge bird hovering almost directly above them. They were so startled that all they could do was gape at it.

The engine was running very quietly. They could barely hear the hum of the large propeller above the sound of the wind and the rushing water.

"Here they are!" Jacob shouted in a hoarse voice.

Breathlessly they watched as the helicopter dropped lower and lower, circling all the time.

"We are saved," Mr. Wielemaker said, grasping his wife's shoulders. "We are saved."

Kees watched in silence as the helicopter came down lower still. It was only about twenty-five feet above them now. And it was quite motionless, except for the propeller. They could see the pilot sitting in his cabin. He waved at them and smiled encouragingly.

They watched the helicopter descending until it was no more than eight feet above them.

Then the pilot let down a rope-ladder.

Jacob, who was nearest to it, caught hold of it. Now the cabin door opened and the pilot leaned over and called out: "Children first. I can take the two children together, but I only have room for one adult at a time." His voice sounded like music to them.

"Sjaantje first," Mr. Wielemaker said.

"In that thing?" Mrs. Wielemaker asked anxiously.

But Jacob had already taken Sjaantje from her mother's arms. "I'll take her up," he said. He put her on his shoulder and slowly climbed up the rope-ladder. Kees could see that it wasn't so easy. When Jacob had got up high enough, he carefully pushed Sjaantje into the cabin.

Then Jacob came down. "Your turn now," he said to Kees. "You've got to take Sjaantje on your lap. There is only one spare seat in there." Then he turned to Mr. and Mrs. Wielemaker. "He is taking them to Duivenisse. The flood hasn't got that far."

Kees tried to get up, but failed. His legs seemed to be quite useless. He looked imploringly at his father. Father and Jacob held him up under his arms.

"Come on now, I'll help you," Jacob said. Jacob lifted Kees up so that one foot was on the bottom rung.

"Try now," he ordered while he supported Kees with all his remaining strength. Slowly and with a great deal of effort, Kees took the first step. Then he took a second and a third, until he finally flopped into the cabin, utterly exhausted.

"Well, my boy, are you pleased I've come to fetch you?" Two friendly brown eyes looked at him from under a naval officer's cap. "Can you manage to get onto that seat?" Kees was quite dizzy, but he got up and then dropped down heavily onto the seat. He tried to smile but the attempt was rather a failure. There was so much he would have liked to say but he could not open his mouth, he was so terribly tired. The pilot placed Sjaantje on Kees's lap.

"Wave good-bye to your family. Then we'll set off," the pilot said.

Slowly, Kees raised his hand. He could see them all below him, on the roof: Father, Mother, Jacob, and Trui, as well as Miesje and Bob, who was looking up at him and barking loudly.

"Look after Sjaantje," his father called out. Kees nodded. Sjaantje still had her eyes shut. She was so tired that she hardly noticed what was happening to her.

The pilot leaned over Kees and called out to those below, "I'll be back very soon to pick up the rest of you. Keep your chins up!" He pulled up the rope-ladder and shut the cabin door.

The pilot revved up the engine. Kees looked up and saw that the propeller was turning much faster now. The whole helicopter was shaking. Then Kees had a strange sensation, as if he were being pressed down on his seat. And, in fact, that was what was happening for, when Kees looked out, he noticed they were climbing very fast. Soon those on the roof had shrunk until they looked no bigger than small dots.

Then the helicopter shot forward with a jerk. Kees wondered whether he was dreaming. There he was, Kees Wielemaker, high up in the sky, in a helicopter. He was flying! Experiencing himself what he had so often read about, what he had so often longed to do!

He glanced across at the pilot who sat calmly at the controls, just like an ordinary motorist. The pilot noticed, and gave Kees a warm smile.

"How are you feeling?" he asked.

"Wonderful," Kees said, but his lips were trembling.

Below him the earth seemed to be covered with water, water everywhere. Here and there, he could see a roof, a rowboat or the top of a tree. This was the countryside he knew so well, where he had walked so often! Yet now there was hardly a spot he recognized.

"Whatever's happening now?" Kees wondered. The helicopter was behaving strangely; it seemed to be falling. Suddenly there was land below them, rising to meet them. The pilot smiled and said, "We've arrived."

Now Kees could see a number of houses clustered around a church. The village looked like an island in a vast ocean. They had arrived at Duivenisse. He had been there many times but it had never looked like this. The helicopter was dropping all the time. Then Kees recognized a familiar spot. It was the football ground and it was dry. He could see the goalposts quite clearly. In the middle of the field there was a large white area. Kees realized what it was: bed-sheets, to tell the pilot where to land.

There were a lot of people on the edge of the field. A minute ago, they had only been little black dots. Now he could see them quite clearly. As the helicopter passed over them they all waved, and Kees waved back. Slowly the helicopter descended and Kees had a very peculiar sensation in his stomach. Then there was a gentle bump as they landed.

"Right," the pilot said. "That's the end of the journey. The sooner you get out, the sooner I can take off again to fetch the rest of your family."

Suddenly Kees remembered something and a look of anguish crossed his face. "Please, you won't leave Bob and Miesje behind, will you? Please don't."

The pilot looked surprised. "Who are they?"

"The dog and the cat."

"Don't worry, I shan't forget to bring them along."

Then the helicopter took off. Soon, Kees thought, soon they would all be together again. They had lost a great deal. But still, they had all managed to survive. Kees realized that there was a lot to be thankful for.

1. In the morning, the Wielemaker family could see boats and airplanes. How was this a turning point?
2. What things did the Wielemaker family do that made it possible for them to survive on the roof?
3. Describe the part of the story that you felt was the most discouraging.
4. How was the family finally rescued?
5. Find the part of the story that told you how worried Mr. Wielemaker had been and how relieved he was at seeing the helicopter.

A newspaper headline is designed to tell what the news story is about. It sums up the story.

Select the best headline for a newspaper article about this story. Explain your choice.

1. The Tide in the Attic
2. Boy Rescued by Helicopter
3. Helicopter Rescues Family on Roof
4. Flood Family Rescued After Night on Roof

Prewrite

This illustration shows the Wielemaker family about to be rescued from the roof of their house. If you study the illustration and raise questions about it, your answers will tell a good deal about what happened in "The Tide in the Attic." For example, you might ask: *Who are the people? Where are they? Why are they on a roof?* Make up at least two more questions about the illustration. Then use the story to answer each question.

Compose

Write a news story to tell about the illustration. Use the answers to the questions as facts in your news story. You may want to reread the story for specific information.

Revise

Read your news story. Check to see that you have included facts to answer the questions that were raised about the illustration. As you revise, add any facts that were left out.

Comparison and Contrast

Authors often use comparison and contrast to make their stories or articles clear and interesting. To compare, or to make a **comparison,** means to tell how two or more things are alike. To **contrast** means to tell how two or more things are different.

Understanding comparison and contrast will help you understand what you read.

Making Comparisons: Using Clue Words

You probably make comparisons frequently. When you say, ''Maria is the same height as Johnny,'' you give people who know Johnny an idea of how tall Maria is. When you say, ''The Smiths' house looks like a castle,'' even people who do not know the Smiths get a picture in their minds of how the Smiths' house looks. When you say, ''The story I read today is similar to the one I read last week,'' you are making a connection in your own mind between two things.

Look at the example sentences again. One contains the word *as*, one contains the word *like*, and one contains the word *similar*. These words are often used to signal comparisons. Other words that may give you a clue that a comparison is being made are *too, also, in the same way,* and *in comparison*.

Recognizing Comparisons

You will often come across comparisons in your reading. Sometimes authors make comparisons in order to help readers understand a new idea.

What is the new idea in each of the following sentences? To what familiar things is the new thing compared? What word signals the comparison?

1. The plesiosaurus looked like a turtle shell with a snake threaded through it.
2. Many ancient mollusks were similar to the snails and clams today.

Did you find the comparisons? In sentence 1, the comparison is signaled by the word *like*. An unfamiliar thing, a plesiosaurus, is compared to two familiar things, a turtle shell and a snake. The author realizes that you may not know what a plesiosaurus looked like, but you can imagine a turtle shell with a snake threaded through it.

In sentence 2, the word *similar* signals the comparison between ancient mollusks, which are unfamiliar, and snails and clams, which are more familiar. The comparison shows that if you know what snails and clams look like, then you know what ancient mollusks were like.

Sometimes authors give reasons for the comparisons they make. What things are compared in the next pair of sentences? What word signals the comparison? What reason is given for the comparison?

1. The modern Olympics are very much like the ancient Greek Olympics.
2. Then, as now, contestants had to train for a long time.

In sentence 1, the word *like* signals a comparison between the modern Olympics and the ancient Greek Olympics. Sentence 2 tells how the contestants' long training makes the two Olympics alike.

Using Clue Words to Recognize Contrast

You use comparison to show how things are alike. You use contrast to show how things are different. For instance, you might say, "I like adventure stories, but my sister prefers mysteries." You are contrasting your taste in books with your sister's taste in books.

Did you notice the word *but* in the example sentence? That is a clue that a contrast is being made. Other words that often signal contrasts are *however, nevertheless,* and *although.*

Authors sometimes use contrast to help you understand a new idea. What two things are being contrasted in each of the following pairs of sentences? What words signal the contrasts?

1. The first Olympics were held to honor the Greek gods and goddesses. However, the reason for today's Olympics is to build a spirit of world friendship.
2. In the northern half of the world, July is a summer month. But in the southern half of the world, July is a winter month.

In the first pair of sentences, the word *however* is a clue to a contrast. The reason for the first Olympics is contrasted with the reason for the modern Olympics. In the second sentence pair, the word *but* signals the contrast between July in the northern half of the world and July in the southern half of the world.

Time words can also be clues to contrasts. In the following paragraph, two different times are contrasted. Notice the time words.

Long ago, most sports equipment was made from natural products like wood and leather. Today, artificial products such as fiberglass and plastic are often used.

In the paragraph you just read, the materials used long ago to make sports equipment are being contrasted with what is often used today. Time words such as *long ago, today, now, then,* and *used to* are often clues that two different times are being contrasted.

Comparison and Contrast Used Together

Sometimes authors use comparison and contrast together. In a paragraph, or even in a single sentence, an author may tell you what is the same and what is different about two things.

As you read each of the following sentences, ask yourself, "What two things are being compared and contrasted in this sentence?" "How are they alike?" "How are they different?" Use the clue words to help you.

1. Steve's sweater is the same style as Jo's, but it's a different color.
2. Although Mom's car is smaller than Pat's, it uses a similar amount of gas.

In sentence 1, the word *as* gives you a clue that Steve's sweater is being compared to Jo's sweater. The sweaters are alike in style. The word *but* tells you that the sweaters' colors are different. This is a contrast.

In sentence 2, the word *although* signals a contrast: Mom's car and Pat's car are different in size. The word *similar* signals a comparison: the cars' use of gas is alike.

Textbook Application: Comparison and Contrast in Science

Authors often use comparison or contrast to help readers understand new ideas. A comparison tells how two or more things are alike. A contrast tells how two or more things are different. Recognizing comparisons and contrasts will help you understand what you read.

Sometimes authors use clue words that make it easier to recognize a comparison or a contrast. Some words that may signal a comparison are *like, as, similar, too, also, in, the same way,* and *in comparison*. Words that often signal contrasts are *but, however, nevertheless,* and *although*. Time words such as *long ago, today, now, then,* and *used to* may also signal contrasts.

Read the following selection from a science textbook to yourself. The sidenotes will help you find comparisons and contrasts.

What does the word *too* signal? What things are being compared?

What does the word *difference* alert you to look for?

Think of a dog. A dog is a complete living thing, an **organism.** It is an organism made up of millions of cells: muscle cells, nerve cells, blood cells, and many other kinds of cells. A dog is a **many-celled organism.**

A paramecium is a complete living thing, too. A paramecium is an organism, though it is made up of just one cell. A paramecium is a **one-celled organism.**

What is the difference between a one-celled organism, like a paramecium, and a single cell, such as a muscle cell in a dog?

The paramecium can get its own food. The muscle cell in the dog depends on the blood to bring it food. The single cell of the paramecium moves about on its own. The single muscle cell of a dog, however, moves along with millions of other muscle cells.

What things are contrasted here? How many differences are mentioned? What signal word is used?

One-celled organisms like the paramecium carry on all life activities in one cell. A one-celled organism is a complete organism. Yet a muscle cell is only one kind of cell in an animal like a dog. In a many-celled organism, a single cell is only part of the organism.

Does the word *yet* signal a comparison?

Shaped like a slipper, the paramecium is covered with cilia. The cilia on the paramecium steer bits of food into its mouth. The cilia also help the paramecium move about. They beat against the water like oars.

Two things are compared in the first sentence. What are they? What clue word is used? What things are compared in the last sentence? How are they alike?

— *HBJ Science*
Harcourt Brace Jovanovich

When you read a textbook, look for comparisons and contrasts. Recognizing how things are alike or different can help you understand and remember what you read.

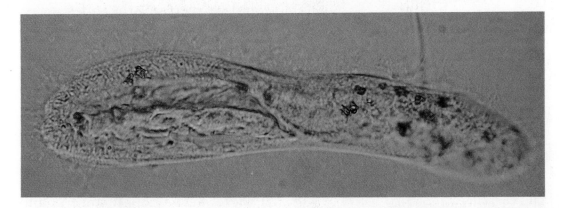

Samuel Morse had several turning points in his career as an inventor. Read to find out what they were.

Samuel Morse made a great contribution to the field of communication. How was his invention like the invention of Blissymbols?

Signals and Messages
by William Wise

Even in the earliest times, people had tried different ways of communicating quickly. Sometimes they sent letters by messenger. Sometimes they communicated by using signals.

Greek soldiers sent messages by turning their shields toward the sun. The flashes of reflected light could be seen several miles away. The enemy did not know what the flashes meant. But other Greek soldiers understood what the message said.

In some places, Roman soldiers built long rows of signal towers. When they had a message, the soldiers shouted it from tower to tower. If there were enough towers, and

enough soldiers with loud voices, important news could be sent over a long distance.

American Indians used smoke signals to send messages. First they built a smoky fire on the top of a hill, then held a blanket over the fire. Each time the blanket was lifted, a puff of smoke rose in the air. Different numbers of puffs had different meanings. Watching from a distant hill, other Indians counted the number of puffs and understood the message.

In Africa, people learned to send messages by beating on a series of large drums. Each drum was kept within hearing distance of the next one. The drum beats were sent out in a special code that all the drummers understood. Though the messages were simple, they could be transmitted at great speed for hundreds of miles.

In Europe, people found another way to send short messages. They built towers and signaled one another by using semaphore code. Each position of the arms had a different meaning, known to the people who worked the semaphore.

For thousands of years, people sent messages by all of these different methods. But as little as two hundred years ago, most people in the world still could not communicate quickly enough.

To call a doctor or to ask for assistance in fighting a fire, you had to go on foot or on horseback. Mail service was very slow. Letters went by mail-coach, or were carried in the pockets of a single horseback rider.

On land, therefore, letters or messages hardly ever traveled faster than the speed of a horse. At sea, a vital message could not travel faster than the speed of a sailing ship.

At times, people suffered a great deal because information could not be sent more quickly. In the year 1815, during the War of 1812, a fierce battle was fought near the city of New Orleans between American and British soldiers. Only later was it learned that the battle should never have been fought. Both sides had agreed to make peace — two weeks before the first shot had been fired. But word of peace had traveled too slowly, and more than a thousand soldiers had been killed or wounded by the time the news of peace had arrived.

"A Patient Waiter Is No Loser"

In 1832, an American painter named Samuel Morse left England to return home. Although he was primarily an artist, Morse had long been interested in the idea of fast communications. One evening while on shipboard, he began talking to another passenger about electricity. The passenger told him how an electric current could be made, and how far and how quickly the current would flow along a wire.

That night Morse was so excited he hardly slept. He seemed to see wires stretching around the world carrying messages at great speed. For Morse realized almost immediately that the flow of an electric current could be controlled simply by raising or lowering a key at one end of a wire. By using a code, and by stopping and starting the current, messages could be sent to distant areas.

While still aboard ship, he worked out a simple code of short and long signals, which he called "dots" and "dashes." Later, Morse improved his code. Today, it is known as the International Morse Code. Here it is:

The International Morse Code

A · −	N − ·	Á · − − · −	8 − − − · ·
B − · · ·	O − − −	Ä · − · −	9 − − − − ·
C − · − ·	P · − − ·	É · · − · ·	0 − − − − −
D − · ·	Q − − · −	Ñ − − · − −	, (comma) − − · · − −
E ·	R · − ·	Ö − − − ·	. · − · − · −
F · · − ·	S · · ·	Ü · · − −	? · · − − · ·
G − − ·	T −	1 · − − − −	; − · − · − ·
H · · · ·	U · · −	2 · · − − −	: − − − · · ·
I · ·	V · · · −	3 · · · − −	' (apostrophe) · − − − − ·
J · − − −	W · − −	4 · · · · −	- (hyphen) − · · · · −
K − · −	X − · · −	5 · · · · ·	/ − · · − ·
L · − · ·	Y − · − −	6 − · · · ·	parentheses − · − − · −
M − −	Z − − · ·	7 − − · · ·	underline · · − − · −

Once back in the United States, Morse eagerly built the first model of what he called the "telegraph." As with most inventors, he found it difficult to interest anyone in his invention.

He wanted very much to keep on working on his invention, but he needed income to support himself and his family. So, in 1835, he accepted an appointment as professor of art and design at a university. This did not mean he lost interest in his dreams of fast communication. He kept on working and experimenting.

One of Morse's students, Alfred Vail, became interested in the telegraph. Vail's father was wealthy and, because of his son's enthusiasm, advanced Morse enough money to build a small laboratory. There Morse and young Vail built a better model. When it was ready, Vail's father came to the laboratory. He didn't believe the invention would work. He wrote a message on a slip of paper: "A patient waiter is no loser."

"Send that to Professor Morse," he said, "and see if he gets it at the other end!"

His son began to tap out the message with his telegraph key. In the next room, Morse received the signals, and wrote down the message. Then he carried it back and showed it to the student's father. He had written, "A patient waiter is no loser."

Luckily, Morse himself was a patient man. From 1838 to 1844, he tried to get the first telegraph line built. He showed people his model and proved that it worked. But strangely enough, businessmen did not think the telegraph would be very useful. Neither did President Martin van Buren and his Cabinet when Morse showed them how easy it was to send messages "instantly" over a wire.

Morse went to England, France, and Russia. None of these countries was willing to spend the money to build a telegraph line. At last, back home, Congress agreed to give him $30,000 to build a test line from Washington to Baltimore.

At this point, with success so near, Morse made a mistake. He laid his wire underground in pipes. The wires were not insulated, though, which meant that the electric current could escape freely into the ground. The wire "went dead"— it would not carry a message. More than $20,000 had been spent, and there was absolutely nothing to show for it.

But Morse still had almost $10,000. This time, he and his helpers strung the wire above ground on poles. To keep the electricity from escaping, they insulated the wires with the necks of glass bottles. At last the test line, just forty miles long, was ready.

A friend of Morse dictated the first message in Washington. "What hath God wrought?" the message said.

The letters tapped out, and at the other end of the line, the Baltimore operator received them. Newspaper reporters crowded around as the telegraph key clicked away. Finally the operator handed them the message: "What hath God wrought?"

It had worked! In a few seconds, a message in dots and dashes had been sent from one city to another. Before long, telegraph lines were strung between other cities, both in America and Europe. Thanks to the artist and inventor, Samuel Morse, the age of rapid communications had begun.

Since then, other inventions have been developed, such as the telephone, the radio, and the teleprinter. These inventions now do much of the work first done by Samuel Morse's telegraph. But for many years the wires he had dreamed of did stretch around the world, the only way of carrying messages at great speed.

239

1. What were the turning points in Morse's career as an inventor?
2. Name five ways people sent messages before the invention of the telegraph.
3. How did you feel when Morse's underground wire went dead?
4. Samuel Morse had a problem supporting himself while he worked on his invention. How did he solve his problem?
5. When did you first begin to think that Morse would change communication? Find that part of the story.

Apply

the

Skills

A comparison explains how two things are alike. A contrast tells how things are different.

The invention of the telegraph and the invention of Blissymbols both helped people communicate. How are these inventions alike, and how are they different?

Prewrite

Early Methods of Communication	Modern Methods of Communication
1. smoke signals	1. radio
2. signal towers	2. telephone
3.	3.
4.	4.

The chart above lists some of the early methods of communication and some of the modern methods in use today. Copy and complete the chart by adding two more methods of communication to each category.

Compose

Use the information on the chart to write two paragraphs that compare and contrast early methods of communication with modern methods. In the first paragraph, contrast methods of communication. In the second paragraph, compare them. Begin with a good topic sentence and include at least one sentence that describes each method listed on the chart. You may wish to use this topic sentence for your first paragraph: *Early methods of communication were very slow compared to the methods in use today.*

Revise

Reread your paragraphs. As you revise, make sure that you have included information about each method of communication listed on the chart.

Characterization and Dialogue

When you read a story, you often feel that the characters are real people. An author tries to make the characters in a story seem real to you. To do this, the author gives the characters qualities, such as kindness or grumpiness, that a real person might have. These qualities are called **character traits**.

It would be simple for an author to write, "Bill is a grumpy person." But that would make the story dull. Instead, the author might let you discover for yourself that Bill is grumpy. One way an author does this is by describing what Bill does. Read this description of Bill. Look for clues that tell you that Bill is grumpy.

> Bill stomped into the room and flopped into the chair. He opened the newspaper and held it up in front of his face as he read. He didn't want to see anyone, and he didn't want anyone to see him.

Another way an author might let you find out about a character is through the words of other characters. Read these sentences to see what Bill's friends have to say about him.

> "I need to ask Bill about our homework," said Rich. "But I hate to bother him. I don't think he had a good day at band practice."

"He didn't," said Tammy. "Bill found out that he practiced the wrong song, so he's grumpier than ever."

A third way you can find out about a character is through the character's own words. Here's what Bill said to his cat. Can you tell what kind of mood Bill is in?

> "Get out of here," Bill said to Tiger, his cat.
> Tiger rubbed against Bill's foot.
> "Go away, Tiger," said Bill. "I don't want to play with you right now."
> The kitten jumped into Bill's lap.
> "Oh, all right," said Bill. "You can sit here, but don't expect me to pet you."

The words that are spoken by the characters in a story are called **dialogue**. In a play, there are no descriptions. All of the action is told through the dialogue of the characters. Here is some dialogue from a play. What can you tell about the characters?

> **Liz:** Hey! Look what I found under this bench! It's a wallet.
> **Sandy:** Look inside. Maybe there's a card that tells the owner's name.
> **Liz:** There's $10.00 in here! Wow! Now I can buy that new record album.
> **Sandy:** No you can't. That money belongs to someone. We have to give it back. Is there a name in the wallet?
> **Liz** *(Sighs)*: Yeah. Steve Jones, 267 Maple Street.
> **Sandy:** Let's go call Mr. Jones. The money is his.
> **Liz:** I guess you're right. I would feel bad if I kept the money. Let's go call Mr. Jones.

What can you tell about the kind of person Sandy is? What can you tell about Liz? As you read, look for the ways the author tells you about the kind of person a character is.

Lewis Carroll

When Charles Dodgson wrote *Alice in Wonderland*, he did not use his real name, but instead made up what we call a "pen name." This name was Lewis Carroll.

Dodgson lived about a hundred years ago. He taught math to college students in Oxford, England. He was tall and slender with blue eyes and a crooked smile. He had an uneven walk because of a tilted shoulder. He was also deaf in one ear.

With adults, he felt awkward and he stammered, but when he spoke to children, he came alive. It was easy for him to talk to them, and he always had new games and puzzles to show them.

One Friday, he and a friend took three little sisters on a boat trip. The girls were Lorina, Alice, and Edith Liddell; they were thirteen, ten, and eight years old. The little group rowed down the river for a few miles and then pulled up beside the river bank to rest.

That was when Dodgson first told the girls about Alice's adventures in Wonderland. You will be reading some of these adventures for yourself. The real Alice Liddell was thrilled to be the heroine of the make-believe story.

At times Dodgson would stop the story and say, "And that's all till next time." Then all three girls cried, "Ah, but it is next time." So he had to keep on making up more adventures as he went along. Sometimes he would pretend to fall asleep in the middle of the story. He would always pick an exciting or scary moment to do this. He loved to tease in that way. Then the three girls would plead until he went on with the tale.

Dodgson added more details to the story on other picnics. Alice begged him to write it all down, and at last he agreed. After a while, parents who had read the story said that it should be made into a book and published. That way, other children could enjoy it also. No one had any idea that it would become an all-time classic. An artist named John Tenniel did illustrations that went along with the story. He pictured Alice as a girl with long blond hair. In fact, Alice Liddell had brown eyes and dark brown hair, cut short, with bangs across the forehead.

When it was published, *Alice in Wonderland* was an instant success. Adults as well as children loved it. They also wanted to read more adventures of Alice. At last, Dodgson wrote a sequel to the first story. A sequel tells what happens after the end of an earlier story. This book was called *Through the Looking Glass*. This second book was also a big success.

Later, Dodgson became ashamed of *Alice in Wonderland* and *Through the Looking Glass*. He called them "nonsense books." Using his real name, Dodgson then wrote serious books for adults. He finally wrote one last nonsense book, filled with silly and wonderful rhymes, called *The Hunting of the Snark*. Of course, this was immediately popular. Children still read it today.

Getting into Looking-Glass House was a turning point for Alice. How does everything change on the other side of the looking glass?

Each character that Alice meets has a strange way of looking at the world. What does the dialogue tell you about each character?

Through the Looking Glass

by Lewis Carroll

Adaptation by Lewy Olfson

Characters

Alice	**Humpty Dumpty**
The Red Queen	**The White Knight**
The White Queen	**Narrator**

Narrator: Alice was sitting in the big easy chair, playing with Dinah, her cat, and wondering what the best thing to do might be. If Dinah had been a person, instead of a cat, they might have had a game of chess. Alice was very fond of chess. Or perhaps they could play make-believe, for Alice was very fond of make-believe, too. She was trying to decide which would be better — chess or make-believe. She thought she might consult Dinah herself on the matter.

From *Classics Adapted for Acting and Reading* by Lewy Olfson. Copyright © 1970 by Lewy Olfson. Published by Plays, Inc., Boston, MA.

Alice: Kitty, can you play chess? Now don't smile, my dear. I'm asking it seriously. Whenever I play, you watch me so closely that I almost think you understand the game. And when I say "Check," you always purr with pleasure. Kitty dear, let's pretend that you're the Red Queen. Do you know, I think if you sat up and folded your arms, you'd look exactly like her.

Narrator: The Red Queen—as Alice was sure her kitty understood—is one of the figures used in playing chess. And "Check" is something one says quite often while playing chess.

Alice: *Do* try to look like the Red Queen, Kitty. Oh, you bad cat, why don't you cooperate? If you're not good directly, I'll put you right into Looking-Glass House. What's that, Kitty? Don't you know what Looking-Glass House is? Come here and I'll show you. You see, it's the house just on the other side of our looking glass. The room on the other side, of course, is just like our drawing room on this side, only with everything reversed. But that's just to fool us. Just beyond the looking-glass part

you can't see—I'm sure there are the most wonderful things anyone could ever imagine.

Oh, how I wish I could get into Looking-Glass House. Let's pretend that there *is* a way. Let's pretend that the glass has become as soft as gauze, so that we can get through. Why, Kitty, *look*! The glass *is* getting soft. It's turning into a sort of mist, I declare. Kitty, I'm going through the glass. What fun! I'm going through the looking glass!

Music: *Happy theme.*

Narrator: Sure enough, Alice found herself able to step through the looking glass over the mantel and right into Looking-Glass House. She looked around. Everything in the room was just the same as in her own drawing-room at home, but it was all reversed. Was it *really* the same, she wondered, or did it just appear to be? She spied a book on the table and turned over a few pages.

Alice: What curious writing! It's not like proper writing at all. I wish I could read it—but I don't know the language. Why, it's a looking-glass book, of course. I'll have to hold it up to the glass to see what it says. Oh, I see. It's a poem. "Jabberwocky."

> 'Twas brillig, and the slithy toves
> Did gyre and gimble in the wabe:
> All mimsy were the borogoves,
> And the mome raths outgrabe.

How funny, it *seems* to be English, and yet somehow it doesn't quite make sense. Somehow it seems to fill my head with ideas—only I don't know exactly what they are. Oh, it's all as new and different as I imagined! What a wonderful, curious place is Looking-Glass House!

Music: *Happy theme.*

Narrator: Anxious to see what lay behind the door she had always thought so much about, Alice dashed out of the room. Without thinking twice she ran down the stairs and out into the garden. Imagine her surprise when she collided with—of all people—the Red Queen herself. She looked just like the Red Queen in Alice's chess set, crown and all; but by some miracle, she had grown, so that she was now as tall as Alice herself.

Red Queen: Well, young lady, where do you come from? And where are you going?

Alice: I—I'm not quite sure, ma'am. I seem to have lost my way.

Red Queen: I don't know what you mean by *your* way. All the ways around here belong to me. Curtsy while you're thinking what to say. It saves time. And always say "Your Majesty."

Alice: I only wanted to see what your garden was like, Your Majesty. I declare, it's marked out just like a large chessboard.

Red Queen: Of course it is, my dear.

Alice: Oh, I see! It's a great huge game of chess that's being played. Oh, what fun it is. I wish I could play. I wouldn't mind being a Pawn, if only I might join — though of course I should like to be a Queen best.

Red Queen: That's easily managed. You're in the Second Square to begin with. When you get to the Eighth Square, you'll be a Queen. Now, take my hand, my dear, for we must begin to run.

Alice (*Beginning to pant for breath*): Where are we — running to?

Red Queen: Faster, faster! Don't try to talk!

Alice: My — goodness. I've never — run so fast — in my life. Are we almost there?

Red Queen: Almost there? Why, we passed it ten minutes ago. Faster! There now. You may rest a little.

Alice: Oh, I'm so glad. But — but we're under the same tree we were under when we started. Everything's just as it was.

Red Queen: Of course it is. What did you expect?

Alice: Well, in *our* country, you generally get to someplace else if you run very fast for a long time as we've been doing.

Red Queen: A slow sort of country! *Here*, you see, it takes all the running you can do just to keep in the same place. If you want to get somewhere else, you must run twice as fast. Now then: at the end of two yards I shall give you your directions. (*Pause*) You have nothing to say?

Alice: I didn't know I was supposed to say anything.

Red Queen: You *should* have said, "It's extremely kind of you to tell me all this." But we'll pretend you have said it. Your instructions are to get to the Eighth Square as fast as you can. Then you'll be a regular Queen. Now, a few words of advice. Speak in French when you can't think of the English for a thing; turn out your toes as you walk; and remember who you are. That's all you need to know. Goodbye!

Alice: Goodbye, Red Queen. And thank you ever so much for starting me off.

Red Queen: Think nothing of it, my dear. I shall see you again in the Eighth Square, when we are Queens together. And won't that be feasting and fun! Goodbye.

Alice (*In amazement*): I declare! She's running faster now than she did before. How complicated it is to play chess when you're one of the pieces yourself. I wonder, how am I supposed to begin?

Narrator: It was not a very difficult question for Alice to answer, as there was only one road. As she walked along, the wind blew somebody's shawl in her direction, and Alice caught it. Farther along the road she saw a funny little lady running toward her. It was, without doubt, the owner of the shawl—and Alice noticed that she looked very much like the chess piece of the White Queen.

Alice: I'm very glad I happened to be in the way, ma'am, when your shawl came floating along. Here, let me help you adjust it. Tell me, am I addressing the White Queen?

White Queen: Well, yes, if you call that a dressing. It isn't *my* notion of the thing at all, for you're doing it all wrong.

Alice: If Your Majesty will only tell me the right way to begin, I'll do it as well as I can.

White Queen: I don't know what's the matter with that shawl. It's out of temper, I think. I've pinned it here, and I've pinned it there, but there's no pleasing it. And look at the mess my hair is in.

Alice: Perhaps what you need is a lady's maid.

White Queen: I'm sure I'll take *you* with pleasure. Two pence a week is what the position pays — and, of course, jam every other day.

Alice: I don't want you to hire *me* — and I don't like jam.

White Queen: It's very *good* jam.

Alice: Well, I don't want any jam.

White Queen: You couldn't have it even if you *did* want it. The rule is, jam tomorrow and jam yesterday — but never jam today. It's jam every *other* day. Today isn't any other day, you know.

Alice: I don't understand you. It's all so confusing.

White Queen: That's the effect of living backwards. But there is one great advantage in it: my memory works both ways. In that way, I can remember things before they happen.

Alice: I'm sure *mine* works only one way.

White Queen: How sad for you. (*Shrieking*) Oh, oh, oh. My finger's bleeding! Oh, oh, oh, oh, oh.

Alice: What is the matter? Have you pricked your finger?

White Queen: I haven't pricked it yet — but I soon shall. Oh, oh, oh. There, you see? The pin of my brooch has come undone, and I must fasten it up again.

Alice: Take care, you're holding it all crooked. Oh, you've stabbed yourself with it.

White Queen (*Calmly*): That accounts for the bleeding, you see. Now you understand the way things happen here.

Alice: But why don't you scream *now*?

White Queen: I've done all the screaming already. What would be the good of having it all over again? Now then: how old are you?

Alice: I'm seven and a half.

White Queen: I believe you. Now I'll give *you* something to believe. I'm just one hundred and one, five months, and a day.

Alice: I can't believe that.

White Queen: Can't you? Try again. Draw a long breath and shut your eyes.

Alice: There's no use trying. I just *can't* believe impossible things.

White Queen: Poor girl, you probably haven't had much practice. When I was your age, I always did it for half an hour each day. Why, sometimes I've believed as many as six impossible things before breakfast. But we have talked enough, my dear. It is time for you to move on to the next square.

Alice: Will I see you again, Your Majesty?

White Queen: By and by, perhaps. One never knows in chess. But we must part for the moment. You go that way, and before you know it you'll be in the next square.

Alice: I do hope I meet somebody nice there.

White Queen: Why, what a silly girl you are. You'll meet the nicest one of all: Humpty Dumpty!

Music: *Happy theme.*

Narrator: Sure enough, when she reached the next square, there was Humpty Dumpty, perched on his wall. Humpty Dumpty himself! Alice could hardly believe it. She ran forward with her arms outstretched, for she felt that at any moment he might fall and break into a million pieces.

Alice: It *is* Humpty Dumpty, it is! And how exactly like an egg he is.

Humpty: It's very provoking to be called an egg — very.

Alice: I said you looked like an egg, sir. And some eggs are very pretty, you know.

Humpty: Some people have no more sense than a baby. Tell me your name and your business.

Alice: My name is Alice.

Humpty: It's a stupid enough name. What does it mean?

Alice: Must a name mean something?

Humpty: Of course it must. Now *my* name means the shape I am—and a very good shape it is, too. With a name like yours, you might be any shape.

Alice: Why do you sit here all alone?

Humpty: Because there's nobody here with me. Did you think I didn't know the answer to that riddle? Ask another.

Alice: Don't you think you'd be a lot safer on the ground?

Humpty: What tremendously easy riddles you ask! Of course I don't think so. If I ever did fall off—which there's no chance of—but *if* I did, the King has promised me . . . .

Alice (*Promptly*): To send all his horses and all his men.

Humpty: Shame on you. You must have been eavesdropping to know that.

Alice: I haven't indeed! It's in a book.

Humpty: Ah, that's different. They may write such things in a book if they like. Now let's get back to the last remark but one.

Alice: I'm afraid I can't quite remember it.

Humpty: In that case it's my turn to choose a new subject. So here's a question for you. How old did you say you were?

Alice (*Brightly*): Seven years and six months.

Humpty: Wrong! You never said a word about it!

Alice: I thought you meant "How old *are* you?"

Humpty: If I'd meant that, I'd have said it. Seven years and six months. An uncomfortable sort of age. If you'd asked my advice, I'd have said, "Leave off at seven." But it's too late now.

Alice: But one can't help growing, you know.

Humpty: One can't, perhaps, but two can. Now it's your turn to pick a subject.

Alice: That's a very nice belt you have on. Or rather, necktie. Or is it a belt? That is, it looks like a tie . . .

Humpty: It is a very provoking thing when a person doesn't know a belt from a necktie. It's a necktie, my child. The White Queen gave it to me as an unbirthday present.

Alice: I beg your pardon, but what is an *un*birthday present?

Humpty: A present given when it isn't your birthday, of course.

Alice: Oh, I like birthday presents best.

Humpty: You don't know what you're talking about. There is only one day in the year when you may get a birthday present, but three hundred and sixty-four days when you might get an *un*birthday present. There's glory for you.

Alice: I don't know what you mean by glory.

Humpty: Of course you don't—till I tell you. I meant, "There's a nice knock-down argument for you."

Alice: But glory doesn't mean "a nice knock-down argument."

Humpty: When *I* use a word it means just what I want it to mean: neither more nor less. But this is all impenetrability. By which, of course, I mean that we had better change the subject and it would be just as well if you'd mention what you're going to do next, as I suppose you don't mean to stand here all the rest of your life.

Alice: You're so good at explaining things. I wonder if you could explain the poem "Jabberwocky" to me.

Humpty: I'm not very good at explaining poems, I'm afraid. But I can *repeat* poetry. Shall I recite a poem for you now?

Alice: That would be very nice.

Humpty: "In winter, when the fields are white, I sing this song for your delight." Only I don't sing it.

Alice: I see you don't.

Humpty: If you can *see* whether I'm singing or not, you've very sharp eyes. "In spring, when woods are getting green, I'll try and tell you what I mean." There now, wasn't that lovely?

Alice: Is that all?

Humpty: That's all. Goodbye.

Alice: Oh, I suppose then, that I must go. Goodbye, till we meet again.

Humpty: I shouldn't know you again if we *did* meet. You're so exactly like other people.

Alice: The face is what one goes by, generally.

Humpty: That's just what I mean. You have the same face everybody has—two eyes, nose in the middle, mouth under. Now, if both eyes were on one side of your face . . . or if your mouth were at the top . . . . But it's too late to do anything about that now. So goodbye till we *never* meet again. It's been very nice talking with you.

Alice: Thank you, sir. But before I go, can you tell me in which direction I am next to move?

Humpty: Why, straight ahead. Incidentally, at this very moment the White Knight is in the middle of his move. If you run straight ahead, you may catch up with him.

Alice: How wonderful to meet a real Knight! Thank you very much, Humpty Dumpty, for a lovely conversation.

Humpty: Not at all, my dear. Impatience!

Alice: I suppose that means something different, too?

Humpty: Of course it does. Impatience always means goodbye. Impatience, Alice. Impatience!

Music: *Rollicking theme.*

Narrator: Alice waited a moment, but as Humpty had closed his eyes, she said goodbye once more and quietly walked away. She couldn't help thinking to herself about Humpty Dumpty.

Alice: Of all the unsatisfactory . . .

Narrator: But she never finished the sentence. At that very moment a heavy crash shook the forest from end to end. Poor Humpty Dumpty! Alice had no time to think further about his fate, however, for by now she had reached the next square. And sure enough, just as Humpty had predicted, there was the White Knight. How kindly he looked as he rode up on his white horse.

Knight: It was a glorious victory, wasn't it? I can even take one more person prisoner.

Alice: I hope it won't be me, sir. I don't want to be anybody's prisoner. I want to be a Queen.

Knight: So you will, when you've crossed the next brook. I'll see you safe to the edge of the wood — and then I must go back, you know, for that's the end of my move.

Alice: Thank you very much. Perhaps I shouldn't mention it, sir, but I notice there are a great many curious objects fastened to your horse's saddle.

Knight: Ah, yes — my inventions. I see you're admiring the little box. It's my own invention to keep sandwiches in. You see I carry it upside down, so that the rain can't get in.

Alice: But the things can get *out* that way. Did you know the lid was open?

Knight: I didn't know it. Well, the box is of no use now. I'll just hang it on this tree. Can you guess why?

Alice: No, sir, I can't.

Knight: In hopes that some bees may make a nest in it. Then should I get the honey.

Alice: But you have a beehive — or something like one — tied to the saddle.

Knight: Yes, and it's a very good beehive, too. But not a single bee has come near it yet. And the other thing is a mousetrap. I suppose the mice keep the bees out — or the bees keep the mice out.

Alice: It isn't very likely, is it, that there would be any mice on a horse's back?

Knight: Not *very* likely. But if they *do* come, I don't choose to have them running all about. It's best to be prepared

for everything. That's why the horse has those anklets 'round his feet.

Alice: What are *they* for?

Knight: To guard against the bites of sharks. It's an invention of my own. I say, I hope you have your hair well fastened on.

Alice: Why—only in the usual way.

Knight: That's hardly enough. You see, the wind is so very strong here. It's as strong as soup.

Alice: Have you invented a plan for keeping hair from being blown off?

Knight: Not yet. But I have a plan for keeping it from *falling* off. First, you take a stick. Then you make your hair creep up it, like a vine. The reason hair falls off is because it hangs down. Things never fall upward, you know. It's my own invention. You may try it if you like.

Alice (*Dubiously*): Perhaps I will . . . someday.

Knight: My newest invention is a way of getting over a gate. You see, I said to myself: The only difficulty is with the feet, for the head is already high enough. So first I put my head on the gate—then the head's high enough. Then I stand on my head—and that makes the feet high enough. And then I'm over, you see.

Alice: Yes, I suppose you would be over when that was done.

Knight: Well, here we are at the end of my move. I must leave you now.

Alice: But what am I to do next?

Knight: You've only a few yards to go. Down the hill and over that little brook, and then you'll be a Queen. But you'll stay and see me off first, I hope. It would encourage me so.

Alice: Certainly, if you'd like me to.

Knight: Goodbye, then. Remember, just over the brook, and you've reached the Eighth Square.

Narrator: Alice waited until the kindly White Knight had turned his horse around. Then they shook hands, and he trotted off. Alice waved until he was out of sight, then turned and ran down the hill. A very few steps brought her to the edge of the brook, and before she could think, she was flying across it. In a moment, she had come to rest on a lawn as soft as moss, with little flower beds dotted about it here and there.

Alice (*Delightedly*): The Eighth Square at last! How lovely! Oh, how glad I am to get here. And what is this on my head? It feels—it feels as though—it *is*! A crown, a crown, my very own crown. I've reached the Eighth Square. I have become a Queen!

Music: *Merry theme.*

Narrator: At last she was a Queen—the most important piece in the whole game of chess. She looked around proudly, and was amazed to discover the Red Queen and the White Queen sitting close to her, one on either side. She wanted to ask if the game was over, but thought it might not be polite. So, instead, she said:

Alice: Please, would you tell me—

Red Queen (*Interrupting*): Speak when you're spoken to.

Alice: But if everybody obeyed that rule, and if you spoke only when you were spoken to, and if everybody else waited till *they* were spoken to, nobody would ever say anything.

Red Queen: Ridiculous! Why, don't you see, child . . . .

Alice: I'm not a child anymore. I'm a Queen.

Red Queen: Nonsense. You aren't a Queen until you've passed the examination.

Alice: I'm sure I didn't mean . . . .

Red Queen: That's just what I complain of. You *should* have meant. What is the use of a child without meaning? Even a joke has meaning, and a child is of more importance than a joke. You couldn't deny that, even if you tried with both your hands.

Alice: I don't deny things with my hands.

Red Queen: Nobody said you did. I said, you couldn't if you tried. But let us get on with the examination. White Queen, ask the first question.

White Queen: Can you do Addition, Alice?

Alice: Oh yes, I was very good at Addition in school.

White Queen: Then tell me what one . . . and one . . . and one . . . and one and one (*Very fast*) and one and one and one and one add up to.

Alice: I don't know. I lost count.

Red Queen: She can't do Addition. How about Subtraction? Take nine from eight.

Alice: I can't take nine from eight because . . .

White Queen: Can't do Subtraction, either. Can you do Division? Divide a loaf by a knife — what's the answer to that?

Alice: I suppose —

Red Queen: Bread-and-butter, of course. You can't do sums at all!

Alice (*Angrily*): Can either of *you* do sums?

White Queen (*Ashamed*): No, I can't, though Red Queen is very good at them.

Red Queen: Let us try useful questions. How is bread made?

Alice (*Confidently*): I know that. You take some flour . . . .

White Queen: Where do you pick the flower? In a garden or a hedge?

Alice: It isn't picked at all. It's ground.

White Queen: How many acres of ground? Don't leave out so many things.

Red Queen: That's enough of useful things. Let us try languages. What is the French for fiddle-dee-dee?

Alice (*Protesting*): But fiddle-dee-dee's not English.

Red Queen: Who ever said it was?

Alice (*Defiantly*): If you tell me what language it is, I'll tell you the French for it.

Red Queen: Queens never make bargains.

Alice: I wish Queens never asked questions.

White Queen (*Yawning*): Oh dear, I am sleepy.

Red Queen (*Yawning*): Yes, so am I. We shall have to postpone the examinations.

Alice: Until when?

Red Queen: Until a year from next Thursday.

Alice: But that isn't fair! I've succeeded in getting as far as the Eighth Square. I don't want to have to wait until next year to become Queen.

White Queen: But you don't have to wait until next year. My backward memory tells me that you didn't pass the examination until the third time around — *three* years from half-past last Monday.

Alice (*Almost in tears*): But it isn't fair. I've worked so hard to become Queen, getting all the way from the Second Square to the Eighth. I nearly lost my temper trying to fix the White Queen's shawl. I had to listen to Humpty Dumpty's nonsense and admire the White Knight's worthless inventions. I've answered your horrid questions and been bullied about by you, but no matter what I do it doesn't seem to please you. And now you say I must wait three years before I become Queen.

Red Queen: Tut, tut, my dear. Queens never lose their tempers.

Alice: I can't stand this any longer. And as for *you*, Red Queen, you're the cause of it all.

Red Queen (*Disturbed*): Alice! What are you doing?

Alice: I'm shaking you, that's what I'm doing. I'm going to shake you and shake you and shake you. I only wish I could shake some sense into you. I'm going to shake you

until you turn—until you turn into an animal. I'm going
to shake you until you turn into a cat!

Red Queen: No, no, no!

Alice: Yes, yes, yes. I'm going
to shake you—and shake
you—and shake you. (*She
sounds sleepy*). Going to
turn you into a kitten . . .
shake you . . . and turn
you . . . and shake you . . .
and turn you . . . into a
kitten.

Music: *Dreamlike music,
played softly enough so that
Alice can be heard speaking
above it.*

Alice (*Sleepily*): Into a kitten!
I'm going to shake you
into a kitten!

Sound: *Cat purrs.*

Alice: (*Awake*): Why—why,
Dinah! It's you! I did shake her into a kitten. I did, I
did—and it's you. I—I'm home again. Yes, home in my
own house, by the fire. Oh, Kitty, I've had the most
marvelous dream. I dreamed I went into Looking-Glass
House. And the Red Queen was there—and the White
Queen, too. I saw Humpty Dumpty, and the White
Knight, and oh, Kitty, how strange it all was. And how
real it all was to me then—but now I can see that I didn't
really step through the Looking Glass after all. It was a
dream—it was all a wonderful, wonderful dream, Kitty.
A dream!

Looking-Glass Characters (*Softly*): Alice! Alice!

Alice: Where are those voices coming from? It *was* a dream. I *know* it was a dream.

Looking-Glass Characters (*Their voices more distant*): Alice.

Alice: Or—or was it?

Music: *Happy theme.*

1. How did everything change on the other side of the looking glass?
2. What did Alice have to do in order to become a queen?
3. Which character did you find most unusual? Why?
4. Alice was upset because the Red Queen was keeping her from becoming a queen. How did Alice solve this problem?
5. Why are unbirthday presents better than birthday presents? Find the part of the story that explains this.

Apply the Skills

In a play, you find out what a character is like through the character's dialogue.

Two statements in the list below were spoken by the Red Queen. Identify them and explain what each tells you about the Queen's character.

1. "Impatience always means goodbye."
2. "Speak when you're spoken to."
3. "The reason hair falls off is because it hangs down."
4. "I don't know what you mean by *your* way. All the ways around here belong to me."

Thinking About "Turning Points"

As we have seen, there are many kinds of turning points. Turning points change people's lives forever.

In "The Big Wave" a sudden tragic turning point forever changes Jiya's life. There is a happy turning point in "The Tide in the Attic," when Kees and his family are saved by a helicopter during the flood. In Ramona's life, there is an even more joyous turning point. As she welcomes the tiny new Quimby into the family, Ramona herself makes a great leap in growing up. Alice's imaginary leap through a looking glass turns her world, if only for a time, backwards.

There have been turning points in the world of communication. Samuel Morse's invention of the telegraph, the work of many years, was a turning point in communication history. Kari Harrington's learning to use Blissymbols to communicate was a major turning point that opened up entire worlds to her.

Our lives are filled with turning points, large and small. Some turning points bring unexpectedly wonderful surprises. What turning points do you think are ahead for you?

1. A turning point might change a person's whole life. Which character in these stories do you think experienced the greatest change? Tell why you think so.

2. Which character from "The Price of Eggs" or "Through the Looking Glass" do you like the most? Find a piece of dialogue that shows off that character. Tell why you would like to play that role.

3. Friends helped both Jiya and Kees at turning points in their lives. Compare how each character was helped by friends.

4. Two of the stories you read —"The Price of Eggs" and "Through the Looking Glass"—are plays. What makes them plays?

5. Describe the symptoms of "siblingitis." Why does Ramona have it? How would you cure it?

6. In "The Big Wave," Kino finds that he has a new brother in Jiya. In "The Fifth Quimby," Ramona gets a new sister. Both Kino and Ramona have to adjust to the changes in their families. Is this family change more difficult for Kino or Ramona? Why?

7. If you had never been able to speak and someone gave you a symbol board and explained how to use it, what would be your first message?

Read on Your Own

The Big Wave by Pearl Buck. John Day. Kino and Jiya become closer friends than ever after tragic events change Jiya's life.

Jed: The Story of a Yankee Soldier by Peter Burchard. Coward McCann. Jed realizes that an enemy in war is not necessarily a bad person.

Dear Mr. Henshaw by Beverly Cleary. Morrow. Leigh writes to his favorite author, and a pen pal becomes a real friend. The story is told in the form of letters.

Ramona Forever by Beverly Cleary. Morrow. Spunky Ramona comes through the problems, adventures, and other big changes in her life.

The Scribner Anthology for Young People edited by Anne Divan. Scribner. In this collection the short story, "The Bracelet," by Yoshiko Uchida, is of special interest.

The Oxford Book of Children's Verse in America edited by Donald Hall. Oxford. This book has poems about many subjects including baseball and crocodiles.

Blissymbolics; Speaking Without Speech by Elizabeth S. Helfman. Elsevier Nelson. Helfman describes the system of symbols that enables some handicapped children to communicate.

A Flock of Words collected and annotated by David MacKay. Harcourt Brace Jovanovich. The author has collected poems about many subjects.

How Juan Got Home by Peggy Mann. Coward McCann. Juan makes friends through his batting ability.

Classics Adapted for Acting and Reading by Lewy Olfson. Plays, Inc. These plays, adapted from such classics as *Rip Van Winkle*, *Through the Looking Glass*, and *Kidnapped*, are suitable for acting and for reading.

The Case of the Sabotaged School Play by Marilyn Singer. Harper & Row. Who is trying to sabotage the school play—and why?

The Alfred Summer by Jan Slepian. Macmillan. Alfred (who's retarded), Lester (who has cerebral palsy), and Myron (who is always laughed at for his clumsiness) become good friends while building a boat.

The Tide in the Attic by Aleid Van Rhijn, translated by A. J. Pomerans. Criterion. This is the true story of how a family is rescued by helicopter during a flood.

From Scrolls to Satellites: The Story of Communications by William Wise. Parents Magazine Books. Learn about ways to send messages, from smoke signals and flashing shields to telephones and satellites.

Unit 3

Dialogues

People talking, telling stories, telling jokes, asking questions, giving answers—these are all part of dialogue. **Dialogue** is a conversation between two or more people. If you talk with anyone other than yourself, you are having a dialogue.

Think about how much you learn from dialogue every day. Before you could read, almost all of your knowledge came either through your dialogue with others or from listening to other people's dialogues. In a story, you can find out much about the characters' thoughts and feelings through dialogue. You can also learn about a story's setting and plot from what the characters say.

In this unit you'll read dialogue between a few mean ogres, a very unusual dragon, and some funny people. You'll also find out about a real chimpanzee who can actually communicate with people. And you'll read dialogue between some storytellers and their listeners.

Dialogue can open up new worlds. What new worlds will the dialogue in these stories open up for you?

Fantasy

Fantasy is a kind of fiction. In fantasy you read about characters that could not possibly exist in real life. You meet animals such as Peter Rabbit, who talks and drinks tea, and Babar the elephant, who drives a car. You also meet human characters who have superhuman powers and qualities, such as Superman and Wonder Woman. Fantasies can take you to the far reaches of an unknown past or to unexplored places in a future world. Fairy tales and folktales, myths and legends, some cartoons and comics, some adventure tales, and all science fiction stories are examples of fantasy.

Magic things often happen in fantasy — things that could not happen in real life. Things appear and disappear. Characters sleep for a hundred years, or even die, and then come back to life. Humans are turned into animals.

Sometimes, though, not all characters and events in a fantasy are magical. Some fantasy stories are a blend of the real world and a fantastic world. In *The Wizard of Oz*, for example, a realistic character, Dorothy, and her realistic dog, Toto, live in the state of Kansas. They are blown by a tornado to the land of Oz, a magical place with witches, a wizard, and some amazing characters. In *Through the Looking Glass*, Alice, a realistic girl, steps through a magical mirror into a topsy-turvy world filled with such strange creatures as Humpty Dumpty.

Although fantasy stories have unrealistic characters and events, they often deal with real human problems. Think about *The Wizard of Oz*. A fantastic character such as the

276

Cowardly Lion struggles with the fear of being hurt. In the fantasy stories you read — from fairy tales to science fiction — you can often recognize human feelings about human problems.

Read the following dialogue from another popular fantasy, *Charlotte's Web* by E. B. White. In the story, Wilbur the pig is horrified to find out that he will be killed and turned into Christmas ham and bacon. Then he meets a spider named Charlotte who says she has a plan to save his life.

"I just love it in the barn," said Wilbur. "I love everything about this place."

"Of course you do," said Charlotte. "We all do."

The goose appeared, followed by her seven goslings. They thrust their little necks out and kept up a musical whistling, like a tiny troupe of pipers. Wilbur listened to the sound with love in his heart.

"Charlotte?" he said.

"Yes?" said the spider.

"Were you serious when you promised you would keep them from killing me?"

"I was never more serious in my life. I am not going to let you die, Wilbur."

If this dialogue were carried out between two human characters, it would not be fantasy. E. B. White imagined a barnyard where animal characters feel and talk about their situations in a human way. This element of fantasy makes the story funny. But generations of readers also have sympathized with Wilbur's fear and Charlotte's efforts to save him.

Perhaps E. B. White knew that only through fantasy could we ever sympathize with a pig and a spider. For fantasy often opens up our hearts as well as our minds.

Sometimes stories can help you to learn about yourself. Read to find out what Lee Edward asks Mama Luka when she finishes telling him the story. What does his question help him learn about himself?

As you read, look for the realistic and the fantastic elements of the story.

How Jahdu Became Himself

by Virginia Hamilton

Mama Luka liked to sit in her tight little room in a fine, good place called Harlem. She had black skin and a nose as curved as the beak of a parrot. She wore her hair in one long pigtail down her back. She called the pigtail her plait, and she could sit on it. She sat on it whenever she felt like telling tales.

Mama Luka took care of Lee Edward after his school was out for the day and until his mother came home from work. And Mama Luka sat all the while in her little room in the good place, telling Jahdu stories to Lee Edward. She told them slow and she told them easy while Lee Edward listened. He sat on the floor with his eyes tight shut, which was the best way for him to imagine Jahdu.

Summer had come to the good place called Harlem, so the window was open wide in Mama Luka's hot little room. Mama Luka had moved her chair closer to the window. Yes, she had. She had raised her blind so that she could see what happened in the street below.

"Yes, child," she said to Lee Edward, who sat on the floor, "I have seen fifty summers come to the street down

278

there and with each summer will come Jahdu just running along."

"Will I get to see him this summer?" asked Lee Edward.

"You might have a hard time seeing him, Little Brother," Mama Luka said, "because Jahdu is never the same."

"Not even his face?" asked Lee Edward.

"Anyone who has seen the face of Jahdu will tell you only that it is never the same," said Mama Luka carefully, "but there is a steady light from his eyes. There is pride in his face that is always the same."

"I will look for Jahdu," said Lee Edward. "I will look for the pride in every face I see."

"You know, I start baking bread in the summertime," Mama Luka told Lee Edward. "I always think that maybe this time Jahdu will stop and visit with me and tell me what he has been up to."

"Has Jahdu ever stopped by to visit with you?" asked Lee Edward.

Mama Luka stared out her window. She spoke softly to Lee Edward. "I am baking bread right now," she said. "I am baking bread and I am hoping."

"I can smell the bread," Lee Edward said, "and it smells very good, too."

"Yes, child," said Mama Luka, turning from the window. "I never told you before, but Jahdu was born in an oven beside two loaves of baking bread." Mama Luka smiled. "One loaf baked brown and the other baked black. Jahdu didn't bake at all, but since that time black and brown have been Jahdu's favorite colors and the smell of baking bread is the sweetest smell to him."

"Now here we go, Little Brother," Mama Luka said.

"There are many a-thousand Jahdu stories," she told Lee Edward, "and I know about two hundred of them. I've told you a roomful of Jahdu stories, so that leaves one more roomful of Jahdu stories to tell. Now, you pick out of the air in this room one more Jahdu story."

Then Lee Edward pointed to the window sill all of a sudden. Mama Luka understood and she cupped her hands around the place Lee Edward had pointed to. Mama Luka opened her mouth and swallowed what had been in her hands.

"Oh, yes," she said. "Little Brother, that's the best old story you picked out of the air. It makes me feel cool and fresh inside."

"Then tell it," Lee Edward said to Mama Luka.

"I'm getting myself ready," said Mama Luka.

THIS IS THE JAHDU STORY SO COOL AND FRESH
THAT MAMA LUKA TOLD TO LEE EDWARD.

Jahdu was running along and he was telling everybody
to get out of his way. Everybody always did get out of
Jahdu's way, except this time somebody wouldn't and that
somebody was Grass.

Grass lay on the ground in one dull shade of gray as far
as the eye could see. Jahdu shouted at him, "Get out of the
way, Grass, for Jahdu is coming through."

Grass didn't move at all. No, he didn't. Jahdu lay down
on Grass and stretched himself out as far as he could.

"How do you like that, Uncle No-Color?" Jahdu said to
Grass. "Jahdu is heavy, isn't he?"

Grass didn't say a word, but Grass couldn't feel the
sunlight with Jahdu stretched out on him and he grew cold.
And when Jahdu called him Uncle No-Color, he became
very angry.

Grass lifted all his young gray blades straight as arrows
and pushed them against Jahdu with all his might. The
strain on his young gray blades turned each and every one
of them green. To this day you can tell Grass whenever you
chance to see him, for each of his blades is still green.

Well, Jahdu laughed and he got up slowly. He yawned
two or three times and gave no more thought to Grass, who
had turned green.

Jahdu kept right on running along. He was running
eastward, for he had been born in the East. And Jahdu had
an idea he might like to be born again into something else.
He ran and he ran until he came to dry, hot sand.

"Woogily!" Jahdu whispered. "This sand is hotter than anything I know that is hot."

Jahdu saw Ocean lying as calm as could be on the horizon where the hot sand ended.

Jahdu screamed in his meanest voice, "Hey, Uncle Calm Ocean! Why don't you once in a while get up and give the sand something to cool itself with? Lying around all day, watering the clouds and cooling off the birds. Why don't you get yourself together long enough to help out the hot sand?"

Old Ocean wasn't bad, but he was used to being the biggest somebody around under the sky. He was used to not moving, just lying there as cool and blue as he pleased.

Ocean knew he was bigger and wetter and deeper than anything under the sun, and when Jahdu said what he had, all grew still.

The wind stopped its blowing. Ocean himself stopped being lazy long enough to think about what Jahdu had said.

All at once Ocean gathered himself together right across his middle and gave a heave that lifted his body higher than he had ever lifted it before. Ocean started moving from the horizon over the sand in a white, foaming line treetop tall.

"Woogily!" said Jahdu, and he went on running.

Old Ocean leaped right in front of Jahdu, but Ocean didn't catch him, for Jahdu surely knew how to keep running along. Every time Ocean slid back to the horizon to gather himself together again, Jahdu would run away somewhere else. Ocean would hit the hot sand with all his might only to find that Jahdu had run by.

To this day Ocean keeps on moving up and back and up and back again, trying to catch anything passing by.

Jahdu kept right on running along. He was growing tired and he felt like stopping to rest, but he had no friend he could stop along with. He had played so many tricks nobody trusted him.

Mrs. Alligator used to give Jahdu free rides on her back. But not anymore, for Jahdu had come along one time with a can of blue paint on his head. He had put Mrs. Alligator to sleep and then he had painted her skin with two coats of blue paint. The paint hadn't worn off for a year. Now Mrs. Alligator thought Jahdu had manners worse than a crocodile's, so whenever she heard Jahdu running along, she would dive deep to the bottom of her pool. Yes, she would.

Jahdu came alongside a shade tree. The shade tree had leaves as big as elephant's ears. It had a trunk smooth to lean against, so Jahdu sat himself down. He leaned against the tree trunk and rested and he let the leaves as big as elephant's ears fan him. Jahdu soon felt like taking a nap. He was almost asleep when he heard a voice next to him.

"Stranger, kindly move off my tail!" said the voice. "Hey, you, sir, who will lean against a body without a pardon me!"

"Woogily!" said Jahdu, and he jumped five feet away from the tree.

It wasn't the shade tree who had spoken. Shade trees do not speak and do not care who leans against them. It was old Chameleon who had spoken. Chameleon was a lizard six inches long. He had not seen Jahdu for many a month, but when Jahdu said "Woogily!" Chameleon knew him right away.

"Jahdu," Chameleon said, "I wish you would learn to ask somebody when you want to lean on somebody."

Jahdu looked all around, and it took him a minute to see the lizard on the tree trunk. Jahdu had always liked Chameleon because Chameleon could change the color of his skin any time he felt like it. If Chameleon sat down on a green leaf, he would turn himself green and nobody could tell he was sitting on the leaf. If he wanted to sit on a flat stone, he would turn himself the color of the flat stone and nobody need know he was resting awhile.

At last Jahdu saw Chameleon on the trunk of the shade tree. Chameleon was brown as was the dark brown tree trunk.

"Well, how are you doing?" Jahdu said, coming closer.

"You stay right where you are!" shouted Chameleon. "Don't come any nearer until you promise you won't tie my tail in a knot."

"Oh, my goodness," Jahdu said, sitting down.

"I mean what I say," Chameleon told Jahdu. "The last time you tied my tail up I had an awful time getting it untied."

"How did you get it untied?" Jahdu wanted to know. He spoke to the lizard in his kindest voice, for Jahdu knew now that he wanted something special from the lizard.

"Never you mind how I got myself loose," said Chameleon. "You just promise."

So Jahdu promised, and then he and the lizard sat against the trunk of the shade tree.

"I've just been running along," Jahdu told his friend Chameleon.

"All right," said Chameleon.

"I had a little fun with Grass," said Jahdu.

"That's good," said the lizard. "Grass is always so gray and sad."

"Not anymore," Jahdu said. "Grass is now green as he can be!"

"All right," Chameleon said. "Green is brighter than gray."

"I had a little fun with Ocean," Jahdu told his friend.

"That's all right," said Chameleon. "Ocean always did lie too far back on the horizon."

"Not anymore," Jahdu told him. "Now Ocean rises treetop tall. He runs over the hot sand hilltop high and then he falls down trying to catch anything running along."

"That's good, too," said the lizard. "Now the hot sand will get a chance to cool itself."

"So I have stopped awhile from running along," said Jahdu.

"All right," Chameleon said.

"I have stopped and now I know why I was running along and what I want from you," said Jahdu.

"Tell me then," said the lizard.

"I want to know how you work your magic," said Jahdu.

"You already have your own magic," Chameleon told Jahdu. "You can put anything to sleep and wake anything up again."

"But I need to know the magic you have," said Jahdu to his friend.

"What magic is that?" Chameleon asked Jahdu.

"You can change to look like a stone or even a leaf," Jahdu told him.

"Sure," said the lizard, "but I can't let you do that, too."

"Well, I know you can't, my friend," Jahdu said. "I only want to know how you do it. If I know how it is you can change and hide, maybe I can learn how to just change into something else."

"Change into what?" Chameleon wanted to know.

"Change myself into whatever I want," Jahdu told him. "If I see a deer, I can be a deer running through the woods, and if I see a fox, I can be as swift and clever as a fox."

Chameleon smiled. "It's not hard," he told Jahdu. "I will tell you what I do, and with a bit of practice maybe it will work for you."

"Tell me then," said Jahdu.

"First I see a place where I want to sit," Chameleon said. "Then I think about what it feels like sitting there. Next I run as fast as I can to get there. Then I sit, and the color of the thing I'm sitting on comes over me right away."

"That's all you do?" Jahdu asked. "Woogily!" he said. "Changing is going to be easy!"

Suddenly Jahdu looked unhappy. "How am I going to run fast enough to catch up with a deer and climb on his back?" he asked the lizard.

"Maybe you won't have to run at all," said Chameleon. "Maybe you will only need to see the deer running fast."

"Then what?" Jahdu asked.

"Then you think hard," said Chameleon. "You say to yourself, 'Jahdu is running as fast as the deer. Jahdu is on that deer. Jahdu *is* that deer!'"

"Woogily!" said Jahdu.

"Try it," Chameleon told Jahdu.

Jahdu left his friend Chameleon dozing against the trunk of the shade tree and went running along. He had not seen anything yet that he wanted to be and he was still running eastward to where he had been born.

"The first thing I see that I like, I will be," Jahdu said to himself, and he kept right on running along.

Jahdu came to an island. The island had buildings higher than high. Jahdu liked the buildings. Yes, he did.

He said, "Woogily!" and kept on running. "I'm going to make myself into a building."

Jahdu picked out for himself a building higher than a hilltop and he thought very hard. "Jahdu is running to that building," he said to himself. "Jahdu is on top of that building. Jahdu *is* that building!"

Jahdu became a building made of steel and concrete. He was very tall, but he could not move. Jahdu did not like standing still.

"Woogily!" said Jahdu. He thought very quickly and he said to himself, "Jahdu is jumping off this building. Jahdu is running away from this building. Jahdu is not a building anymore!"

Jahdu kept right on running along. He ran and he ran through the city on an island. He saw a stray cat and he became the cat. But Jahdu didn't like being a cat. He was always hungry. He was sick and he was tired and he slept where he could. Jahdu was thrown out of a supermarket for trying to get at the frozen fish.

"Woogily!" said Jahdu. "Cats have a hard time getting along. Jahdu is jumping off this cat. Jahdu is running faster than this cat. Jahdu is not a cat anymore!"

Jahdu kept on running and saw a yellow-and-black taxicab.

"Woogily!" said Jahdu. "I'm going to be that taxicab." And so he was.

Now Jahdu was busy taking people from one place to another, but he didn't much like being a taxicab. People sat down too hard on his seats and tracked dirt in on his floor. People were afraid when he went very fast. Jahdu worked for long hours. Yes, he did. And the bright lights of the city hurt his eyes.

"Jahdu is jumping off this taxicab," Jahdu said at the end of a long day. "Jahdu is moving faster than that pretty yellow-and-black taxicab. Jahdu is not a taxicab anymore!"

The taxicab drove away, but Jahdu kept right on running along. He found himself in a fine, good place called Harlem.

"Woogily!" said Jahdu. "All the people here are brown and black."

Jahdu came upon a group of children playing in a

playground. He saw a small, black boy who was running around making noise.

"Woogily!" said Jahdu. "Jahdu is running as fast as that black child. Jahdu is jumping on that black child. Jahdu *is* that black child!"

Black was Jahdu's favorite color and Jahdu was now a strong, black child. He didn't own a baseball or a bat, but he had a dog. Yes, Jahdu did. The dog's name was Rufus, and the dog was black all over, just like Jahdu. Jahdu had a sister and a brother too. And Jahdu had a good time in the city on the island.

Jahdu was happy, because he was a strong, black boy. For a while he stayed in the neighborhood, just enjoying himself.

THIS IS THE END OF THE JAHDU STORY SO COOL
AND FRESH THAT MAMA LUKA TOLD TO THE CHILD,
LEE EDWARD.

"You picked the story," Mama Luka said. "It was a good
story and Jahdu was happy being a strong, black boy."

"The way I am happy?" asked Lee Edward.

"Just the way you are happy," said Mama Luka.

"Did the strong, black boy have the Jahdu magic?"

"The strong, black boy was still a small, black boy," said
Mama Luka, "and, Little Brother, a small, black boy doesn't
have too much magic, even when he's Jahdu. He could put
his mama to sleep by making her read him one storybook
after another, and he could wake his papa up fast enough
by saying he had been a building once upon a time. But he
didn't have much more magic than that."

"I don't see how Jahdu of all the Jahdu stories could like
being a small, black child," said Lee Edward. "I would think
he'd rather be a building."

"You think about it for a while," Mama Luka told Lee
Edward, "and I'll take myself a little nap for five or six
minutes." Mama Luka always did like sleeping after telling
a good Jahdu story.

Mama Luka went right to sleep in her chair and sitting
on her long black braid. The smell of baking bread was
strong and sweet in the room.

Lee Edward went to Mama Luka's kitchen not much
bigger than a closet on one side of the room and he peeked
into the oven. The large loaf of bread he found had baked
brown and was done, so Lee Edward took the loaf of bread
out of the oven and placed it on the counter. He turned off
the oven and stood sniffing the bread that smelled sweeter

than anything. And then Lee Edward lay on his back on the floor beside Mama Luka's chair and thought about Jahdu.

Pretty soon Lee Edward closed his eyes and smiled. A little later he opened his eyes and laughed. He knew why Jahdu was happy being a strong, black boy.

Lee Edward imagined Jahdu's changing from a strong, black boy into a bigger, stronger boy. As Jahdu grew, he had more and more magic power. Something Mama Luka had said about Jahdu came to him.

"There is pride in his face that is always the same."

Little Brother had to smile.

"Once he's grown up he'll be a black Jahdu with all his power," whispered Lee Edward.

He pointed to a space of air close to Mama Luka's right foot. He thought he felt himself growing.

"I can have the pride and power, too," Lee Edward said, and he waited for Mama Luka to wake up.

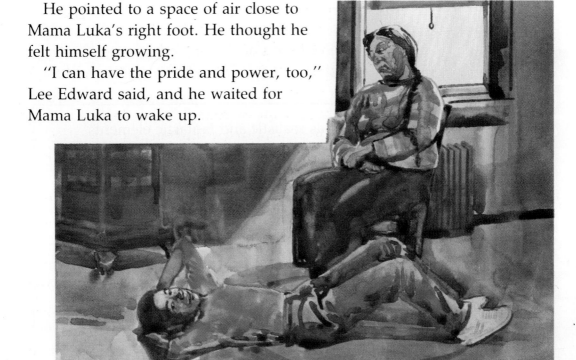

1. What did Lee Edward ask Mama Luka after she had finished telling him the story?
2. How did Lee Edward find out the answer to his question?
3. Jahdu often played tricks on other characters. For example, he tied Chameleon's tail in a knot. Why do you think Chameleon liked Jahdu and helped him out?
4. Lee Edward found out through the story that he had power. How was Lee Edward's power as a black boy like Jahdu's magic?
5. How did Lee Edward's dialogue with Mama Luka help him understand the story of Jahdu? Find parts of the story that tell you.

Apply

the

Skills

Fantasy often has realistic and fantastic elements in it. Read the following items from the selection. Tell which are realistic and which are fantastic.

1. Mama Luka wore her hair in a long pigtail that hung down her back.
2. Jahdu was born in an oven beside two loaves of bread.
3. Grass used to be a dull shade of gray.
4. Lee Edward sat on the floor with his eyes shut and imagined Jahdu.
5. Mama Luka liked to take a nap after telling a good story.

Prewrite

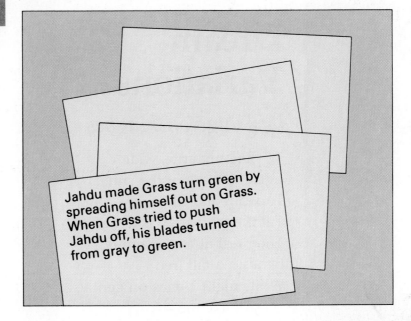

Jahdu made Grass turn green by spreading himself out on Grass. When Grass tried to push Jahdu off, his blades turned from gray to green.

The note card above describes a trick that Jahdu played on a character in "How Jahdu Became Himself." Use the story to make three more note cards about Jahdu's tricks. On each card explain what the trick was and how Jahdu played it.

Compose

Using your note cards, write a paragraph about how Jahdu liked to play tricks. Begin your paragraph with a topic sentence that summarizes your main idea. You may wish to use a topic sentence such as the following: *Jahdu loved playing tricks on everyone he ran into.*

Revise

Read your paragraphs. Make sure your summaries include the necessary information. If not, revise your work.

Dream Variations

by Langston Hughes

To fling my arms wide
In some place of the sun,
To whirl and to dance
Till the white day is done.
Then rest at cool evening
Beneath a tall tree
While night comes on gently,
  Dark like me —
That is my dream!

To fling my arms wide
In the face of the sun,
Dance! Whirl! Whirl!
Till the quick day is done.
Rest at pale evening . . .
A tall, slim tree . . .
Night coming tenderly
  Black like me.

In this story, an old woman must defend herself against some mischievous ogres. Read to see what her dialogue with them shows about her character.

As you read, think about what makes this story a fantasy.

The Old Woman and the Rice Cakes

retold by Ethel Johnston Phelps

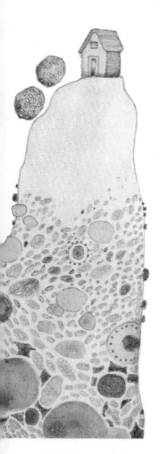

Long ago, in Japan, there was a cheerful old woman who lived alone in a small house halfway up a steep hill. She had a few chickens and a pig, but very little else. Quite often she had only one meal a day.

One evening she had just finished making a bowl of round rice cakes for dinner, when the bowl slipped and the rice cakes fell on the floor. To her dismay, they rolled right out the doorway. The old woman ran after them.

Once outside, the rice cakes rolled down the steep hill, bouncing over rocks, going faster and faster. The woman scurried down the hill behind them, but she could not catch up with them until they came to rest at the very bottom, near a large slab of rock.

Just as the woman bent over to pick up her rice cakes, a long, blue, scaly arm with a three-fingered, clawlike hand reached out from behind the rock and snatched them from her.

"That's my dinner!" she cried. She peered behind the rock slab, and seeing a small opening, in she went right after her rice cakes.

She found herself in a narrow tunnel. Ahead of her was a large shambling creature hurrying away.

"Sir!" she called loudly, trotting after him. "My dinner! You've taken my dinner!" But the creature went right on, with the woman close behind him, until they reached a large cave.

The old woman stopped short in surprise. In the cave were several more large creatures. They had horns on their heads, wide mouths that stretched from ear to ear, and three red, staring eyes. She realized she was in a den of Oni, ogres who lived under the ground and came forth only at night. The Japanese Oni, like trolls in other parts of the world, are always bent on mischief.

She was, however, more angry than frightened, for the Oni had greedily shared her rice cakes among themselves and gulped them down.

"You're no better than thieves!" she cried. "You've eaten my rice cakes and now I have no dinner!"

But they only sat licking their large, clawlike hands, staring at her so hungrily that she wondered if they were going to eat her next.

Then one of them said, "Did you make the rice cakes?"

"Yes, I did," retorted the old woman. "I make very tasty rice cakes, if I do say so myself."

"Come along, then, and make more!" said he, and he clumped away through a maze of tunnels and caves. The old woman followed, for she was hungry and she thought it only fair that the ogres should give her dinner.

But by the time they arrived at the cave full of huge round cooking pots, she realized she was hopelessly lost. She doubted she could ever find the small hole in the rock where she came in.

The Oni dropped a few grains of rice into a large pot of water.

"That will never make enough rice cakes!" she said crossly.

"Of course it will, stupid creature," he scowled. He picked up a flat wooden stirrer. "Put this into the pot and start stirring."

The woman did as she was told. At once the few grains of rice increased until almost the whole pot was filled. So the old woman made the ogres a huge pile of rice cakes — taking care to eat some herself first, before handing them over.

"I'll be going home now," she announced firmly, "if you'll show me the way back to the entrance."

"Oh, no," growled the Oni. "You will stay here and cook for us."

This did not suit the little old woman at all, but as she looked at the large monsters crowded about, licking their claws, she thought she had better not say so.

Nevertheless, while the woman worked to make piles of rice cakes for the hungry Oni, she thought and thought about how to escape. She soon discovered that the source of the water for cooking the rice was a stream nearby, flowing along between the rock caverns. She thought this must be the same stream that flowed out of the bottom of the hill below her home. Farther on, it became a river, and the people of the village fished from its banks.

But there was no boat to be seen.

"The Oni would not have a boat," thought the old woman. "It's well known the wicked creatures cannot go over water!"

Without a boat, how could she escape? She thought of this as she cooked and stirred — until she saw that one of the large round pots might do very well. They were as big as she was.

The Oni, being night creatures, slept during the day, sprawled in the many caves under the hill. The next day, as soon as they were all asleep, she put the magic stirring paddle in a huge pot and dragged the pot down to the stream.

It floated very nicely, so she hopped in and started to paddle. But the grating sound of the pot being dragged to the stream had wakened a number of Oni nearby. Suddenly they appeared on the side of the stream shouting in rage.

The old woman paddled faster and faster. Ahead she could see a patch of sunlight where the stream made its way out into the world.

But the stream began to shrink, and grew smaller and smaller. Then she saw that the Oni were drinking up the water, swelling up like monstrous balloons as they sucked in the stream. Rocks and stones began to show in the bed of the stream. The huge pot ground to a halt. All around her, stranded fish flopped about helplessly on the stones.

It seemed the ogres could soon walk across the gravel to seize her. Quick as a wink, the old woman picked up the fish and tossed them, one after another, to the ogres on the banks.

"Have some fish stew!" she called.

The Oni caught the fish in their claws—and because they were always hungry, they opened their wide mouths to gulp down the fish. As soon as they did this, the water rushed out of their mouths again, back into the stream —which, of course, was just what the old woman had hoped would happen.

The round pot floated free, and off the old woman paddled, out of the hill and into broad daylight.

When she had floated down the stream to a safe distance, she paddled over to the nearest bank. Hopping ashore, she pushed the big pot back into the water to drift farther downstream. This, she thought, would mislead the Oni if they should come looking for her. But she kept the magic stirrer with her and climbed safely back up the hill to her house.

The old woman never went hungry again, for with the magic stirrer she was able to make as many rice cakes as she could eat—and she had enough left over to share with her neighbors.

But if any rice cakes fell to the floor and rolled away down the hill, she never went after them.

"Let the Oni have them," she'd say cheerfully. And so, with her chickens, her pig, and plenty of rice for her dinner, she lived very happily the rest of her days.

1. From the way she talked to the Oni, what can you tell about the old woman's character?
2. How did the old woman escape the Oni den?
3. How would you describe the Japanese Oni? Were they smart? Were they frightening? What would you have done in the old woman's place?
4. The Oni had some strange habits. How did the old woman manage to turn those habits against the Oni and make her escape?
5. Find the part of the story that tells what the old woman gained from her experience with the Oni.

In realistic stories you read about things that could happen in real life. In fantasy stories you read about things that could not happen in real life.

Answer the following questions about the story "The Old Woman and the Rice Cakes."

1. Is this a realistic story or a fantasy story?
2. How are the characters in this story fantastic?
3. What happens in the story that could not possibly happen in real life?

Prewrite

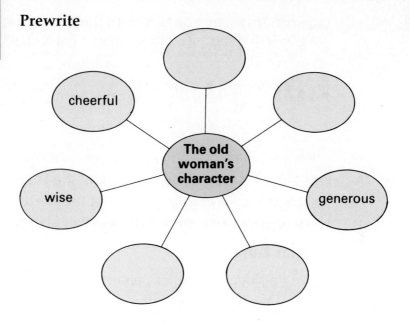

This diagram is called an "ideaburst." The words in the center, *the old woman's character*, are the central idea. The phrases around them all relate to the central idea; they describe the old woman's character. Copy the ideaburst and complete it with words that describe other character traits of the old woman.

Compose

Use words from the ideaburst to write a paragraph describing the old woman. Give an example of the old woman's behavior in the story for each character trait from the ideaburst.

Revise

Read your paragraph. Check to make sure that you gave an example of the old woman's behavior for each character trait. If not, revise your work to include the examples.

Formal and Informal Language

We use different kinds of language at different times and for different reasons. The President of the United States making a speech, for example, does not use the same kind of language as two friends talking together about a TV show.

Formal Language

The President and other public speakers use **formal language**. That is language that carefully follows the rules of correct usage as stated in dictionaries. Read the following sentence spoken by Martin Luther King, Jr.:

> Injustice anywhere is a threat to justice everywhere.

King's sentence is carefully worded and follows the rules of language usage. Yet it is simple, direct, and powerful.

Generally, people use formal language in books, newspapers, magazines, speeches, business letters, and reports. Your teachers probably use formal language in teaching you, and you use it whenever you write an assignment. Think of formal language as a public language. It is something that is said or written for most people to understand.

Informal Language

Two friends talking about a TV show would probably use **informal language**. Notice the slang terms and incomplete sentences in the following dialogue:

Joe: Hey, did you catch the Jacky Button Show
   last night?

Claire: Yeah, I died laughing. What a trip!

Joe: When Button plopped the waffle . . .

Claire: . . . right in Tommy's lap! Could you
   believe it? The guy's a maniac!

Someone overhearing this dialogue may not understand some of the words and so not understand the meaning. But it is perfectly appropriate for Joe and Claire to talk that way, or even to write that way in a personal letter, because they both understand the words they're using.

You may come across informal language in some stories — especially in dialogue — on TV, and sometimes in newspapers and magazines. Usually, though, informal language is used in small groups of people who are related by age, region, or family.

How can you tell if a word is formal or informal? You probably know the slang you use. But if you're not sure, look up the word in a dictionary. Most dictionaries will print the labels *informal* or *slang* if the entry word is informal.

Some words in the dictionary are labeled **archaic**, meaning old and seldom used today. For example, the word *thou* was used to mean *you* a long time ago. The dictionary will print *archaic* after the word or otherwise explain that it is seldom used today. If there is no usage label printed after the word, you can assume that the word is used in formal language.

Copy the following words. Look up each one in a dictionary. After each word, write *I* if it is informal, *A* if it is archaic, and *F* if it is formal.

1. snippy
2. thee
3. persnickety
4. slurp
5. mash
6. burp
7. grit
8. caitiff

Roosevelt's parents are migrant farm workers who move to follow the crops they pick. Read to find out how Roosevelt changes a situation by starting a dialogue in yet another new school.

As you read, notice the kind of language the author uses. Is it primarily formal or informal?

Roosevelt Grady

by Louisa Shotwell

The Opportunity Class: that's where the migrant bean-pickers got put. Roosevelt Grady wondered what it meant.

Roosevelt knew about schools. Fourth grade, fifth grade —things like that. He knew about schools from experience: three weeks here, six weeks there, a day or two somewhere else. But Opportunity Class. This was something new.

Looking around the schoolroom, he decided that Opportunity Class must mean mixing up the little children and the big boys and girls in the same room. But he couldn't figure out why. Opportunity for what?

The teacher, Miss Gladys, wore a black dress all wrinkles and chalk dust; she was skin and bones strung together—no soft places anywhere. She had a voice like the horn on Cap Jackson's beat-up truck, trembly but plenty raucous and loud.

Roosevelt saw that Miss Gladys taught with a stick. In oral reading, tap tap tap went that strong, slender stick on the blackboard, three taps for every word. When two girls fell to giggling, Miss Gladys held the stick straight up in the air and high. It worked like magic: the room got still as a piney woods. One thing was plain to Roosevelt Grady: nobody in this class wanted a licking.

When the time came for figures, Roosevelt glanced down at his work sheet and saw a whole page full of nothing but taking away. Take 12 away from 17. A cinch, Roosevelt muttered to himself; he licked his stubby pencil and in the answer space wrote a nice fat 5. Take 28 away from 33. Same old answer. He began to get bored; he made another fat 5 and this time put a curly tail on it.

Roosevelt nibbled the eraser of his pencil. He was sick and tired of all this taking away; what he really wanted to know about was putting into. At the last school where he'd been, they'd finished taking away and begun on putting into, and that he liked.

So here he was in a new school, all ready to learn more about putting into and not a thing to work on but the same old taking away. He sighed and went back and added curly tails to another 5.

The boy behind him pinched his shoulder and whispered: "What's that you're making?"

Roosevelt covered his paper with both hands and refused to answer. The boy made a dive for the paper; in nothing flat the two of them were in the aisle, wrestling.

Crack, smack, down on their two heads came Miss Gladys's stick! "We don't tolerate any nonsense here," she announced. The boys slunk back into their seats and rubbed their heads. Miss Gladys went on, "Here we never forget that we are the Opportunity Class."

That was when Roosevelt said it; he had no idea he was going to speak, but he did. "Please, ma'am," he asked, "opportunity for what?"

Silence.

Somebody tittered, and all at once the whole class burst out laughing. They roared and then rocked in their seats; the boys thumped each other; the girls poked their elbows into their neighbors' ribs and shrieked with delight.

Shame burned inside Roosevelt's head and his eyes smarted. He hadn't meant to be funny or fresh or anything: he simply wanted to know.

Up in the air went the slender stick and they all got quiet. "Exactly what, young man," said Miss Gladys, "do you want opportunity for?"

Roosevelt felt miserable, but he couldn't see any way to back down. "For putting into," he said; "please, ma'am, I want opportunity to learn about putting into." He plunged on, explaining, "I'm tired of taking away; I want to know about putting into."

Another silence. Then came the surprise of the day. Roosevelt couldn't believe his ears: Miss Gladys giggled. And then she began laughing so hard she dropped the stick. She had to go and sit down behind her desk. She opened a drawer and took out a white handkerchief; she wiped her eyes and then she blew her nose, loud.

"Hands up," she said, "all those who are tired of taking

away." All over the room hands shot up. "Hands up," she said, "all those who want to learn about putting into." Again the air shivered with waving hands.

Miss Gladys studied the class and said, "Very well. Tomorrow all the big boys and girls will begin studying putting into—that is a promise." Roosevelt felt good—as if he belonged.

After school, the boy who'd grabbed his paper stopped
him on the way to the bus. For the first time Roosevelt
had a good look at his wrestling mate. He was a big boy,
a good two sizes bigger than Roosevelt; he had on a green
corduroy jacket. "Take it easy, man," he said, "be seeing
you." And he loped off.

On the bus Roosevelt looked around, but the green
jacket was nowhere in sight. To the boy in the seat beside
him, he said: "Who was that kid? The one I tangled in
the aisle with."

"Oh, him? His name's Manowar."

As the bus rolled along beside the irrigation ditch,
Roosevelt sank down into the cushy seat low on his spine
and shut his eyes. Manowar: what a name!

Tomorrow Miss Gladys would explain about putting into; maybe she wasn't such a bad teacher after all, even if she did have a voice like a trembly truck horn, even if she did teach with a stick. Maybe the Opportunity Class was a good place for bean-pickers, a place where they could find out things — if they asked.

Back home in camp came the second surprise of the day, and this one was unpleasant: the Grady family was packing up their possessions.

"Bean crop's all run out," said his father, "and there's nothing more to pick here, so Cap Jackson says we'll pull out early tomorrow morning and head north."

Roosevelt's heart dropped: here it was, happening all over again. Not ever, probably, would he get to stay put long enough in school so he'd really belong.

Roosevelt bunched his sweater underneath him to soften the jouncing floor of the moving truck. He leaned his head back against his mother's arm. If the air got any chillier, he'd have to take his sweater out from under him and put it on to keep warm, but it wasn't quite that cold yet.

Along with three other families, the Gradys rode in the back of the truck, all but Papa, who sat up front to spell Cap Jackson. Cap was the crew leader; he owned the truck and in it he carried the people to places where the crops were ready for picking.

The truck had a canvas roof that sloped up on each side to a peak, like the top of a barn, and it prevented you from seeing the sky. Anyway, it was dark outside — it was the middle of the night, but the truck kept right on going.

Between sleeping and waking, Roosevelt thought about the question that kept running around his head the way a mosquito teases you in the dark. This was the question that had bothered him for so long: When you put something into something else and it doesn't come out even, what do you do with what's left over?

What had happened yesterday was exactly what had happened at the last school. The teacher came to the point of explaining putting into. That time it wasn't the beans that ran out—it was the celery. But it didn't matter what the crop was; if it ran out, it ran out and that was the end. The whole family packed up and piled into Cap Jackson's sputtery old truck and away they went to find a place where onions or tomatoes or some old thing was coming along ready to harvest. And same as yesterday, Roosevelt never got back to school to hear what the teacher had to say.

His next school was called Willowbrook. There were four separate classes and the one you went into depended on how old you were. Roosevelt was put in with the nines, tens, elevens. He was happy to see that Manowar had showed up in this class, too.

Roosevelt's class wasn't ready yet for putting into, but on the blackboard the teacher, Mrs. Dinwiddie, showed him privately how to fix up the left-over number.

Mrs. Dinwiddie had no stick, and she did not look teachery, either: too young for one thing; too small for another. She had cornsilk hair and if she hadn't worn shoes with spiky heels, she wouldn't have been much taller than Roosevelt. Her sweater and her skirt were both sky blue, and she kept pushing her sweater sleeves up above her elbows. When she walked around the room, her high heels went click-click-click on the floor so you knew where she was whether you were looking in that direction or not.

Mrs. Dinwiddie was great on stories. How you tell if a story is good, she said, is if people keep quiet and listen while you tell it to them. If the story is good enough, you don't have to tell them to keep still. They won't remember to wiggle; they'll be too interested. A story doesn't have to be true. It may be true or it may not be true — it's nice to know which — but what's important is, does the audience like it.

Everyone in the class had a chance to tell a story. Roosevelt called his "My Brother Matthew." He made it true because he wasn't so good at inventing stories. He told about old Matthew and his jokes and how he bumped his head on purpose on the attic roof and how he was always finding something interesting everywhere he went and especially about him crawling around the junk pile at Quimby's Quarters and coming up with a beat-up old harmonica that squawked. The boys and girls liked that story quite well. Anyway they listened without a wiggle, and at the end, they laughed and clapped their hands.

When Manowar's turn came, he stood up and announced: "Mine's a whopper."

His story took off something like Jack and the Bean-stalk. He told about a boy named Joshway, who found an old tomato can and filled it with dirt and planted a sunflower seed in it. At least it looked to Joshway like a sunflower seed, but later on, he was not so sure. Joshway watered the dirt every day and after a while the seed sprouted. Then it grew very fast and very big. Some days it grew as much as a foot before lunch.

Wherever Joshway went, from one ripe crop to another, he toted his plant along, from carrots to onions to cauliflower and so on. Finally, the plant got as tall as a telephone pole, and it grew such fine spready branches that Joshway built a platform high up on a couple of branches and fixed himself a small house among the shiny green leaves.

One day a pair of catbirds flew in and asked him if he minded if they built themselves a nest in his tree. On the opposite side from his own house, of course, they explained. Joshway decided he'd let them do it, thinking if they weren't too close, he might enjoy their company.

Another day he woke up in the morning and found a possum hanging from a branch by its tail. The possum didn't ask permission; he stayed on without a by-your-leave and he was no bother to Joshway because he appeared not to do anything ever except sleep.

All this time the tree was growing at the bottom, too. Tough, snaky roots broke through the tomato can and split it all to pieces and they crept down into the ground. These roots did their growing at night, mostly. Every morning Joshway would pull them out of the ground, and every night the roots would go back down in, each time a little deeper. Came a morning when Joshway found he couldn't pull them out. They were stuck fast. It was time to move on to another crop, but he couldn't leave the tree behind and his house and all. So there was nothing for it but he had to stay and live there in his tree house. He got rather hungry, not having any work, but by and by folks took to coming along and wanting to pay rent for branches to build houses on for themselves. Pretty soon Joshway had every pocket full of paper money and he had enough people living in his tree to make two sides for a softball game.

Here Manowar stopped talking and walked over to the drinking fountain and took a good long gulp. "Is that the end?" asked Lulubelle.

"No," said Manowar, coming back from the fountain, and he continued.

A bulldozer came rolling along and a cat was driving it — a big fierce cat he was, black-and-yellow stripes and extra-long whiskers. The cat said, "I'll give you five minutes to move out, and then I'm going to run right over your tree, houses and all."

Joshway had to think fast. He thought for three minutes and then he whispered something to the catbirds and that took another minute. The birds bobbed their heads and chirped and fluttered their wings. Then he whispered something to the possum, who kept his eyes shut and gave no more sign of life than he ever had.

Right at that instant the cat decided the five minutes were up. He started the bulldozer bearing down on the tree.

"Go," Joshway shouted, and the catbirds flew straight at the bulldozer, and the cat leapt up in the air to catch them and their feathers flew. The possum leaped down from his branch and coiled his tail around the steering wheel. The bulldozer slipped sideways and scraped past the tree, taking only a small chip out of its trunk. Faster and faster went the bulldozer, the possum still hanging on and the cat racing after it until they were all clean out of sight.

Joshway breathed long and deep. "The possum doesn't fret me," he said, "because he can look after himself, but it's a real shame about the catbirds; I'll miss having them around."

And right then he heard "Meow, meow," and he glanced up and there were the catbirds sitting on their nest with their breasts all swelled up looking as though they'd swallowed the bulldozer.

"Hi," said Joshway, "glad you made it back. Great job you did—much obliged." He climbed up into his tree house and sat down and began to eat his lunch. "I guess I was wrong," he said to himself.

"Wrong about what?" the catbirds asked, both at once, expecting more praise.

"Wrong about that seed I planted in the tomato can," said Joshway. "I guess it couldn't have been a sunflower seed, after all."

That afternoon, Roosevelt was the last one to get on the school bus. He had to take the only seat left — next to Manowar. "Where you been?" asked Manowar. "I been saving this seat for you."

Roosevelt slid into the seat and relaxed. Some days, he thought, work out better than most.

1. How did the dialogue that Roosevelt started with Miss Gladys change the classroom situation?
2. How did the life of the Grady family make school difficult for Roosevelt?
3. Why do you think Manowar and Roosevelt became friends? What did they have in common? Did they share any other character traits?
4. What part of Manowar's story of Joshway reflects his background as part of a migrant family always on the move?
5. Find the part of the story that tells how Roosevelt learned to divide.

Apply

the

Skills

Formal language carefully follows the rules of correct usage. Informal language uses everyday words and phrases.

Read the examples of informal language from "Roosevelt Grady" in the left column below. Copy both columns. Complete the second column by writing the formal language equivalent of each informal example that is given.

Informal	*Formal*
1. taking away	subtraction
2. a cinch	an easy task
3. nobody wanted a licking	
4. fixed himself a house	
5. mine's a whopper	

Prewrite

 This is an illustration of the tree in Manowar's story. Make up five questions about the tree. The answers to the questions should tell everything about the tree. For example, you might begin with the questions *"How did the tree start growing?"* and *"Who owns the tree?"*

Compose

 Write a short paragraph that will serve as a caption for the story illustration above. Use the answers to your questions as information in the paragraph caption.

Revise

 Read your paragraph. Check to see that you have included answers to your questions about the illustration. As you revise, add any information that you left out.

Listen!

by Toni de Gerez

I am the singer
  I am singing
the pictures of the book
I am the blue-and-green
  bird
I make the pages speak
I am the quetzal

  What is my song?
my song is a piece of
  jade
I cut into it
it is my song
look how I string beads of jade
  into a necklace
it is my song
it is my jade song

As quetzal feathers
beautiful is my song
look how my song
bends down over the earth
in the house of butterflies my song
    is born

    The true storyteller
says things boldly
with the lips and mouth of an artist
the true storyteller uses words of joy
flowers are on the lips
the language is strict
the language is noble

Draw Conclusions

Imagine that you see a little boy in the park who is crying and looking up at the sky. In his hand is a piece of string. High above him a helium balloon is floating away. Why is the little boy crying? If you say that he is unhappy because he lost his balloon, you are a drawing a **conclusion**.

How do you know the boy is sad? You know that children who cry are usually unhappy. How do you know he is crying about his lost balloon? The boy is holding a piece of string, and you know that balloons are usually tied with string. And from the way the boy watches it, you can figure that the balloon floating away belonged to him.

You draw conclusions all the time, often without realizing it. What if you opened the door to your home and smelled something delicious? You would probably conclude that someone was cooking something good in the kitchen. Suppose you heard a crash of thunder and then the sound of rain. You would conclude that a storm had begun, even if you did not see it.

In a way, drawing conclusions is like doing a simple addition problem. You take all the facts you are given and add them together. The answer you get when you add them up is your conclusion.

For example, imagine you are visiting a friend's house for the first time. Standing in the kitchen alone, you see a collar and a leash on the table. On the floor you see a water bowl with the name "Fido" printed on it. In the corner is a dog's bed. You needn't actually see a dog to draw the conclusion that your friend has a dog named Fido.

If you learn new facts in addition to the ones you already know, you might draw a different conclusion. For instance, suppose you saw a note taped to your friend's refrigerator that said, "Thanks for volunteering to take care of Fido. I'll be back next week. Love, Aunt Susie." What new conclusion would you draw? You would probably conclude that your friend is not Fido's owner but is taking care of Fido until Aunt Susie returns.

Adding Up the Facts

When you read, you constantly draw conclusions: you add up the facts and come to conclusions about them. Read the paragraph below and decide what conclusions you can draw from the facts given.

> The common cold has been around a long time. There are more than one hundred types of viruses that can cause colds. When you catch a cold, you may have a stuffed nose. You may get chills, a cough, or a headache. You may sneeze and your eyes may water. Some people drink orange juice or eat chicken soup to feel better. Some just go to bed and stay there until they feel better. Most doctors don't prescribe medicine for colds. They say the best thing to do for a cold is to rest and let it run its course.

Which of the following conclusions can you draw from the facts given in the paragraph?

1. A cold can make a person very uncomfortable.
2. Scientists have stopped looking for cold cures.
3. Most doctors believe cold medicines don't cure colds.

Sentence 1 is a good conclusion because the paragraph lists many ways a cold can make a person feel uncomfortable.

The paragraph does not contain enough information to draw the conclusion in sentence 2. What about sentence 3? This also seems to be a good conclusion. Find the sentence or sentences in the paragraph that support the conclusion in sentence 3.

Using What You Know to Draw Conclusions

You often use more than just the facts you read to draw conclusions. You rely on your knowledge and experience. Perhaps even without thinking about it, you use your own background to "fill in the blanks." For example, read the following sentence and draw a conclusion.

Paul raced to the mailbox, yanked open the door,
and sorted frantically through the bills and letters.

Did you conclude that Paul was expecting something special in the mail? The sentence doesn't say so, but you probably drew that conclusion anyway. Three clues in the sentence help you figure this out: (1) Paul raced to the mailbox; (2) he yanked open the door; (3) he sorted frantically through the bills and letters. You know from personal experience that people who race, yank, and do things frantically are usually eager. You also probably know from experience that waiting for something special can make you anxious. You used the clues in the sentence and your own experience to draw the conclusion that Paul was looking for a special piece of mail.

Textbook Application: Draw Conclusions in Science

The purpose of textbooks is to give you information about particular subjects. Textbooks are filled with facts.

When you read a textbook you often find that the author draws conclusions. Sometimes the author arranges the facts so that they lead you to the conclusion the author wants to communicate.

It is important to be aware that an author has moved from giving straight facts to stating a conclusion. Then you can observe the way the author has backed up conclusions with facts. It is also important to be aware of when an author simply states the facts and lets you draw your own conclusions. Whether or not the author states a conclusion, you should think about the facts and what conclusion you can draw yourself.

You may not always agree with an author's conclusions. You may feel that the facts do not support the conclusion, or you may think that the author is not telling the entire story. You may decide that you need more facts than the author has supplied.

The following selection includes facts and the author's conclusions. But you will have the opportunity to draw your own conclusions. The sidenotes will help you understand what to look for as you read.

What Is It Like on Other Planets?

One reason why we can live on Earth is because of the Earth's place in the solar system. The Sun's energy travels 150 million kilometers to the planet Earth. The amount of energy that reaches the Earth is just enough for us to live here.

What conclusion does the author begin with?

The Earth has an **atmosphere** (AT-muh-sfeer) that supports life. An atmosphere is a layer of gases surrounding a planet. The Earth's atmosphere is made up mostly of nitrogen, oxygen, and water vapor. The clouds on Earth are full of water vapor. Because there is oxygen and water we can live here on Earth.

What facts support this conclusion?

Mercury is so close to the Sun that it is very hot. On the side of Mercury that faces the Sun, it is hot enough to melt lead. Are you surprised, then, that there is no water on this planet? Mercury has no atmosphere to shield the planet from the rays of the Sun. Clearly, we could not live here.

What facts support the conclusion that we couldn't live on Mercury?

Could living things exist on Mars? There is a little water on this planet. It is frozen into ice caps like the North and South Poles of the Earth. Mars has an atmosphere made up mostly of carbon dioxide and nitrogen. The atmosphere, however, is thin and doesn't trap much of the Sun's heat. So, although a day on Mars might feel like spring, night on the planet can be as cold as −70 degrees Celsius.

The author wants you to answer the question in this paragraph. What conclusion can you draw from the facts?

— HBJ Science
Harcourt Brace Jovanovich

Drawing conclusions is something people do every day. Being aware of the conclusions in what you read and how they are arrived at can make you a better reader. Then you'll be better able to think for yourself and draw your own conclusions.

Here's a folktale that begins as a dialogue between two people. Read to find out what the dialogue reveals about the people of Lagos.

As you read, think about whether the story supports the conclusion that the storyteller draws about the townspeople of Lagos.

The Holes of Lagos

retold by M. A. Jagendorf and R. S. Boggs

"Lagos! Where is Lagos?"

"Far, far away."

"How far?"

"As far as far can be in Mexico."

"How far is that?"

"Well . . . I can't tell exactly."

"What part of Mexico?"

"I can't tell. Maybe any part of Mexico. Some people say one place; some say another; but, wherever that town is, it is full of foolish people."

"Aren't there foolish people everywhere?"

"Yes, but in Lagos everybody is a *bobo*. The townspeople of Lagos are different from those of any other town in Mexico. Everywhere there are some fools; but in Lagos they are all fools."

"That can't be."

"Oh, yes it can! In Lagos they do things people would do nowhere else. Take, for example, the time they found a deep hole in the center of the plaza, not far from the church."

"What happened?"

"Well, this is what happened."

One morning the mayor of the town was walking across the plaza on his way to the city hall. When he got near the church, he discovered an immense hole, big enough for three people to fall into. He stopped and gazed at the hole for a long time.

"How did this hole come to be in the plaza of Lagos?" he cried. "Who put it there?"

When no one responded, he called to the town police officer, who had a big torn sombrero on his head and a thin stick in his hand.

"How did that hole get there?" cried the mayor.

"I don't know, Señor Alcalde."

"If you, the guardian of peace in Lagos, do not know, then nobody knows."

"That is true, Señor Alcalde."

"It's dangerous to have a hole like that in our town plaza. If our townspeople walk to church or to the city hall, they might fall into it and get hurt."

"Quite true, Señor Alcalde."

"Well, then, it must be closed immediately."

"That's right, Señor Alcalde."

"Get the men of Lagos immediately and have them fill up the hole."

"Sí, Señor Alcalde."

The mayor went into the city hall to attend to business, and the police officer went to assemble all the men of Lagos. They took shovels and began digging up the earth from a place nearby and threw it into the hole. When the sun sank behind the hill, the hole was filled and the earth over it was smooth as a leaf. Everyone was satisfied with the day's work and went home to eat.

Later, when the mayor came out of the city hall, the officer said politely, "Señor Alcalde, you see that the hole is filled and that the men did a superb job."

"I'm glad to hear it. We have excellent men in our town, better than any in Mexico."

"Thank you, Señor Alcalde. *Buenas tardes*."

"Buenas tardes."

The mayor walked away, but he hadn't walked far before he came to a second hole, the one from which the earth had been taken to fill the first hole. He stopped and looked at it in surprise.

"Another hole!" he exclaimed. "How did *this* hole get here? I didn't see it this morning. . . . Carlos! Carlos!" he shouted.

The police officer came running.

"Sí, Señor Alcalde."

"There is a hole here. Look!"

"Yes, Señor Alcalde, there is," replied Carlos, looking at it.

"Townspeople going to church or to the city hall could fall into it and break a leg, or even a neck."

"Well they might, Señor Alcalde; they certainly might."

"It must be closed immediately, Carlos."

"Yes, it must be closed immediately, Señor Alcalde," agreed Carlos, taking off his sombrero and scratching his head, "but the men have all gone home to eat and go to bed. Everybody will be sleeping now."

"That's true," replied the mayor. "Then *mañana.*"

"Tomorrow it will be done, Señor Alcalde."

Early next morning Carlos had the men of Lagos digging up the earth not far from the new hole. The mayor passed by on the way to his office, watched the men at work, and smiled in satisfaction.

"There are no workers in all Mexico better than the workers of Lagos," he said aloud, and went to the city hall.

The men all heard the mayor's words of praise and were pleased; then they continued their work with greater

zeal. Soon the second hole was filled and the earth smoothed down.

At the setting of the sun, the mayor came by and saw the hole filled and the ground over it as smooth as a church floor.

"Carlos, that is good work."

"The men of Lagos are good workers, Señor Alcalde," agreed Carlos.

The mayor walked on; but he hadn't walked much of a distance when he came to a new hole.

"Holes grow in Lagos like weeds in a corn patch! How did this hole come to be here? Carlos! Carlos!"

Carlos came running.

"What's happened, Señor Alcalde?"

"There's another hole here in the ground, look!"

Carlos peered into the hole and replied, "Yes, Señor Alcalde, there is another hole in the ground."

"It must be filled."

"Yes, it must be filled, Señor Alcalde."

"Townspeople crossing the plaza might fall into it and break a leg."

"They might indeed break a leg, Señor Alcalde."

"Fill it immediately."

Carlos removed his sombrero and scratched his head.

"The men have gone home to eat, and soon they'll be asleep."

"True," said the mayor, "absolutely true. Well then, *mañana*."

"Sí, Señor Alcalde."

Next morning, bright and early, the good men of Lagos were out digging again. From a spot nearby they dug up earth and filled the hole, and by the time the sun set, the task was done.

The mayor passed by on his way home.

"This is superb work, indeed," he said when he saw the hole filled, smooth as glass. "What excellent workers these men of Lagos are! There are none finer in all Mexico."

"That's true, Señor Alcalde," Carlos agreed.

The mayor continued on his way and soon came to a new hole.

"A new hole!" he cried. "There is a curse of holes on our town. Carlos! Carlos!"

Carlos came running.

"There is a new hole, see!"

"So there is, Señor Alcalde."

"It must be filled immediately. But the men will be asleep, so then *mañana*, Carlos."

This went on and on as everyone in Lagos tried to figure out how it happened and why there were so many holes in their town, but they couldn't. They were just that kind of foolish people. So they kept on filling holes by digging new holes until they came to the edge of town.

Now, the people of the next town had been watching the ridiculous work of Lagos day by day, laughing among themselves and saying nothing. But when the hole was next to their own town, they filled it with things lying around that they had been wanting to bury for a long time.

When the mayor of Lagos saw the last hole filled and could not find another, he was overjoyed and declared, "The men of Lagos never give up a job until it is completely finished."

The men of Lagos were happy, too, for they said they were getting a little tired of so much digging every day. So everyone was happy, and there were no more holes in Lagos.

1. Why did the storyteller think the people of Lagos behaved foolishly?
2. Why did the holes keep appearing in Lagos?
3. Did you think this folktale was funny? Why do you think people generally enjoy hearing stories about foolish behavior?
4. How was the problem of the holes in Lagos finally solved?
5. Find the point in the selection where it changes from a dialogue to a single person telling a story.

Apply the Skills

Good conclusions are always supported by facts. The storyteller's conclusion that the people of Lagos behaved foolishly is supported by events in the story. The mayor of Lagos also draws conclusions, but he draws the *wrong* conclusions. Listed below are two of the mayor's conclusions. For each one, state the facts or events from which the mayor draws those conclusions. Then explain why those are the wrong conclusions.

1. "There is a curse of holes on our town."
2. "There are no workers in all Mexico better than the workers of Lagos."

Prewrite

Character 1:	Look at those people of Lagos digging a hole in the plaza.
Character 2:	Why are they doing that?
Character 1:	
Character 2:	
Character 1:	
Character 2:	

Imagine that you are from a neighboring town to Lagos. You and a friend have been watching the workers digging and filling up holes. Copy and fill in the chart by writing a dialogue between the two of you about what you have seen. In your dialogue, explain what's going on in Lagos and what both of you think about it.

Compose

Use your dialogue to write a story of your own about what has been going on in Lagos. Be sure to state the story's setting at the beginning. Add an ending that explains what you intend to do when the holes get close to your town.

Revise

Read your story. Make sure you stated the setting at the beginning. Check to see that you have used correct punctuation in your dialogue. If not, revise your work.

Labels

Most things we buy have labels that serve many useful purposes. All labels name the product and tell what it is made of. Some tell how to use the product. Others warn of dangers. Still others explain how to handle emergencies.

Some products can be dangerous when misused. So there are laws requiring many manufacturers to put detailed labels on their products. Think of labels as short directions that tell you how to use the things you buy. Labels are useless if you don't read and understand them.

Clothing Care Labels

Look at the clothing care label below. Labels such as this are most often found in the necks of shirts and the waists of pants or skirts. They tell a great deal about the clothing.

☆ **T O P P S** ☆
_____

SIZE 12
_____

60% cotton, 40% polyester. Do not dry clean.
Machine wash. Wash colors separately in cold water.
No bleach. Iron with cool iron. Made in U.S.A.

This label tells you that the Topps Company made this shirt in the United States. It is a size 12. The label also says that this shirt is made of cotton and polyester. Shoppers know that clothing made of this fabric is easy to care for. Notice all the cautions on the label. You are not to dry clean or use bleach. You are to use cold water and a cool iron. What do you think would happen if you didn't follow these directions? Here is the care label from a jacket. Read it carefully.

HOBAN 🏠 HOUSE

100% Pure Wool	SIZE 38	Dry Clean Only

The label says this jacket is made of wool. That means it will keep a person warm and dry. It must never be put in the washing machine. A wool jacket would be ruined if it were washed along with cotton-polyester shirts.

Clothing labels are very useful. They help you find the kind of clothing you want. They also tell you how to take care of the clothing you buy.

Cleaning Products

Labels on the boxes of cleaning products—such as soaps, sprays, cleansers, polishes, and waxes—tell what they are made of and how to use them. Look at this label from a box of laundry detergent.

YERBEST LAUNDRY POWER

CONTAINS NO PHOSPHORUS	BIODEGRADABLE

Use ¼ cup detergent for top and front loading washers. Use more for heavily soiled clothes. Ingredients: Cleaning agents, water softener, fabric brightener, perfume.

What can you learn by reading this label? You see that soap contains no phosphorus. That means it is biodegradable and will not pollute rivers and streams. The next line tells how much to use in each load of washing. The ingredients line tells what is in the detergent. Perhaps these ingredients are exactly what a shopper wants. Then again, another shopper may not want water softener, fabric brightener, or perfume. That shopper may be looking for a less expensive product without those ingredients. By comparing labels, shoppers can find exactly the product they want.

Some cleaning products contain strong chemicals. They are poisonous and can be dangerous if swallowed or splashed in the eyes. So cleaning products often have warning labels, too. Study this warning label.

▶**CAUTION**: This product can hurt skin or eyes. Flood at once with plenty of water. If taken internally, drink milk or egg white. Call doctor.

Be sure to read the labels and follow what they say. Then you can use any cleaning product safely.

Medicine Labels

Many medicines are strong drugs that are carefully controlled by the government. A prescription medicine is given by a doctor to one person for a certain illness. The label must state the person's name, the doctor's name, the name of the medicine, and how often it is to be taken. One person cannot give his or her medicine to someone else. Study the prescription label below. Notice the warnings.

TARCO DRUGS (232) 222-2222

NO. 844108	DATE: 5-30-86

FOR: Thomas Rose
    Larynol — 2 teaspoons every 4 hours.
    Prescription may not be refilled.
    Caution: May cause drowsiness.   Dr. White

Many medicines can be bought over the counter. That means you do not need a prescription. Labels on these medicines usually tell you several things:

- what illnesses the medicine helps
- how much to take and how often
- when *not* to take it
- what to do if too much is taken
- the date after which it should not be used

Many of these instructions are printed on the box. They may be explained further on a sheet of paper inside the box.

Read these labels. Which ones tell you how to use the product? Which warn you of dangers? Which give you information to help you decide what to buy?

◀◀◀ B O X O N E ▶▶▶
BICARBONATE OF SODA

- To help overcome heartburn, sour stomach, and acid indigestion.
- Average dosage: ¼ teaspoon in ½ glass of water.
- Warnings: Do not take more than 8 doses in a 24 hour period. Do not use this product if you are on a sodium-restricted diet.
- Keep this and all medicines out of reach of children. In case of accidental overdose contact doctor or poison control center at once.

EXP 9-87

SUNNY SHAMPOO

Wet hair. Apply. Rub in, rinse. Repeat.

PROTAPRO
TV SET

Avoid fires or shock. Do not take back off set. Keep set away from rain and water. Do not attempt to repair unless trained.

EUREKA
NOTEBOOK

8-½ x 10 inches
70 Sheets
Wide Rules

A EUREKA PRODUCT

SUPER BIKE

Welded steel frame.
3-speed.
20" Racer Model

WEMBERLY SPORTSTER, INC.

Smiler's
TOOTHPASTE

Recommended by Dentists of America, Inc. For best results, squeeze tube from bottom and flatten as you go.

Is a dialogue possible between an animal and a human? Read the selection to find out how an animal learned to communicate with humans.

As you read, decide what conclusion you can draw from the facts given.

The Story of Nim

by Anna Michel

Can an animal learn to "talk"?

We know that animals communicate with each other. People and animals can also communicate ideas to each other in various ways. Your dog or cat learns what you want it to do. Elephants, horses, and other animals can understand word commands from people.

But using language—words and different combinations of words—to communicate has always been thought of as something only humans can do. Recently, we have learned that this is not so. A gorilla named Koko, a chimpanzee named Washoe, and several other apes have been taught to use signs to communicate.

This is the story of a chimpanzee named Nim and how he learned to talk to people.

On November 21, 1973, at the Institute for Primate Studies in Oklahoma, a baby chimpanzee was born. Although he was just like any other newborn chimp, he would someday be very special. He would become one of the first chimps who could "talk" to people.

Dr. Herbert Terrace, a scientist at Columbia University in New York City, was interested in how language is learned. He knew how Koko the gorilla, Washoe the chimp, and several other apes had been taught to use words. He wanted to see for himself how an ape could communicate through human language.

Chimpanzees and other apes are very intelligent animals. But the way their larynx, their "voice box," is constructed makes it physically impossible for them to make the sounds people make when speaking and forming words. Dr. Terrace hoped to teach a chimpanzee to "talk" in another way — by making certain motions with its hands, the way hearing-impaired people do. This is called "signing," and is the way Koko and Washoe had learned.

Two weeks after the baby chimp was born at the Institute for Primate Studies in Oklahoma, he was sent to New York to take part in this amazing experiment. Since the little chimp was named Nim, the experiment was called Project Nim.

Dr. Terrace thought that if Nim were going to learn language and talk about the things people talk about, he should be raised like a human child. So Nim was going to live with a family where he would be cared for and played with, talked to and loved. He would wear clothes, sit in a highchair, and be toilet trained. These would all be things for him to talk about.

Dr. Terrace arranged for Nim to live in the home of one of his Columbia University students, Stephanie LaFarge. The LaFarge household was big and lively. Both Stephanie and her husband, WER, had been married before. Their household included Stephanie and her children, fifteen-year-old Heather, fourteen-year-old Jennie, and eleven-year-old Josh; WER LaFarge and his children; a friend of the family, Marika; and a German shepherd named Trudge. They would all play a part in bringing up Nim, as would the many teachers and volunteers who joined the project to help care for Nim and teach him sign language.

Taking care of baby Nim was very much like taking care of a human baby. He slept in a crib. Every few hours, day and night, he woke up

Part of Nim's training involved learning about human things — in this case, a necklace of beads.

and cried until someone gave him his bottle. He was fed and burped and diapered. He was held and rocked, tickled and tossed into the air. He smiled and cooed, he kicked and cried, he sucked his thumb — or his toe — and behaved in many ways like a healthy human baby.

From his first day with the La-Farges, Nim was "talked" to in American Sign Language, the language of the hearing-impaired. And slowly, in the way a baby begins to understand words, Nim began to understand signs. Every time Ste-

phanie brought Nim his bottle, she touched her thumb to her lips making the sign for *drink*. Nim's response was to grunt hungrily and look for his bottle. And when she made the sign *up*, he would reach out his arms for her to pick him up.

Though Nim was beginning to recognize the signs, he made no effort to imitate the signs with his own hands. He had to be shown how to do this. When Nim was two months old, Dr. Terrace and Stephanie and his other teachers began to gently shape — or mold — his hands into different signs. Before Stephanie, or anyone else, gave Nim his bottle, she first signed *drink* and then molded Nim's hands to make the drink sign. If he wanted to be picked up, she molded his hands to sign *up*. When he reached for a toy, she molded *give*.

Throughout the project Nim's teachers molded his hands whenever they were teaching him a new sign. Eventually Nim even offered his hands to be shaped when he wanted to be shown the sign for something.

One day, when Nim was two-and-a-half months old, Stephanie held up his bottle, and Nim put his thumb to his lips and signed *drink*. This was the first time Nim had made a sign

Nim has a lesson outdoors on the grass with one of his teachers.

tickling session or pillow fight. Soon Nim was much too lively to stay in his crib. So a little tent was made out of netting and set up in a corner of the dining room. A hammock was hung inside for Nim to sleep in. At first Nim screamed when he was left alone for the night but then quieted down and fell asleep with a bottle or pacifier.

Nim's first summer was spent at the seashore. As long as he could keep one of his human friends in sight, Nim ran around happily out-of-doors. He touched, smelled, and sometimes ate the flowers. He tried to catch birds flying in the sky and wild rabbits as they dashed across the grass — always without success. Like all chimpanzees he was afraid of the water, so no one could tempt him into the swimming pool or the ocean, but he liked to play in the sand with his pail and shovel. Efforts to teach Nim were relaxed during this vacation time, and the only new sign he learned that summer was *eat*.

all by himself. Stephanie was very surprised, for no one had expected Nim to begin signing at such an early age. In the next six weeks Nim's vocabulary grew, and he made the signs for *up, sweet, give,* and *more*.

Nim was growing fast and becoming more active every day. By his second month, he could both crawl and walk, climb and jump. One of his favorite games was chasing Trudge, the family dog, all over the house. And he always loved a good

When Nim returned to New York City in September, he was ten months old and he knew how to make six signs: *drink, sweet, give, more, up,* and *eat*. Dr. Terrace decided it was now time to begin a more intensive teaching program — Nim would go to

351

school. There would be fewer distractions in school than at home, so Nim could concentrate more on learning to sign.

Nim's school was a group of rooms in the psychology department at Columbia University. There was a tiny classroom which would be kept bare so that Nim would not be easily distracted. When Nim started school, his teachers decided it was as important for him to understand sign language as it was to learn to make the signs himself. So throughout the day, his teachers signed the names of things around him and talked in sign language about what Nim was doing. On a typical day, Nim would arrive at his school by eleven o'clock. *Hang up your coat,* Nim's teacher signed as she helped Nim take off his coat and hang it on his own hook, just three feet from the floor. Later, she would sign *time to eat.*

Eat, eat, Nim repeated enthusiastically, making the *eat* sign with his own hand. And he made food grunts that sounded like "uh-uh-uh." Then Nim signed *up,* and climbed up into his highchair. His teacher tied on his bib, identifying it in sign language, and as Nim ate, she showed him the sign for each food. Mealtimes were Nim's favorite parts of the day.

Nim learns to sign for orange.

Looking at pictures is part of learning, too.

To interest Nim in his lessons, his teacher often had to make them seem as much like playing as possible. Every morning Nim's toy bag would be brought out. As the teacher peered into the bag of toys, Nim sat down on her knee, bouncing energetically. There was always something new in the bag—a ball, flashlight, tennis shoe, puppet, mirror—so Nim never knew what to expect. Everything that was pulled out of the bag then became the object of a lesson. It would be named and played with and talked about until Nim grew tired of it.

Nim's attention span was short, so his teacher was always ready to move on to a new activity if he became bored or restless. When he was finally tired of the bag of toys, it was put away and a new activity was started. It might be time to look at picture books or work with picture cards, or to draw or paint.

The best way to teach Nim was to tie signing to activities he liked. For example, Nim enjoyed taking a tea break every day, and this provided an opportunity to learn to sign for tea and to use some of the signs he already knew. Nim's teacher would use the new sign in many different ways: *Time to make tea; You want tea? I drink tea,* and so on. When it seemed that Nim understood the meaning of the tea sign, the teacher would then mold his hands so he could make it himself. For days or even weeks, Nim only made a new sign right after he had seen a teacher make it. Or he would make the sign at the wrong time, when he really meant something else. Or he would make the sign incorrectly, like baby talk. But eventually Nim reached the stage where he made the sign correctly in the right situation without any help.

The LaFarges became very attached to Nim — he was almost like one of the family — but by the time he was eighteen months old, it became clear that their home was not designed for a growing chimpanzee. Nim needed much more space. Dr. Terrace learned about a large house that had been given to Columbia University. It had many rooms, and outside there was grass to play on, trees to climb, and even a pond with fish and ducks. It wasn't being used

Work and play were part of the daily routine. And there was always something to talk about.

at the time, so Dr. Terrace rented it for Project Nim. Here Nim would live with four of his teachers. They would become his new family.

There was much to see and do and talk about in the new house, and Nim spent those first days exploring and discovering — switching lights on and off, turning on the water faucets, going up and down stairs, opening all the doors, and playing outside. Though at first everything was new and different and confusing, within a few weeks Nim was acting as if he had always lived there. Now that Nim's teachers lived with him, more time could be given to talking in sign language, and every daily routine provided something to talk about.

Every morning when it was time to get up, one of Nim's teachers would open the door to his room and greet him in sign language: *Good morning, Nim*. Nim was usually awake but still sleepy, and he didn't answer. As soon as he was ready, he would climb down from his sleeping loft. Then he would take his teacher's hand and lead her down the hall to the bathroom, signing *dirty, dirty*, which was what he had been taught to say when he had to use the toilet. When he was through, he would sign *finish*.

When Nim's teacher held up his toothbrush, Nim signed *toothbrush* eagerly. Brushing his teeth was a task Nim never minded because he loved the taste of toothpaste.

Next came hand washing. First Nim washed his hands and then, as he got more involved, he washed his feet and even his teacher's hands. When he was finished, he asked for hand cream.

When Nim was younger, the skin on his hands became dry and cracked, so applying hand cream had become a daily activity and something else to sign about. Actually the hearing-impaired have no standard sign for *hand cream*, but Nim's teachers noticed that when Nim wanted some he always rubbed his hands together. They decided that would be a good sign for *hand cream*. Nim invented one other sign, *play*. In this case, the real sign for *play* was too hard for Nim to make, but when he began to clap his hands in play situations, they decided clapping would be Nim's sign for *play*.

After Nim had rubbed plenty of hand cream on his hands and feet, and on his teacher's hands too, it was time to get dressed. Nim was expected to name everything he wore before putting it on. Then he dressed himself. When he was dressed, he asked for a hug and was carried down to the kitchen for breakfast.

Nim's weekday breakfast was usually cereal and fruit. Sunday breakfasts were special—banana pancakes—and Nim helped make them.

After breakfast Nim liked to wash the dishes. *Give*, he signed to get a sponge. Then he would turn on the water, squirt dishwashing soap onto a dish, and rub the dish vigorously with the sponge. This routine would continue for twenty minutes or more

Nim learned one or two new signs every week. Old signs were reviewed constantly so that Nim didn't forget them.

until the dishes were all thoroughly cleaned. Then Nim would put them back into the sink and start all over again.

Nim so enjoyed housework that he often misbehaved when he wasn't included. Once when one of his teachers was in a hurry and didn't want to be slowed down by Nim, she told him he must sit and watch while she prepared the meal. Nim hated being left out and threw himself on the floor, screaming. His teacher didn't pay any attention to him. Nim tried another tactic. He waited until his teacher looked at him, then he deliberately knocked over the garbage can.

You're bad! his teacher signed. *I'm angry with you!*

Nim hooted and pouted, signing, *Me sorry! Hug! Hug!*

No! You're bad! Nim's teacher wanted him to know that she was really angry. She knew that Nim had learned that by pouting and signing *sorry* he was often forgiven too quickly and his behavior would be just as bad afterwards. She wanted to be sure Nim meant what he was saying.

Sorry, sorry, repeated Nim, becoming more and more upset. He kept running up to her making the *hug* sign, but she would walk away from him. Finally, he scurried over to the garbage can, picked up all the spilled garbage, and put it back into the can. His teacher was still not satisfied. She signed *clean,* and pointed at the sponge. Nim grabbed it and wiped up the floor. By this time all was forgiven.

When the chores were finished, if it was a weekday it was time to get in the car and leave for school. Nim was expected to sit quietly in the front seat and not jump around or reach for anything, and he usually followed the rules. He was curious about everything they passed along the way, especially police officers on horseback or people on motorcycles. He sometimes named what he saw. *Water,* he signed as they went over a bridge; *light,* when they came to a traffic light; and *out,* when the car came to a stop at Columbia University.

When things were going well, Nim learned one or two new signs every week—but only after his teachers had spent day after day repeating that sign. Old signs were reviewed constantly so that Nim didn't forget them.

By the time Nim was three years old, he could make eighty-eight signs. He knew his own name and the names of some of his teachers. He was putting signs together to make combinations, such as *me hat* or *give hat* if he wanted the hat his teacher was holding. Or he might sign *tickle me* and *tickle me more.* And like a young child, Nim could understand much more than he could say.

Nim's teachers were always thinking of new ways to make his lessons interesting. One day a teacher brought her cat to class in a carrying case. Nim was curious about everything new, and he was especially excited about other animals. He peeked through the window of the case, trying to find out what was inside. When he couldn't open it, he signed, *open, open, open!*

His teacher was in no hurry. *What's in the case?* she asked.

Open me, Nim open! was his response.

There's a cat in the box, she signed to Nim.

As soon as Nim knew what was in the box, he signed faster—*Cat, cat hug, cat me*—anything to get his teacher to open the case.

Nim learned that he could use language not only to name things and get what he needed, but also to get his way. Sometimes he signed *sleep,* even though he wasn't tired. But his teachers learned to tell that Nim was fibbing if he didn't look them in the eye when he made those signs. Sometimes he tried to distract his teachers in the middle of a lesson by starting a game of peek-a-boo or by standing on his head. Other times he just didn't pay attention. He looked bored and stared into space.

Although so much of Nim's behavior was childlike, he also behaved in ways that were pure chimpanzee. He hooted and grunted and walked on his knuckles. He climbed trees and swung from branches.

Nim also behaved in ways that were pure chimpanzee.

Nim, with Dr. Herb Terrace, says good-by.

On September 24, 1977, three years and ten months after Nim's arrival in New York City, his part in Project Nim was finished, and he was returned to the Institute for Primate Studies in Oklahoma. There he lives on an island with other chimpanzees who know sign language, too.

Dr. Terrace has visited Nim since then, and even though over a year had passed, Nim greeted him with hoots of joy and signs for *hug* and *kiss* and *tickle* — not only showing that he remembered Dr. Terrace but that communicating through sign language was still second nature to him. That pleased Dr. Terrace, but more important he also saw that Nim was happily adjusted to his new life among chimpanzees.

By the time Nim was retired, he had a vocabulary of 125 different signs. Project Nim had proved that a chimpanzee could not only be taught words in sign language but could learn how to use language to communicate with human beings. Dr. Terrace is certain there is still more to be learned from studying the language ability of chimpanzees. If he is right, with enough sign language a chimpanzee might someday tell us much — about his feelings and his dreams. Who knows what a chimpanzee might say if he learned the words?

1. How did Nim learn to communicate with humans?
2. In what ways did Nim act like a human child? In what ways did he act like a chimpanzee?
3. Reread the part of the story that describes how Nim's teacher punished him for misbehaving. What do you think about how Nim was treated? Do you think the punishment was necessary? Explain.
4. Why was Nim raised as a child in a human family instead of as a chimpanzee?
5. Nim learned to use language to name things and to get what he needed. But he also used language the way humans do—to try to get his way. Find parts of the selection that show Nim using language to get his way.

Apply
the
Skills

A reader can draw conclusions based on the facts in a selection. The author of "The Story of Nim" draws the following conclusion at the end: "Project Nim had proved that a chimpanzee could not only be taught words in sign language but could learn how to use language to communicate with human beings." List four facts from the selection that support this conclusion.

Prewrite

Who?	What?	Where?	When?	Why?	How?
Nim					

News reporters write about important scientific stories as well as political and economic ones. Their news stories answer the six basic news-gathering questions: Who? What? Where? When? Why? How? Pretend that you are a reporter sent to find out about Project Nim. Copy the chart above and fill it in with information from the selection, "The Story of Nim."

Compose

Write a news story about Project Nim. Include the answers to the six news-gathering questions in your story. You may want to give more information about Nim than the six questions ask for. Be sure to write a title for your story.

Revise

Read your news story. Check to see that you have included the answers to the six basic news-gathering questions. Have you included a title? If not, revise your work.

Ellen Conford has had thousands of dialogues with readers through her books. Read to find out why Ellen Conford started writing books.

What conclusions can you draw about Ellen Conford from what she says about herself?

Ellen Conford: Something Special on Every Page

by Bernice E. Cullinan

Ellen Conford has been writing books for children since 1971, and has she been busy! She has had more than twelve books published, four of which have been singled out for honors. She has also written stories and poems for many magazines.

How did Ellen Conford begin writing? Where does she get her ideas? What kinds of stories does she like to write? As with most authors, the answers to these questions involve personal experiences, a sense of purpose, and great imagination.

Conford said she became interested in writing in the third grade. "That year," she said, "my teacher asked us to write our spelling words in sentences. As I played with the words, I noticed that my first two sentences rhymed. I thought, 'Why not do the whole list that way?' When the teacher handed back our papers, she gave everyone else their papers, but she kept mine. Then she asked me to come to the front of the room to read mine out loud. Everyone clapped and, naturally, I put my spelling words into a poem every week after that. I don't think those poems were very good, or even made much sense, but my teacher was pleased with them and encouraged me with praise and enthusiasm."

Conford remembered another early experience that involved writing. "In the same year I wrote my spelling words in a poem," she explained, "I wrote a poem for my dentist. When I gave it to him, he put it up on a little bulletin board he had in the office. Just recently, when he retired, he sent it to my mother and said, 'I thought you might like to have this piece of Ellen's early writing.' That kind of encouragement is very important to a writer. It shows that people appreciate what you write."

Ellen Conford's first book for young children grew out of a personal experience. It was written for a particular reason. She had been looking in the library for a book for her four-year-old son and was not satisfied with any of the books she found. She felt that she could write a better story. So she decided to do so. Her first book, *Impossible Possum*, was published in 1971.

Since that time, Ellen Conford has created a variety of memorable characters. Some of her books include *Dreams of Victory* (1973), *Felicia the Critic* (1973), *Me and the Terrible Two* (1977), *The Revenge of the Incredible Dr. Rancid and His Youthful Assistant, Jeffrey,* (1980), *If This Is Love, I'll Take Spaghetti* (1983), and *Lenny Kandell, Smart Aleck* (1983).

When asked where she gets ideas for her books, Conford said she really doesn't know. But she did offer this explanation: "Usually the stories develop from the personality of the main character, such as Felicia, the critic, in *Felicia the Critic*, and Victory, the dreamer, in *Dreams of Victory*. When I get an idea for a book, I just jot it down in one sentence and let it stay in the back of my mind for a while. If it's a good idea, it usually begins to take shape as a book without my even consciously working at it. And it stays in my mind until I do something about it—write it. If it doesn't keep coming back to me, if it doesn't get bigger and better, it doesn't become a book. For an idea to turn into a book, it has to bother you and haunt you until it forces you to write it."

One idea of Conford's came from a dream. She said that she woke up one morning and had the entire plot in her head. Another idea came from hearing an interesting name while watching TV. Still other ideas came from things that have happened to her son and his friends.

Some of Conford's characters and stories are autobiographical. The main character, Victory, in *Dreams of Victory* is very much like Ellen Conford. "I was a big daydreamer," Conford admits. "I still am. Not everything that happens to Victory happened to me, but her feelings and reactions are the same as mine were at her age. Most often, my characters are not duplicates of anyone I know, but their personalities, mannerisms, and characteristics come from those of adults and children I have known."

With all the writing that she does, one might wonder if Ellen Conford has time for anything else. She certainly does! She likes to cook, do crossword puzzles, watch old movies on television, read, and eat! She particularly likes to read mysteries and cookbooks. She also likes to play word games.

To keep her company, Ellen Conford has a dog and a cat. Her dog's name is Emma, and her cat's name is Children's Room. The cat was so named because she was found under the card catalog in the children's room of a public library. Conford explained that the reason she didn't name her cat Card Catalog was because Card Catalog would be a silly name for a cat!

Conford's view of words and of her own writing can best be summed up in her own words, "I write the kinds of books I like to read. I like books with zippy dialogue and funny incidents on every page. I want instant payoff when I read, so I try to put something special on every page."

Once you have read any of Ellen Conford's stories, you know she has done just that.

1. Why did Ellen Conford start writing books?
2. In your own words explain how an idea develops for one of Conford's books.
3. Conford said she appreciated the encouragement she got as a child from her teacher and her dentist. Why do you think this kind of encouragement is important for a writer? What other kinds of encouragement can you think of for a writer?
4. Where does Conford get ideas and characters for her books?
5. The author of this article chose a quotation from Conford to use as a title. Look through the selection and find another quotation that describes Conford as a writer. Then explain why you made that choice.

To draw a conclusion about something, you use the information you are given plus your own knowledge and experience. Tell which of the following conclusions you can draw from the selection. Then find sentences in the selection that support each conclusion.

1. Enthusiasm and appreciation by others are extremely helpful in encouraging a young writer.
2. Authors should only write about people they know.
3. Imagination can be awakened in many ways.

Prewrite

Kind of pet:	
What it looks like:	
Where it was found:	
Tricks it can do:	
Name of the pet:	

In the selection "Ellen Conford: Something Special on Every Page," you learned about Ellen Conford's cat and why Conford chose the name Children's Room. Think about your pet or a pet you know, or make up an imaginary pet. Copy the chart and complete it with information about the pet.

Compose

Using the information on the chart, write a paragraph or two describing the pet and explaining how it got its name. Be sure to use topic sentences. If possible, draw a connection between your pet's name and some special thing about it. For example: *We named our dog Freckles, because he has spots on his nose.*

Revise

Read your paragraphs. Did you explain how the pet got its name? If not, revise your work.

Fact and Opinion

Recognizing Fact and Opinion

A **fact** is something that can be proved. An **opinion** is something that a person or group of people believes to be true. Opinions may be supported by facts, but they cannot be proved as facts can. Read the sentences below and decide which statements are facts and which are opinions.

1. All cats have thirty sharp teeth.
2. Cats are more attractive than dogs.
3. Cats make better pets than dogs because they are easier to care for.

If you decided that sentence 1 states a fact, you are correct. It's a fact because it is possible to prove. What about sentence 2? Some people might agree with that statement; others would certainly disagree. Which pet is more attractive is a matter of opinion. It is not possible to prove or disprove the statement. Sentence 3 is tricky. Part of the sentence is factual; the other part is an opinion based on that fact. Can you tell one from the other? It is a fact that cats are easier to care for than dogs. You can prove it. But whether cats make better pets *because* of that fact is an opinion — what someone believes.

When you read, you often find facts and opinions mixed together. It is important to be able to tell what is fact and what is opinion. You cannot argue with facts. But you can choose what opinions to believe and come up with opinions of your own. Read the following paragraph carefully and decide which statements are facts and which are opinions.

Today bicycle riding is becoming more popular. And it's a good thing, too. Bikes are a very efficient means of transportation, and they don't pollute. If more people rode bikes today, we would clear the skies and clean up our cities.

The first sentence can be proved by studying recent sales of bicycles. Therefore, it is a fact. The second sentence states an opinion that that fact is "good." Whenever you read or hear someone say something is good or bad, better or worse, wonderful or terrible, you are being given an opinion. It is a fact that bicycles are efficient and don't pollute the air. The last sentence, however, is an opinion.

Weighing the Author's Opinion

Separating facts from opinions is an important part of reading. Writers, just like other people, often try to convince you to agree with their opinions. However, sometimes you may find that you disagree with a writer's opinion. You might feel that a writer is not telling you the entire story. Perhaps certain facts that don't support the opinion have been omitted. You might think that the writer is reading the facts incorrectly, or you might not share the writer's opinion.

The following paragraph is about jigsaw puzzles. What is your opinion of jigsaw puzzles? Do you think they are fun to do, or do you think they are silly and boring? As you read the paragraph, ask yourself: *What is the author's opinion of jigsaw puzzles?*

Putting together a jigsaw puzzle is very enjoyable. It's a great way to spend an evening or a rainy Saturday afternoon. You can work on the puzzle with family or friends, and you can listen to music or talk while you assemble the puzzle. When you finish, you can take it apart and use it again.

The first two sentences are opinions. The rest of the paragraph lists facts to support the opinions. Do you share the author's opinion? What was your opinion of jigsaw puzzles before you read this paragraph? Did the paragraph encourage you to change your mind?

Evaluating the Sources of Opinion

Sometimes opinions can be as helpful and informative as facts are. Suppose you want to buy a radio, for example. You would want other people's opinions about which is the best kind of radio to buy. Look at the following sources of opinion on new radios. Think about which one would give you the most valuable opinion.

1. an advertisement for a certain radio
2. an article in an electronics magazine
3. an article in a consumer magazine

How good a source of opinion about a radio is its ad? Have you ever seen an ad say anything negative about its product? What about an electronics magazine? Usually, the writers for such magazines are well informed about the quality of many different products. They may give you facts that would be difficult for you to find yourself. So, an electronics magazine would be a valuable source of opinions about a radio. Consumer magazines are other good places to find valuable opinions. Often a consumer magazine will test products for quality and compare prices for you. Then you can decide for yourself the best radio to buy for your money.

Textbook Application: Fact and Opinion in Social Studies

Textbooks help you learn by teaching you facts. Textbooks sometimes also include the opinions of others. Authors of textbooks don't state their own opinions directly. They report other people's opinions so that you can make up your own mind.

The following selection from a social studies textbook includes both facts and opinions. The sidenotes will help you recognize the opinions as you read.

The Rights of Women

What fact is given in the first paragraph?

Another major achievement of the twentieth century has been the continuing growth of democracy. In 1920 women got the right to vote.

The right of women to vote had first been proposed in 1848 at a women's rights meeting. This meeting which was held in Seneca Falls, New York, was organized by Lucretia Mott and Elizabeth Cady Stanton. They had met each other while working for the abolition of slavery.

What was Elizabeth Cady Stanton's opinion of Lucy Stone? Notice the quotation marks around Stanton's words.

Lucy Stone, like Stanton and Mott, was both an abolitionist and a defender of women's rights. As a young woman, she traveled the country giving speeches. "She was the first who really stirred the nation's heart on the subject of women's wrongs," according to Stanton.

In 1872 the Supreme Court had supported Illinois in its refusal to let women practice law. Women, said the Court, were naturally timid and delicate. Therefore they were unfit for many occupations. This was a popular idea among people of the time. The facts, however, did not support it.

What was the Illinois Supreme Court's opinion of women in 1872?

Settling America would have been impossible without numbers of strong and brave women. The American Revolution would not have been won without the active help of women. Women worked to end slavery and bring about reforms. At telephone switchboards, at typewriters, at cash registers, women were helping American business to grow. Other women became teachers, scientists, writers, and doctors.

What do the facts say about women?

Working for the Vote

By 1910 the suffrage movement had gained the support of most American women. Women started wearing yellow, the color of the cause. Women started holding rallies and parades. In 1912, 15,000 women marched up Fifth Avenue in New York in a demand for women's suffrage.

Are there any opinions expressed in the last two paragraphs?

The Nineteenth Amendment to the Constitution became law in 1920. For the first time adult women could vote nationwide for President. Another step toward a fuller democracy had been taken.

— *The United States: Its History and Neighbors,*
Harcourt Brace Jovanovich

People communicate their feelings and thoughts in different ways. Read to find out what thoughts are communicated in the unusual dialogue in this story.

As you read, form an opinion about the main characters.

Clever Carmelita

retold by Frances Carpenter

This happened, people say, in a Chilean town, which had a young Spanish Governor. It was long ago, but also it was after the conquerors from over the sea began ruling the land. This young Governor, whose name may well have been Don Pedro, set great store by cleverness. He himself had the sharpest mind in all the land. Not one of his counselors could get the best of him in a matching of wits.

Now Don Pedro was not married. When people suggested that he should take a wife, he would always reply, "I shall wed only a maiden who is as clever as I am. Find me such a one, and you shall have your wedding feast."

The people of that city shook their heads. There were plenty of beautiful girls to be had—Spanish girls and daughters of Indian Chiefs—but how would they ever discover one half as clever as their young Governor, when no man was a match for him?

Don Pedro liked a joke. When he was out riding, he often reined in his horse to ask a trick question of some maiden—just for the fun of seeing her eyes grow wide and her jaw drop, as she stood speechless before him.

One day as he walked his horse through a village just outside the city, he came upon a young woman who was watering a basil plant near the gate of her garden. The garden belonged to a well-to-do man who had three pretty daughters. On this afternoon it was Teresa, the oldest, who was taking her turn with the watering.

Don Pedro greeted her with this little verse.

Good day, fair maid, 'tis good to see,
A plant cared for so tenderly.
Upon its stalk, pray tell to me,
How many small green leaves there be.

At these words of the handsome young Governor, the girl's face grew scarlet. She hung her head and rushed to her house. Of course she did not know how many leaves the basil plant had, and she could not think what to reply.

The next time the young horseman came past the garden, the middle sister, Floriana, was watering the basil plant. Again the joking Don Pedro put the same question, and like Teresa, Floriana stammered and blushed and ran into the house.

But when the young man stopped at this garden gate a third time, it was Carmelita, the youngest daughter of the family, who was tending the green plant. She was as fair as her sisters, and she was known all through the neighborhood for her clever wit.

Carmelita did not hang her head when Don Pedro called out teasingly:

Good day, fair maid, 'tis good to see,
A plant cared for so tenderly.
Upon its stalk, pray tell to me,
How many small green leaves there be?

No, Carmelita did not blush; she did not run indoors to hide. Instead she looked up at the young man on his prancing horse, and using a verse, just as he had, she said:

First, do you who question me,
Tell how many fish swim in the sea.

This time it was Don Pedro who was silent, for he did not know how he could respond to her question. He rode away, half angry and half pleased with the clever maiden.

"I'll get the best of her another time," he promised himself. And he thought, and he thought until he had a plan that was sure to embarrass her.

When he reached home, the young Governor called for the head cook in his household, an old blind man.

"Tomorrow," he gave the order, "you must dress yourself like a street cake-seller. Take a basket of hot, fried cakes on your arm and go to this House of the Three Sisters. I want you to sell your cakes to Carmelita, the youngest one. Take no money from her, but see that she pays you with a kiss instead! And take care that you do not say it was I who sent you."

"Cakes for sale! Hot fried cakes for sale! Who'll buy my cakes!"

377

When the two older sisters heard the cake-seller's call, they ran to the door to answer his knock.

"We have no money to buy your hot cakes, old man," Teresa said regretfully. "But our youngest sister, Carmelita, who is washing clothes in the brook—she always has pesos in her apron pocket. Perhaps she will buy."

"Cakes for sale! Hot fried cakes for sale! Who'll buy my cakes?"

Carmelita rose from her knees on the bank of the brook when she heard this tempting call. She put her hand in her apron pocket to take out a coin to give to him.

"No, *niña*," said the old cake-seller, "I do not sell these good, hot, fried cakes for money. I sell only for kisses."

"For kisses, indeed! Only for kisses! Then you can just take them away from here," exclaimed Carmelita with a ringing laugh.

"Why not kisses, my pretty one? What is a kiss? And for a harmless old man like me? Besides who would know? We are hidden here by the brook? I myself—I am blind. Even I could not see you, and my cakes—they are very hot and very good."

The hot fried cakes smelled so good that they made Carmelita's mouth water, so she gave the old man a fleeting kiss for each one in his basket. Then she ran home to share the feast with her two sisters.

Next day the young Governor rode past the house of the three sisters once more. Carmelita was near the garden gate, and the young horseman stopped.

Good day, fair maid, 'tis good to see,
A plant cared for so tenderly.
Upon its stalk, pray tell to me,
How many small green leaves there be.

Carmelita laughed. This was a good game. As before she gave him back her own verse:

First, do you who question me,
Tell how many fish swim in the sea.

Now the young man had another verse in reply. With twinkling eyes and teasing voice, and watching Carmelita's pretty face, he said:

Ho, Carmelita, down by the brook,
How many times did you kiss my cook?

Then Carmelita's cheeks burned like fire. She shook her head, and speechless, she ran into the house and slammed the door. She was very angry, and she vowed that she would get even with this proud young man who had played such a trick to embarrass her.

For weeks Carmelita thought of nothing else but Don Pedro. Each day she had a new idea, but none seemed to please her. Then one afternoon, she learned that the young man had fallen ill.

"He is not very sick," people said, "but he greatly fears he will die."

Carmelita dressed herself in a gray wig and a long robe, so as to resemble Saint Anthony. Leading a fat pig, as the good saint was known to do, she made her way to the Governor's house.

"Saint Anthony! Saint Anthony!" Don Pedro's servants fell on their knees when they saw the familiar bent figure leading the pig. They took these two travelers at once to the room where Don Pedro lay on his couch.

"I have been sent to you, my poor friend." Carmelita's voice sounded just like that of a man. "You have been faithful. Now that you are about to die, I come to help you get ready."

"Good Saint Anthony, I beg you. I am too young to die. Help me to live instead."

The false saint's head was bowed. No words came for a moment, then Carmelita spoke slowly, "God loves the meek, my son, so show that your heart is humble. Perhaps then God will be pleased and will grant you longer to live.

"This poor creature by my side is my friend and companion, yet it is only a pig, one of the lowliest of all the creatures. Show your meekness by treating it as your brother. For each kiss you give my pig, I will pray that you will be granted one more year of life."

The young man was eager to live, so he leapt up from his couch and pressed a full hundred kisses on the pig's bristly head. Then still bending over, in her saint's disguise, Carmelita led the animal away.

Of course Don Pedro soon was well again. In truth, he had never been very sick. On the first day he could mount his horse, he rode past the house of the fair Carmelita. Though he would not yet admit it, he had fallen in love with this young woman who was so pretty and so clever.

Good day, fair maid, again I see,
Your plant is cared for tenderly.
Upon its stalk, pray tell to me,
How many small green leaves there be.

Carmelita laughed merrily as their game began. She had a surprise for this joker! First she replied as before.

First, do you who question me,
Tell how many fish swim in the sea.

Pleased to think he was to have the last word in teasing the maiden, Don Pedro repeated his rhyme.

Ho, Carmelita, down by the brook,
How many times did you kiss my cook?

But this was not the last word. Ah, no! To the young man's great surprise, Carmelita tossed her head and cried:

A saint can be made with robe and wig,
How many times did you kiss my pig?

Don Pedro laughed until his sides ached. This witty Carmelita had beaten him at his own game. He called his counselors together and said, "At last I have found a woman who is as clever as I. I shall make Carmelita, from the House of the Three Sisters, my beloved bride."

Clever Carmelita consented to marry the young Governor of her land.

1. What thoughts were Don Pedro and Carmelita communicating in their dialogue?
2. What was Don Pedro trying to prove with his verses?
3. Do you think that the exchange of verses and tricks was a good way for Don Pedro and Carmelita to get to know one another? Explain why or why not.
4. Why was Carmelita's trick a good one to play on Don Pedro? Explain.
5. Find parts of the story that show that Carmelita was a good match for Don Pedro.

Every story is made up of facts—what happens, who the characters are, where the story is set, and so on. As you read a story you develop opinions about it. Listed below are sentences about "Clever Carmelita." For each one, tell whether it is a fact about the story or an opinion about the story.

1. Don Pedro tricked Carmelita into kissing his cook.
2. Carmelita was more clever than Don Pedro.
3. Carmelita liked hot fried cakes.
4. Don Pedro looked totally foolish when he was tricked by Carmelita.
5. Carmelita agreed to marry Don Pedro.

Prewrite

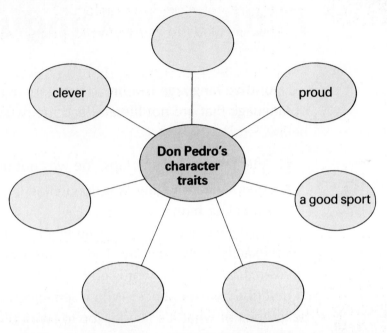

The words in the center of this ideaburst—*Don Pedro's character traits*—are a central idea. The words surrounding them describe some of Don Pedro's character traits. Copy the ideaburst and complete it with other words that describe Don Pedro.

Compose

Use the information on your ideaburst to write a paragraph about Don Pedro's character. Use examples of his behavior from the story to explain each of his traits.

Revise

Read your paragraph. Check to make sure you gave examples of Don Pedro's behavior for each character trait. If not, revise your work.

Figurative Language

Figurative language is a broad category that refers to uses of language that are not literal. Read the two sentences below.

1. After swimming fifty laps, Joe was out of breath.
2. After swimming fifty laps, Joe felt as if his lungs were strangling him.

The first sentence uses language *literally;* that is, the words mean exactly what they say. The second sentence uses words *figuratively;* the words go beyond the literal meaning to describe an experience. Which sentence gives you a better idea of what it's like for Joe to swim fifty laps?

Figurative language often tries to make you see, hear, feel, even smell or taste what's being described. Think about the five senses when you read figurative language.

Metaphor and Simile

Metaphors and similes are probably the most common forms of figurative language. They compare things. A **metaphor** usually makes a comparison only with a verb connecting two things. A **simile** uses *like* or *as* in a comparison. Read the following examples from two poems.

1. A train is a dragon that roars through the dark.
2. Fast as foxes,
   buzzy as bees,
   down the slope
   on our silver-tipped skis —

The first sentence uses a metaphor to compare a train with a dragon. How is a train like a dragon? It's strong and powerful; it "roars." The metaphor makes you think about a train in a special way—as a rather scary creature of the dark. The second example describes how skiers feel about what they are doing. Notice the use of *as* in the two similes Do you get the feeling of speed (fast as foxes) and the crowds of people on the slopes (buzzy as bees)?

Exaggeration

An **exaggeration** (also called **hyperbole**) is a statement making something greater than it is. It is used for effect and emphasis rather than to fool people. Read this example:

> Jan ran like greased lightning.

This is an exaggeration meant to emphasize the speed of Jan's running. Notice that the exaggeration is also a simile. Exaggerations are often in the form of comparisons.

Personification

Personification is a comparison in which a thing is given human qualities. For example, if you say the wind sings, you are using personification. Wind doesn't sing; a person does. You mean the sound of wind is like a person singing. Look for the personification in this verse:

> The Night was creeping on the ground!
> She crept and did not make a sound.

Notice that the word *Night* is capitalized like a person's name. Night is also called *she*. So *night* in this verse is personified as a woman.

These examples of figurative language all use words in different ways for greater meaning. Once you understand figurative language, you'll be able to get more meaning out of what you read.

Author Profile

Kenneth Grahame

When Kenneth Grahame first began writing about growing up, no one thought he was writing for young people. Only adults read his stories. It never occurred to anybody that he might be writing *for* the people he wrote *about*. Adults assumed his writing was too difficult for young people to understand. It wasn't until *The Wind in the Willows* was published in 1908 that younger people began to read Kenneth Grahame's work. And that's also when some adults finally saw that his writing can be read with pleasure by people of every age.

Kenneth Grahame was born in Edinburgh, Scotland, in 1859. When he was five years old, his mother died of scarlet fever. Kenneth, his two brothers, and his sister moved to England to live with their grandmother in a large, old house close to the Thames River. Kenneth spent many happy hours exploring the riverbanks, the fields, and the woods nearby. He discovered many different wild animals in the countryside — water rats along the riverbanks and moles in the fields. He was to remember these long walks many years later when he wrote *The Wind in the Willows*.

Within a few years, Kenneth Grahame's grandmother moved, and he was sent to school in the town of Oxford. Grahame decided that more than anything else, he wanted to go to Oxford University when he was old enough. But his grandmother had other plans. She flatly refused to let him go to the university, and sent him to work in a bank instead.

At the age of sixteen, Grahame moved to London and became a clerk in the Bank of England. He was very unhappy there. Then, by chance, he met a group of writers. He began to do some writing himself.

Grahame's first pieces of writing were published in literary magazines. His writing was very unusual for his time. When Grahame was writing, there were few authors who wrote for young people. Have you ever heard the expression, "Children should be seen and not heard"? This was a favorite expression in the nineteenth century. It's easy to understand, then, why adults believed that Kenneth Grahame was writing only for them.

Grahame wrote only three books, which is quite a small amount for a writer. He continued to work at the bank, which meant that he didn't have much time for writing. Originally, the next story you will read, "The Reluctant Dragon," was a chapter in Grahame's second book, *Dream Days*. It wasn't until many years later that the story was printed on its own. *The Wind in the Willows* was his third and last book. It came from stories that he told to his son, Alistair (whose nickname was "Mouse"). It is a classic and is Grahame's most beloved book.

Kenneth Grahame died in 1932 at the age of seventy-three, twenty-four years after he had written his last book. He had become more famous with each year, and his books are still widely read by young and old alike.

Talking can help enemies to solve their problems. How does talking help the two traditional enemies —St. George and a dragon—in this story?

As you read, notice how the author uses different kinds of figurative language.

The Reluctant Dragon

by Kenneth Grahame

Long ago in a cottage halfway between an English village and the Downs, a shepherd lived with his wife and their son. Now the shepherd spent his days up on the wide Downs, with only the sun and the stars and the sheep for company. But his son, when he wasn't helping his father, spent much of his time buried in big books that he borrowed from people round about. His parents were very fond of him, and rather proud of him too, though they didn't let on in his hearing, so he was left to go his own way and read as much as he liked. He was treated more or less as an equal by his parents, who sensibly thought it a very fair division of his labor that they should supply the practical knowledge, and he the book-learning. They knew that book-learning often came in useful in a pinch. What the Boy chiefly read was natural history and fairy tales.

One evening the shepherd came home all a-tremble. Sitting down at the table where his wife and son were sitting quietly, she with her sewing, he following out the adventures of a Giant with no Heart in his Body, the shepherd exclaimed: "It's all up with me, Maria! Never no more can I go up on them there Downs!"

"Now don't you take on like that," said his wife, who was a *very* sensible woman, "but tell us all about it first. Whatever it is has given you this shake-up, between us, we ought to be able to get to the bottom of it!"

"It began some nights ago," said the shepherd. "You know that cave up there. I never liked it, somehow, and the sheep never liked it neither, and when sheep don't like a thing there's generally some reason for it. Well, for some time past there's been faint noises coming from that cave — noises like heavy sighings, with grunts mixed up in them; and sometimes a snoring, far away down — real snoring, you know!"

"I know," said the Boy quietly.

"Of course I was terribly frightened," the shepherd went on. "Yet somehow I couldn't keep away. So this very evening, before I came down, I took a look round by the cave, quietly. And there — Oh my! There I saw him at last, as plain as I see you!"

"Saw who?" said his wife, beginning to share in her husband's terror.

"Why him, I'm a-telling you!" said the shepherd. "He was sticking halfway out of the cave, and seemed to be enjoying the cool of the evening. He was as big as four cart horses, and all covered with shiny scales — deep blue scales at the top of him, shading off to a light sort of green below. As he breathed, there was that sort of flicker over his nostrils that you see over our chalk roads on a windless day in summer. He had his chin on his paws, and I should say he was meditating about things. Oh, yes, a peaceable sort of beast enough, and not doing anything but what was quite right and proper. I admit all that. And yet, what am I to do? Scales, you know, and claws, and a tail for certain, though I didn't see that end of him. I ain't used to 'em, and I don't hold with 'em, and that's a fact!"

The Boy, who had apparently been absorbed in his book, now closed the volume, yawned, and said sleepily: "It's all right, Father. Don't you worry. It's only a dragon."

"Only a dragon?" cried his father. "What do you mean? Only a dragon indeed! And what do you know about it?"

" 'Cause it *is,* and 'cause I do know," replied the Boy quietly. "Look here, Father, you know we've each of us got our line. You two know about sheep, and weather, and things. I know about dragons. I always said, you know, that that cave up there must have belonged to a dragon some time, and ought to belong to a dragon now. Well, now you tell me it *has* got a dragon. I'm not half as much surprised as when you told me it *hadn't* got a dragon. Now, please, just leave this all to me. And I'll stroll up tomorrow evening and have a talk with him. You'll find it'll be all right. Only please, don't you go worrying round there without me. You don't understand 'em a bit, and they're very sensitive, you know!''

"He's quite right, Father," said the sensible mother. "As he says, dragons is his line and not ours. He's wonderful knowing about book-beasts. And to tell the truth, I'm not half happy in my own mind, thinking of that poor animal lying alone up there, without a bit of hot supper or anyone to exchange the news with. Maybe we'll be able to do something for him. If he ain't quite respectable our Boy'll find it out quick enough."

Next day, after he'd had his tea, the Boy strolled up the chalky track that led to the Downs. There, sure enough, he found the dragon, stretched lazily on the grass in front of his cave. The view from that point was a magnificent one. To the right and left lay the bare and billowy Downs. In front was the valley, with its clustered homes, its white roads running through orchards and tilled fields. And far away was a hint of gray old cities on the horizon. A cool breeze played over the grass, and the silver moon was showing above distant trees. No wonder the dragon seemed in a peaceful and contented mood.

Indeed, as the Boy came close he could hear the beast purring with a happy regularity.

"Hullo, dragon!" said the Boy quietly.

The dragon, on hearing the footsteps, made the beginning of a courteous effort to rise. But when he saw it was a Boy, he set his eyebrows severely. "Now don't you hit me," he said, "or throw stones, or squirt water, or anything. I won't have it, I tell you!"

"Not goin' to hit you," said the Boy, dropping on the grass beside the beast. "And don't, for goodness sake, keep on saying 'Don't.' I hear so much of it, it makes me tired. I've simply looked in to ask you how you were, but if I'm in the way I can easily clear out."

"No, no, don't go off in a huff," said the dragon hastily. "Fact is—I'm as happy up here as the day's long. And yet, between ourselves, it is a bit dull at times."

The Boy bit off a stalk of grass and chewed it. "Going to make a long stay here?" he asked politely.

"Can't hardly say at present," replied the dragon. "It seems a nice place enough—but I've only been here a short time, and one must look about and consider before settling down. It's rather a serious thing, settling down. Besides—now I'm going to tell you something! The fact is, I'm such a very lazy fellow!"

"You surprise me," said the Boy politely.

"It's the sad truth," the dragon went on, settling down between his paws and evidently delighted to have found a listener at last. "I fancy that's really how I came to be here. You see all the other fellows were so active and *earnest* and all that sort of thing—always rampaging, and fighting and chasing knights all over the place. Whereas I liked to get my meals regular and then to lean my back against a bit of rock and snooze a bit, and wake up and just think of things. So when it happened I got fairly caught."

"When *what* happened, please?" asked the Boy.

"That's just what I don't exactly know," said the dragon. "I suppose the earth sneezed, or shook itself, or the bottom dropped out of something. Anyhow there was a shake and a roar. Then I found myself miles away underground and wedged in as tight as tight. Well, thank goodness, my wants are few, and at any rate I had peace and quiet and wasn't always being asked to come along and *do* something. And I've got such an active mind—always occupied, I assure you! But time went on, and there was a certain sameness about life, and at last I began to think it would be fun to work my way up and see what you other fellows were doing. So I scratched and dug and at last I came out through this cave here. And I like the country, and the view, and on the whole I feel inclined to settle down here."

"What's your mind always occupied about?" asked the Boy. "That's what I want to know."

The dragon colored slightly and looked away. Then he said shyly: "Did you ever—just for fun—try to make up poetry?"

"Course I have," said the Boy. "And some of it's quite good, I feel sure, only there's no one here cares about it. Mother's very kind and all that, when I read it to her, and so's Father for that matter. But somehow they don't seem to—"

"Exactly," cried the dragon, "my own case exactly. They don't seem to, and you can't argue with 'em about it. I should just like your opinion about some little things I wrote when I was down there. I'm awfully pleased to have met you, and I'm hoping the other neighbors will be equally agreeable. There was a very nice old gentleman up here only last night, but he didn't seem to want to intrude."

"That was my father," said the Boy. "He *is* a nice old gentleman, and I'll introduce you some day if you like."

"Can't you two come up here and dine or something tomorrow?" asked the dragon eagerly.

"Thanks awfully," said the Boy, "but we don't go out anywhere without my mother. To tell you the truth, I'm afraid she mightn't quite approve of you. You see there's no getting over the fact that you're a dragon, is there? And when you talk of settling down, I can't help feeling that you don't quite realize your position. You're an enemy of the human race, you see!"

"Haven't got an enemy in the world," said the dragon cheerfully. "Too lazy to make 'em."

"Oh, dear!" cried the Boy. "I wish you'd try and understand. When the other people find you out, they'll come after you with spears and swords and all sorts of things. You're a scourge, and a pest, and a baneful monster!"

"Not a word of truth in it," said the dragon. "Character'll bear the strictest investigation. And now, there's a little sonnet I was working on when you appeared . . ."

"Oh, if you *won't* be sensible," cried the Boy, getting up, "I'm going off home. No, I can't stop for sonnets; my mother's sitting up. I'll look you up tomorrow, sometime or other, and do for goodness' sake try and realize that you're a pestilential scourge, or you'll find yourself in a most awful fix. Good night!"

The Boy found it an easy matter to set the mind of his parents at ease about his new friend. They took his word without a murmur. The shepherd was formally introduced and many kind inquiries were exchanged. His wife, however, though expressing her willingness to do anything she could — to mend things, or set the cave to rights, or cook a little something for the dragon — could not be brought to meet him. She made no objection, however, to her son spending his evenings with the dragon quietly, so long as he was home by nine o'clock. So many a pleasant night they had, sitting on the grass while the dragon told stories of old times, when dragons were quite plentiful and the world was a livelier place than it is now, and life was full of thrills and jumps and surprises.

What the Boy had feared, however, soon came to pass. The most modest and retiring dragon in the world, if he's as big as four cart horses and covered with blue scales, cannot keep altogether out of the public view. And so down in the village the fact that a real live dragon sat in the cave on the Downs was naturally a subject for talk. Though the villagers were extremely frightened, they were rather proud as well. It was a distinction to have a dragon of your own. Still, all were agreed that this sort of thing couldn't be allowed to go on. The dreadful beast must be exterminated. The countryside must be freed from this pest, this terror.

The fact that not even a hen-roost was the worse for the dragon's arrival wasn't allowed to have anything to do with it. He was a dragon, and he couldn't deny it, and if he didn't choose to behave as such, that was his own lookout. But in spite of much talk, no hero was found willing to take sword and spear and free the suffering village. Meanwhile the dragon lolled on the turf, enjoyed the sunsets, and told ancient stories to the Boy.

One day the Boy, on walking into the village, found everything wearing a festive appearance which was not to be accounted for in the calendar. Brightly colored banners were hung out of the windows, the church-bells clamored noisily, the little street was flower-strewn, and the whole population jostled each other along either side of it, chat-

tering and shoving. The Boy saw a friend in the crowd and hailed him.

"What's up?" he cried. "Is it the players, or bears, or a circus, or what?"

"It's all right," his friend hailed back. "He's a-coming."

"*Who's* a-coming?" demanded the Boy.

"Why, St. George, of course," replied his friend. "He's heard of our dragon, and he's comin' on purpose to slay the deadly beast, and free us. Oh my! Won't there be a jolly fight!"

Here was news indeed! The Boy felt that he ought to make quite sure for himself, and he wriggled himself in between the legs of his elders. Once in front, he breathlessly awaited the arrival.

Soon, from the faraway end came the sound of cheering. Next, the measured tramp of a great war-horse made his heart beat quicker, and then he found himself cheering with the rest, as amid welcoming shouts and waving of handkerchiefs, St. George paced slowly up the street. The Boy's heart stood still, the beauty and the grace of the hero were so far beyond anything he had yet seen. His armor was inlaid with gold, his plumed helmet hung at his saddlebow, and his thick fair hair framed a face gentle beyond expression till you caught the sternness in his eyes. He drew rein in front of the little inn, and the villagers crowded round with greetings and thanks and long statements of their wrongs and grievances. The Boy heard the gentle voice of the Saint, assuring them that all would be well now, and that he would stand by them and free them from their foe. The Boy made off up the hill as fast as he could.

"It's all up, dragon!" he shouted as soon as he was within sight of the beast. "He's coming! You'll have to pull yourself together and *do* something at last!"

The dragon was licking his scales and rubbing them with a rag the Boy's mother had lent him, till he shone like a great turquoise.

"Don't be *violent*, Boy," he said without looking round. "Sit down and get your breath, and then perhaps you'll be good enough to tell me who's coming?"

"That's right, take it coolly," said the Boy. "Hope you'll be half as cool when I've got through with my news. It's only St. George who's coming, that's all. He rode into the village half an hour ago. Of course you can lick him—a great big fellow like you! But I thought I'd warn you, 'cause he's sure to be round early, and he's got the longest, wickedest-looking spear you ever did see!"

"Oh deary, deary me," moaned the dragon. "This is too awful. I won't see him, and that's flat. You must tell him to go away at once, please. Say I'm not seeing anybody at present."

"Now, dragon, dragon," said the Boy, "don't be perverse and wrong-headed. You've got to fight him, you know, 'cause he's St. George and you're the dragon. Better get it over, and then we can go on with the sonnets."

"My dear little man," said the dragon solemnly, "just understand, once for all, that I can't fight and I won't fight. I've never fought in my life, and I'm not going to begin now. In old days I always let the other fellows — the *earnest* fellows — do all the fighting, and no doubt that's why I have the pleasure of being here now."

"But if you don't fight he'll cut your head off!" gasped the Boy.

"Oh, I think not," said the dragon in his lazy way. "You'll be able to arrange something. I've every confidence in you. Just run down and make it all right. I leave it entirely to you."

The Boy made his way back to the village in a state of great despondency. First of all, his dear friend the dragon hadn't shown up in quite such a heroic light as he would have liked. And second, whether the dragon was a hero at heart or not, it made no difference, for St. George would most undoubtedly cut his head off. "Arrange things indeed!" he said bitterly to himself. "The dragon treats the whole affair as if it was an invitation to tea and croquet."

The villagers were straggling homewards as he passed up the street, all of them gleefully discussing the splendid fight that was in store. The Boy made his way to the inn where St. George now sat alone, musing over the sad stories of wrong that had poured into his sympathetic ears.

"May I come in, St. George?" said the Boy politely, as he paused at the door. "I want to talk to you about this little matter of the dragon, if you're not tired of it by this time."

"Yes, come in, Boy," said the Saint kindly. "Another tale of misery and wrong, I fear me. Is it a kind parent, then, the tyrant has taken from you? Or some tender sister or brother? Well, it shall soon be avenged."

"Nothing of the sort," said the Boy. "There's a misunderstanding somewhere, and I want to put it right. The fact is, this is a good dragon."

"Exactly," said St. George, smiling pleasantly, "I quite understand. Believe me, I do not in the least regret that he is an adversary worthy of my steel, and no feeble specimen."

"Oh dear, oh dear!" cried the Boy. "How stupid men are when they get an idea into their heads! I tell you he's a good dragon, and a friend of mine, and tells me the most beautiful stories, all about old times and when he was little. And he's been so kind to Mother, and Mother'd do anything for him. And Father likes him too, though Father doesn't hold with poetry much, and always falls asleep when the dragon starts talking about style. But the fact is, nobody can help liking him when once they know him."

"Sit down, and draw your chair up," said St. George. "I like a fellow who sticks up for his friends, and I'm sure the dragon has his good points, if he's got a friend like you. But that's not the question. All this evening I've been listening, with grief, to tales of murder, theft, and wrong. History teaches us that the greatest rascals often possess all the domestic virtues; and I fear that your friend, in spite of the qualities which have won your regard, has got to be speedily exterminated."

"Oh, you've been taking in all the yarns those fellows have been telling you," said the Boy impatiently. "Why, our villagers are the biggest storytellers in all the country round. It's a known fact. You're a stranger in these parts, or else you'd have heard it already. All they want is a *fight*. It's meat and drink to them. Dogs, bulls, dragons — anything so long as it's a *fight*. And I've no doubt they've been telling you what a hero you were, and how you were bound to win, in the cause of right and justice, and so on. I assure you, St. George," he said earnestly, "the dragon's a real gentleman, every inch of him."

"Well, perhaps I've been over-credulous," said St. George. "Perhaps I've misjudged the animal. But what are we to do? Here are the dragon and I, each supposed to be thirsting for each other's blood. I don't see any way out of it, exactly. What do you suggest? Can't you arrange things, somehow?"

"That's just what the dragon said," replied the Boy, rather nettled. "Really, the way you two seem to leave everything to me — I suppose you couldn't be persuaded to go away quietly, could you?"

"Impossible, I fear," said the Saint. "Quite against the rules."

"Well, then, look here," said the Boy. "It's early yet. Would you mind strolling up with me and seeing the dragon and talking it over? It's not far, and any friend of mine will be most welcome."

"Well, it's irregular," said St. George, rising, "but really it seems about the most sensible thing to do. You're taking a lot of trouble on your friend's account," he added good-naturedly, as they passed out through the door together.

"I've brought a friend to see you, dragon," said the Boy rather loud.

The dragon woke up with a start. "I was just — er — thinking about things," he said in his simple way. "Very pleased to make your acquaintance, sir."

"This is St. George," said the Boy, shortly. "St. George, let me introduce you to the dragon. We've come up to talk things over quietly, dragon, and now for goodness' sake do let us have a little straight common sense, and come to some practical businesslike arrangement."

"So glad to meet you, St. George," began the dragon rather nervously, "because you've been a great traveler, I hear, and I've always been rather a stay-at-home."

"I think," said St. George in his frank, pleasant way, "that we'd really better take the advice of our young friend here, and try to come to some understanding. Now don't you think that after all the simplest plan would be just to fight it out, according to the rules, and let the best man win?"

"Oh, yes, *do* dragon," said the Boy delightedly.

"Believe me, St. George," said the dragon, "there's nobody in the world I'd sooner oblige than you and this young gentleman here. But the whole thing's nonsense. There's absolutely nothing to fight about. And anyhow I'm not going to, so that settles it!"

"But supposing I make you?" said St. George.

"You can't," said the dragon triumphantly. "I should only go into my cave and retire for a time down the hole I came up. You'd soon get sick of sitting outside and waiting for me to come out and fight you. And as soon as you'd really gone away, why, I'd come up again. For I tell you frankly, I like this place, and I'm going to stay here!"

St. George gazed for a while on the fair landscape around them. "But this would be a beautiful place for a fight," he began again. "These great, bare rolling Downs for the arena —and me in my golden armor showing up against your big, blue scaly coils! Think what a picture it would make!"

"Now you're trying to get at me through my artistic sense," said the dragon. "But it won't work. Not but what it would make a very pretty picture, as you say," he added, wavering a little.

"We seem to be getting rather nearer to *business*," put in the Boy. "You must see, dragon, that there's got to be a fight of some sort, "'cause you can't want to have to go down that old hole again and stay there till goodness when."

"It might be carefully arranged," said St. George thoughtfully. "I *must* spear you somewhere, of course, but I'm not bound to hurt you very much. There's such a lot of you that there must be a few *spare* places somewhere. Here for instance, just behind your foreleg. It couldn't hurt you much, just here!"

"Now you're tickling, George," said the dragon. "No, that place won't do at all. Even if it didn't hurt, it would make me laugh, and that would spoil everything."

"Let's try somewhere else, then," said St. George patiently. "Under your neck, for instance—all these folds of thick skin. If I speared you here you'd never even know I'd done it!"

"Yes, but are you sure you can hit the right place?" asked the dragon anxiously.

"Of course I am," said St. George, with confidence. "You leave that to me!"

"Look here, dragon," interrupted the Boy on behalf of his friend, who seemed to be getting all the worst of the bargain, "there's to be a fight, apparently, and you're to be licked. What I want to know is, what are you going to get out of it?"

"St. George," said the dragon, "just tell us, please— what will happen after I'm vanquished?"

"Well, according to the rules I suppose I shall lead you in triumph down to the market-place," said St. George.

"Exactly," said the dragon. "And then—?"

"And then there'll be speeches and things," continued
St. George. "And I shall explain that you've changed, and
see the error of your ways."

"Quite so," said the dragon. "And then—?"

"Oh, and then—" said St. George, "why, and then there
will be the usual banquet, I suppose."

"Exactly," said the dragon, "and that's where I come in.
Look here," he continued, addressing the Boy, "I'm bored

to death up here, and no one really appreciates me. I'm going into Society, I am."

"Remember, you'll have to do your proper share of the fighting, dragon!" said St. George, as he rose to go. "I mean ramping, and breathing fire, and so on!"

"I can *ramp* all right," replied the dragon confidently. "As to breathing fire, it's surprising how easily one gets out of practice; but I'll do the best I can. Good night."

Next morning the people began streaming up to the Downs at quite an early hour, in their Sunday clothes, every one intent on getting a good place for the combat. This was not exactly a simple matter, for of course it was quite possible that the dragon might win and in that case it might not be safe to be too close. Places were chosen, therefore, with a view to a speedy retreat in case of emergency.

The Boy had secured a good front place, and was feeling as anxious as a stage-manager on a first night. Could the dragon be depended upon? He might change his mind. Seeing that the affair had been so hastily planned, without even a rehearsal, he might be too nervous to show up. The Boy looked at the cave, but it showed no sign of life. Could the dragon have made a moonlight flight?

The higher parts of the ground were now covered with sightseers, and presently a sound of cheering and a waving of handkerchiefs told that something was visible to them. A minute more and St. George's red plumes topped the hill, as the Saint rode slowly forth on the level space which stretched to the mouth of the cave. Very gallant he looked on his tall war-horse, his golden armor shining in the sun, his great spear held erect. He drew rein and sat motionless. The lines of spectators began to give back a little, nervously; and the boys in front leaned forward expectantly.

"Now then, dragon!" muttered the Boy. He need not have distressed himself. The dramatic possibilities of the thing had tickled the dragon immensely, and he had been up from an early hour, preparing for his first public appearance with as much heartiness as if he had been again a little dragonlet, playing with his sisters on the floor of their mother's cave, at the game of saints-and-dragons, in which the dragon was bound to win.

A low muttering now made itself heard, rising to a bellowing roar that seemed to fill the plain. Then a cloud of smoke hid the mouth of the cave. Out of the midst of it the dragon himself, shining, sea-blue, magnificent, pranced splendidly forth; and everybody said, "Oo-oo-oo!" His scales were glittering, his long spiky tail lashed his sides, his claws tore up the turf and sent it flying high over his back, and smoke and fire jetted from his nostrils. "Oh, well done, dragon!" cried the Boy excitedly. "Didn't think he had it in him!" he added to himself.

St. George lowered his spear, bent his head, dug his heels into his horse's sides, and came thundering over the turf. The dragon charged with a roar — a great blue combination of coils and snorts and clashing jaws and spikes and fire.

"Missed!" yelled the crowd. There was a moment's clash of golden armor and blue-green coils and spiky tail. Then the great horse carried the Saint, his spear swung high in the air, almost up to the mouth of the cave.

The dragon sat down and barked viciously, while St. George with difficulty pulled his horse round into position.

"End of Round One!" thought the Boy. "How well they did it! But I hope the Saint won't get excited. I can trust the dragon all right. What a regular play-actor the fellow is!"

St. George had at last made his horse stand steady, and was looking round him as he wiped his brow. Catching sight of the Boy, he smiled and nodded.

The dragon used the time to give a ramping performance for the crowd. Ramping, it should be explained, consists in running round and round in a wide circle, and sending waves and ripples of movement along the whole length of your spine, from your pointed ears right down to the spike at the end of your long tail. When you are covered with blue scales, the effect is particularly pleasing; and the Boy recollected the dragon's recently expressed wish to become a social success.

St. George gathered up his reins and moved forward.

"Time!" yelled everybody excitedly. The dragon, leaving off his ramping, sat up on end, and began to leap from one side to the other with huge ungainly bounds. This naturally

upset the horse, who swerved violently, the Saint only just saving himself by the mane. As they shot past, the dragon delivered a vicious snap at the horse's tail which sent the poor beast running madly over the Downs.

Round Two brought friendly feeling toward the dragon. The spectators were not slow to appreciate a combatant who could hold his own so well and clearly wanted to show

good sport. Many encouraging remarks reached the ears of the dragon as he strutted back and forth, his chest thrust out and his tail in the air, hugely enjoying his new popularity.

St. George had dismounted and was tightening his girths, so the Boy made his way to the Saint and held his spear for him.

"It's been a jolly fight, St. George!" he said, with a sigh. "Can't you let it last a bit longer?"

"Well, I think I'd better not," replied the Saint. "The fact is, your simple-minded old friend's getting conceited, now they've begun cheering him. He may forget all about the arrangement and there's no telling where he would stop. I'll just finish him off this round."

He swung himself into the saddle and took his spear from the Boy. "Now don't you be afraid," he added kindly. "I've marked my spot exactly, and *he's* sure to give me all the assistance in his power, because he knows it's his only chance of being asked to the banquet!"

St. George now trotted smartly toward the dragon, who crouched, flicking his tail till it cracked in the air like a great cart whip. The Saint circled warily round him, while the dragon adopted similar tactics. So the two sparred for an opening, while the spectators maintained a breathless silence.

Though the round lasted for some minutes, the end was so swift that all the Boy saw was a lightning movement of the Saint's arm, and then a whirl of spines, claws, tail, and flying bits of earth. The dust cleared away; the spectators whooped and ran in cheering. The Boy made out that the dragon was down, pinned to the earth by the spear, while St. George had dismounted, and stood astride of him.

It all seemed so genuine that the Boy ran in breathlessly, hoping the dear old dragon wasn't really hurt. As he approached, the dragon lifted one large eyelid, winked solemnly, and collapsed again. He was held fast to the earth by the neck. But the Saint had hit him in the spare place agreed upon, and it didn't even seem to tickle.

"Ain't you goin' to cut his head off, mister?" asked one of the applauding crowd.

"Well, not *today*, I think," replied St. George pleasantly. "You see, that can be done at *any* time. There's no hurry at all. I think we'll all go down to the village first, and have some refreshment. Then I'll give him a good talking to, and you'll find he'll be a very different dragon!"

At that magic word *refreshment* the whole crowd stood up and silently awaited the signal to start. The time for talking and cheering was past; the hour for action had arrived. St. George, hauling on his spear with both hands, released the dragon, who rose and shook himself and ran his eye over his spikes and scales and things, to see that they were all in order. Then the Saint mounted and led off the procession, the dragon following meekly in the company of the Boy. The spectators kept at a respectful distance behind.

There were great doings when they got down to the village again, and had formed up in front of the inn. After refreshment, St. George made a speech, in which he informed his audience that they shouldn't be so fond of fights, because next time they might have to do the fighting themselves, which would not be the same thing at all. Then he told them that the dragon had been thinking over things and if they were good perhaps he'd stay and settle down there. So they must make friends, and not go about making up stories and fancying other people would believe them. Then he sat down, amid much cheering, and the dragon nudged the Boy and whispered that he couldn't have done it better himself. Then everyone went off to get ready for the banquet.

Banquets are always pleasant things, consisting mostly, as they do, of eating and drinking; but the especially nice thing about a banquet is that it comes when something's over, and there's nothing more to worry about. Tomorrow

seems a long way off. St. George was happy because there had been a fight and he hadn't had to kill anybody; for he didn't really like killing, though he often had to do it. The dragon was happy because there had been a fight, and far from being hurt in it he had won popularity and a sure place in society. The Boy was happy because there had been a fight, and in spite of it all his two friends were on the best of terms. And all the others were happy because there had been a fight.

The dragon was able to say the right thing to everybody, and proved the life and soul of the evening. The Saint and the Boy, as they looked on, felt that they were helping at a feast of which the honor and the glory were entirely the dragon's. But they didn't mind that, being good fellows, and the dragon was not in the least conceited or forgetful. On the contrary, every ten minutes or so he leaned over toward the Boy and said, "Look here! you *will* see me home afterward, won't you?" And the Boy always nodded, though he had promised his mother not to be out late.

At last the banquet was over, the guests had dropped away with many good nights, and the dragon, who had seen the last of them off, left with the Boy, wiped his brow, sighed, sat down in the road, and gazed at the stars. "Jolly night it's been!" he murmured. "Jolly stars! Jolly little place this! Think I shall just stop here. Don't feel like climbing up any old hill. Boy's promised to see me home. Boy had better do it then! No responsibility on my part." And his chin sank on his broad chest and he slumbered peacefully.

"Oh, *get* up, dragon," cried the Boy. "You *know* my mother's sitting up, and I'm so tired." And the Boy sat down in the road by the side of the sleeping dragon.

The door behind them opened and St. George, who had come out for a stroll in the cool night air, caught sight of the two figures sitting there—the great sleeping dragon and the Boy.

"What's the matter, Boy?" he asked kindly, stepping to his side.

"Oh, it's this great *pig* of a dragon!" cried the Boy. "First he makes me promise to see him home, and then he goes to sleep! Might as well try to see a haystack home! And I'm so tired, and Mother's —"

"Now don't take on," said St. George. "I'll stand by you, and we'll *both* see him home. Wake up, dragon!" he said sharply, shaking the beast.

The dragon looked up sleepily.

"Now look here, dragon," said the Saint firmly. "Here's this fellow waiting to see you home, and you *know* he ought to have been in bed these two hours, and what his mother'll say *I* don't know, and anybody but a selfish pig would have *made* him go to bed long ago —"

"And he *shall* go to bed!" cried the dragon, starting up. "You give me hold of your hand, Boy. Thank you, George, an arm up the hill is just what I wanted!"

So they set off up the hill arm-in-arm, the Saint, the Dragon, and the Boy. The lights in the little village began to go out; but there were stars, and a late moon, as they climbed to the Downs together. And, as they turned the last corner and disappeared from view, snatches of an old song were borne back on the night breeze. I can't be certain which of them was singing, but I *think* it was the Dragon!

1. How did talking help St. George and the dragon to solve their problem?
2. Why did the people of the village tell lies about the dragon to St. George?
3. How did you feel about the dragon's reluctance to fight? Did you feel frustrated as the Boy did?
4. Why did St. George and the dragon agree to a fake fight instead of no fight at all?
5. Find parts of the story that show how all three characters got what they wanted in the end.

Metaphor, simile, exaggeration, and personification are types of figurative language. Below are sentences containing figurative language from "The Reluctant Dragon." Tell what kind of figurative language each sentence contains. Then give the literal meaning of each sentence.

1. A cool breeze played over the grass.
2. The dragon crouched, flicking his tail till it cracked in the air like a great cart whip.
3. "I'm bored to death," said the dragon.
4. "It's this great *pig* of a dragon!" cried the Boy.

Thinking About "Dialogues"

In this unit you were introduced to different kinds of dialogue. Storytellers such as Mama Luka and Manowar used dialogue to tell stories. And listeners such as Lee Edward asked questions to understand stories. There were characters in this unit who talked to fantastic creatures like ogres and dragons. There was also a real chimpanzee who learned to talk to humans in sign language.

Dialogue can be important because of what it can tell us about a character. The dragon in "The Reluctant Dragon" was described as being as big as four cart horses and covered with shiny blue scales. And yet it was through his dialogue, not his appearance, that we came to understand his true character. In "Clever Carmelita," although Carmelita is pretty, it is what she says that wins Don Pedro's heart.

The opinions we form about real people are often based on what they look like. Opinions about characters in stories are based on what they say and do. Perhaps writers are trying to tell us to listen before we look or judge. Writers know that words are very powerful. They know, too, that the words a person speaks can be the most powerful of all.

1. The old woman in "The Old Woman and the Rice Cakes" was strong, clever, and brave. She was not what she might have seemed on the outside. Describe two other characters in the unit who are not what they seem on the outside.

2. In which of this unit's stories are the personalities of animals shown through dialogue? Name the animals and describe their personalities.

3. Because Nim learned to use our language to express himself, people learned a lot about what he thought and felt. What other animal do you think would be important for us to know about? How could we teach this animal to communicate with us?

4. The old woman in "The Old Woman and the Rice Cakes" escaped from the Oni by using trickery. What other characters in this unit's stories use trickery to solve their problems? In your opinion, which of these characters is the most clever?

5. "The Holes of Lagos" contains a story within a story. Name two other stories in the unit that contain stories within stories. Who are the storytellers in those stories?

6. Which stories in this unit are fantasies? Which are realistic? What is the difference between the two kinds of stories?

7. What was your favorite story in this unit? Give reasons to support your opinion.

Read on Your Own

The Wizard of Oz by L. Frank Baum. Scholastic. Dorothy and her dog, Toto, are blown from Kansas into the magical land of Oz. There they share adventures with a Tin Woodman, a Scarecrow, and a Cowardly Lion as they go to see the famous Wizard.

Black Fairy Tales by Terry Berger. Atheneum. These fascinating stories from South Africa tell about princes and princesses, monsters and good fairies, magic spells, and other forms of enchantment.

Giant Kippernose and Other Stories by John Cunliffe. Andre Deutsch. Here are stories of giants who steal the world, swallow the wind, and do other funny, mischievous, or nasty things.

Seven-Day Magic by Edward Eager. Harcourt Brace Jovanovich. Barnaby, John, Susan, Abbie, and Fredericka find a special kind of magic book. Flying houses, dragons, and a wizard are just some of the things they encounter.

The Reluctant Dragon by Kenneth Grahame. Holiday. This small book gives the complete text of the story of the dragon who refuses to be fierce.

The Oxford Book of Children's Verse in America edited by Donald Hall. Oxford. Poems old and new feature varied subjects, such as baseball, tree-climbing, and crocodiles.

The Time-Ago Tales of Jahdu by Virginia Hamilton. Macmillan. Read more of Mama Luka's tales of Jahdu, the mysterious trickster.

The Dragon Circle by Stephen Krensky. Atheneum. The Wynd family practices magic. When Jennifer, Perry, Alison, Edward, and Jamie meet some dragons, it takes all the family magic to get them out of their predicament.

The Story of Nim, the Chimp Who Learned Language by Anna Michel. Knopf. Read more about the chimpanzee who was taught to communicate with people by using American Sign Language.

Roosevelt Grady by Louisa R. Shotwell. World. Roosevelt and his family are migrant workers who follow the crops. Along the way, Roosevelt makes a good friend and has some important questions answered.

Where the Sidewalk Ends by Shel Silverstein. Harper & Row. Funny, rhythmic, read-aloud poems celebrate acrobats, battles, toucans, peanut butter, and a wide variety of other matters.

Stuart Little by E. B. White. Harper & Row. Another animal fantasy by the author of *Charlotte's Web*, this tells the adventures of a mouse with very human ways.

Heirlooms

Many families have special things that have been handed down from their relatives. One family may have the trunk Grandmother used when she came to the United States from the Old Country. Another family might be proud of Great-Grandfather's watch—more than a hundred years old and still ticking! Special dishes, old pictures and letters, a ring, well-worn toys and dolls, all are valued because of their roots in the past. These family treasures are called heirlooms.

But there are other kinds of heirlooms that belong to all of us: songs, stories, works of art. Everything from people's earliest history is part of our heritage. We treasure our pasts and pass them on for future generations to enjoy and learn from.

In this unit, you'll read about heirlooms of different kinds. Some stories are historical fiction: made-up stories about real or imagined people at different times in the past. Other stories are nonfiction. These also give facts about things and ideas that are part of our heritage.

As you read, ask yourself how these selections are heirlooms from an earlier time.

Historical Fiction

A story about real people and real events from the past is history. A story about historical events or a historical time, but with made-up characters, is called **historical fiction**. Another kind of historical fiction is a story about real people from the past, but with fictional details and dialogue.

An author who writes historical fiction has to know about history, the events and people from the past. In *America's Paul Revere*, Esther Forbes wrote about Paul Revere and his part in the Revolutionary War. Read the author's words below, about a time just before Paul Revere's famous ride. Revere would soon warn the Americans that the British were arriving by sea.

> Paul Revere had suggested that if the regulars left by land, one lantern would be shown in the spire of Christ Church. If by sea, two. The British would try to stop all messengers from Boston who might warn the Minute Men. However, two men would try to get out. One was Billy Dawes, who would leave by the town gate. The other, Paul Revere, who would, if he did not get caught, cross the Charles River to Charlestown.
>
> That afternoon he saw that the *Somerset*, British man-o'-war, was being moved into the mouth of the Charles to stop people like himself who might want to cross the river.

This story about Paul Revere is factual. The people are real. The events really happened.

In *Johnny Tremain*, Esther Forbes wrote another story about the Revolutionary War. Paul Revere and other historical figures of the time are included. However, Johnny Tremain, the main character, is fictional. Only the author's imagination could make Johnny appear at the home of Paul Revere. As you read the excerpt below, see if you can tell why *Johnny Tremain* is historical fiction.

From Ann Street Johnny ran toward North Square. This he found crowded with light infantry and grenadier companies, all in full battle dress. They got in his way and he in theirs. He could not get to the Reveres' front door, but by climbing a few fences he reached their kitchen door, and knocked softly. Paul Revere was instantly outside in the dark with him.

"Johnny," he whispered, "the *Somerset* has been moved into the mouth of the Charles. Will you run to Copp's Hill and tell me if they have moved in any of the other warships? I think I can row around one, but three or four might make me trouble."

The conversation between Johnny Tremain and Paul Revere could never have happened because Johnny never lived. The author made up the character and the conversation as a way of making history come alive. This story is historical fiction; it is part history and part fiction.

In this unit, you will read some examples of historical fiction. Some events and persons in a story you will recognize from your knowledge of history. But sometimes you won't be able to tell what is factual in a story. The author of a story will often tell you whether a person actually existed or whether an event actually occurred. Look for clues in the information you read before the story, as well as within the story, to find out what is historical and what is fiction.

When the Hamiltons moved west, they brought along some family heirlooms. What place will these treasures have in a rough log cabin?

Look for details the author used to make a part of history come alive.

The Cabin Faced West

by Jean Fritz

The days just after the Revolutionary War are the setting for this work of historical fiction. Early pioneers headed west across the Allegheny Mountains to homestead and turn the wilderness into farmland. The Hamiltons, who once lived in the East, decide that they, too, will make the move West. At first, Ann, the next-to-youngest, is not very happy about the move. Ann's older brothers, Daniel and David, set great store by the way things were done in the East, and they are determined to bring the manners of the old, civilized world with them to the new, rough territory. The youngest family member, Johnny, is just a baby and the first to be born on the frontier.

Author Jean Fritz tells us, "Most of it is just story, but some of it is true. There really was a Hamilton family, and Ann Hamilton was my great-great-grandmother." Ann Hamilton's memories of growing up became a family heirloom on which the author based her story.

Ann Hamilton swept the last of the day's dust out of the door into the sunset. Even the cabin faces west, Ann thought, as she jerked the broom across the flat path the daylight made as it fell through the open doorway. It was the only place the daylight had a chance to come in. The cabin was solid logs all the way around without another opening anywhere. Its back was turned squarely against the East just as her father had turned his back. Just as her older brothers, David and Daniel, had.

"We've cast our lot with the West," her father had said as he stood in the doorway the day the cabin was completed. "And we won't look back."

That was the time Daniel and David had made the Rule. Ann supposed she must have been pouting, because Daniel had looked straight at her when he had spoken.

"The first one who finds fault with the West," he had said in that important voice he used more than ever since he had passed his eighteenth birthday, "will get . . ."

He had hesitated a moment and David had finished the sentence. "Will get a bucket of cold spring water on top of his head." He had laughed as he pulled one of Ann's brown braids. Still, both the boys had taken the Rule seriously. They were always trying to catch each other complaining, though neither one had been caught yet.

As for Ann, she had made her mouth into a tight line when Daniel had stated the Rule. She knew she had complained too much. All up and down the endless mountains to this lonely hill last spring, she had complained. But the day Daniel made the Rule she stopped.

Ann sighed as she leaned the broom against the wall near the hearth where her mother was rocking the baby.

"Ann." Mrs. Hamilton looked up with a little frown between her eyes. "Ann, there's no more work for you today. I can finish alone. You run along, if you've a mind to."

Ann kneeled down on the floor beside her mother. She held a finger for the baby to catch, but he wasn't interested. He was only ten weeks old, too little to do much but sleep and eat.

"Howdy, little Johnnycake," Ann whispered softly. Then suddenly she jumped up and ran to the old stump David had sawed off for a stool. She dragged it over to the long log wall and, climbing on it, stood on her tiptoes. She reached above the row of pegs where the clothes were hanging to the top log just under the sleeping loft. This log jutted out a bit and was wide enough, Ann had discovered, to hold the few dear possessions that in all the family belonged only to her. She ran her hand along the log. Yes, there were her blue Gettysburg shoes that she was saving for winter and special occasions. Only there didn't appear to be any special occasions here. Nothing was special enough even for her mother to use the linen tablecloth or the twelve china plates that were stored away.

The next morning, Ann jumped out of bed and in a few minutes was in the room below, helping her mother ladle out the breakfast mush into wooden bowls.

Mrs. Hamilton set the first bowl of mush down in front of her husband.

"Are you still planning to go down to the McPhales'?" he asked.

"Yes, Ann can pick the peas while I'm gone and shell them and get the potatoes ready and cooking. The baby will nap most of the morning, and I'll be back by noon."

After the men had gone to the fields, Mrs. Hamilton packed a basket of food. "Be sure to build up the fire," she reminded Ann as she went out the door. "Remember it's a fresh fire this morning and won't last long without care."

That was probably the most important job of all, Ann thought as she went out to the vegetable patch. She hated to think of her father's face and Daniel's face if she ever let a fire go out and had to call them in from the fields to start a new one.

She tied the bottom corners of her apron to her waist band to form a long pocket across her lap. Vegetables grew around the cabin, up to the barn, and to the edge of the clearing. Ann walked up one row of peas and down another, picking and dropping them into her folded apron pocket. It was a nice feeling to go between the straight rows, her yellow dress brushing the plants on either side, and remember that she helped to plant these peas. Now they marched right across Hamilton Hill to where the trees began!

Her apron full, Ann sat down on the doorstep and began to shell the peas into a large wooden bowl. Some time later, out of the forest came Andy McPhale, his tousled head bent down, his arms behind him. Even so, there was a kind of swagger to Andy as he made his way between the rows of peas and came to a stop in front of Ann.

Then, as if he couldn't hold his secret another minute, Andy suddenly brought his hands from behind his back—and there was a wild turkey! He held it high by its feet, its head dangling.

"Just killed it with a sling shot," he said. "Big one, isn't he?" He tried to make his words matter-of-fact and everyday, but he couldn't keep the pride out.

And no wonder. A wild turkey with a sling shot! Ann

smiled up at this strange boy who sometimes almost surprised her into liking him. "He's a beauty," she said.

In a burst of enthusiasm she went on. "Oh, Andy, why don't you folks plant? You could have a nice farm down there. I could show you how to grow peas, too."

"We're not farmin' folk," he said, his chin jutted out. "We likely won't be stayin' here long anyway. We'll probably pull out when my pa gets back."

"But you don't want to, do you? You wouldn't want to quit, would you?" Ann hit the word *quit* hard like you would a nail.

"Why not?" Andy laughed. "Just what you want to do too, isn't it?"

"I would not," Ann replied, but even as she spoke, she felt her face growing hot. Wouldn't she? Wasn't that just what she had secretly been wanting all the time? No, she

told herself, it wasn't the same at all. She didn't want to quit; she just wanted to go back to Gettysburg.

"I would not," Ann repeated louder than she needed to, and she marched off into the cabin. "I have to see about dinner," she called over her shoulder.

As soon as she stepped inside, she had a sinking feeling in the bottom of her stomach. She had forgotten about the fire. Quickly she ran over to the hearth and sank down on her knees before a pile of black ashes and a half-burned log. In desperation she blew into the fireplace, hoping to revive a hidden spark. Ashes flew out into the room and up in her face, but there wasn't a tiny glow of red anywhere.

And then the baby woke, letting out a sharp cry for attention.

"Oh, Johnny, Johnny, what will I do?" Ann moaned as she picked him up. "I can't call Father. I just can't."

She looked at the tinderbox beside the fireplace with its piece of steel and flint. She had never made a fire from the beginning. She went to the door to tell Andy, but he was gone.

"Maybe I could borrow some. But if I went down the hill to Uncle John's, I'd have to take the baby. It wouldn't be so bad going, but coming back—carrying the baby and a pot of fire—I don't know if I could manage."

Then as Ann thought again of calling her father, she quickly made up her mind.

"I'll go to Uncle John's," she said firmly.

It was harder to carry Johnny and an empty iron pot than Ann had imagined. By the time she reached the road, her arms were aching, and when she came to her favorite sitting spot she wanted so much to stop and forget all about fires and peas and potatoes and dinner-on-time. It would be a perfect morning to sit in her half-circle of trees and look down the road and dream.

A moment later a great chestnut-colored horse climbed into sight. On the back of the horse sat a man with matching chestnut hair, and he was singing. When he reached Ann, he stopped his horse and his song at the same time.

"I wondered what I would see when I came up this hill," he said. "Last thing in the world I expected was a pretty young lady with a baby in her arms."

Ann smiled, realizing that she was as much a surprise to this young man as he was to her. Before she knew it, Ann had told him who she was, where she lived, where she was going, and that the fire was out.

"Miss Ann," he said, talking serious and as if Ann were a grown lady, "if your fire is out, there isn't much time for

a proper introduction. I am Arthur Scott of Lancaster County, come to the Western Country to find land and settle, and I am at your service. Now let's go build that fire."

At the cabin, using his own tinderbox to start the fire, Mr. Scott seemed just as eager as Ann to have dinner ready on time.

"I don't know why your folks need know anything about your fire going out," he said. "Why don't we keep it our secret?"

"You mean you won't tell?" Ann asked gratefully.

Mr. Scott's eyes twinkled as he leaned down close to Ann. "Never," he whispered, and suddenly they were both laughing like fellow conspirators.

"That is," Mr. Scott went on, "if you'll put my name in those pots while I walk up to your father's fields and make the proper introductions." In the Western Country putting someone's name in the pot meant he was staying for dinner.

Other travelers had stopped from time to time at Hamilton Hill for a meal, but never anyone like Arthur Scott, Ann thought as she watched him stride across the clearing to the lower fields where her father and brothers were working. Ann wished there were something for dinner besides peas and potatoes and johnnycake.

Maybe they could make the dinner very special, Ann thought with mounting excitement, and use Mother's linen tablecloth and china plates with the little flowers on them.

All at once she knew something she could do right now. She climbed up to her private shelf and reached down her two blue satin hair ribbons. She tied a bow at the end of each of her braids and smiled to think how much difference those two little bows must make. There was no mirror on Hamilton Hill, but sometimes, Ann had discovered, if she caught the light just right, she could find her reflection in a pail of water. She moved a pail over to the light by the doorway and was looking in the water, first on one side, then on the other, when her mother came up behind her.

"Oh, Mother," Ann exclaimed, pushing the pail aside, "can we have a party dinner? And can we, please, use the tablecloth and china plates?" Once Ann started to tell her mother about Arthur Scott and her plans for dinner, her words tumbled out faster and faster, picking up more words as they went—the way a few pebbles sometimes start a landslide down a mountain.

"No, Ann," her mother said patiently. "We can't have a party in the middle of the day with work to be done. Arthur Scott is welcome to share whatever we have, the way we always have it, and I expect even he would think we were mighty foolish to set a fancy table on a Monday noon."

Ann hadn't thought of it that way, and although she secretly suspected her mother might be right, still it was disappointing and tiresome.

When Arthur Scott tramped into the cabin with the three Hamilton men, however, Ann forgot her disappointment. The men were all laughing together, and Ann could tell right away that her father thought Arthur Scott was nicer than most travelers. Meeting Mr. Scott seemed to make Mrs. Hamilton feel better, too.

"This is our daughter, Ann," Mr. Hamilton said.

Mr. Scott bowed, giving Ann a private wink. "I have had the pleasure," he said. "I stopped in at the cabin and Miss Ann agreed to put my name in the pot."

But when they sat down at the table, Ann felt like a little girl again. Everyone began talking politics, and Ann couldn't find her way into the conversation at all. Ann let her mind wander off by itself until something Mr. Scott said suddenly made her take notice. He was talking about the war that was just over. "When I was at Valley Forge—" he said. Without thinking, Ann jumped right into the middle of his sentence.

"Were you a soldier at Valley Forge?" Even if Daniel did scowl at her for interrupting, Ann didn't care. As far back as she could remember, she had heard stories about the terrible winter at Valley Forge, but never before from anyone who had been there.

"I was only thirteen years old," Mr. Scott said. "They wouldn't take me as a soldier, so I drove an ammunition wagon."

"How were you ever brave enough to stay all winter?" Ann asked, hoping no one would stop her.

"Ann, you forget yourself," Daniel began, but Mrs. Hamilton put her hand quietly on Daniel's arm and leaned forward to hear what Arthur Scott had to say.

Mr. Scott spoke slowly, as if he were sending his mind back six years to remember just how it was. "I guess I would have been ashamed to quit when there was so much bravery all around me. I remember a girl," he said, speaking directly to Ann, "who wasn't as big as you are. Her name was Rachel Peck and she lived nearby. All winter she used to save food from her own plate and make gingerbread every chance she had. She would walk through the snow up to her knees to bring that food to the soldiers."

Ann swallowed hard. She would have done that, too, she thought. If she'd been there, she would have gone in snow up to her waist.

She was so deep in her thoughts that she didn't notice that dinner was over, and that while the men were standing in the doorway, talking, she was sitting at the table alone. Then she thought of one more question.

"Mr. Scott," she said and jumped up from the table and ran to the doorway, "you are going to stay for a while, aren't you?"

Ann didn't know what the men had been talking about before she interrupted. All she knew was that all at once it was very quiet. Daniel was standing on the steps in front of the others. He turned on her.

"If no one else will correct you, I will," Daniel said, his eyes flashing. "You have done nothing but interrupt your elders and act as if you had never been taught otherwise. You've lost your Eastern manners, Ann Hamilton, and talk as bold as any common Western girl." Daniel turned his back on the group. He had said his say, and even the way he held his shoulders showed that he knew he was right.

Ann cringed. She didn't dare look at Mr. Scott. The silence seemed to grow so thick, she felt choked by it and wanted to run away — far away. But then she felt a hand on her arm and there was David. He had stepped back beside her and was grinning and winking and secretly pointing to the pail of water Ann had left near the door. He put his finger over his lips. David was going to try to catch Daniel in some fault-finding.

"I haven't noticed anything wrong with Western ladies," David remarked innocently, reaching down with one hand toward the pail.

"They are not ladies," Daniel snapped, his back still turned. "The only ladies here are those fresh from the East. Most girls who have been here a spell shed their manners with their shoes. And I don't want any sister of mine taking on unbecoming Western ways."

Daniel started to stride away when all of a sudden there was a great hoot from David. A pailful of cold spring water hit Daniel square on the back, dripped down his collar, rolled down the length of his sleeves, and settled in a pool around his feet.

Daniel swung around to face David. He must have said some angry words, but no one could hear them. Everyone was laughing. David was shouting that this was what happened if you found fault with Western ways. The laughter didn't seem to be so much at Daniel as it was the laughter that comes at the end of a long-standing joke. Daniel, as he calmed down and shook off water, had to admit he had been caught fair and square. Mr. and Mrs.

Hamilton and Arthur Scott smiled as they watched the two brothers spar, half in play, half in earnest. Ann sat down on the steps, filled with gratitude and relief. Everyone had forgotten about her. She grinned as she remembered the loud smack the water had made as it hit Daniel in the back.

1. What place did the family heirlooms have in the family's life in the West?
2. What did Mr. Hamilton mean when he said, "We've cast our lot with the West, and we won't look back"?
3. Why do you think Ann was so upset when the fire went out? What else could she have done to get it started again?
4. How did Daniel and David's Rule eventually help Ann?
5. What did Ann do before dinner which showed that she felt Arthur Scott was a special person? Find that part of the story.

Apply
the
Skills

In historical fiction, some details really happened or were true at the time, and other details were made up by the author. Read the following items from the selection. From what you know about history and the story, tell which items you think are historical and which are fiction.

1. Ann Hamilton had two older brothers.
2. David Hamilton laughed as he yanked on one of Ann's long braids.
3. During the Revolutionary War, the American soldiers spent a harsh winter at Valley Forge.
4. "Howdy, little Johnnycake," Ann whispered softly to her baby brother.

Prewrite

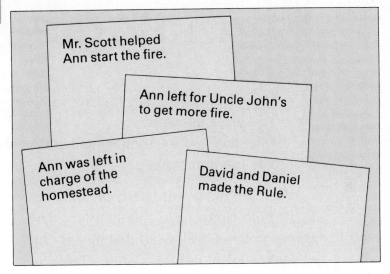

Mr. Scott helped Ann start the fire.

Ann left for Uncle John's to get more fire.

Ann was left in charge of the homestead.

David and Daniel made the Rule.

Each note card above describes a major event in "The Cabin Faced West." Look back at the story. Make notes about other incidents. Then use your notes and the ones above to make a list. Arrange the events in the correct time order.

Compose

Use your list to write a summary of the major events in "The Cabin Faced West." Try to use words such as *first, next, then, following,* and *finally* to tie your ideas together. Your first sentence might be: *Ann's brothers, David and Daniel, made the Rule against complaining about the West.*

Revise

Read your story summary. Check to see that you have included all the events on your list and that one sentence leads to the next in a sensible way. If your summary does not reflect this, revise your work.

Etymologies

How can you see stars that are far away in the sky?
You use a telescope.
How can you see something that is very tiny?
You use a microscope.

Where do the words *telescope* and *microscope* come from? Both words have a long history. The word-part *scope* comes from a Greek word that means "to see." The first part of each word is also from Greek. *Tele* means "far off" and *micro* means "small."

You can see why an instrument that makes far-off objects appear closer is called a *telescope*. You can also see why *microscope* is the name for an instrument that makes small objects look larger.

These facts about *telescope* and *microscope* give the etymology of each word. An **etymology** is the history, the origin, of a word. Many dictionaries give the etymology of a word if it is known.

Knowing the history of a word can help you understand how many words in our language are related. Knowing the history of certain word-parts can also help you figure out the meaning of other words with the same word-parts.

The words in boldface in the following sentences have the same word-part. It is *port*, from a Latin word that means "to carry."

1. Tony moved the **portable** television into the kitchen.

2. A large van was needed to **transport** the family's furniture across the country.

3. The artist showed her **portfolio** to the magazine's editor.

Match each word in boldface above to one of the following meanings:

a. a case for carrying drawings

b. easily carried

c. carry from one place to another

If you explore the history of words, you will find that the language is always changing. For example, *space shuttle* was not in dictionaries twenty years ago. But even new words come from old languages.

The word *space* comes from a Latin word that means "to expand or spread out." The word *shuttle* comes from an Old English word that means "to shoot."

Think of some other modern words you know. Check their etymologies in a dictionary.

Give the meanings of the following words. The Greek or Latin word-parts presented in this lesson will help you. Then check the meanings in a dictionary.

1. televise

2. microfilm

3. porter

The painting on the wall in Giles's great aunt's house was a family heirloom. Read to find out why Giles was fascinated by it.

Sometimes ordinary words have an interesting history. As you read, think of words whose etymologies you would want to look up.

Cherry Ripe

by Ruth Ainsworth

"Giles, you're ready for a holiday."

Giles looked up and saw his mother smiling at him from the doorway. She was holding a letter in her hand.

"London is no place for a boy who has been very sick and is almost well," his mother went on. "Your Great Aunt Flo has invited you to come for a visit. She lives in the country with a garden as big as a park, and you could be out-of-doors all day long. You'd get well twice as quickly if you went."

Giles looked at his two little sisters. He had never been away from his family before. "If I don't like it, can I come home?" he asked.

"Of course," his mother told him.

"Then I'll go and see if I like it," Giles decided.

Great Aunt Flo met him at the train station. Giles had expected her to be very old indeed. She had white hair, it was true, but she walked quickly with long strides and carried his suitcase to the car as if it weighed nothing.

They went up a long drive and stopped in front of a red brick house. It had rows and rows of windows and very tall chimneys, and it looked very grand to Giles.

After he had washed his hands, he found Great Aunt Flo in the drawing room. "Go into the kitchen and have tea with Mrs. Best," she said. "She'll take care of you. She's brought up ten children of her own, so you'll be all right with her."

Giles went into the kitchen, and Mrs. Best welcomed him as if she had known him all his life. "Come along, Giles, I've boiled you an egg and here's a plate of banana sandwiches. You'll soon get better if you eat well and sleep well."

While Giles ate, she told him funny stories about her five girls and their five teasing brothers. Before he had heard half enough, he had eaten everything, and Mrs. Best said he looked fatter already.

The next day Giles woke with a start and felt, at once, that everything was different. There was no rumble and roar of buses and cars, and not even the noise of his mother busy in the flat, clinking china and shutting doors. Outside there was only the crowing of a rooster, the occasional barking of a dog, and the distant hum of a tractor. Giles got out of bed and went toward the stairs.

The halls and the staircase were hung with dark portraits in dingy gold frames. The portraits were all of old people in old-fashioned clothes. But halfway downstairs there was a small landing, and here hung the portrait of a girl.

Giles stood still and looked with pleasure at the girl in her long white frock with a red sash and a bunch of red cherries in one hand. She had dark curls and dark eyes and a mischievous expression. Her lips were parted, perhaps because she was going to burst out laughing, or perhaps pop in another cherry.

The artist had painted the girl sitting down, but she appeared ready to jump up any moment and run off. Giles went on downstairs, deciding to come back often and look at the lively little cherry girl. She seemed out of place among all the elderly ladies and gentlemen, as he felt out of place in this large, silent house.

Breakfast was a cheerful meal in Mrs. Best's sunny kitchen. When he had eaten, Giles wandered about the garden, past flower beds and vegetable plots. But there was nothing to do to pass the time. The trees did not look right for a boy to climb, and the lawns were useless without a ball or someone to play with.

During the morning the doctor came. He asked Giles a few questions, listened to his chest, and told Great Aunt Flo to see that he had plenty of food, fresh air, and sleep. "You'll be fit as a fiddle in no time," he told Giles.

"But what can I *do*?" Giles asked despairingly. "There's nothing to do, here!"

"Ah, you're missing your sisters," the doctor said. "Well, if someone mends the old swing, will that do for a start?"

"Oh, yes," said Giles. He'd never had a swing of his own.

After lunch, the gardener put his head around the door and said the swing was mended. Giles hurried out to the field where it hung from the bough of a tree. It was only a wooden seat with new ropes attached, but the seat was polished smooth as if many children had played on it.

Giles swung gently to and fro, then higher and higher. He soon got hot and tired and had to stop for a rest, but the rests got fewer and shorter and he found he could swing almost up to the tree bough.

The next few days seemed long ones in spite of the swing. Every day he wrote to his family, and every day he looked at the girl with the cherries as he went up and down the stairs.

One day, Giles found the swing gently moving. When he sat on it, the seat felt warm. It was as if someone had been sitting on it and had run away when they saw him coming. He told himself it was warm from the sun, and the wind might have blown it. Only it was a calm, dark day, so that was not a very suitable explanation.

Another time he had the same feeling he was not alone. When he had worked himself up really high, he let go of the ropes and jumped off into the long grass. He was sure someone nearby gave an "o-o-oh" of surprise.

Then, when he had been playing by himself for two weeks, he actually saw someone. It was a girl about his own age, and she was sitting on his swing.

"Why aren't you at school?" asked Giles.

"Why aren't you?" answered the girl.

"I've been ill and I'm getting better."

"I'm getting better, too," said the girl. But her cheeks were so rosy it was hard to imagine her ever having been ill. "My name is Caroline," she added.

"My name is Giles, and I'm staying here," he told her. "Where do you live?"

"Very near, I'm almost at home," and she laughed.

"Does your mother know my Great Aunt Flo?"

"I expect so. She knows most of the people around here," Caroline said, and laughed again.

Giles gave up asking questions because Caroline only put him off with her answers. She seemed to be making fun of him.

"I'll show you how to do a twizzle on your swing," Caroline offered. "Sit on the swing and hold tight." She turned Giles and the swing around and around until the two ropes were twisted together as if they were one thick rope. Then she spun him in the opposite direction and Giles whirled around and around until he felt dizzy.

"Shall I give you one?" he asked when the ground had stopped going around.

"Yes, please," she said, and when the spinning was over her cheeks were redder than ever.

"Now let's play hide-and-seek," she said, "I know all the good places."

"Yes, but—" began Giles. "But I'm only supposed to play quiet games until I'm well."

"We'll leave hide-and-seek until later on," Caroline said cheerfully. "I'm only supposed to play quiet games, too. They want me to grow up to be a fine lady who likes pretty clothes and doesn't romp about. But I shall romp about as much as I like!"

"Did you say you'd been ill, too?" Giles asked.

"So I did. I remember the doctor was there, and my father and mother. But I can't remember what happened next. They put a spoonful of something horrid between my lips, and I remember I tried to spit it out," Caroline said. She looked so worried Giles felt sorry for her.

"Never mind," he told her. "I expect you went to sleep. Then you must have waked up much better or you wouldn't be here, would you?"

She looked much happier. "I must have gotten better without knowing it." And she jumped up and turned a cartwheel in spite of her long dress. "Bother my dress! It gets in the way. I wish I were dressed like you." Caroline looked enviously at Giles's gray shorts and blue sweater.

"But lots of girls wear shorts," Giles told her. "Don't you have any clothes besides that party dress?" She looked worried again. "I used to, but I'm not sure where they are. I don't think I could find them, now."

"Let's gather fir cones," Giles said, to change the subject. "We can put them in the hollow tree to dry, and one day we'll make a bonfire of them and roast potatoes in the ashes."

Giles said nothing about Caroline as he ate his supper that night. He wasn't sure if she should be in the garden at all. He was certain Great Aunt Flo didn't know about her. Where could she live? There were no other houses near, yet she had said, "I'm almost at home."

When Giles went up to bed he stopped as usual on the little landing. The girl in the picture seemed livelier than ever. It's the best picture in the whole house, he thought. She looks so alive. I like her better than anyone here, except Mrs. Best.

The next day was sunny and warm, and Giles met Caroline by the swing. They had swings in turn, and gave each other twizzles. Then they began to make a house for themselves in the thicket, using dead branches and ferns from the ditch. The floor was laid with moss. Caroline took her sash off and tied it over the doorway. "It's the House of the Red Banner," she said.

They worked on the house again in the afternoon, making all kinds of improvements. When the gong sounded for tea, Caroline could not untie her sash.

"Help me," she cried. "Help me, Giles!" They both pulled, but the knots only got tighter. Then the gong sounded again, for the second time.

"Never mind. You must go, and so must I," said Caroline. "Good-by, Giles."

"Good-by, Caroline, and never mind about the sash," Giles told her.

"Oh, I don't mind, but *they* may," said Caroline sadly. "They are always minding about something or other."

That night as Giles went up to bed he looked at the portrait for a long time. It looked different. She hasn't her sash on, said Giles to himself. She's lost her sash. So she couldn't untie it after all. What am I thinking? Why did I say that? But I've always known the portrait was Caroline. So if Caroline has lost her sash, the girl in the portrait has lost hers, too. I don't understand, I just know.

The next day Giles said, "There's a nice picture of you halfway up the stairs, Caroline."

"I remember sitting for it," she laughed. "Oh, how tired I used to get! And the cherries looked so good. I sometimes ate one when no one was looking."

"But that must have been ages ago," said Giles. "The picture is old, I'm sure. It must have been painted before I was born."

Caroline seemed ready to cry. "It couldn't be," she said. "It was only last summer, before I was sick. It couldn't have been ages ago! Oh, Giles, please don't frighten me!"

She clutched his hand, and he squeezed her cold fingers. "It doesn't matter," he said. "Let's do something different. Let's look for a sack in the stable and see if we can find enough hen and duck feathers to stuff a pillow. We can sit on it in our house."

Caroline rubbed against a post in the hen run and it left a brown stain on her dress. They tried to wash it out, but the stain only got worse, so they gave up.

As Giles went up to bed that night he was not surprised to see a stain on the white dress in the portrait. He would have been more surprised if it hadn't been there.

The days went quickly now and Giles and Caroline played all over the garden. But though the gardener and Mrs. Best waved to Giles when they saw him, no one took any notice of Caroline. No one ever asked her name or what she was doing there.

Once Giles went indoors to fetch something and he noticed that the portrait on the stairs was empty. The frame was still there, and the background of trees and flowers, but there was a space where Caroline should have been in her white dress. He was surprised that no one had noticed and asked questions.

Giles began to have an idea. At first he pushed it aside as unkind and dangerous, but it kept coming back. At last he told himself it was a joke and no harm would come. Or if it did, he could easily put things right again. So one afternoon when Caroline was making daisy chains in the garden, he hurried indoors and lifted the picture off the wall. It was very heavy, but he managed to hide it on the window seat in his bedroom, behind one of the heavy curtains. Then he ran back into the garden.

Giles felt uneasy about his plan, and he was especially nice to Caroline. He even let her make a daisy crown for his head. When the gong sounded, he stayed beside her until she said, "You'd better go before Mrs. Best gets cross."

"I didn't hear the gong," Giles lied. "Come inside with me and I'll show you something interesting."

"Tell me instead," Caroline said. "I only go indoors when I have to, when they call me."

"I can't tell you, I can only show you. Please come." He took her hand but she pulled it away.

"Don't bother me," she said angrily. "I can't come, and you could tell me if you wanted to."

Giles knew he must go. There was no hope of getting Caroline indoors and showing her where her picture was.

"See you tomorrow, Caroline."

"Yes. Good-by, Giles," she said.

Giles went to sleep that night unhappy and unsettled. But at the same time he felt excited. What would Caroline do? Would she find the picture hidden behind the curtain? If not, might she turn into an ordinary girl? He meant to stay awake all night, watching and listening, but he fell asleep.

It was pitch dark when Giles woke to the sound of someone crying bitterly in the darkness. He pounded on the wall shouting, "Mrs. Best, Mrs. Best!"

"I'm coming, Giles. Just a minute." He heard the click of her light and a moment later she was in the room. "Why are you crying, Giles? Have you a pain? Was it a bad dream?"

"I heard someone crying. Listen!"

They both listened, but there was nothing to hear.

"She's quiet now," Giles said. "She isn't crying anymore."

"It wasn't anyone outside," said Mrs. Best. "It was you, yourself. I heard you crying when you called me. There's no one here except you and me."

"We must put the picture back at once," Giles said. "We may be too late. Will you help me? I moved it and she couldn't get back!"

"I think you are still dreaming," said Mrs. Best gently, "but of course we'll put it back. You must have moved that picture in your sleep. You couldn't have carried such a heavy thing by yourself if you'd been awake."

They hung the picture back on its hook.

Next morning Giles tiptoed downstairs and looked at the portrait. Caroline was in her usual place. So all was well, and she was safely back where she belonged.

After breakfast Giles ran to the swing as fast as he could. Caroline was not there. He called her name, but there was no answer. Once he thought he caught a glimpse of her white dress between the bushes, but it was only white flowers.

He went indoors and looked at the portrait again. Caroline was there smiling, with her red sash on. He ran back to their little house. Yes, the red sash had gone from above the door. He whispered urgently to Caroline, "Please, please come back, if only for once. I'm going home soon and we must say good-by."

The next morning by the swing he gave up hope. He knew he would never see Caroline again. She had gone back to wherever she had come from, and he couldn't follow. He knew it was his own fault for trying to bring her into his world to live. She could only live where she belonged, and he must live where he belonged, without her.

On his last evening, Giles sat with Great Aunt Flo in the drawing room. "I'm not used to children, but I must say you have been a very good boy," she said. "You've been no trouble at all. I hope you'll come again and bring your little sisters."

"I'd love to," said Giles.

"I want to give you a present to take home. Is there anything here that has taken your fancy? This house is so full of things," Great Aunt Flo said.

Giles blushed and hesitated. "There is something but I can't possibly ask," he said at last. "You see, it's big and valuable." He took a deep breath and spoke quickly, "It's the portrait of the girl in white, halfway up the stairs."

"You can have that with pleasure," said Great Aunt Flo. "It was done by some unknown painter and is of no special value. I'll have it packed up and sent."

"Who is the girl?" Giles asked.

"Lady Caroline Peel. She died of smallpox, poor child. That was over a hundred years ago. She used to live here."

When the portrait arrived and was hung in his bedroom, it took up most of the space over Giles's bed. At first he felt shy with Caroline so near, but he soon got used to her. It was like sharing the room with a friend.

1. Why was Giles fascinated by the painting in his great aunt's house?

2. Why do you suppose Giles was able to see Caroline as a real girl?

3. Why do you think Giles took the picture off the wall and hid it in his room? Was that a good thing to do? Explain.

4. Why did Giles want the painting of Caroline even though he knew she would never come back?

5. When did you first realize that the girl in the painting and the girl in the garden were the same person? Find the part of the story that helped you decide.

Apply

the

Skills

Because all words come from someplace, they all have etymologies. But the meaning and spelling of words often change. Look at some words taken from "Cherry Ripe," listed below at the left. Match each word with its etymology, listed below at the right.

1. bonfire

2. sash

3. fashion

a. from Middle English *bonefire*, a fire of bones

b. from Middle English *facioun*, shape, manner

c. from Arabic *shash*, muslin (cotton cloth)

Prewrite

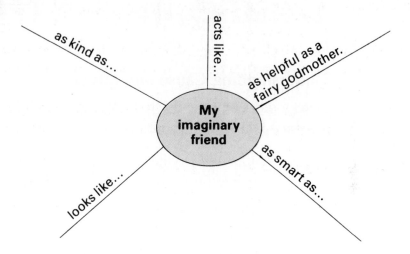

as kind as…

acts like…

as helpful as a fairy godmother.

as smart as…

looks like…

My imaginary friend

Giles's friend, Caroline, was a most unusual character. Use your imagination to create your own unusual make-believe friend. Copy the ideaburst above. Complete the unfinished similes with original and unusual comparisons, or create your own similes to fit your imaginary friend. Remember that similes are comparisons using *like* or *as*.

Compose

Write a paragraph describing your imaginary friend. Use at least five similes. You might start with this topic sentence: *My imaginary friend has vast powers.*

Revise

Read your paragraph. Are there any similes that you can improve to make your character even more unusual or lifelike? If so, revise your work.

Cause and Effect

Understanding Cause and Effect

Why did Wilbur and Orville Wright watch birds? Read the sentence below to find out.

> Wilbur and Orville Wright watched birds because they wanted to learn the secret of flight.

When you read, you often find out why things happen. The reason *why* things happen is called the **cause**. *What* happened is called the **effect**. Notice that the second sentence about Wilbur and Orville Wright gives a cause and an effect. You learn something that happened (the effect), and you learn why it happened (the cause).

Sometimes, word clues help you to see how cause and effect work together. The word *because* in the sentence about the Wright brothers is such a clue. Other word clues are *so, when, since,* and *therefore.*

Authors don't always use word clues to show cause and effect. You have to ask questions to find the cause and its effect. You can ask, "What happened?" to find the effect and "Why did it happen?" to find the cause. Read the following sentences.

> Wilbur and Orville Wright watched birds. They wanted to learn the secret of flight.

Wilbur and Orville Wright test one of their gliders at Kitty Hawk, North Carolina, 1901.

Try using the *what* and *why* questions. What did Wilbur and Orville Wright do? They watched birds. Why did they do it? They wanted to learn the secret of flight. It's easy to find the answers to the *what* and *why* questions. You only have to look in the sentences you are reading.

See if you can find a cause and an effect in the following sentence.

When people became interested in flight, they started to build flying machines.

In the sentence, one thing that caused another thing to happen is given. The cause is "people became interested in flight." The effect is "they started to build flying machines." The word *when* at the beginning of the sentence is a clue that you will find a cause and an effect in the sentence. Remember that you can find a cause and an effect by asking yourself "What happened?" and "Why did it happen?"

On December 17, 1903, the Wright Brothers made the first heavier-than-air flight. Orville Wright was at the controls. Wilbur Wright was on the ground.

One Cause Leading to Several Effects

Sometimes one cause can lead to more than one effect. See if you can find a cause and three effects in the following paragraph.

> Wilbur and Orville Wright always wanted to fly. First they worked with kites; then they tried air gliders. Finally, they invented an engine light enough for an airplane.

The cause in the paragraph is given in the first sentence: *Wilbur and Orville Wright always wanted to fly*. Their wish to fly had three effects: a. They worked with kites. b. They tried air gliders. c. They invented an engine light enough for an airplane.

Find a cause and two effects in the following paragraph.

> Wilbur and Orville Wright made the world's first flight on December 17, 1903. The Wright brothers became well known. Their first airplane is in the National Air and Space Museum in Washington, D.C.

1. What is the cause?
2. What is the first effect?
3. What is the second effect?

Textbook Application: Cause and Effect in Science

Textbooks often contain many examples of cause and effect. Remember that a cause is *why* something happened and an effect is *what* happened. Authors will often ask questions to help you understand causes and effects. Use the sidenotes to help you as you read the textbook selection below.

The third sentence describes an effect. The author then asks if you know the cause. Find the causes and effects in the rest of the paragraph.

The first sentence of this paragraph tells the effect. You are then asked to find the cause. The rest of the paragraph describes the cause.

Kinds of Electricity

It is a cold day in the winter. You walk across a wool carpet and reach out to turn a doorknob. You feel a shock. What happened? When you moved across the carpet, you gained electrons. The electrons built up on your body and stayed there. This buildup of electrons gave your body an electric charge. An electric charge that does not move is called *static* (stat′ ik) *electricity*.

When you touched the doorknob, electrons moved from you to the doorknob. Why did this happen? Electrons move from a place where there are many electrons to a place where there are fewer electrons. Your body had more electrons than the doorknob. When you touched the doorknob, the extra electrons moved from your body to the doorknob. This movement of the extra electrons is called an *electric discharge* (dis′ charj). After the electric discharge, you became neutral again.

— *Science*, Silver Burdett

Read the next textbook selection. Use the sidenotes to help
you find causes and effects.

Wind Changes the Land

Like water and ice, wind carries materials
from one place to another. When the wind
blows, it lifts and carries small dry particles.
Most of the particles carried by wind are sand,
soil, and dust. When these particles are blown
against rock, they can cause physical
weathering of the rock.

> The second sentence contains a cause and an effect. What is the cause? What is the effect?

> Notice the cause and effect in this sentence.

As wind blows sand from one place to
another, the speed of the wind may be slowed
by rocks or plants. When the wind slows, it
deposits the sand it carries. This causes the
sand to pile up. The deposition of wind-carried
sand causes piles of sand, called *sand dunes*,
to form. Some sand dunes may be as much as
50 m high. Sand dunes have many shapes.
The forming of sand dunes is another way the
earth is changed by building up.

> What is the effect of the wind's carrying the sand and depositing it?

In some places in the desert, wind blows
away all loose sand. Only coarse pebbles and
other small rocks are left behind. Such areas
are known as desert pavement.

> The first sentence in this paragraph gives the cause. The effect is explained in the next two sentences.

— *Science*, Silver Burdett

Looking for causes and effects as you read can help you
understand a selection. Asking yourself "What happened?" and
"Why did it happen?" can help you remember information.

Joe High Elk and his sister, Marie, discover an important family heirloom. What secrets does the heirloom reveal?

The heirloom, because of its value, could have an effect on the High Elk family's lives. Read to find out what effect it might have.

High Elk's Treasure

by Virginia Driving Hawk Sneve

The High Elks have raised horses for generations on the Sioux reservation in South Dakota. Through years of hardship, however, the great herd has been reduced to two: the last remaining mare, named Śungwiye, and her filly, Star. Śungwiye will soon give birth a second time, and the High Elks hope to start raising horses again.

One day thirteen-year-old Joe High Elk and his younger sister Marie get trapped in a storm on their way home from school. They find shelter in a cave. The cave has special meaning to the High Elk family, for it was there that Great-grandfather High Elk had bred his first horses. Joe discovers a bundle covered in old and rotting rawhide buried in the wall of the cave. Joe wraps the bundle in Marie's sweater and the two of them carefully carry it home to their parents, William and Marlene.

Joe handed the sweater-wrapped package to his father and told how he had discovered it in the cave.

"Well, let's go take a look at what old High Elk hid away," said his father William, leading the way to the house.

Inside, Marie was setting the table. Grandma was peeling potatoes.

"Joe," asked his mother, "where is Marie's sweater?"

"Here, Marlene," said William to his wife. "Move the dishes over for a while, Marie, so that we can see what old High Elk's treasure is."

Marie had told Marlene and Grandma about Joe's finding the leather-wrapped bundle and they came closer to see, but Grandma hung back a little.

"Tehinda, forbidden," the old woman said. She still believed many of the old superstitions. "Careful," she warned, "there may be a wanaǵi, ghost, in it." But she moved a little nearer.

"Do you know of this?" William asked his mother as he began to remove Marie's sweater.

Hands to her face, ready to shut out the sight of a ghost if one appeared, Grandma nodded. "My husband's grandfather told of how he had hidden a story thing in the cave. He warned of not disturbing it until a hundred years had passed."

"A hundred years," mused her son. "Why, it must be past that now. Did he say the year he had hidden it?"

"No, he had no use for the year's number. It must have been after he moved into the cave."

"Let's see. We're pretty sure that he came to the reservation about 1876, for didn't he tell that it was the time of the barren autumn after the Little Big Horn?"

"Yes," said Grandma, lowering her eyes, "he knew of that battle."

"He didn't fight Custer, did he, Grandma?" excitedly asked Joe.

Grandma covered her mouth with her hands, her eyes became blank and she mumbled, "We must not speak for a hundred years."

William looked at his mother in surprise. His mind was busy with speculations about what was in the package he was unwrapping, but he suddenly comprehended what his mother had said. He took his hands from the bundle which, free of the sweater, lay in what only seemed to be a rotten roll of rawhide. He gazed into his mother's eyes as if trying to force her to say more, but she looked away and shook her head.

Joe sensed the tension between them. "What is it? What's the matter?" he cried.

William still stood, quietly staring at his mother; then he looked at Joe as he decided what to do.

"Years ago," he explained, "about one hundred years ago, a large gathering of the Sioux and Cheyenne defeated General Custer at the battle of the Little Big Horn."

"I know that," Joe said, wanting to forestall a history lesson and get back to whatever was wrapped in the rawhide.

William held up his hand to signify patience. "The soldiers who came to punish the Indians after the battle wanted very much to know who killed Custer. The warriors, who were in the battle and who knew which brave killed the general, vowed not to speak of it again for a hundred years."

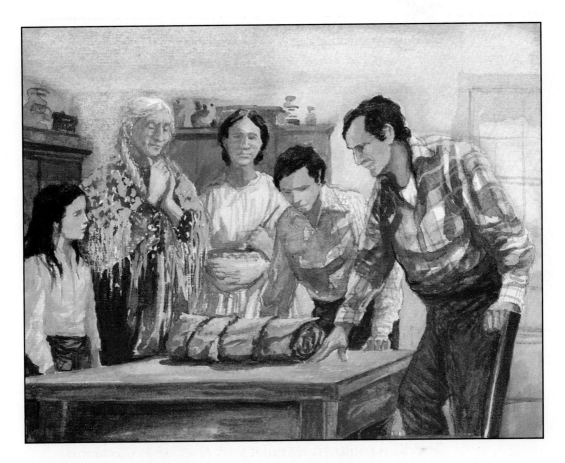

Joe was awed. "Do you think it was Grandpa?"

"*Hinh, hinh*," wailed Grandma. "Do not say such a thing. We will be punished!"

"Do not worry, *Ina*," William comforted. "Whatever High Elk hid in here," he reverently put his hand on the bundle, "will not bring punishment on us. Those bad days are gone. It may," he went on, thinking aloud, "bring us good instead."

"Aren't you going to open it now, Dad?" Joe asked hopefully, already sensing that his father was holding back for some reason.

"Not yet. I think it is important that when we do open it, we do so in the presence of someone whose word will not be doubted."

"What do you mean?" Joe asked.

"Too often in the past our people have lost valuable tribal treasures. Whatever is in here," William said, placing his hand on the bundle, "may be valuable historically, as well as being worth money. We don't want to lose it."

"I don't understand," said Joe.

William answered, "Today there are men who pose as experts and take a treasure from an innocent Indian, promising to prove its history. They are thieves, because they never return the article. So when we open the bundle we must do so in the presence of someone who knows about historical items, but we must make sure that he is also an honest man."

"What are you going to do?" asked Joe.

"Tomorrow I'll go to the tribal office and tell the council and the chairman, Frank Iron Cloud, of your discovery. They'll want to know what is in the bundle, and they should know an expert from the university to contact to be here when we open it.

"But first," William continued, going to an old trunk where the family kept some things that had belonged to High Elk, "we will wrap it in High Elk's buffalo robe." He took out an old tanned hide which showed much wear, but was still intact.

"We will give it to Grandma to keep and guard," he said, handing the bundle to his mother, "for she is always at home to see that it is safe."

The old woman held it in her arms, and then carried it to her room.

Two days later, Joe and his cousin Howard were riding home together.

"Look," Howard said as the High Elk house came into view, "aren't there two cars at your place?"

"Yes," agreed Joe, peering ahead. "Mom and Dad must be home early and—oh, hurry! It must be Mr. Iron Cloud and someone from the university."

Howard kicked the horse into a canter as Joe told him of the mysterious bundle and how he wanted to be present when it was opened.

Riding up fast into the yard they saw that the whole family, Mr. Iron Cloud, and a tall, gray-haired white man were gathered around the horse shed.

"Śungwiye!" yelled Joe. "Has she had a colt?"

"No, not yet," answered William, emerging from the mare's stall. "But I don't think it will be long. No," he said, taking Joe's arm as the boy started into the shed, "we'll leave her alone. She knows what to do and our presence will just make her nervous. Come into the house now. We'll check on her in a little while."

"Gosh, Dad, I can't begin to sit still. Everything happens at once!"

Joe's father laughed at the boy's agitation. "I know, but don't you want to greet Mr. Iron Cloud and Dr. Scott, who are here to open the High Elk bundle?"

"How do you do," said the tall white man.

"Hello, Joe," greeted Mr. Iron Cloud.

Joe, remembering his manners, shook hands with the men. "Hello, Dr. Scott, Mr. Iron Cloud. I'm sure glad you're here."

The group moved into the house, but Joe noticed that Howard stayed behind.

"Dad, I told Howard about the High Elk thing," Joe said, wanting his relative to share the family's discovery.

William turned and called, "Come with us, Howard. This is your heritage too."

The group quietly seated themselves around the kitchen table. Grandma brought the bundle, from which she had gently taken the buffalo hide, and placed it in the center of the table. She remained standing, a little distance from them.

"Open it, Joe," William said, motioning to his son. "You should have the honor, since you discovered it."

"No, I can't," Joe said, shaking his head. "I'm too nervous. Dr. Scott, you open it."

William nodded at the white man to go ahead. Dr. Scott began to undo the leather thongs, but they were rotten and fell apart in his hands.

"Was it in this condition when you found it?" he asked Joe.

"Yes. It was buried in the wall of the cave, and looked just like it does now."

The thongs off, Dr. Scott began carefully to unroll the rawhide. There were several layers of it; some peeled away easily; but in spots it tore away as if it had been glued together.

"It seems to have been partially sealed with something. It is a sticky, oily substance, I'm not sure, but it may be creosote."

"It might be the tar pitch of a pine tree," guessed William. "The old Indians knew how to use it for waterproofing."

"That could be," said Dr. Scott. "I'll have it chemically analyzed, but whatever it is, it seems to have protected the inner layer of the rawhide."

He removed the last of the outer covering and disclosed a bulky, oblong, envelope-shaped bag. "Why, it's a parfleche," he said, excitement sounding in his voice.

Parfleches were heavy duty storage packets used to store dried food or personal belongings. They were made, as was this one, by folding a single wet sheet of rawhide into the desired form.

"Why, you can still see the design on it," marveled Marlene.

"Yes, someone, probably High Elk's wife, took great pains to paint it carefully as well as artistically," said Dr. Scott, gently lifting the parfleche to examine it. "It is in surprisingly good shape, just a little decay on the corners."

He opened it and found another leather-wrapped package inside.

"This," he said, taking the smaller bundle out, "is of tanned hide, probably elk or deer. It is very soft and smells sweet," he mused as he unrolled it. The pungent odor reached the group gathered around the table. Dr. Scott found the source of the spicy scent in a braided stalk of grass rolled in the leather wrapping.

"Sweet grass," he said. "Didn't the Indians use this as we use a sachet?"

"Yes," answered Marlene, "we still do. We have some that Grandma braided in our storage trunk."

Dr. Scott nodded. "Now," he breathed, "we come to whatever was precious enough to merit such care."

A smaller piece of tanned hide was rolled within the outer one. Gently, with extreme care, he spread it flat on the table.

"Look, there are pictures painted on it," Joe said. "What is it?"

"This is fantastic!" The historian was amazed at the discovery. "It is a pictograph narrative." He bent closer to examine it. "It must be the record of some important event."

"Aren't those soldiers?" Joe asked, placing his finger on the crudely drawn figures which seemed to be scattered in one section. "They look like they have the kind of uniforms that the army used to wear long ago."

"You're right," Dr. Scott answered, clearly excited. "And look here, in the center must be the general. Good Heavens," he said unbelievingly, "I think this is Custer

An account of the Battle of the Little Big Horn. Indians were the only survivors.

and the drawing must be an account of the Battle of the Little Big Horn."

"It must be Custer," said William. "See, he is dressed differently than the soldiers. Didn't he wear a buckskin jacket?"

"Where?" Joe asked. "I don't see, which one?"

"Here," Dr. Scott said, putting his finger on the figure, "this one with the long yellow hair." Then pointing to another figure, "And this must be the Indian who shot him. See, he is holding a gun."

"How can you tell who it is?" asked Joe. "His face is all covered with what looks like drips of water or blood."

"Rain-In-The-Face," said the historian softly.

He was silent, gazing at the wondering faces around him.

"I won't be sure until I review the information on this battle, but there was a Sioux warrior called Rain-In-The-Face who was suspected of killing both General Custer and his brother. In fact, if I remember right, I believe he bragged of doing so. But there were many conflicting stories from Indians who were at the Little Big Horn, and those who may have really known, would not say. . . ."

". . . for a hundred years," William finished for him.

"Yes, one hundred years," repeated Dr. Scott. "Did High Elk participate in this battle?" he asked William.

William looked at his mother. "So my husband was told," she said quietly.

"High Elk must have made this record of the killing of Custer," the historian said, "and then to keep the vow he and other warriors made, he buried it in the cave."

"Did you know of this, *Ina*?" William asked his mother.

She nodded. "My husband told me, whose father told him, I was to tell you before I died."

"This can't be true," Mr. Iron Cloud broke in. "My great-grandfather, who was in this battle, said that Custer killed himself."

"As I said," Dr. Scott looked at Mr. Iron Cloud, "there were so many conflicting stories of what happened on that day. There was also much confusion and a thick dust enveloped the battlefield, making observation difficult."

"What do you suppose this means?" asked Joe, who had been studying the pictures. "This man with antlers on his head, who looks like he's taking funny steps, he's leading a horse—why, it looks like Śungwiye." He looked at his father. "Do you think that's supposed to be High Elk leading a horse away from the battlefield?"

"Why, I know about this," Howard said in surprise. "Grandpa told me that near the end of the battle High Elk found the wounded mare, led her to safety, and then bred the great High Elk herd. I never thought I would ever see a picture of it."

"Yes," agreed Grandma, "the mare was taken from the soldiers on that day. She was wounded in the leg and lamed after it healed."

"Didn't the army put big 'U.S.' brands on their stock?" Howard asked Dr. Scott. "I wonder how High Elk kept the soldiers from seeing it."

"Yes," Dr. Scott answered, "the animals were branded. Do you know about this, Mrs. High Elk?" he asked Grandma.

She shook her head.

"But look," Mr. Iron Cloud interrupted. "How could High Elk know who killed Custer if he was leading a horse away from the battleground? See, he has his back to the whole thing."

The group around the table fell silent.

"Gee," Joe said quietly, "this is more mysterious than ever. What *does* it all mean?" he asked, looking at his father and then at Dr. Scott.

Dr. Scott smiled. "It means that you have found a very valuable historical record, even with all its mystery. It is probably worth hundreds, or perhaps thousands of dollars, depending on which museum wants it badly enough."

Wordlessly the family stared at him.

"The horses, the herd . . ." William murmured, thinking of what the money could do.

Dr. Scott began rolling the leather back up. "If it meets with your approval, I would like to take this, and the wrappings, back to the university with me. I need more time to examine it and do a thorough study. When I have done so I will make a public announcement of the discovery. Can I assume you would sell the pictograph?"

William looked at his wife, who smiled at him, then at the tribal chairman. "Frank," he began, and then he said to Dr. Scott, "I don't know."

Mr. Iron Cloud cleared his throat. "The tribe wouldn't be able to pay you anything, William, but we would be honored to have this in our new Tribal Museum."

"Well, think about it," said Dr. Scott. "There will be plenty of time in which to make a decision. In the meantime, I will give you a receipt showing that I am borrowing the pictograph from you. I hope you will trust me to take good care of it."

"Dad! Dad!" Marie came screaming into the house. Startled, William leapt to his feet. In his concentration on the unwrapping of the bundle, he hadn't noticed the little girl's absence.

"Dad," she called again. "Śungwiye had her baby. Oh, come see!"

"Yahoo!" Joe yelled, following his father out the door. "Come on, Howard," he called to his cousin, "see a new High Elk horse!"

William ran into the shed and knelt by the mare to examine the new foal.

"It is a male," he announced.

Joe was close to tears as he watched Śungwiye gently licking and nuzzling the colt which lay snuggled close to her side. The mare carefully stood and began nudging the perfect little horse to his feet. He struggled to untangle his long, thin legs, not yet sure what they were for. He gained his footing on delicate front hooves, straddled before him. Śungwiye nudged encouragingly at his rear, and awkwardly, but surely, he stood. He swayed and staggered, staring curiously at the people watching his

progress. He took a cautious step, turned to his mother and began to nurse.

"Oh, isn't it beautiful," Marie said softly. "Why, he looks just like Star."

The colt did resemble his sister. The same golden color, the same star-shaped blaze on his forehead and four identical white stockings.

"What will we call him?" asked Marie. "He can't be 'Star', too."

"He should have a Lakota name," said Joe. "One that means 'hope' or 'beginning,' because that's what he is, isn't he, Dad?"

William nodded, his throat too tight to speak.

"The colt will be called '*Otokahe*,'" said Grandma. "Beginning."

Sioux Artifacts

The buffalo and the horse were the mainstay of the Sioux, also known as the Lakota. The buffalo was the source of their food, clothing, shelter, and tools. The horse gave the Sioux the freedom to follow the buffalo that roamed the vast grasslands of South Dakota.

This woman's dress was made from the hide of a buffalo and decorated with colored glass beads obtained from white traders. The geometric patterns had specific meaning and referred to particular objects, animals, or concepts.

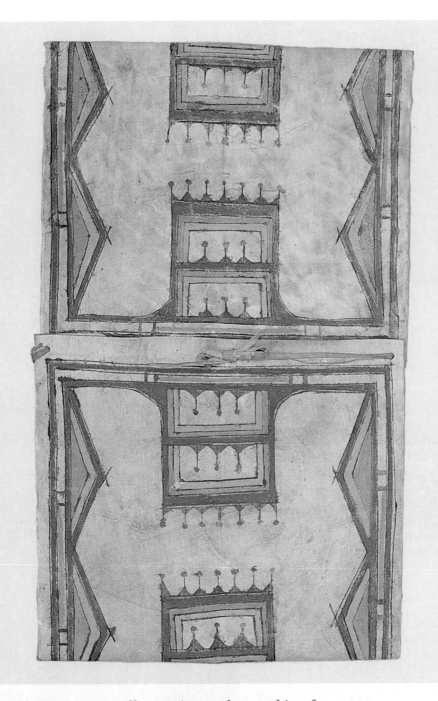

The parfleche was a carryall, or suitcase, for anything from food to clothing to sacred objects. It was decorated with beadwork, using geometric designs. These designs were traditionally done by the women of the tribe.

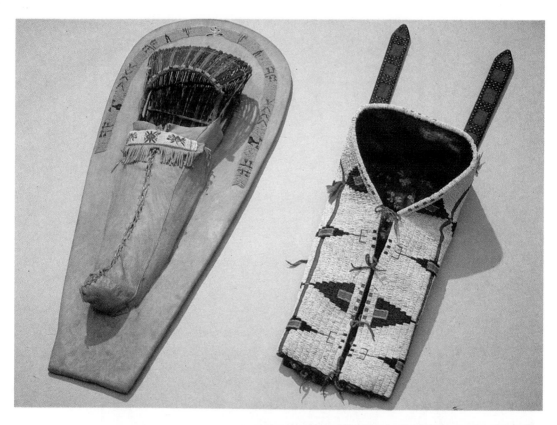

The cradle board, made of wood, leather, and beadwork, could be hung from poles and could be carried on long journeys. It gave warmth and security to Sioux babies. The tribal designs on the cradle board were usually an expression of a family's pride in their child.

The horse was often used as a design on Sioux articles. The men artists of the Sioux usually created the representational art work, as shown on this bag.

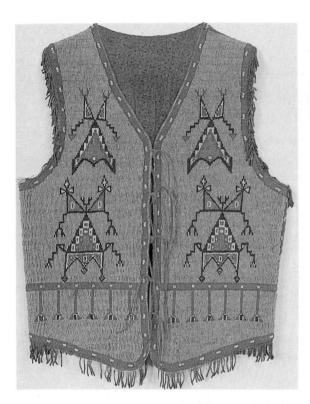

Fringes were often added to Sioux clothing, as shown on this vest. The design appears to be teepees, the shelter of a people who lived a nomadic life style.

This child's dress and moccasins show the fine beadwork of the Sioux. The pendant necklace appears to be symbolic of the sun.

1. What secrets about the past did the heirloom that Joe and Marie discovered reveal?

2. Why did William want to wait until he was in the presence of an honest historical expert to open the leather-wrapped bundle?

3. The High Elks could sell the pictograph or donate it to the new Tribal Museum. What do you think they will do? What would you do in their place? Why?

4. Why did Grandma High Elk name the new colt *Otokahe*, "Beginning"?

5. Grandma High Elk did not think that the bundle that Joe and Marie found should be opened. Find the part of the story that explains why she thought this.

Events in a story cause other things to happen. What happens is called an effect. Sometimes one cause can have several effects.

At the beginning of the story, "High Elk's Treasure," Joe and Marie High Elk have found a leather-wrapped bundle in a cave wall. Name two effects that their discovery has on their family during the story or might have on their family's future after the story ends.

Prewrite

Who?	What?	Where?	When?	Why?	How?
The High Elk Family					

Radio and television newscasters report in a brief, factual, and interesting way events that have recently taken place. Their news stories answer the six basic news-gathering questions: Who? What? Where? When? Why? How?

Imagine that the High Elk family has decided what to do with the pictograph. You are a newscaster assigned to write a TV or radio news story about their decision. Copy the chart above and finish it with information about the decision.

Compose

Write a TV or radio news story about the High Elk family's decision. Be sure to include answers to the six basic news-gathering questions. You may wish to give some background about the discovery of the pictograph in your news story, too.

Revise

Read your news story. Check to be sure that you have included the answers to the six basic news-gathering questions. If not, revise your work.

You may collect stamps or have a stamp collection as a family heirloom. Think about designing a stamp. Then read to find out about some of the stamps that Chris Calle designed.

Chris Calle started art classes when he was very young. As you read, look for causes of his interest in drawing.

Meet Chris Calle, Illustrator

by Miriam Lee

Chris Calle was just twenty-two years old when the U.S. Postal Service asked him to design a stamp honoring President Harry S. Truman. That stamp was voted "best design" in its class for that year, and Chris has since designed more stamps. One is a portrait of the great nature artist, John J. Audubon. Another is of World War II hero Admiral Chester W. Nimitz. Chris has become so well known as a stamp designer that he now designs stamps for many countries.

Today Chris illustrates books and magazines as well as stamps. He works with his father, Paul Calle, also an illustrator and stamp designer. Their studio is an old, converted barn near Stamford, Connecticut, where Chris grew up.

"Having a father who is an artist was great when I was little," he remembers. "At that time his studio was right in our home, and I could watch him work. During the time of the first moon shot, he was doing illustrations for NASA of Cape Kennedy. I drew a lot of spaceships, trying to copy him! He's been my best teacher, all the way."

Chris designed and created these stamps.

When Chris was about seven years old, he and his brother went to Stamford Museum's Nature Center for Saturday morning classes in art. "My brother got interested in the animals and became a veterinarian. But I kept on drawing," Chris says, with a laugh. He went on with after-school art lessons and graduated with honors from the University of Michigan School of Art in 1983.

What happens when Chris gets a commission to do an illustration? "First I have to find out what kind of illustration they want," he explains. "For example, do they want black and white or full color? I need to know the size and the technique they want me to use." Chris works in pencil and watercolor. He also makes prints. "If it's a book or short story, I read it carefully to get a sense of what the author is thinking. Sometimes the art director tells me exactly what is wanted. Other times I can use my own ideas, and that's more fun."

Research is very important to an illustrator. Chris spends a lot of time in libraries and art museums. He goes looking for pictures and old prints to make sure the

Chris and his father, Paul, review finished art work in their studio.

backgrounds of his drawings are exactly right. When he designed the Audubon stamp, he worked from oil paintings by Audubon's son, looked at prints from the Chicago Historical Society, and studied books on the artist's life.

Chris uses real people as models for his work. For a children's book, he visited a nearby school and took pictures of children who fit the author's descriptions. "I use my friends, my father—even myself, sometimes," he says, grinning.

It can take days or even weeks of research before Chris is ready to go back to the art director. "Some artists like to do rough sketches. I like to do as final a sketch as possible," he says. "It helps us both if the art director can see almost-finished art and make any changes needed."

Once his idea is approved, Chris goes back to his drawing board in the old barn studio. There he finishes the illustration—as it will look in a book or magazine, or as the stamp that will go out on thousands of letters.

Chris is working on illustrations for the story "Cherry Ripe."

1. What are some of the stamps that Chris Calle designed?
2. What does Chris need to know before he can begin an illustration?
3. Why do you think Chris prefers to use his own ideas from a story to do an illustration rather than what the art director tells him?
4. Once he has gotten an assignment, why does it take so long for Chris to come up with the art for the director to approve?
5. Read what Chris says in the third paragraph of the selection. What does this quotation tell you about how Chris feels about his father? Why do you think this was included in the article?

Causes and effects are everywhere — in nature, in history, in stories, and in people's everyday lives. Listed below are events, or effects, from "Meet Chris Calle, Illustrator." For each effect, ask "Why did it happen?" Try to find a cause in the article for each effect.

1. Chris Calle was asked to design more stamps, including one of John J. Audubon and one of Admiral Nimitz.
2. During the time of the first moon shot, Chris drew a lot of spaceships.
3. Chris spends a lot of time in libraries and museums.

Prewrite

Interview Information Sheet

Classmate's name: _____

Age: _____

Career or job ideas: _____

_____

_____

_____

Current interests or hobbies: _____

_____

_____

Chris Calle started art lessons as a boy and later became an illustrator. Copy the form above, and use it to interview one of your classmates. Ask questions about what he or she wants to do as a career or job. Next, find out what his or her current interests are. Complete your interview form. Then have your classmate interview you.

Compose

Use the information you gathered from your interview to write a brief essay about your classmate's ideas for a career or job and his or her current interests. State the connection between your classmate's career ideas and current interests.

Revise

Read your essay. Make sure you have included the information gathered in your interview. If you have not done so, revise your work.

Forms and Applications

You have probably been asked to fill out many forms and applications. Maybe you have completed an **application** for a library card or a **form** subscribing to a magazine. You may have filled out a form when you joined a club or group, such as a soccer league or swim team. If you ever ordered something through the mail or entered a contest, you probably completed a form.

It is important to know how to fill out forms and applications. These basic steps will help you complete them correctly.

1. Read all directions carefully and have all the information you need before starting to write.
2. Use a pen unless the form or application asks you to use a pencil.
3. Write or print clearly and neatly.
4. When the form or application is finished, check it for errors.

The following application was completed by someone who wanted to become a member of a museum. See if you can find three errors he made because he did not follow the steps mentioned above.

Children's Museum of Hartford

West Hartford, Ct. 06119

please print

Name: *John Michael Simmons*

last   first   middle initial

Address: *10 Oak Street*

street

Union, Alabama   *04321*

city   state   zip

Phone: *043*   *555-9101*

area code   number

Birthdate: *3* — *14* — *74*

year   month   day

Did you find these three errors?

1. John did not print.

2. He did not put his name in the right order.

3. His date of birth was not written correctly.

Now look at the magazine order form below, and pretend that you are doing the ordering. On a separate piece of paper, copy the form and fill in the necessary information.

★★★

Heirloom Magazine

San Diego, California 92101

Please print
Use pen

Name: _____

First   Last   Middle Initial

Address: _____

Mailing

_____

City   State   Zip

Payment: You will be billed.

Forms often look very different from one another. The directions for filling them out vary widely, too. Some forms ask you to leave spaces between certain words, but other forms don't. Some tell you to use all capital letters or to use only pen or pencil. Because some forms are used with computers, the information must be complete so that the computer can process the information.

You may have seen forms that ask you to print your information in small boxes rather than on lines. Maybe you filled one out when you took a test at school and had a special answer sheet to use. Look at the next example.

Achievement Test 5

Use pencil
Leave a space between words
One space per letter

Name

Last																	First													
C	a	r	s	o	n												A	l	i	c	e								

Address

Street										City														State	
1	1		L	a	k	e		D	r	R	o	u	n	d	t	r	e	e	N	Y					

zip							month	day	year	Age		area code	number								
0	0	1	3	4			0 3	1 5	7 3	1 0		0 8 3	5 5 5	2 4 1 1							

Birthdate — Use two numbers for each part of the birthdate

Phone — Area code first

Many stores and businesses have order forms to fill out if you want to buy something. Look very closely at the fine print on the forms to be sure you know exactly what you are buying. Be careful to write clearly the order number, the name of the item, and the quantity you want.

Look at the order form below. Notice that the fine print explains how the order should be placed and what you must do if you want to return something. It also explains how to order by mail or in person at the store. Study the order form closely and answer the questions that follow the form.

Museum Gift Shop

The Cowboy Museum
Dallas, Texas

To purchase merchandise from showroom or catalog complete the form and present it to the information desk. Please Print.

For prompt service on specialty items, jewelry or photographs, place your order on a separate piece of paper and present it to the cashier.

name			
address			
city	state	zip	
phone	order to be paid by ☐ Check ☐ BankCard ☐ Cash		

Complete catalog number from catalog or sample tags.	Qty.	Item description: Specify color, size, etc.	Price
1 2 6 S L E (example)	1	Museum Poster	4.00

All returns must be accompanied by sales receipt and in their original carton and packing (no returns after 10 days).

1. Could you return the poster in two weeks if you weren't satisfied with it? Explain your answer.

2. Why is it important to save your receipt?

3. Would you need three different forms if you were ordering three items?

Filling out forms and applications correctly and completely can help you get what you want without confusion or delays.

Stories and books can become heirlooms just as old objects can. In this selection, you will learn how some classic books and stories got their start.

What application might you have to fill out to borrow some of the books mentioned in this selection?

Treasures from the Past

by Bernice E. Cullinan

My father taught me to love stories. My earliest memories include the stories he told me about his own childhood. He told scary stories about noises in the night that would give me the shivers even though I was snug on his lap and knew I was safe. I cried when he described saying good-by to the two little fox cubs he raised and sent back to the wilderness when they were grown. And he told me and read me the stories he had loved when he was small.

I didn't realize it then, but my father was giving me heirlooms. He was giving me a love of literature.

Today, in everything I do, I share the love for stories my father handed down to me many years ago.

Different types of stories from the past make up our literary heritage. Stories our parents tell us about themselves when they were young are heirlooms; so, too, are stories told by people who lived many years ago. We keep the stories alive because we enjoy them so much.

There have been stories as long as there have been human beings. Before there were books, children sat around the fire and listened to the same stories adults heard. These stories were not written down, because almost no one could read or write. Instead, they were memorized and passed on for hundreds of years. We can imagine the excitement in a little town when someone came with new stories to tell! Then the good storytellers learned the new stories and retold them in their own special ways. That was how stories moved from town to town and even from country to country.

Nobody really knows when stories were first written down. Aesop's fables came from ancient Greece, and they were probably first told, then written down. Later they were hand-copied for scholars and rich people who could read.

We do know that in 1697, almost three hundred years ago, a Frenchman named Charles Perrault published a book of traditional stories told in the villages of his country.

A wood engraving, 1881, of a scene from A Christmas Carol *by Charles Dickens.*

A wood engraving, 1861, of a scene from Cinderella.

Among those old, old stories were *The Sleeping Beauty, Little Red Riding Hood, Cinderella,* and *Puss in Boots.*

In 1812, two brothers named Grimm traveled about Germany listening to people's stories, and wrote the stories down — more than two hundred of them! You know some of them today: *Hansel and Gretel, Tom Thumb, The Fisherman and His Wife, Rumplestiltskin,* and *Snow White and the Seven Dwarfs.*

In Denmark, in 1835, Hans Christian Andersen was both collecting old stories and writing new ones of his own. He wanted his stories to be liked by both children and adults, and he became a favorite storyteller in his own country. His story *The Ugly Duckling* is said to be about his own life. He was unhappy in his early years, and he only came to be recognized and accepted when he was grown up. Another of his well-loved stories, *The Nightingale*, reflects his love for Jenny Lind, a popular singer of his day. Andersen wrote about winning and losing, about courage and disappointments, and about good overcoming evil. These ideas still appeal to us, and Andersen's stories are among our favorite literary heirlooms.

The earliest children's books we know of were written to teach the young how to behave. Children were told to be good, kind, neat, and honest, or terrible things would happen to them. But exciting books for grown-ups were being written, and children found them. *Robinson Crusoe, The Swiss Family Robinson,* and *A Christmas Carol* are among the books for adults that were adopted by young people.

It is believed that the first book to have been written just for chil-

An illustration of Robinson Crusoe on a raft from Robinson Crusoe *by Daniel Defoe.*

An illustration by Sir John Tenniel, 1865, of the Mad Tea Party from Alice in Wonderland *by Lewis Carrroll*

dren's pleasure is *Alice in Wonderland*. It began as a story told to two little girls by a young professor who took them on a boat ride in 1862. That night he wrote the story down just as he had told it as they rowed along.

Perhaps he used the pen name of Lewis Carroll because he thought it wasn't dignified for an Oxford professor to tell such a story, but *Alice* and his next book, *Through the Looking Glass*, are the reasons he is remembered today.

The author of some other classics, Beatrix Potter, was born in London in 1866. She was a lonely little girl, with few playmates but many pets. In the summer she loved to go to the country with her family, and there she drew pictures of wildflowers and animals. *The Tale of Peter Rabbit* was first written as a letter to a little boy, with drawings. He saved it, and later Beatrix made it longer and added more illustrations. No publisher would buy it, so Beatrix had it printed at her own expense. Children loved her stories, and soon a publisher came asking for more. Her tales of Jeremy Fisher, Flopsy, Mopsy, Cottontail, and Peter Rabbit have been read by millions of children. They have become part of the literary heirlooms that we all share.

There is a literary classics guessing game some students like to play. Often they are surprised to find that so many books they know are classics, books their parents and grandparents loved also. Here are some guessing game questions. (Answers are upside-down at the end of this essay.)

1. Who was the mean old miser who hated Christmas?

2. Who was the little girl who lived in the Swiss mountains with her grandfather?

3. Who was the spider that was Wilbur the pig's best friend?

4. Who was the English nanny with the magic umbrella?

5. Who was the bear that was Christopher Robin's best friend?

6. Who was the wooden puppet whose nose grew longer when he lied?

7. Who was the giant lumberman whose working partner was a big blue ox?

8. Who was the Polynesian boy who set off alone in a canoe to prove his bravery?

You can play this literary classics game with many books you have enjoyed. Here are the rules: A book is called a "classic" when it has been enjoyed by more than one generation. Check the copyright page in the front of a book to find the copyright date, the date when the book was first published. Then add twenty years to that date, plus your age. Does the total come to less than this year's date? If so, you have been reading a book that is a classic. It is one that has been passed down for at least one generation.

Heirlooms are valuable possessions left to us by people who lived before us. Old stories are a special kind of heirloom we treasure for ourselves and for our children. Some books written today will be classics for your grandchildren. Which ones do you think they will be?

1. Ebenezer Scrooge
2. Heidi
3. Charlotte
4. Mary Poppins
5. Winnie the Pooh
6. Pinocchio
7. Paul Bunyan
8. Mafatu

1. How did many classic stories get their start?
2. Why are classic stories considered heirlooms? To whom do they belong?
3. Some early children's books were written to teach a valuable lesson. Which books have you read that you think teach a lesson?
4. How did children learn stories before books were written just for them? What kinds of books did they read?
5. Who are three authors whose books and stories have become part of our literary heritage? Find the part of the selection that tells about each author.

Knowing how to fill out a form or application is important. Reading directions is a key to filling them out correctly.

Copy and then fill out the application for a library card. Then list two books you would like to check out.

First	Middle	Last Name
School	Grade	Age

Prewrite

Title:	
Setting:	
Characters:	
Plot:	

Think about one of your favorite stories. Copy the chart and fill it in with the elements of that story or an episode from that story.

Compose

Using the information on your chart, write down your story. Write it as if you were going to read it to a small child. Try to express the wonder and excitement of the story that you felt when you first heard or read it.

Revise

Read your story. Does the action flow smoothly? Would a small child be able to follow the plot? Do your characters come alive? Think of some words you could add to make your characters seem more real. Revise your work.

Author's Purpose

Finding the Author's Purpose

Authors write with a **purpose**, a reason, in mind. Sometimes an author simply wants to **entertain** readers with a humorous tale or an exciting story. At other times, an author's purpose is mainly to **inform** or teach readers about something. Some writers express their opinions in their writing and write primarily to **criticize** something or someone. Others try to **persuade** their readers to think or act a certain way.

To Entertain

Many authors write just to entertain. Most of the stories you read were written for you to enjoy. Whether you prefer funny stories, scary stories, or adventure stories, the authors mean to entertain you in their own special ways. Read the following example.

> My friend Drew was playing chess with his dog Topper. I'd never seen a dog play chess before. "Topper is a very smart dog!" I said. "Not really," Drew replied, "I've already beaten him in three out of five games."

Did this story make you laugh? Then the author succeeded in his purpose, to entertain you.

To Inform

Another reason that authors write is to inform or give information about something. Read the following paragraph.

> Chess has interested people for a very long time. A game like chess was played in India around the year A.D. 600. In the 1200's, chess was played in Western Europe. Today the game of chess is played all over the world.

In this paragraph, the author informs you about the history of chess. The paragraph doesn't try to entertain you. It doesn't ask you to form an opinion of chess or to make a judgment.

To Criticize

When writers criticize something, they express their opinions either for or against it. Read the following opinion:

> Today, the world chess champion walked out of the first game of the world championship match, giving the victory to the challenger. Many said the champion had lost the lead yesterday. I think he should have stayed in the game and fought it out a while longer. I'm convinced that he got out too early and so lost this important first game.

Clearly, this writer has a negative opinion of the chess champion's action. The writer could just as easily have a positive, or favorable, opinion. Book reviews are good examples of writing meant to criticize. The same book can often be the subject of both positive and negative reviews. Phrases such as *I think* and *in my opinion* are often clues that the author's purpose is to criticize.

To Persuade

Writers sometimes want to do more than criticize. They want to convince you to feel or act a certain way. Then they write to persuade you. Read the following example. What is the writer trying to persuade you to feel or do?

> Chess is the most interesting game in the world. It teaches you how to think and plan ahead. Everyone should learn how to play chess.

In this paragraph, the author tells you that chess is the most interesting game in the world. That is the author's opinion rather than a fact. The author's purpose in telling you this is to persuade you to learn to play chess. The word *should* in the last sentence is a clue that the author wants his or her readers to do something.

Sometimes a piece of writing can have more than one purpose. For example, something entertaining may also inform you by giving important facts. A critical piece of writing, such as a movie review, often tries to persuade you to see a certain movie. To determine the author's overall purpose, ask yourself these questions: What is the author's main reason for writing this? What does the author want me to get out of this writing?

Read the following two paragraphs. As you read, think about the author's purpose in writing each.

A. James Naismith, a gym teacher, made up the game of basketball in 1891. He hung up two peach baskets. Each team had its own basket where it threw the ball. Someone had to climb a ladder to get the ball out each time. From this beginning, basketball became the game we know today.

B. Exercise is one of the most important things you can do for yourself. Far too many young people today are out of shape. Too much time is spent in front of the TV set and the video screen. Young people should be playing organized sports with others their age. They should get involved in after-school sports or other activities. Why don't you get involved in some kind of exercise today!

1. What is the author's purpose in the first paragraph? What clues helped you decide?
2. What is the author's purpose in the second paragraph? What clues helped you decide?

Textbook Application: Author's Purpose in Health

Textbook authors have a purpose for writing. In textbooks, the author's purpose is usually to **inform**. You may also read some paragraphs in which the purpose is to **persuade**.

What fact is explained in the first paragraph?

What are some words in this paragraph that are clues to the author's purpose?

Are there any opinions in this paragraph?

When Nutrients Are Missing

Suppose a certain nutrient is missing from your diet. You may not notice the difference for a few days. You may even go for weeks without feeling any harm. But after a while, your health will be damaged. The lack of each nutrient causes a different kind of illness.

You are not likely to become ill in any of these ways. You probably eat at least a little of each nutrient that you need. But you may not get as much of each nutrient as your body really needs. Perhaps you could be somewhat healthier. For example, you should eat more fruit than cookies. Then you would get the vitamins you need and not too much sugar. If you did eat too many cookies, it would be because you chose to. You could easily get a piece of fruit from a nearby store if you wanted to.

In some parts of the world, people do not have any choice about what they eat. They may have little to eat except grains, such as rice and corn. Many people in other parts of the world can rarely get fruits or vegetables.

They only rarely see meat or eggs. These people have unbalanced diets. They get too little protein. They may be missing many of the minerals and vitamins they need.

Scientists are working on ways to help people improve their diets. For example, they are finding new foods that can give people protein. Many people now get protein from a plant called the *soybean*. Soybeans are rich in protein, and they cost much less than meat. Soybeans may be one answer to the problem of hunger and poor nutrition in the world.

> What are some clues to the author's purpose in this paragraph?

— *HBJ Health*
Harcourt Brace Jovanovich

1. What is the author's purpose in the first paragraph?

2. Summarize what the author says in the second paragraph. Does the author want you to do something? If so, what?

3. What is the author's purpose in the second paragraph? Name some words that are clues.

4. What subject does the author want you to know about in the last paragraph?

5. What is the author's overall purpose?

Understanding an author's purpose for writing can help you determine what to pay attention to when you read.

Stories about George Washington are heirlooms from this country's past. In this story, Phillis Wheatley, a famous poet, writes a poem in Washington's honor. Read to find out what happened to the poem.

As you read, decide what the author's purpose was in writing the story.

A Poem for George Washington

by Shirley Graham

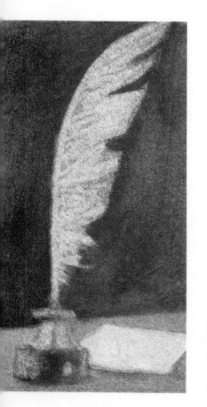

In 1761, Mrs. Susannah Wheatley paid three pounds to rescue a terrified little black girl from the slave-auction block in Boston, Massachusetts. The teenaged Wheatley twins, Mary and Nathaniel, named her Phillis, and decided to educate her—something unheard-of for slaves in those days. Mary began teaching her English and the alphabet, and it became clear that Phillis was an exceptionally bright child. Soon Nathaniel taught her Latin and Greek.

Phillis wrote her first poem in 1766, when she was about eleven years old. As this story begins, it is 1775, and the American War for Independence has begun. Phillis has already become famous in Boston and in England as "the Black Poetess."

There was rejoicing in Boston when the news spread that General Washington, Commander-in-Chief of the Continental Army, was camped just across the river.

"Now the redcoats will be running back to England!" people said.

One night Mary was awakened by a little cry from her baby. As she was about to slip back into her room she noticed a light under Phillis's door. Could she be sick? Mary listened but could hear no sound. She knocked gently and pushed open the door.

Phillis was sitting at her table fully dressed, with a quill pen in her hand. When she looked up, startled, Mary whispered, "Phillis, you've written a new poem. I can see it in your face!"

Phillis nodded her head. "I — I — guess I've been writing all night," she said apologetically. Then she said, "It's for General Washington." Mary leaned over her shoulder and read in a low voice:

> Celestial choir, enthroned in realms of light
> Columbia's scenes of glorious toils I'll write;
> While freedom's cause her anxious breast alarms,
> She flashes dreadful in refulgent arms.
> See mother Earth her offspring's fate bemoan
> And nations gaze at scenes before unknown!

"Oh, Phillis! This is wonderful!" Mary picked up another sheet:

> Shall I to Washington their praise recite?
> Enough thou knowest them in field of fight.
> Thee first in place and honors, we demand
> The grace and glory of thy martial band.
> Famed for thy valour, for thy virtues more,
> Hear every tongue thy guardian aid implore!

"How many sheets are there? Phillis, he should see this!" Mary said.

"You like it then?" A happy smile was spreading over Phillis's face. "If you think it's good I'll take it to him."

"Like it? Oh my dear! But now do go to bed," Mary said leaning over and hugging the tired girl.

Later that day Phillis copied all the lines carefully on clean sheets of paper. She asked Mary not to say anything to the men about it. "Master Wheatley might forbid me to go through the lines!" she exclaimed.

Mary thought this quite likely. "Wouldn't it be better to send it, Phillis?" she asked.

"By whom?" Phillis asked. "Indeed, Miss Mary, I'm sure the soldiers won't bother me at all. They would stop a man."

Phillis washed and pressed the frilled white maid's cap she seldom wore now, and tied on a clean apron. Then, with a little basket on her arm, she set out on an errand for her "master." When questioned she spoke timidly, with eyes downcast, and the soldiers hardly bothered to hear what she said. It was not until she was across the river and inside the Continental Army lines that she drew attention. A black serving girl was something new in this camp of Yankees, and there was laughter and shouting.

"Look you! A woman!"

"Where is your master?"

Phillis was looking around a little frightened when she heard a loud command: "Quiet, there!"

She looked up gratefully as a thin, young-looking man came toward her. "What do you want, girl?" he asked.

"I seek General Washington, sir," she said, and made a little curtsy.

The soldier looked hard at her. After a moment he said, "The general is not here. I am his aide and will take the message from your master."

Phillis hesitated. The soldier's hawklike eyes were studying her, and she felt her cheeks burning.

"It is—" she began, and then her words came in a rush. "I have a poem for him!"

"A poem? Oh, a poem!" The soldier slapped his thigh. "I knew I'd seen your face before. You're the Black Poetess! I saw you riding in a carriage, one day in England."

A sudden suspicion shot through Phillis's mind. "You are an Englishman?" she asked. When he nodded she asked quickly, "What are you doing in *our* camp?"

The soldier's eyes twinkled. "You'll likely find me where men are fighting for freedom. The general will be honored to receive your poem, miss, and I shall ask him to let me publish it."

Phillis's eyes opened wide. "You are a printer?"

"Among other things." He grinned and then added, "I write sometimes, too."

Phillis no longer distrusted the soldier. As she took the folded sheets from her sleeve, she said shyly, "I should like to know your name, sir."

He took off his three-cornered hat and bowed low. "My name is Tom Paine," he said, "and I am at your service."

"I take it, sir, we did not meet in London," Phillis said.

"We did not, miss." He smiled. "I should be happy to invite you to tea now — but we have no tea."

She smiled back at him. "I would have brought you some tea — but there is none on our shelf. I bring only a poem."

When he told her good-by, Tom Paine said, "It will mean much to Washington to know that he is first in your hearts."

Many weeks later an army courier brought a letter for "Miss Phillis Wheatley." Mr. Wheatley took it from him and called, "Phillis! Where are you, Phillis?"

She came running down the stairs.

"What is it, Phillis?" Mary appeared in the kitchen door.

"Well, open it! Open it!" Mr. Wheatley said impatiently. Letters brought by courier were apt to be important.

Phillis opened the letter. Her eyes went first to the bottom of the sheet and she looked up quickly.

"It's from General Washington!"

"General Washington?" Mr. Wheatley looked at their beaming faces as if he thought they were mad. "Washington?" he asked again.

"Yes, Father," Mary said, trying to speak calmly. "Don't look so surprised. Remember Phillis is a poetess! Read it, Phillis. What does he say?"

Phillis skipped through the letter. "Your favor of the 26th of October did not reach my hands till the middle of December . . . I apologize for the delay . . . I thank you most sincerely for your polite notice of me in your elegant lines . . . I would have published the poem had I not been apprehensive that while I only meant to give the world this new instance of your genius, I might have incurred the imputation of vanity. . . ."

She looked up with shining eyes. "How could anyone think General Washington was vain! He invites me to visit him if I am ever near his headquarters. And it's signed, 'Your obedient humble servant, George Washington!' I'll keep this letter all my life!"

The British had drained Boston dry. They had torn up the Commons, and pulled down fences and houses and steeples. But they had not subdued the people. Early in March, 1776, when Washington took two large hills overlooking the southern part of Boston, the British quietly sailed away.

On March 20, General Washington marched into the town at the head of his troops. All the bells the townspeople could salvage began to ring, and everyone rushed out to cheer him.

When Washington left a few days later for New York, he took most of the Massachusetts troops with him.

The next morning as Phillis walked along King Street she saw the Englishman, Tom Paine. She smiled as he approached her. "Welcome to our town, good sir," she said, extending her hand.

He took off his hat and bowed elegantly, but Phillis noted that his clothes were stained and threadbare.

"Good morning, Miss Phillis," he said. "This is a good meeting because I owe you an apology."

"No need, Mr. Paine," she said. "Mr. Washington thanked me for the poem, and he said why he had stopped its publication."

"I still think he's wrong," said Tom Paine. "All people should know how highly some of his countrymen regard him. Not all his enemies are with the British."

Phillis had heard people speak against Washington. Now her face was troubled as she listened to his aide.

"Could I see his letter?" Paine asked abruptly.

"My house is only a few steps down the street, sir. Will you come with me?" Phillis said.

When he read the letter, Paine said, "If this letter were published with the poem, Washington's objections would be removed. Will you trust me with your letter?"

Phillis did not want to let the letter out of her hands, but Tom Paine's plan was so clear and so good that she nodded her head.

"I'll talk to Washington again." He smiled his crooked smile and said, "We shall see."

"It seems strange that we must fight Englishmen when *he's* an Englishman," Mary said when their visitor had gone.

Phillis thought of her friends in England. She thought of the fine old colonial homes and churches that had been demolished in Boston, and she spoke slowly. "There must be a lot of different kinds of people in the world, and I don't think fighting anybody helps to understand them."

In May Phillis received a copy of the *Pennsylvania Magazine*, or *American Monthly Museum*. It was dated April 1776. In it appeared her "Poem to George Washington," accompanied by the short note she had written to him and the letter the general had written to her. The people of Massachusetts read the magazine and boasted of "the poet in their midst."

And on July 4, a new nation was born in Philadelphia.

Discuss

the

Selection

1. What happened to the poem Phillis Wheatley wrote about General Washington?
2. Why did Phillis Wheatley want to write a poem about General Washington and give it to him?
3. How did you feel about General Washington's decision not to let Tom Paine publish the poem at first?
4. How did Tom Paine solve the problem of publishing the poem?
5. How did Tom Paine help Phillis Wheatley? Find the parts of the story that tell what he did.

Apply

the

Skills

Think about the author's purpose in writing the story, "A Poem for General Washington." A story writer's main purpose is usually to entertain, but parts of a story may also inform or persuade the reader.

Find five sentences in "A Poem for General Washington" that inform by giving factual information about George Washington or about the Revolutionary War. Then find two sentences that the author might have written to persuade the reader that wars are not good.

Prewrite

Problem	Resolution
Phillis wanted to deliver her poem to General Washington personally.	
Tom Paine wanted to publish Phillis's poem.	

All good stories present problems that must be solved. Think about the story, "A Poem for General Washington." What were the problems? How were they resolved? Copy the chart above and fill it in.

Compose

Write two paragraphs about "A Poem for General Washington." In the first paragraph, write about the story's first problem and how it was solved. Add more sentences that give details about the problem and the solution. In the second paragraph, write about the story's second problem and solution. Add sentences with further details.

Revise

Read your paragraphs. Check to make sure that each paragraph gives the problem and the solution as well as details. If it does not, revise your work.

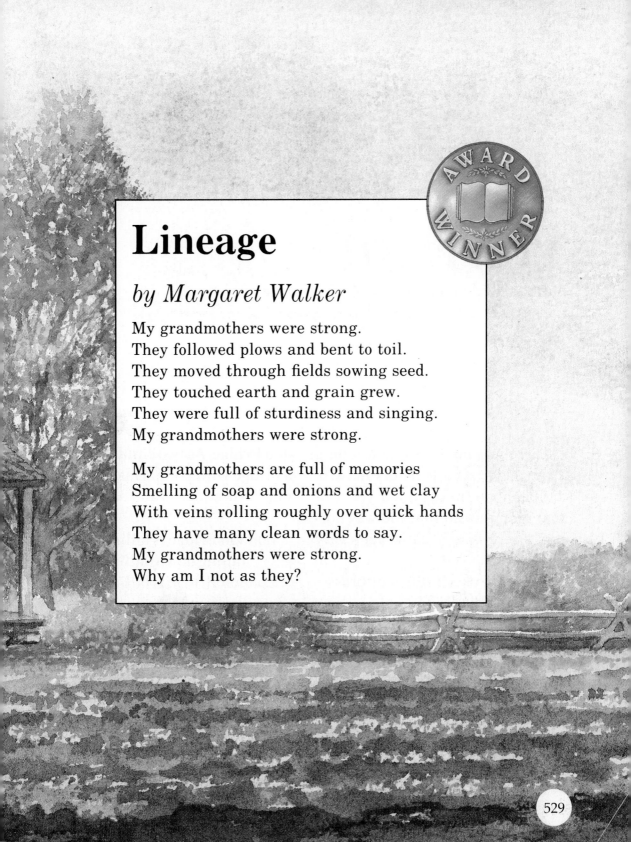

Lineage

by Margaret Walker

My grandmothers were strong.
They followed plows and bent to toil.
They moved through fields sowing seed.
They touched earth and grain grew.
They were full of sturdiness and singing.
My grandmothers were strong.

My grandmothers are full of memories
Smelling of soap and onions and wet clay
With veins rolling roughly over quick hands
They have many clean words to say.
My grandmothers were strong.
Why am I not as they?

Some of the games and toys you have enjoyed may be heirlooms from the 1800's. What did children in the 1800's do for fun?

As you read, see if you can identify the author's purpose in writing this selection.

You're It!
Games Kids Played on the Frontier

by James E. Cook

There was no Saturday morning TV in the Arizona Territory in 1870. TV hadn't been invented yet. But that didn't mean that life was boring. There was a game for every kind of day.

Children of all the cultures—Mexican, Indian, and Anglo—knew plenty of games by heart. Many games had come across the oceans and then across the United States. Others had come north through Mexico.

In Phoenix, one of the younger children's favorite games was London Bridge. As two children formed a bridge with their arms, the others marched under it and sang:

London Bridge is falling down,
    falling down, falling down.
London Bridge is falling down,
    my fair Lady.

Mexican children in the old town of Tucson, many miles to the south, had the same game. Only the words were different. The game, called La Víbora, was about a huge sea monster.

A la víbora, víbora de la mar,
    de la mar.
Por aquí pueden pasar.
Los de adelante corren mucho.
Los de atrás se quedarán, rán,
    rán.
Campanita de oro
Déjenme pasar
Con todos mis hijos.
Menos él de atrás, trás, trás.

Which means, roughly:

Oh monster, monster of the
    sea,
They can pass here.
Those who run fast get through.
Those who hold back remain.

Bell of gold
Let me pass through
With all my children
Except the slow ones.

The one who was caught as the arms fell was asked which side he or she wanted to be on. In London Bridge, it could be gold or silver; in La Víbora, *sandía* (watermelon) or *melón* (cantaloupe). The game ended when all the players stood behind one side of the bridge or the other.

Matarile was another Mexican game. The children formed two lines, facing each other, about fifteen feet apart. The first line walked forward four steps, then back, singing a chorus that had no meaning:

Agua té matarile, rile, rile
Agua té, matarile, rile, ron.

The second line then moved back and forth, singing:

¿Qué quiere usted? (What do you want?)
Matarile, rile, ron.

The first line responded with the name of a job it had chosen: farmer, carpenter, cleaning woman.

Quiero un cocinero (I want a cook)
Matarile, rile, rile, etc.

The second line answered:

Escójalo usted (Choose again),
Matarile, rile, rile, etc.

Then the first line said:

Escojo a (I choose) lava platos (dishwasher),
Matarile, rile, rile, etc.

This continued until the players in the first line had chosen a job title both lines could agree on.

The game ended with all joining hands in a circle and singing:

Celebremos todos juntos
(Let's all rejoice together)
Matarile, rile, rile, etc.

Yaquí Indians from Mexico and Arizona played a game called Hita Kolorim? (What Colors?). Leaders chose two teams of players, and goal lines were scratched in the dirt about twenty-five yards apart.

The teams formed two straight lines, standing face to face halfway between the goal lines. One team had a secret: something it had chosen, such as a melon, a cooking pot, or an ear of corn.

The other team asked about its color, its shape, its texture. If that team guessed what the thing was, the members of the other team had to try to run back to their goal line without being captured.

Another Yaquí game was called Totim (Chickens). One person was chosen to be a mother hen, and another was the coyote.

The remaining players lined up behind the hen, each holding onto the person just in front. The hen held her arms out and squawked and clucked like a chicken. The

coyote tried to pry the chicks loose, usually trying to catch the one on the end of the line. But the chicks moved around in a weaving snake of a line, trying to elude the coyote. Sometimes the whole line fell to the ground giggling as the coyote closed in. The game ended when the hen had lost all her chicks.

Navajo children learned early to play a game called Shoe. It is still played, by children and adults, at healing ceremonies called "sings."

Two rows of the players' shoes are placed on the ground a few feet apart, and each group stands behind its row of shoes. A ball carved from yucca root, about the size of a marble, is hidden in the toe of one shoe.

While the people laugh and sing, one player from the other side advances to the row of shoes with a stick bent to the shape of a P. The player taps the shoe he or she thinks contains the ball.

If the correct shoe is tapped, the player wins a prize. The winner gets to take the ball back for his or her side to hide. If the player fails, another player tries.

There is a story to go with this game that is told only in winter, never in summer. It seems the animals which always appear in Navajo stories were playing Shoe, but no one could find the wooden ball. The animals decided that Owl was hiding the ball in his hand. If the ball was found by the other players, daylight would come. But Owl wanted the night to remain.

Finally one of the animals tapped Owl's hand with his stick. As Owl dropped the ball, dawn broke. But winter nights are still longer than summer nights because Owl hid the ball so long.

On the frontier, most toys were homemade—a doll made by stuffing a sock with wool, a stick horse, a boat carved of wood.

Navajo girls made their own dolls of cloth, stuffing the heads with wool from the sheep they tended. Another piece of cloth was pulled apart to form hair for the doll.

The metal bands which held wooden barrels together became other toys—hoops. A stick two or three feet long, with a much shorter stick nailed across the end of it, was used to push the hoop along. The idea was to see who could keep the hoop upright the longest as it rolled over rocks and through weeds.

Papago children also had a toy made of things they found around them. It was called Dia Wolo (Ring and Pin). A stick about a foot long had a string of yucca fiber or deerskin tied to one end of it. Along this string were placed rings of different sizes, sliced from a squash. The largest ring was nearest the tip of the stick, and the smallest at the far end of the cord, where a solid plug of squash rind kept it from flying off the string. The object of the game was to swing the cord and catch as many rings as possible on the stick.

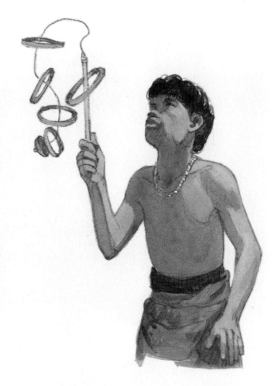

If the schoolhouse or milk house had a peaked roof, a group of children might play Annie Over. Players divided into teams on each side of the building, and someone called, "Annie, Annie over!" while throwing the ball over the roof. Players on the other side tried to catch the ball as it rolled off the sloping roof, then tried to run around the building and tag the first team. Of course, the first team didn't know which end of the building the runners would come around.

Red Rover was another lively game, and it caused some skinned knees and elbows. Two lines of players joined hands and faced each other. The leader of one line would call for someone — Margie, for instance — from the other line:

Red Rover, Red Rover, let Margie come over.

There was a lot of whooping and hollering as Margie ran at the opposing line. If she could break through, she got to take one of its members back to her side, and if she couldn't get through, she joined that line. The game ended when one line had all the players, or when the teacher rang the bell that meant recess was over.

There were many ways to play hide-and-seek and other chasing and capturing games. But always the person who was "It," with closed eyes, had to count to ten, or fifty, or one hundred, while everyone else ran and hid.

A different "It" game was played on moonlight nights at the Copper Glance mining camp in southern Arizona. "It" was the Tiger, who had to run and hide while everyone else stayed at the base and counted.

Then the others prowled through the rocks and bushes, looking for the tiger. The catch was that they all had to call out as they went, "All the tigers are gone." The tiger pounced from the hiding place and captured the other players, who then became tigers.

There were a couple of ways to play a game called Statue Tag, or Freeze. In one version, the player who was "It" chased the other players and tried to tag them out. A player who froze like a statue couldn't be tagged. But any player who moved at all was tagged and became "It."

A livelier way to play the game was for "It" to swing each of the other players around and around by the arm, then turn them loose. As the player reeled away, "It" called out, "Freeze!" The player had to stop, no matter how silly the position was, and stay there. The first "statue" to get caught moving became the new "It."

One day in spring, some boys would bring their marbles to school. Soon "marble season" would be on, and the boys would play nothing else for weeks and weeks.

Yaqui boys, who had no marbles, played a game with flat, smooth river stones. They collected good stones just as Anglo boys collected marbles. They drew a line about ten feet long on the ground. Then they backed off several yards and tried to land their stones near the line. The boy whose rock landed nearest to the line was the winner.

One of these lazy Saturday mornings, when you're looking for something different to do, you might try some of the games kids played on the frontier.

Discuss the Selection

1. What did children in the 1800's do for fun?
2. How were the toys used by children on the frontier different from most toys used today?
3. Which of the games mentioned in this selection do you remember playing?
4. How does the Navajo story of Owl playing the game Shoe explain the length of winter nights?
5. Find the part of the selection where the Anglo game London Bridge and the Mexican game La Víbora are compared. How are the two games alike, and how are they different?

Apply the Skills

The author's purpose in writing this selection was to inform the reader about frontier games. Many details in the selection give information about how the games are played.

Go back through "You're It!" and look for sentences with details describing how the games ended. Here is the sentence for London Bridge: "The game ended when all the players stood behind one side of the bridge or another." Find the same kind of sentence for the following games.

1. Matarile
2. Totim (Chickens)
3. Red Rover

Prewrite

Name of the game:
How many players and how they are arranged:
Steps of the game:
How the game ends and the winner is determined:

"You're It!" explains how to play many of the games that frontier children played. Pretend that you are going to teach someone from another culture how to play your favorite game. Copy and fill in the form above to help you organize the parts of the game in a way that someone else can follow.

Compose

Using the information on your chart, write two or three paragraphs of instructions explaining how to play your game. Imagine that you are writing to someone who has never heard of the game before. Don't leave anything out or you might cause confusion for the reader.

Rewrite

Read your instructions for playing the game. Is everything in the right order? Are your instructions clear and simple? If not, revise your work.

Direction

by Alonzo Lopez

I was directed by my grandfather
To the East,
   so I might have the power of the bear;
To the South,
   so I might have the courage of the eagle;
To the West,
   so I might have the wisdom of the owl;
To the North,
   so I might have the craftiness of the fox;
To the Earth,
   so I might receive her fruit;
To the Sky,
   so I might lead a life of innocence.

Point of View

An author writes a story from a certain point of view. The **point of view** demonstrates who is **narrating,** or telling, the story. When you read a story, ask yourself, "Who is telling the story?" Keep that question in mind as you read the following story.

> I like to solve mysteries. For example, today my friend Lily and I solved the mystery of the creaking door. We found an empty shed and were looking around inside when suddenly, the door creaked. Lily gasped, and I jumped up so fast I hit my head on a low beam. Then I heard Lily laughing. "Look who's here, Jim!" she exclaimed. I saw my cat, Clarence, gently push the door open. Clarence must have followed us.

Who is telling this story? The narrator is Jim, a character in the story. The events in the story are presented through Jim's eyes and ears. When an author writes a story as if a character were telling it, that story is written from a **first-person** point of view.

How can you recognize a story with a first-person point of view? You can use clues. The most important clue is your answer to the question "Who is telling the story?" If it is one of the characters, then you know that the story has a first-person point of view.

Look at the pronouns for another clue to the point of view. The pronouns *I, mine, me, we,* and *us* are called first-person pronouns. A story with a first-person point of view uses many of these pronouns outside the dialogue.

An author may also use the **third-person** point of view. In this point of view, the story is told by a narrator who is *not* a character in the story. The pronouns *he, she, his, hers, him, her, they, theirs,* and *them* are called third-person pronouns. These pronouns appear outside the dialogue in third-person point of view stories. Read the following story and answer the questions.

Today Jim and his best friend Lily solved the mystery of the creaking door. They were looking around in an empty shed when suddenly, the door creaked. Lily gasped in fright and froze in her tracks. Jim jumped up so fast he hit his head on a low beam. Then as Lily looked at the bottom of the door, she relaxed and started to laugh. "Look who's here, Jim!" she exclaimed. Jim's cat, Clarence, gently pushed the door open. He had followed them.

1. Who is telling the story?
2. What pronouns are used?
3. Is it written from a first-person or third-person point of view?

Authors use different points of view for different purposes. For example, one author may decide that a story will be more exciting if a character tells it. A third-person narrator can often tell a reader more about what characters are feeling than a first-person narrator can.

Each point of view gives a reader a different outlook. Each point of view even creates a different feeling in a story. Knowing about different points of view can help you understand a story better.

Author Profile

Barbara Brenner

Barbara Brenner, author of *On the Frontier with Mr. Audubon*, has written more than forty books for young people. Most of her stories, such as *The Gorilla Signs Love* and *A Snake Lover's Diary*, are based on her love of animals and of the wilderness, and on her extensive nature studies. She and Fred Brenner, her husband and a noted painter, spent many years camping throughout the United States and Canada with their two sons.

How do writers of historical fiction get their ideas for characters? Here Barbara Brenner tells how she learned about Joseph Mason, a character you will meet in the next story. She wrote an imaginary journal describing his travels with John J. Audubon.

"Although his journal is my creation, Joseph Mason was a real boy. I first learned about him from a note under an Audubon painting at the New York Historical Society. It said Joseph Mason had done the flower background for some of Audubon's work when he was thirteen.

"That caught my interest. I began to look for other proof that Audubon had a young assistant. I found it, in all the Audubon biographies. Joseph Mason *had* really lived. John James Audubon *was* his drawing teacher. And they *had* traveled together down the Mississippi and Ohio rivers.

544

"Now that I knew Joseph was real, I needed more facts. They were hard to find. Joseph was like a shadow, appearing and disappearing from the pages. It wasn't until I located an unedited diary of Audubon's travels during 1820 and 1821 that Joseph began to come alive. There, in Audubon's own words, was the detailed story of their life together. He wrote of the hunting for birds, the hard times, the long hours of drawing. And the good times, too — the fine dinners in New Orleans, the hikes, the beautiful Pirrie plantation where they stayed. I could feel the friendship growing as they worked and traveled over the months.

"Using Audubon's diary as a factual base, I began to write a new diary: Joseph's Journal. I went to other Audubon biographies to check facts. And I drew on other Audubon writing, especially his *Ornithological Biographies*. In these books, Audubon tells in great detail about every bird he painted.

"The result is a story as 'true' as I could make it. Almost everything Joseph and Audubon do in the book really happened. Their words are fiction but they are based on facts I found in the books about them or on Joseph Mason's statements later in his life."

John James Audubon painted beautifully detailed pictures of birds. He left heirlooms in the form of paintings. Read the selection to find out why Audubon's birds have always looked so real.

Joseph Mason tells about a long journey he took with Audubon. As you read, notice the point of view in the selection.

On the Frontier with Mr. Audubon

By Barbara Brenner

October 11, 1820
The Beginning

My name is Joseph Mason.

Most likely you never heard of me. Or of my teacher, Mr. John James Audubon. He is a painter around these parts and teaches drawing to young persons like myself. He also works at the museum here in Cincinnati, where his job is preparing birds for the museum's displays.

Mr. Audubon has a regular passion for birds. He has a notion to paint *every bird* in America and make a big book or portfolio of them for folks to marvel at. Right now he is planning a trip down the Ohio and Mississippi to search for birds to paint. And now here is where Joseph Mason comes into the picture. John James Audubon has asked me to go with him!

I am to help Mr. Audubon find bird specimens and to do other chores for him as he may need me. In return, he will

John James Audubon is best known for his watercolors and paintings of birds, but he also painted portraits of himself.

provide my board and also teach me drawing. I hope to be a painter when I grow up, but while Mr. Audubon's specialty is birds, mine is plants and flowers.

Both Mr. Audubon and I like nothing better than to hunt and fish and tramp through the woods; we are much alike in that. I think that may be why Mr. Audubon chose me to go on this trip with him.

I aim to set down in this journal all that happens to us on this trip. I shall do it as truly and faithfully as I can, because I know that although Mr. Audubon is only a poor painter now, someday he will be famous. Then people will want to know all about how he made his bird paintings. And maybe they will also want to know something about Joseph Mason and this frontier journey.

October 12, 1820
All Aboard

At half past four this afternoon we stepped aboard a flatboat bound for New Orleans. The dock was crowded with boxes and bales, as well as with voyagers and their families come to see them off.

Seemed like before we knew it, the crew was casting off. A few last words and our families were hustled ashore. By five o'clock we were drifting into the channel — on our way.

Now it's late. Way past my bedtime at home. I'm in the cabin of the flatboat, sitting with Mr. Audubon. We are both writing in our journals.

I guess I'm lucky. Not many thirteen-year-old boys get the chance to travel down the Ohio and Mississippi all the way to New Orleans. Scares me a mite, though. Never was this far from home before. I keep thinking of my mother and father. Mama's cheek was wet with tears when she kissed me. And Papa suddenly looked so old and frail.

I wonder when I'll see them again. I asked Mr. Audubon how long he figured we'd be away. Maybe six months, maybe a year, he says. Mr. Audubon says he misses his family already.

We're going to sleep now. Mr. A. says we shall sleep on deck. The air is better out there, he says. We have buffalo robes to roll ourselves in, so we shouldn't be cold.

And so to bed. More about this boat tomorrow, when it's light enough for me to see.

October 13, 1820
The Flatboat

Sun in my eyes woke me this morning. Mr. Audubon was already up and off somewhere. I sat on the deck for a spell, getting a closer look at my new home. I've seen many a flatboat from the shore, but this is the first time I've seen one from the deck.

A flatboat is really a large raft with sides. It's about 40 feet long. Both ends are squared off, and it has some cabin space as well. Most of the passengers stay on deck. Many of them are taking their livestock down the river to sell or to trade, so the deck looks like a regular Noah's Ark or a traveling barnyard. *Smells* like a barnyard, too. Can't hardly get a whiff of the river for all the pig and chicken smell.

This kind of boat has no sails or steam, so we're at the mercy of the wind and the river current. On a brisk day we can travel up to fourteen miles or so. But if there's no wind, we have to sit like a big clumsy cow in a mudhole, until the breeze or current takes us again.

The flatboat, with passengers and livestock.

Mr. Audubon and I spent a good part of this day sitting on deck sketching. And Mr. Audubon told me more about his plans for this trip.

Now here I got a surprise. It seems that Mr. A. hasn't a penny to his name. He has got us passage on this boat with the promise that we will supply game for the captain and his crew! So I shall be *hunting*, if not *singing*, for my supper. And for everyone else's, too.

Now about the birds for Mr. Audubon's paintings. He needs examples of every species of bird common to these parts, including those which have never been named in other bird books. He calls these nondescripts — which means that no one has described them. Mr. A. has a book with him by a Mr. Alexander Wilson, which he uses as a guide. But Mr. Audubon hopes to include in *his* bird book many species that Mr. Wilson does not picture. If I find a new species, Mr. Audubon says he may name it for me. Mason's hawk! Mason's flycatcher! Even Mason's eagle! How fine that sounds. I shall look sharp for new birds, you may be sure.

We are all ready. Powder dry, boots greased, guns in order. Tomorrow we start hunting in earnest. I hope that game is plentiful, otherwise two artists and the crew of this flatboat will be going hungry.

I can't help thinking what a long way I am from my cozy bedroom under the eaves.

October 20, 1820
Hunting

Mr. Audubon and I have gone hunting every day this week. We start out as soon as the sun is up. We leave the flatboat and arrange to meet it at an appointed place downstream. The first day we did this I couldn't believe that the boat wouldn't move faster than we did. But at dusk, when we came out of the woods, there it was.

We have found plenty of game as well as many birds to draw. Today, for example, we started out by taking care of our food supply. We shot seven partridges and a few grebes, which are a kind of duck. Later we came on a group of wild

Audubon's paintings are very realistic. These grebes are shown in their natural surroundings.

Audubon carefully measured each bird's parts so that he could draw, and later paint, its true size. Shown here are ivory gulls.

turkeys. Mr. Audubon showed me how he calls them. He has a whistle of bone on which he blows. As soon as they hear the sound, they begin to flock around. He shot one, and it went into our game bag with the other birds.

As for our drawing collection, I first shot a fish hawk, which I wounded. When I went to fetch it, the bird jabbed me in the hand with its talons. Then in its frantic twisting to get away it ran one of its claws through its own beak! Poor creature. Mr. Audubon killed it with a pin through the breast, so it would be whole for him to draw.

Soon after this, we added a hermit thrush to our collection.

Audubon's painting of this turkey is both colorful and lively.

When the game bag became heavy, we decided to head back toward the river. That walk back to the boat seemed powerfully long to me, but Mr. A. stepped along as sprightly as if we were just starting out. By the time we saw the outlines of the boat looming out of the dusk, we had covered more than thirty miles. How does Mr. Audubon do it? He is almost forty years old, but I confess he can outlast me.

Right now he is sitting across from me in the cabin, setting up his drawing materials. He has everything the best — Whatman's paper, chalks, brushes, watercolor paints of the finest quality. When I marveled at his rich supplies, he told me, "Joseph, these are the tools of my trade. For these and a good gun I will spend my last penny."

He lays out his supplies so lovingly — the way a man about to have a feast would set his table. How Mr. Audubon loves his work! He will labor all evening drawing the fish hawk and the hermit thrush. *He* is not a bit tired. But Joseph Mason is more than ready for sleep.

October 21, 1820
Working

Worked all day today. Practiced my flower drawing. Audubon is still drawing the fish hawk and the hermit thrush. He only made sketches of the hawk, but he has drawn the hermit thrush in detail and plans later to make a painting of it. Mr. A. makes sketches of everything as preparation for painting later. But if he makes a painting of a bird and later feels he can do it better, he will abandon or destroy the first one. At this rate I wonder, will he ever finish his portfolio?

It is very interesting how John James Audubon does his bird drawings, so I will tell it here. He has a wooden frame

Audubon made notes about every bird he painted. Shown here are two wrens.

A long, slender down-curved bill and long legs are noticeable features
of the curlew. Audubon painted these curlews near the water because
they are wading birds.

which is covered with wire. The wire is made of small squares. He wires the bird on this frame in some interesting and lifelike position. Sometimes he attaches threads to the wings and tail so he can raise or lower them. Then he takes fresh paper and rules it into squares the exact size of those on the frame. He then begins to draw the bird, true size, using the squares as a guide. He pays careful attention to every part, measuring bill and claw and length of wing. You might think all this measuring would make the drawing stiff and dull. But no. When Mr. Audubon is finished with the drawing, the bird looks so lively it seems that any moment it will fly off the paper.

After Mr. Audubon finished the drawing of the hermit thrush, he cut it open to examine the contents of its stomach. This way he can see what a bird has been eating and make note of it. Mr. A. makes a note of everything. He may someday write a book of life histories of the birds of America to go with his paintings.

I learned that we still weren't finished with the hermit thrush. After he had finished examining it, Mr. A. put it into the fire and roasted it for our lunch! It was hardly enough for two, but what there was tasted tender and delicious. Still . . .

I think I would rather hear a thrush sing than eat one. Mr. Audubon agreed.

November 10, 1820

I never did see a man work as *hard* as he does. I have watched him sometimes sixteen hours a day, bent over the little drawing table in the cabin. And this place so cramped he can't even stand up straight to stretch his legs!

I hope to copy Mr. Audubon's ways and work harder at my own drawing.

I feel sorry for Audubon. I think it a shame that he works so hard and makes such fine pictures, yet is so poor. Perhaps when these paintings are finished, he will get the fame he deserves.

December 5, 1820
The Eagles' Day

We have left the Ohio River and are on the broad, muddy waters of the Mississippi. Today we launched the skiff and floated ahead of the flatboat.

Now we began to see eagles all around. They were sitting in the low branches of trees along the river. They did not move as we drifted by in our little boat.

We didn't even fire our guns at other birds for fear of disturbing the eagles. Mr. Audubon said this was to be his day for observing them. We noticed that some eagles have brown heads. Others are white on top. Mr. Audubon's notion is that they are two different species. He looked at them all carefully through his spyglass and let me try it once or twice. Truly, that is a wonderful tool. It makes everything you look at seem close at hand.

We had put out a fishing line as we were drifting, hoping to catch something. In the late afternoon we felt a tremendous tug on the line. After much sweat and muscle, we finally hauled aboard a monster catfish. I think it must have been close to sixty pounds—truly a magnificent fish. We stared at it as it slapped about in the bottom of the skiff. Suddenly Audubon said, "Ah! Yes! I have it! I will draw my eagle with the catfish. I will put the fish in the eagle's talons." As soon as he said it, I realized what a good idea it was. Most of the bird paintings I have seen show the creature simply sitting on a branch. But Mr. Audubon is talking about painting *scenes* of birds doing what they do in the wild.

Sitting there in the boat, he made his first sketches, just as he saw it in his imagination. But he was handicapped without an eagle to draw from. It was then that we decided

The power of the eagle as a hunting bird is captured in this painting by Audubon.

to try to bring one down without killing it. We both tried, but I am no match for John Audubon in shooting skill. He finally pointed out an eagle, told me which wing he was going to hit, and proceeded to do it, *from 150 yards away*!

The eagle fell, wounded. Our faithful dog Dash (who had accompanied us on our adventure) plunged into the water and started after it. We followed in the skiff and succeeded in hauling both dog and eagle back into the boat. The eagle, safely captured, sat glaring at us, while his mate circled our boat shrieking with rage and sorrow, in a most pitiable way.

Audubon's painting of a blue heron.

When we arrived back at the boat, we showed everyone our prize. Then we fastened him to a perch. But we neglected to fasten the perch securely, and the next thing we knew, friend eagle had departed, dragging the long pole behind him. He skimmed, half fluttering, half swimming, across the water. I had to go out after him again in the small boat, and once again make him captive.

What a magnificent, brave bird. He sits on his perch and glares at the world. When anyone comes near, he ruffles up his feathers like an owl. Tonight we cut up the catfish and fed him some, offering it to him at the end of the stick.

Once, when Mr. Audubon was leaning forward to feed him, he suddenly shot out a talon and caught Mr. A. a nasty blow on his right thumb. I hope it won't interfere with his drawing. A drawing of the eagle should be splendid.

Speaking of drawing, I keep asking Mr. Audubon when I shall be ready to do some work on his paintings, like a real apprentice. Why won't he let me paint in a background or draw the feet of a bird? I'm sure I could do some of the flower background, and well, too.

"Not yet, Joseph," he tells me. "You must do a bit more work with the pen. More accurate. More rhythm. You must *look* more and get your hand to do the bidding of your eye." What a taskmaster John James Audubon is.

February 18, 1821
Bird Life

We are off the flatboat and are now living in a room in New Orleans. We have been watching the migration of birds. This is a subject in which Mr. Audubon is very interested. To tell the truth, until I met John James Audubon, I didn't even know that birds travel from one part of the country to another. When I was small, I was told that I didn't see certain birds in winter because they were sleeping under the mud or even under the water! There are plenty of folks who still believe this way, although Mr. Audubon says it is absolutely not true.

He says that birds migrate to warmer climates to get food. Sometimes they travel hundreds of miles without stopping to get to their winter homes. But I asked Mr. Audubon, "How do they know where to go and how to get there? And do they go to the same place every year?"

He admits that is a puzzle. But someday, he says, scientists will have a system for marking birds and following their movements. He says he once marked a phoebe by tying a string on its leg. Through this device he discovered that the phoebe came back to the same nest the following year.

Today we saw some migrating birds and also a terrible slaughter of them. We were walking along the shore of a lake when we spied a huge flock of golden plovers. There were thousands of them, coming from the northeast and heading south. Ordinarily, Mr. Audubon says, these birds fly over water, but a storm at sea had blown them in toward land.

The hunters, knowing their ways, were waiting for them, stationed all around the woods. They began to use their birdcalls, which imitate the call of the golden plover. The poor birds heard that *Qu-ee-a! Qu-ee-a!* and turned toward the sound. They came directly overhead. As they wheeled, every man raised his gun. At the first volley, hundreds of birds fell. The sound of firing kept up all day, when we were going home, they were still at it. We stopped to talk to them at sunset. One man told us he had shot 750 birds!

Audubon's painting of swallows in their nest.

There were about 400 gunners out there today. According to my sums, if each of them brought down close to what that hunter did, the day's shooting could have accounted for over a quarter of a *million* birds.

Mr. Audubon says he has seen the same massacre of the passenger pigeon. We have decided, Mr. Audubon and I, that while we like hunting as much as the next fellow, this kind of wholesale butchery makes us sick.

"Don't you notice fewer and fewer birds each year?" Mr. Audubon asked the hunters. They said no. Probably what saves the plovers is that they only come this far into shore during a storm. I wish I could tell them, "Brave the storm rather than risk the hunters."

March 15, 1821
Quicksand!

There is a sandy-bottom lake which we can walk to from our house. We decided to go there in search of birds. It was barely daybreak when we left. The mists still hung over the water, and that, with the Spanish moss, gave a ghostly character to the land. I followed Mr. Audubon through the canebrake, listening for bird sounds and trying to avoid snakes. When the sun rose and burned off the mists, we were able to see who was up and about. Now we observed frogs, as well as turtles of several species lying on logs or branches in the water. Innumerable small lizards ran up and down the cypress trees. And we noticed that the Mississippi kites were feeding on them.

"There's an idea for a painting," I said to Mr. Audubon. And he agreed.

I spied an alligator lying like a log on the bank. It looked so still I was sure it was dead. Mr. Audubon said not to be fooled and told me that one alligator had eaten a man's hunting dog. He advised me always to look sharp before I step on any logs along the shore!

Soon we decided to separate, so that we could cover more territory in our search for birds. It was our plan to meet back at that spot in an hour.

Not long after we parted company, I heard a faint whirring of wings. Looking up, I spied a barred owl. I decided to follow it, hoping that it would find a spot, light there and sit quietly, as owls usually do during the day. I hoped to get the owl for Mr. Audubon, who does not yet have a painting of this bird. So, head up to watch my quarry, I plunged through the swamp. I forgot about snakes, alligators, everything. I was watching the owl.

Quiet. Only the sucking sound of my boots going through the muck. At last—I saw the owl through the trees. It was sitting motionless, its head turned away from me. If I hadn't been on the lookout for it, I would have mistaken it for a clump of moss or some dead leaves.

I raised my gun ever so quietly. Then, thinking to get an even closer shot at it, I began to move forward. I took one step, then another, then. . . .

Before I knew it, I began to sink. The most terrible feeling of my life passed over me. I was in quicksand!

I had the presence of mind to toss my gun away, so my hands would be free. I grappled with the twisted roots around me, trying to get a grip somewhere. But it was no use. When the horrid ooze was about up to my armpits, I started to yell. I was surprised to hear the pure terror in my scream for help. But I knew that if Mr. Audubon wasn't around, Joseph Mason wasn't going to be around much longer either.

How fine the sound of someone crashing through the woods can be! In a few minutes Mr. Audubon appeared. He took one look at my situation and knew what to do. He found a stout branch and pushed it out to me. I grabbed it, and by this means he pulled me to firm ground.

"Well, Joseph," says he. "What were you after that made you forget to look where you were going?" I told him about the owl, and nothing would do but we must try to find it again, in spite of the fact that I was covered with mud and more than ready to quit for the day. John James Audubon can be the most persistent man! But I knew that it would have been no different if *he* had been the one to fall in the quicksand. So we continued our search for the owl, and I suffered my muddy clothes in silence.

An hour later we came on the owl again. It was about to swoop down on a squirrel. Mr. A. took aim and brought it down with one shot. As we walked home with our prize, Mr. Audubon said he wanted to draw it as he found it.

And that is the way he has started it, with the squirrel in the picture, too.

All the practice has not been wasted. Today at last I did my first professional drawing.

We had gone out early in search of plants to put in Mr. Audubon's drawings. Found some jewelweed and a lovely pink orchid. And not only did we find several plants in bloom, but I shot what must be the loveliest little bird in the world. It is called the yellow-backed blue warbler. First I found the male and then the female. They are both a wonderful shade of blue and yellow.

Mr. Audubon was very excited. We came straight home, where he began to work on them immediately. About five in the afternoon Mr. A. called me over to see his work. I was astonished to see that he had drawn the birds on a drawing of an iris that I had made the previous day.

I can't tell how proud it has made me to see our work together. There were John James Audubon's beautiful birds, sitting on *my* iris. And down in the corner of the drawing Mr. Audubon has written, " *'Yellow-backed Blue Warbler,' by John James Audubon. Plant by Joseph Mason.''*

May 16, 1821

This day has brought me sad news. My father is dead. I can hardly write of it. All this time, these many weeks, my father has been dead and I never knew it. How is it that I didn't sense somehow that he was gone?

Mr. Audubon is being kind. This evening we sat outside in the street in front of our house, talking quietly. We talked about our fathers. Mr. Audubon's father encouraged him to draw and paint. Just as my father did with me.

"Papa brought me my first book of bird paintings," Mr. Audubon said. He wept and didn't seem ashamed of it. And that made it easier for me to let the tears fall.

Then Mr. A. went in and got his flute and played for a while. He never left my side the whole day. Now he is asleep, but sleep won't come to me. I can't believe I will never see my father again. . . .

October 30, 1821

One full year has passed since we boarded the flatboat. Seems like a century.

"Joseph, it's time for us to take stock of ourselves." That's what Mr. Audubon said last night. So we have taken stock. We discover that we have completed sixty-two drawings and fifty portraits. In addition we have made hundreds of

Audubon positioned these parakeets to show their bright colors and beautiful feathers.

sketches of bees, butterflies, dragonflies, spiders, squirrels, rabbits, snakes, lizards, flowers, seeds, plants, trees, buds —and parts of animals, feet, claws, beaks, eyes. Believe me, if *we* have not drawn it, it is not worth a second glance.

As a result of all this labor, our total combined wealth is $42. We have twenty-seven holes in our clothing (including boots and the seats of breeches) and a collection of bites, scratches, scars, scabs, burrs, thorns, and other tokens of our frontier life that would astonish a town dweller. We are much the worse for wear in every way.

Mr. Audubon has been trying to get a job as a teacher or dancing master—anything—but no one will have him. I am sure it is because of the way he looks. I heard someone say the other day, "Here comes that madman Audubon." Didn't tell Mr. A. this but advised him to get rid of that filthy suit and get himself some new clothes. So he has ordered a new garment, which will cost $40 and will take care of our "wealth."

"I didn't know that forty dollars could make a gentleman," says Mr. A. His tone is bitter.

April 4, 1822

I want to go home. I really want to go home. I must go home. Tonight I will ask him.

Fever

When Mr. Audubon came home last night, he was so pale I didn't have the heart to ask him anything. He went straight to bed and this morning was unable to get up. He sweats and shakes, and I know those signs. He has the fever, the dreaded summer disease of this place. Each year hundreds, maybe thousands of people die of it.

I have sent for Dr. Provan, who is a friend of the family.

Mr. Audubon worse. Dr. Provan stayed the night.

Mr. Audubon very weak. I have sent word to Mrs. Audubon.

Is he going to die? After all he has been through, will he die? Dr. Provan will tell me nothing, but what I see is that John James Audubon is shivering and sweating himself to death.

Better

At last. He is better. Thin and pale, but better.

Something has happened to Mr. Audubon since his illness. He is calmer, more thoughtful. He has decided that he will become a portrait artist and will give up his birds. I cannot believe it; it is as if when the illness passed, his bird fever passed too.

So I have got my wish. I am going home. But I did not figure that all the work we did together would be in vain. It will be a *sin* if those bird paintings never get published. That's what I say, a sin.

August 8, 1822
One Last Trip

Today we took our last trip together. Went out in a bayou, just the two of us. It was as if my teacher were giving me this day to be quietly among my wild friends and to say good-by.

I saw a green snake slither along the top of the water. I reached down and grabbed it, held it for a moment. Its skin was cool against my hand. Then I let it go.

The birds twittered and fluttered above our heads, so many of the ones we had already committed to paper: warblers and flycatchers and the long-legged wading birds that Mr. Audubon loves so much, ibises and spoonbills and herons. They were all there today.

Around dusk we came to a lake. My friend said, "Joseph, let us stay and have our supper here."

"What supper?" I asked, because we had no means to get a meal without our guns.

Then Mr. Audubon reached into his pocket and pulled out a blowgun made of cane which had in it a sharp arrow. He said he had learned how to make these from the Choctaw Indians. Scarcely fifteen minutes later he had stunned a wild duck with it, and the bird was roasting in our fire.

When our bellies were full, we sat on the shore, listening to the tree frogs' chorus and watching the flying squirrels perform their acrobatic leaps among the trees. Once a bull alligator bellowed and we heard the tail of a beaver slap the water.

Mr. Audubon sat quietly, letting me have my fill of the woods. Letting me say my good-bys. And I did say them. Good-by to the wild orchids. Good-by to Spanish moss, to great clumsy alligators and to the delicate little warblers, to the frogs and snakes and all the forms of wildlife that John James Audubon and I shared with each other.

And so today we parted. He cried. I wanted to. He gave me his double-barreled shotgun. He gave me chalks and paints and brushes and paper, so I can work my way home. But this is not the half of it. The biggest things John James Audubon gave me are not things I carry in my bag. They are images I will carry forever in my head and my heart.

So good-by, John James Audubon. Thank you for everything. I hope that you will never give up your dream.

January 30, 1838

It is now eighteen years since I made the trip with John James Audubon.

Today I learned that the last engraving of Audubon's work has been made. He did it; he finished *The Birds of*

Audubon's painting of ducks by a waterfall.

America Folio and a five-volume book, called *Ornithological Biographies*, to accompany it. I understand that he is the toast of England. Both here and abroad, people are clamoring to buy a complete set of the folio for $1,000.

It is just as I thought it would be. John James Audubon has become famous. But a genius is not without his faults. I can never quite forgive him for taking my name off the paintings we did together. I know that often artists do not credit their assistants. But a promise is a promise. And after all, I *did* do the flowers and plants for 50 of the 435 plates.

Are all geniuses scoundrels, I wonder? Oh, let it be, I tell myself. For after all, I have my life here in Philadelphia. I am a portrait painter and well known for it. Perhaps I owe that to John James Audubon.

Our lives will never touch again. But for a little while we were almost as close as a father and son. I will try to remember only those good times. And to think kindly of the man with whom I shared so many frontier adventures.

1. How was John James Audubon able to paint such realistic-looking birds?

2. Why did Joseph Mason go along with Audubon on the journey? What did Joseph expect to learn?

3. What did Audubon accomplish on the long journey? Would you like to have accompanied him? Give reasons for your answers.

4. What happened to make Audubon's dream come true? Why wasn't Joseph completely happy?

5. Joseph Mason admired John James Audubon and his work. Find the parts of the story where Mason described Audubon's dedication to his work.

Apply

the

Skills

A story narrated by a story character is written from a first-person point of view. Stories in the first person use many first-person pronouns.

Which of the following sentences show that "On the Frontier with Mr. Audubon" was written in the first person?

1. Sun in my eyes woke me up this morning.

2. A flatboat is really a large raft with sides.

3. On a brisk day we can travel up to fourteen miles or so.

4. The other people on the boat seem used to our slow progress.

5. Mr. Audubon has been trying to get a job.

Thinking about "Heirlooms"

You've passed through hundreds of years in this unit. Some of the people you met—John James Audubon, Joseph Mason, Phillis Wheatley, Ann Hamilton—were real people from different times in history. They were brought to life by the authors' imagination. In "Cherry Ripe," you met fictional people from the past. In "High Elk's Treasure," you read about how important one family's heirloom can be to history. You've read about heirlooms in the form of children's games and books. Some have traveled across oceans and down through many generations because young people enjoyed them so much.

These heirlooms connect our past with our present. They enrich our lives with knowledge and laughter. They spark the imagination *we* will use to create heirlooms for generations to come. Today, new books are being written, new songs sung, new inventions created. Which of them do you think will be the heirlooms of tomorrow?

1. Think about Ann in "The Cabin Faced West" and Giles in "Cherry Ripe." What things did each do to feel at home in a new place?

2. How might the story "High Elk's Treasure" be different if it were written from the grandmother's point of view?

3. Would you call "Cherry Ripe" a ghost story? How is this story like other ghost stories you have read or heard about? How is it different from others?

4. Which stories that you have read might become heirlooms or classics some day, like the ones mentioned in "Treasures from the Past"? What qualities in the stories could make them classics?

5. If Phillis Wheatley and George Washington had met, what might they have said to each other? Imagine a conversation between them. What might they have talked about?

6. What kinds of children's games do you think last for one hundred years or more? List three important qualities of such games. Which of the characters in this unit's stories do you think might have enjoyed the games described?

7. How are Chris Calle, the illustrator, and John James Audubon, the painter, alike? Name several ways.

Read on Your Own

Nightbirds on Nantucket by Joan Aiken. Doubleday.
A young girl living on Nantucket Island uncovers a wild plot to kill the king of England with a gun that will shoot clear across the Atlantic.

The Phantom Cyclist and Other Ghost Stories by Ruth Ainsworth. Scholastic Press. An exciting collection of ghost stories, some of them historical fiction.

On the Frontier with Mr. Audubon by Barbara Brenner. Coward-McCann. This novel in diary form presents John James Audubon as seen by his young assistant, Joseph Mason. The book tells of their drawing expedition down the Ohio and Mississippi Rivers.

The Cardboard Crown by Clyde Robert Bulla. T. Y. Crowell. Adam answers a knock at the door one night, and finds Olivia, who says she's a princess. Adam believes that she's a princess—but is she really? Why is she asking for a place to stay?

The Secret Garden by Frances Hodgson Burnett. Harper & Row. In this classic story, a girl goes to the country. While there, she discovers a number of secrets, including a wonderful garden.

Who Put the Cannon in the Courthouse Square? by Kay Cooper Walker. This book explains how you can uncover the history of your own town. It takes you from the questions you should ask yourself to a history that you can write yourself.

Johnny Tremain by Esther Forbes. Houghton Mifflin. In this story a silversmith's apprentice in revolutionary America becomes a patriot.

The Cabin Faced West by Jean Fritz. Coward-McCann. In this tale of colonial America, Ann Hamilton's family moves to the Pennsylvania frontier and Ann learns to cope with the resulting changes.

The Story of Phillis Wheatly by Shirley Graham. Julian Messner. A true story of a girl saved from slavery who grew up to be one of America's best-known poets.

Phoebe and the General by Judith Berry Griffin. Coward-McCann. During the Revolutionary War, a young black girl becomes General Washington's housekeeper and foils a plot against the general's life.

Sing Down the Moon by Scott O'Dell. Houghton Mifflin. In this novel, based on a true story, Navajos are forced to move three hundred miles by the U.S. Army. Bright Morning, a young woman, tells of the move and of her longing for the peace of her earlier life.

High Elk's Treasure by Virginia Driving Hawk Sneve. Holiday House. In addition to finding an important family heirloom, Joe High Elk almost loses his horse, Star, and has to rescue her from rustlers.

Sir Bertie and the Wyvern by Nicholas Wilde. Carolrhoda. Sir Bertie, an unusual English knight, likes to garden more than anything else in the world. When he is asked to do what a knight is supposed to do, the results are unexpected.

A Visit to William Blake's Inn by Nancy Willard. Harcourt Brace Jovanovich. This award-winning book creates a poetry world where William Blake runs an inn filled with very unusual people and animals.

Glossary

The glossary is a special dictionary for this book. The glossary tells you how to spell a word, how to pronounce it, and what the word means.

A blue box ■ at the end of the entry tells you that an illustration is given for that word.

The following abbreviations are used throughout the glossary: *n.*, noun; *v.*, verb; *adj.*, adjective; *adv.*, adverb; *interj.*, interjection; *prep.*, preposition; *conj.*, conjunction; *pl.*, plural; *sing.*, singular.

An accent mark (′) is used to show which syllable receives the most stress. For example, in the word *granite* [gran′ it], the first syllable receives more stress. Sometimes in words of three or more syllables, there is also a lighter mark to show that a syllable receives a lighter stress. For example, in the word *helicopter* [hel′ ə•kop′ tər], the first syllable has the most stress, and the third syllable has lighter stress.

The symbols used to show how each word is pronounced are explained in the "Pronunciation Key" on the next page.

Pronunciation Key*

a	add, map	m	move, seem	u	up, done
ā	ace, rate	n	nice, tin	û(r)	burn, term
â(r)	care, air	ng	ring, song	yo͞o	fuse, few
ä	palm, father	o	odd, hot	v	vain, eve
b	bat, rub	ō	open, so	w	win, away
ch	check, catch	ô	order, jaw	y	yet, yearn
d	dog, rod	oi	oil, boy	z	zest, muse
e	end, pet	ou	pout, now	zh	vision, pleasure
ē	equal, tree	o͝o	took, full	ə	the schwa,
f	fit, half	o͞o	pool, food		an unstressed
g	go, log	p	pit, stop		vowel representing
h	hope, hate	r	run, poor		the sound spelled
i	it, give	s	see, pass		a in *above*
ī	ice, write	sh	sure, rush		e in *sicken*
j	joy, ledge	t	talk, sit		i in *possible*
k	cool, take	th	thin, both		o in *melon*
l	look, rule	~~th~~	this, bathe		u in *circus*

*The Pronunciation Key and the short form of the key that appears on the following
right-hand pages are reprinted from the *HBJ School Dictionary*, copyright © 1985 by
Harcourt Brace Jovanovich, Inc.

A a

ab·o·li·tion [ab'ə·lish'ən] *n.* The act of doing away with or ending completely, such as a law or a custom.

ac·cu·ra·cy [ak'yər·ə·sē] *n.* Correctness; freedom from mistakes or errors.

a·cute [ə·kyoot'] *adj.* Sharp, intense, severe, keen: He had an *acute* pain in his right ankle.

a·ged [ā'jid] *adj.* Quite old: Her great-grandmother was *aged* but alert.

a·jar [ə·jär'] *adj.* Slightly open.

a·midst [ə·midst'] *prep.* Amid; among; surrounded by: She stood *amidst* hundreds of daffodils.

an·chor [ang'kər] *v.* **an·chored** To hold in place firmly; fix securely: The mailbox was *anchored* to the sidewalk.

An·glo [ang'glō'] *n.* A white North American whose ancestors were not Hispanic.

an·ni·ver·sa·ry [an'ə·vûr'sə·rē] *n.* A day of the year on which an event took place in a past year: The two-hundredth *anniversary* of the adoption of the Declaration of Independence was on July 4, 1976.

ap·pre·ci·ate [ə·prē'shē·āt'] *v.* To recognize how good something is; to value or enjoy: To *appreciate* paintings, you should go to art museums often.

ap·pre·hen·sive [ap'rə·hen'siv] *adj.* Fearful; worried; anxious: He was *apprehensive* about the interview.

ap·pren·tice [ə·pren'tis] *n.* A person who works for someone else in order to learn an art, craft, or trade.

ap·pro·pri·ate [ə·prō'prē·it] *adj.* Right for the occasion; fitting and proper; suitable: Running shoes are *appropriate* for many activities.

apt [apt] *adj.* Likely: The trees are *apt* to be turning color in early autumn.

ar·ti·fi·cial·ly [är'tə·fish'əl·lē] *adv.* Using something that is made by human labor; not naturally: This soda is *artificially* flavored.—**ar·ti·fi·cial** *adj.*

as·cent [ə·sent'] *n.* The act of going up, climbing, or rising upward.■

as·sume [ə·soom'] *v.* **as·sumed** To suppose to be true; to take as true without proof: You may *assume* that a full moon will occur each month.

at·trac·tive [ə·trak'tiv] *adj.* Pleasing; winning attention: That is an *attractive* window display.

a·venge [ə·venj'] *v.* **a·venged** To repay an insult, a wrong, or an injury: We *avenged* the wrong done to our family name.

B b

back·stop [bak′stop′] *adj. use* Substituting for, in case of an emergency; acting as a backup: a *backstop* party plan.

back·stroke [bak′strōk′] *n.* A swimming stroke made while on one's back.

bar·ren [bar′ən] *adj.* Not able to produce crops: This is *barren* soil.

ba·sic [bā′sik] *adj.* Forming a base or basis of: Flour is a *basic* ingredient of bread.

bass [bās] *n.* **bas·ses 1** In singing, the lowest male voice. **2** A singer having such a voice.

bas·si·net [bas′ə·net′] *n.* A cradle, often with a hood over one end, for use as a baby's bed.

beam [bēm] *n.* A long, heavy piece of wood or metal, used as a horizontal, or crosswise, support of a building. ■

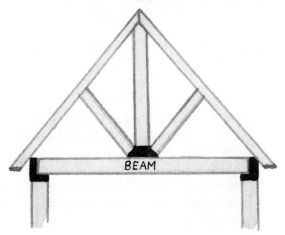

BEAM

bed [bed] *n.* The ground beneath a body of water: The lake *bed* was light-colored and sandy.

be·tray [bi·trā′] *v.* To hand over to the authorities, to give away: I swore her to silence and hoped she wouldn't *betray* my secret.

bill [bil] *v.* **billed** To send a statement of money owed for work done or for things supplied: The store *billed* me for my order.

bit·ter [bit′ər] *adj.* Resentful; having harsh feelings: They were *bitter* over the loss of their house.

bleach [blēch] *n.* A chemical liquid or powder used to whiten something or make it colorless.

bough [bou] *n.* A main branch of a tree: Don't hit your head on the low *bough* of that tree. ■

a	add	i	it	o͞o	took	oi	oil
ā	ace	ī	ice	o͞o	pool	ou	pout
â	care	o	odd	u	up	ng	ring
ä	palm	ō	open	û	burn	th	thin
e	end	ô	order	yo͞o	fuse	th	this
ē	equal					zh	vision

ə =	{	a in *above*	e in *sicken*	i in *possible*
		o in *melon*	u in *circus*	

brace [brās] *v.* **braced** To prepare for a jolt or bump; to support oneself firmly beforehand, in expectation of a jolt.

braid [brād] *n.* Three or more strands, as of hair, woven together; plait. (For illustration, see **plait.**)

brand [brand] *n.* **1** A mark made with a hot iron to show ownership: This *brand* identifies cattle belonging to the the Bar X Ranch. **2** A particular kind, make, or quality, which can be identified by a trademark: My dog likes this *brand* of dog biscuits.

breast stroke [brest'strōk'] *n.* A swimming stroke made while one swimmer lies face downward, moving the arms together from above the head to the sides and making froglike kicks with the legs.

bri·dle [brīd'(ə)l] *n.* The part of a harness that fits around the head of a horse and includes the bit and reins: A rider uses a *bridle* to control the horse. ■

broad·cast [brod'kast'] *v.* **broad·cast** or **broad·casted** To send out by means of radio or television: The World Series was *broadcast* by our local television station.

brooch [brōch] *n.* An ornamental pin, often of gold, silver, or jewels, fas-

tened with a catch and worn near the neck of a garment. ■

buf·fet [boo·fā'] *n.* A meal at which guests serve themselves from dishes or platters laid out on a table.

bur·lap [bûr'lap] *n.* a rough, natural cloth: The rice sat in the storeroom in huge *burlap* sacks.

bur·y [ber'ē] *v.* To cover or conceal by covering with earth: The pirates will *bury* the treasure.

but·ter·fly [but'ər·flī'] *n.* A swimming stroke similar to the breaststroke; in it, both legs are kicked up and down while the arms are moved in a circular motion.

C c

cane·brake [kān'brāk'] *n.* A thick growth of cane plants, such as bamboo, sugar cane, or rattan.

can·vas [kan'vəs] **1** *n.* A heavy, strong cloth made of cotton, hemp, or flax and used for sails, tents, some items of clothing, and for painting on. **2** *adj. use* An item made of such cloth: I often wear *canvas* shoes.

cap·tive [kap'tiv] *n.* A person or animal captured and not allowed to escape.

care·worn [kâr'wôrn'] *adj.* Showing the effects of great worry: Look at that man's *careworn* face.

cat·a·log [kat'ə·lôg'] *n.* A book or pamphlet describing items for sale and listing prices.

cat·e·go·ry [kat'ə·gôr'ē] *n.* A group, class, or division in a classification: Bugs are a *category* of insects.

Cel·si·us [sel'sē·əs] *adj.* According to the Celsius, or centigrade, temperature scale, on which the freezing point of water is set at 0 degrees and the boiling point is set at 100 degrees: It went up to thirty degrees *Celsius* last week.

chain saw [chān'sô'] *n.* A portable power saw with teeth linked together in an endless chain. ■

chal·leng·er [chal'ənj·ər] *n.* A person or team that asks for a contest with another or others: The team from the next town is always the *challenger.*

chaps [chaps] *n.* Strong leather trousers without backs or a seat. They are worn over regular trousers as protection for the legs.

char·ac·ter·is·tic [kar'ik·tə·ris'tik] *n.* A special quality trait, or feature, that helps to distinguish one person or thing from another: The main *characteristic* of my dog is faithfulness.

chem·i·cal [kem'i·kəl] *n.* A substance obtained by or used in a process having to do with chemistry. Chemicals may be solids, liquids, or gases. The simplest chemicals are elements, such as oxygen or copper. Two or more elements may stick, or bond, together to make chemical compounds, such as water, alcohol, or starch.

chimp [chimp] *n.* An informal word for chimpanzee.

chron·o·log·i·cal [kron'ə·loj'i·kəl] *adj.* Arranged in the order in which the events happened; in time order: a *chronological* outline.

chrys·an·the·mum [kri·san'thə·məm] *n.* Any of a large variety of plants having round, showy flowers with many petals. The plants bloom in the fall, in shades of white, yellow, red, and bronze, among other colors.

cil·i·a [sil'ē·ə] *n. pl., sing.* **cil·i·um** [sil'ē·əm] Tiny hairlike outgrowths on leaves and insects' wings or other body parts. They aid some microscopic cells in moving about.

a	add	i	it	o͞o	took	oi	oil
ā	ace	ī	ice	o͞o	pool	ou	pout
â	care	o	odd	u	up	ng	ring
ä	palm	ō	open	û	burn	th	thin
e	end	ô	order	yo͞o	fuse	th	this
ē	equal					zh	vision

ə = { a in *above*   e in *sicken*   i in *possible*
      o in *melon*   u in *circus* }

cinch [sinch] *n.* A slang word for something that is easy and sure: Making peanut butter sandwiches for lunch is a *cinch*.

clam·or [klam′ər] *v.* **clam·or·ing** To make a loud and noisy demand: The children are *clamoring* for these popular dolls.

clas·sic [klas′ik] *n.* A novel, a musical composition, or some other work of art of the highest quality or rank: *Ivanhoe* is a *classic* novel.

coarse [kôrs] *adj.* Made up of large particles, or pieces; not fine: The shore was covered with *coarse* gravel rather than with the fine sand we expected.

com·mu·ni·cate [kə·myoo′nə·kāt′] *v.* To give or exchange thoughts, news, or information; to express or exchange ideas or information: The poem *communicates* the author's thoughts.

com·pa·ny [kum′pə·nē] *n.*, *pl.* **com·pa·nies** A military unit headed by a captain; a body of soldiers of two or more platoons.

com·pe·ti·tion [kom′pə·tish′ən] *n.* A contest between rivals; *also* one's rivals or competitors: The *competition* in this race will be hard to beat.

com·po·si·tion [kom′pə·zish′ən] *n.* **1** A short essay. **2** Something that is put together; an original creation, as a piece of music.

con·fu·sion [kən·fyoo′shən] *n.* Untidyness; disorder: The broken traffic light, the flooded water main, and the repair trucks left our street corner in great *confusion*.

con·test·ant [kən·tes′tənt] *n.* A person who enters or takes part in a contest, such as a race or other competition.

con·tral·to [kən·tral′tō] *n.*, *pl.* **con·tral·tos** **1** The lowest female singing voice. **2** Someone having such a voice.

con·trib·ute [kən·trib′yoot′] *v.* **con·trib·ut·ed** To help in bringing about a result: Many people *contributed* to the success of the book fair.

con·vert·ed [kən·vûrt′id] *adj.* Changed from one use to another: The apartment is a *converted* carriage house.

con·vince [kən·vins′] *v.* **con·vinced** Persuade: The salesman *convinced* me to buy his product.

cor·al [kor′əl *or* kôr′əl] **1** *n.* A stonelike substance formed by the skeletons of many tiny sea animals. **2** *adj. use* Made of coral: a *coral* reef. ■

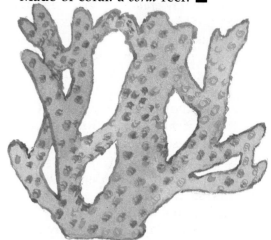

cor·du·roy [kôr′də·roi] *pl.* **cor·du·roys** **1** *n.* A strong cotton cloth with raised velvetlike ridges. **2** *adj. use* Something made of this cloth: a *corduroy* jumper.

corn·silk [kôrn′silk′] *n.* The long, threadlike, silky tuft, or tassel, at the end of an ear of corn.

coun·cil [koun′səl] *n.* A group of elected people who make laws for a city.

cou·ri·er [kŏŏr′ē·ər *or* kûr′ē·ər] *n.* A messenger sent to deliver a message quickly.

crag [krag] *n.* A rough, broken piece of rock jutting out from a cliff. ■

crawl [krôl] *v.* **crawled** To move slowly: Because of the road construction, the cars merely *crawled* along the road.

creak [krēk] *v.* **creaked** To make a loud, squeaking noise: The old wooden floors *creaked* when I walked on them.

crea·ture [krē′chər] *n.* **1** Any living person or animal. **2** Any being created in the imagination: Peter Rabbit is one of many delightful *creatures* in the stories of Beatrix Potter.

cred·u·lous [krej′ŏŏ·ləs] *adj.* Believing too easily; open to being misled: He was so *credulous* that others often tried to fool him.

cre·o·sote [krē′ə·sōt′] *n.* An oily liquid made from coal tar; it keeps wood from rotting.

crit·ter [krit′ər] *n.* A dialect word for creature; a person or an animal.

croc·o·dile [krok′ə·dīl] *n.* A large liz-

ardlike animal resembling an alligator, with long jaws, armored skin, and clawlike feet.

cro·quet [krō·kā′] *n.* An outdoor game in which players use mallets to knock wooden balls through small wire arches called wickets. ■

cross·word puz·zle [krôs′wûrd puz′əl] *n.* A puzzle played on a set of numbered squares, which must be filled with letters spelling words crosswise and downward. Clues are given for words to be filled in. ■

a	add	i	it	o͞o	took	oi	oil
ā	ace	ī	ice	o͞o	pool	ou	pout
â	care	o	odd	u	up	ng	ring
ä	palm	ō	open	û	burn	th	thin
e	end	ô	order	yo͞o	fuse	th	this
ē	equal					zh	vision

ə = { a in *above*   e in *sicken*   i in *possible*
      o in *melon*   u in *circus* }

crum·ple [krum′pəl] *v.* **crum·pled** To fall down, as in a faint; to collapse: She *crumpled* to the floor after hearing the bad news.

cur·sive [kûr′siv] *adj.* Written with the letters joined together, often in flowing strokes. ■

D d

ded·i·ca·tion [ded′ə·kā′shən] *n.* Words written, as in a book or on a musical composition, to honor someone or show respect or gratitude to someone.

de·fy [di·fī′] *v.* to resist, go against: She used to *defy* her father all the time.

de·lay [di·lā′] *n.* Wait; a putting off until a later time: We had so many *delays* in getting to the capital that we missed the ceremony.

de·moc·ra·cy [di·mok′rə·sē] *n.* A form of government that is run by the people, either directly in town meetings or by the election of representatives to manage the government and make the laws.

dense [dens] *adj.* Thick, crowded together; packed: The fog was so *dense*

that we could not see the sides of the road.—**dense′ly** *adv.*

de·pos·it [di·poz′it] *v.* To set down; to put down; to lay down a layer: Floods *deposit* mud over the lawns and streets each year.

dep·o·si·tion [dep′ə·zish′ən] *n.* The action of laying down, as a layer of mud in a flood.

de·sign [di·zīn′] *v.* **de·signed** To work out plans for; to make up plans to fit a special purpose: The bridge was *designed* to carry a heavy load of traffic.

des·per·ate·ly [des′pər·it·lē] *adv.* In an extreme manner: They needed money *desperately* to avoid starvation.—**des·per·ate** *adj.*

dis·a·gree [dis′ə·grē′] *v.* **dis·a·greed** To have a different opinion; not agree: Your plan is a poor one; I *disagree* with it.

dis·may [dis·mā′] *n.* A feeling of uneasiness; alarm; loss of confidence in the face of trouble or danger: The threatening clouds and thunder filled them with *dismay*.

doubt [dout] *v.* **doubt·ed** To be uncertain about; not be sure of; not believe: They *doubted* that the magician could saw his assistant in half.

dra·mat·ic [drə·mat′ik] *adj.* Exciting; impressive; thrilling: Thunder and lightning are *dramatic* when you're safely indoors.

draw·ing room [drô′ing rŏŏm *or* rŏŏm] *n.* A room in which guests are received and entertained; a parlor.

drow·si·ness [drou′zē·nis] *n.* Sleepiness: *Drowsiness* overtook him soon after he had begun to study.

E e

ea·ger [ē′gər] *adj.* Wanting greatly; desiring very much: They were *eager* to see the circus.—**ea′ger·ly** *adv.*

ef·fi·cient [i·fish′ənt] *adj.* Able to get results with the least waste of time and energy; capable: *Efficient* workers turn out much work in little time.—**ef·fi′cient·ly** *adv.*

e·lab·o·rate [i·lab′ər·it] *adj.* Worked out carefully with many details, often fancy and costly: The dress was decorated with *elaborate* embroidery in silver and gold threads.—**e·lab′o·rate·ly** *adv.*

e·las·tic [i·last′tik] *adj.* Able to return to its original shape after being pulled, squeezed, or bent: Sponges are very *elastic*.

eld·er·ly [el′dər·lē] *adj.* Past middle age; somewhat old: His parents are *elderly*, but they have not stopped working.

e·lec·tric charge [i·lek′trik chärj] *n.* An amount of electricity: Rubbing an object such as a carpet will produce an *electric charge*.

e·lec·tron [i·lek′tron′] *n.* A tiny particle of matter; each electron moves around the core (nucleus) of an atom and carries one unit of negative electricity. Different substances have different numbers of electrons: The helium atom has two *electrons*. ■

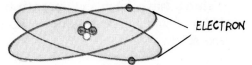

ELECTRON

e·lec·tron·ics [i·lek′tron′iks] *n.* A branch of study that deals with the production and uses of electrons in vacuums and gases: We owe the invention of radios and radar to *electronics*.

el·e·gant [el′ə·gənt] *adj.* Tasteful; fine in quality; luxurious: an *elegant* home.

e·mer·gen·cy [i′mûr′jən·sē] *n., pl.* **e·mer·gen·cies** An unexpected need for quick action: Don responded to the *emergency* by calling the fire department.

em·pha·sis [em′fə·sis] *n., pl.* **em·pha·ses** [em′fə·sēz] Special importance or force given to something: The *emphasis* in a democracy is on freedom.

em·pha·size [em′fə·sīz] *v.* **em·pha·sized** To give special importance to; to point out for special attention: The speaker *emphasized* the need for good health.

a	add	i	it	o͞o	took	oi	oil
ā	ace	ī	ice	o͞o	pool	ou	pout
â	care	o	odd	u	up	ng	ring
ä	palm	ō	open	û	burn	th	thin
e	end	ô	order	yo͞o	fuse	th	this
ē	equal					zh	vision

ə = { **a** in *above* **e** in *sicken* **i** in *possible*
       o in *melon* **u** in *circus* }

en·grav·ing [in·grā′ving] *n.* A picture or print made by printing from a block or plate of metal, wood, or stone, into which marks, letters, or pictures have been cut, or carved: Many *engravings* are works of fine art. ■

en·thu·si·as·tic [in·thoo′zē·as′tik] *adj.* Keenly interested and approving; eager; full of lively excitement: Susan was *enthusiastic* about becoming a cheerleader.

es·say [es′ā] *n.* A short composition on a single subject: Charles Lamb wrote a famous *essay* called "A Dissertation on Roast Pig." *Dissertation* is another word for *essay*.

et cet·er·a [et set′ər·ə] And so on; and other things: *Et cetera* comes from a Latin phrase meaning "and all the rest."

e·ven·tu·al·ly [i·ven′choo·əl·ē] *adv.* In the end; in the course of time; finally: He worked for many years in a lowly position, but *eventually* he got the promotion he wanted.

ex·am·i·na·tion [ig·zam′ə·nā′shən] *n.* A test of knowledge or skill; a list of questions about a subject: I think I passed the *examination* in history.

ex·ist [ig·zist′] *v.* To have life, being, or reality; to be: People cannot *exist* without food, air, and water.

ex·po·sure [ik·spō′zhər] *n.* The amount of time needed for light to act on a photographic film: The day was dark, so I needed a long *exposure* for the pictures.

ex·ten·sive [ik·sten′siv] *adj.* Spreading over a large area; of great extent; wide: The ranch covered an *extensive* part of the county.

F f

fac·tu·al [fak′choo·əl] *adj.* Based on facts.

faith·ful [fāth′fəl] *adj.* Loyal; true; trusting: Even though our team is losing, we're still *faithful* fans.

fan·cy [fan′sē] *v.* **fan·cy·ing** To imagine; to picture in one's mind: Can you *fancy* yourself back in the days of the dinosaurs?

fath·om [fath′əm] *n.* A unit of measure six feet long, used mainly to measure the depth of water.

fern [fûrn] *n.* Any of a large group of plants that have feathery leaves but no flowers or seeds: *Ferns* reproduce by means of spores.

fi·ber·glass [fī′bər·glas′] *n.* A fine, threadlike material of spun glass, used for insulating buildings, making boats, and for weaving into fabrics: *fiberglass* curtains.

flank [flangk] *n.* The side of a person or an animal between the ribs and the hip. ■

flint [flint] *n.* A hard kind of stone that makes a spark when struck against steel.

flop [flop] *v.* **flopped** To fall, drop, or move clumsily or heavily: I was so tired after the long hike that I just *flopped* into bed.

force [fôrs] *n.* Energy that acts on a body or thing at rest, producing, changing, or stopping its motion: Two natural *forces* are magnetic *force* and gravitational *force.*

fore·stall [fôr·stôl′] *v.* To prevent by taking action first, or beforehand: He found that he could *forestall* another lecture on manners by behaving well at the party.

fran·ti·cal·ly [fran′tik·lē] *adv.* In a wildly excited manner: *Frantically,* they tried to find their way out of the thick forest.—**fran′tic** *adj.*

free·style [frē′stīl′] *adj.* In swimming or skating event, using whatever stroke or style the contestant chooses.

fric·tion [frik′shən] *n.* The resistance to motion (tendency to remain at rest) when two surfaces touch or rub together or when one slides over another: Oil, ball bearings, wheels, and rollers help to overcome *friction* and make things easier to move.

frilled [frild] *adj.* Having frills, or ruffles, around the edge.

fron·tier [frun·tir′] *n.* The farthest part of a settled region where unsettled lands begin: Just beyond the *frontier* town lay unexplored wilderness areas.

froth [frôth] *v.* **froth·ing** To cause to form very small bubbles; to foam: He stirred the cocoa rapidly, *frothing* it into light tan bubbles.

fu·ri·ous·ly [fyŏŏr′ē·əs·lē] *adv.* With large excited movements; speedily; greatly energetic: They started digging through the sand *furiously,* trying to find the lost bracelet.

G g

gan·gly [gang′glē] *adj.* Gangling; tall, awkward, and lanky.

a	add	i	it	ŏŏ	took	oi	oil
ā	ace	ī	ice	ōō	pool	ou	pout
â	care	o	odd	u	up	ng	ring
ä	palm	ō	open	û	burn	th	thin
e	end	ô	order	yōō	fuse	th	this
ē	equal					zh	vision

ə =	{	a in *above*	e in *sicken*	i in *possible*
		o in *melon*	u in *circus*	

gen·er·a·tion [jen′ə·rā′shən] *n.* A single step in natural descent, or ancestry; the time between the birth of parents and the birth of their children: The land and the house had been in the family for many *generations.*

gin·ger·ly [jin′jər·lē] *adv.* In a careful manner; cautiously: Karen stepped *gingerly,* as if she were walking on eggs.

gleam [glēm] *n.* A faint light or one that shines for a short time only: We saw a candle *gleam* through the window of the old farm cottage.

gli·der [glī′dər] *n.* A light aircraft without a motor that depends on rising air currents to keep it in the air. ■

grav·i·ty-pow·ered [grav′ə·tē·pou′ərd] *adj.* Supplied with power by gravity; the natural force that causes all objects to move or fall toward the center of the earth.

graze [grāz] *v.* **grazed** To feed on growing grasses: Sheep *grazed* contentedly in the green meadows.

gren·a·dier [gren′ə·dir′] *n.* At one time a soldier assigned to carry and throw grenades—small bombs thrown by hand or fired from a rifle.

grog·gi·ly [grog′i·lē] *adv.* In , an unsteady, shaky manner.—**grog′gy** *adj.*

grudg·ing·ly [gruj′ing·lē] *adv.* Unwilling, resentfully: Patrick washed the windows *grudgingly,* wishing he were at ball practice instead.

grump·y [grum′pē] *adj.* Bad-tempered, grouchy, cranky: Mattie was *grumpy* all morning because she had not slept well last night.

guar·an·tee [gar′ən·tē′] *v.* **guar·an·teed** To declare with certainty; to assure with conviction; to state absolutely, without *ifs, ands,* or *buts:* He wants to become a stand-up comic—and he is *guaranteed* funny!

gut·ter [gut′ər] *n.* A channel along the lower edge of a roof for carrying away rain water. ■

GUTTER

gym·na·si·um [jim·nā′zē·əm] *n.* A building or large room equipped for training athletes or for indoor sports events.

H h

hand·i·capped [han′dē·kapt′] *adj.* Physically or mentally disabled; crippled; having a handicap or disability.

hare·brained [hâr′brānd′] *adj.* Giddy; foolish; reckless: That is a *harebrained* invention if I ever saw one.

haunch [hônch] *n. pl.* **haunch·es** The hindquarter of an animal.

haunt [hônt] *v.* To disturb by coming often to the mind or memory: I can't get the tune out of my mind; it *haunts* me.

hearth [härth] *n.* The floor of a fireplace, usually of stone or brick, and often extending a short way into the room. (For illustration, see **mantel.**)

heave [hēv] *v.* **heaved** or **hove** To rise and fall by turns; to stir and toss: The waves *heaved*, tossing the small boat high at one moment, then lowering it rapidly the next.

he·li·um [hē′lē·əm] *n.* A very light gas that has no odor or color and will not burn. It is an element and is used to inflate airships and balloons. In a liquid form, it is used as a refrigerant.

hide [hīd] *n.* The raw or tanned skin of an animal, especially that of a large animal: Tanning makes a *hide* into leather. ■

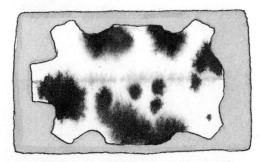

hol·low [hol′ō] *adj.* Not solid; having nothing on the inside.

hov·er [huv′ər *or* hov′ər] *v.* **hov·er·ing** To stay in the air in or near the same place without traveling forward, sideways, or backward: Hummingbirds *hover* while eating nectar from flowers.

hu·man·i·ty [hyo͞o·man′ə·tē] *n.* Human beings; the human race; people.

hum·ble [hum′bəl] *adj.* Modest; not proud: Although she was famous, she remained *humble*.

I i

im·mense [i·mens′] *adj.* Very large, vast; huge: Some whales are *immense*.

im·pu·ta·tion [im′pyo͞o·tā′shən] *n.* An accusation; the charging of a fault or wrongdoing.

in·come [in′kum′] *n.* Money that comes in from work, property rents, investments, or business: Taxes are based on yearly *income*.

in·crease [in·krēs′] *v.* **in·creased** To grow in number or size: These plants will *increase* until they cover the entire lawn.

a	add	i	it	o͞o	took	oi	oil
ā	ace	ī	ice	o͞o	pool	ou	pout
â	care	o	odd	u	up	ng	ring
ä	palm	ō	open	û	burn	th	thin
e	end	ô	order	yo͞o	fuse	th	this
ē	equal					zh	vision

ə = { a in *above*   e in *sicken*   i in *possible*   o in *melon*   u in *circus* }

in·cred·i·ble [in·kred'ə·bəl] *adj.* Too unusual, extraordinary, or strange to be believable; seemingly impossible; unbelievable: The tale was so strange that it seemed *incredible.*

in·cur [in·kûr'] *v.* **in·curred** To be the receiver of something unpleasant especially through one's own actions.

in·di·vid·u·al [in·də·vij'oo·əl] *n.* A swimming competition in which the swimmer races against the clock for a personal time score.

in·fan·try [in'fən·trē] *n.* A group of soldiers who are trained and equipped to fight on foot. ■

in·flam·ma·tion [in'flə·mā'shən] *n.* An infection or irritation in some body part, with symptoms of redness, pain, heat, and swelling.

in·ter·est [in'tər·ist *or* in'trist] *n.* Money paid by a borrower, such as a bank, for the use of the money borrowed: *Interest* is usually figured as a percentage of the amount borrowed.

in·ter·view [in'tər·vyoo'] *n.* A meeting in which a reporter asks questions of someone to obtain information to be published or broadcast.

in·volve [in·volv'] *v.* **in·volved** To have or include as a necessary part: Dentistry *involves* filling cavities in teeth.

J j

jag·ged·y [jag'id·ē] *adj.* Having a notched edge; having points sticking out; jagged.

john·ny·cake [jon'ē·kāk'] *n.* A flat bread or cake made of cornmeal and baked on a griddle.

K k

ker·chief [kûr'chif] *n.* A piece of cloth, usually square, worn as a head covering or as a scarf.

kil·o·me·ter [kil'ə·mē'tər *or* ki·lom'ə·tər] *n.* A metric unit of length equal to 1,000 meters (about five-eighths of a mile).

knap·sack [nap'sak'] *n.* A bag worn strapped to the back and used for carrying clothes, supplies, and so on. ■

knoll [nōl] *n.* A small rounded hill.

L l

land·scape [land′skāp′] *n.* A picture showing a section of natural scenery on land from a single point of view. ■

lan·tern [lan′tərn] *n.* A case with sides of glass, paper, or some other material to protect a light inside from wind and through which the light can be seen: She found her way through the woods by the light of a *lantern*.

lap [lap] *n.* One of several trips up and down a swimming pool or around a race track: Our best track star made the first *lap* around the track in record time.

lar·der [lär′dər] *n.* A place for storing food; a pantry.

lar·ynx [lar′ingks] *n., pl.* **la·ryn·ges** [lə·rin′jēz] *or* **lar′ynx·es** The upper part of the windpipe, where the vocal cords are located.

lib·er·ate [lib′ə·rāt′] *v.* **lib·er·at·ing** To set free: The *liberating* forces moved steadily across the country.

lick·ing [lik′ing] *n.* An informal word for a whipping or a beating.

limp [limp] *adj.* Not stiff; easy to bend; soft; droopy: The swim was so relaxing that she felt as *limp* as a rag.

lo·cal [lō′kəl] *adj.* Of a neighborhood, region, or other small place or area: The garden tools are sold by a *local* store.

lu·mi·nous [lōō′mə·nəs] *adj.* Giving off a glow of light: The full moon was *luminous* in the dark sky.

M m

mag·is·trate [maj′is·trāt′ *or* maj′is·trit] *n.* A government official with power to put the law in force.

mane [mān] *n.* The long hair that grows on or around the neck of some animals such as the horse and the lion.

ma·ni·ac [mā′nē·ak′] *n.* A violently insane person.

man-o′-war or **man-of-war** [man′ə(v)·wôr′] *n.* An armed warship belonging to a country's navy.

a	add	i	it	ōō	took	oi	oil
ā	ace	ī	ice	ōō	pool	ou	pout
â	care	o	odd	u	up	ng	ring
ä	palm	ō	open	û	burn	th	thin
e	end	ô	order	yōō	fuse	th	this
ē	equal					zh	vision

ə = { a in *above*   e in *sicken*   i in *possible*
      o in *melon*   u in *circus* }

man·tel [man′təl] *n.* The shelf over a fireplace: Over the *mantel* hung a large mirror. ■

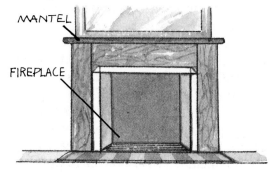

MANTEL

FIREPLACE

man·u·fac·tur·er [man′yə·fak′chər·er] *n.* A person or company in the business of making a product: Mr. Carson is a *manufacturer* of toys.

may·or [mā′ər] *n.* The chief government official of a city or town: Who is the *mayor* of your hometown?

mem·o·ra·ble [mem′ər·ə·bəl] *adj.* Easy to remember; worth being remembered: The class picnic was a *memorable* day.

mend [mend] *v.* **mend·ed** To repair; to put something broken in working order again: The toymaker *mended* Pinocchio's broken nose.

mi·cro·film [mī′krə·film′] *n.* Film used for taking very small photographs of book pages, newspapers, and so on, so that these items can be preserved and stored in a small space: Libraries have old newspapers on *microfilm*.

mist [mist] *n.* A cloud of very fine droplets of water hanging, or suspended, in the air: It wasn't raining, but there was a *mist* in the air.

mod·est·ly [mod′ist·lē] *adv.* In a bashful or humble manner; shyly.—**mod·est** *adj.*

mois·ture [mois′chər] *n.* Small droplets of water, causing slight wetness in the air or on a surface; dampness: The *moisture* that collects on leaves during the night is called dew.

mold [mōld] *v.* To form into a shape: Potters *mold* clay into vases and bowls.

mol·lusk [mol′əsk] *n.* Any one of a group of soft-bodied sea animals without segments and usually with the protection of a hard shell: Oysters, clams, mussels, snails, and squid are *mollusks*. ■

moss [môs] *n.* A very small plant that grows without flowers in clumps in rocks, trees, and the ground.

mouth [mouth] *n.* The part of a river where the water empties into a larger body of water, such as a sea.

mu·ni·tion [myoo·nish′ən] *n.* (usually pl.) guns and other arms or supplies for armies: Without *munitions*, the army could not fight.

muse [myooz] *v.* **mused** To consider thoughtfully at length.

N n

name·sake [nām′sāk] *n.* A person named for someone else: My baby sister Cicely is the *namesake* of Cicely Tyson.

na·tion·al [nash′ən·əl] *adj.* Having to do with a nation as a whole: Congress passes our *national* laws.

nat·u·ral [nach′ər·əl] *n.* An informal word describing a person whose inborn ability especially suits him or her to a particular activity: He is a *natural* on the parallel bars.

neigh [nā] *v.* To make the sound of a horse: The horses in the stable *neighed* loudly.

neu·tral [n(y)o͞o′tral] *adj.* Having neither a positive nor a negative electric charge.

no·tion [nō′shən] *n.* An idea, opinion, or belief: My *notion* of the best time to go is now!

nu·tri·ent [n(y)o͞o′trē·ənt] *n.* A substance that nourishes, or keeps one alive and healthy: Fruits and vegetables have many *nutrients* in them.

O o

o·blige [ə·blīj′] *v.* To owe a debt of thanks to someone for a favor done: I am much *obliged* to you for helping me.

ob·ser·va·tion [ob′zər·vā′shən] *n.* The act of watching, or seeing and noting: The doctor's *observations* gave him clues about the patient's illness.

ob·serve [əb·zûrv′] *v.* **ob·served** To see and take notice of: Henry *observed* a stranger at the square dance.

o·gre [ō′gər] *n.* In fairy tales, a monster or giant who is said to eat people.

o·mit [ō·mit′] *v.* **o·mit·ted** To leave out; not include: I *omitted* an important sentence when I copied my book report.

or·gan·ized [ôr′gən·īzd′] *adj.* Having a formal arrangement; brought together for a special purpose: We spent all afternoon playing *organized* games.

out·look [out′lo͝ok′] *n.* A way of thinking or feeling about something: Terri has a cheerful *outlook* on life.

out·rig·ger [out′rig′ər] *n.* A frame extending from the side of a small boat to a float that prevents the boat from tipping over.

a	add	i	it	o͞o	took	oi	oil
ā	ace	ī	ice	o͞o	pool	ou	pout
â	care	o	odd	u	up	ng	ring
ä	palm	ō	open	û	burn	th	thin
e	end	ô	order	yo͞o	fuse	th	this
ē	equal					zh	vision

ə = { a in *above*   e in *sicken*   i in *possible*
       o in *melon*   u in *circus* }

o·ver·joyed [ō′vər·joid′] *adj.* Very happy; filled with joy: The parents were *overjoyed* at the child's good performance in the dance recital.

P p

par·ti·cle [pär′ti·kəl] *n.* A very small bit or piece; speck: There were *particles* of dust on the furniture.

pay·off [pā′ôf′] *n.* Something in return, as payment; reward: I get a great *payoff* in enjoyment when I read.

peas·ant [pez′ənt] *n.* In Europe, a working-class country person, such as a farmer.

peer [pir] *v.* To look closely in order to see clearly: They *peered* into the well, trying to see if it held water.

per·form [pər·fôrm′] *v.* To give a demonstration of artistic skill, as playing an instrument: The pianist will *perform* a Beethoven sonata.

per·mis·sion [pər·mish′ən] *n.* The act of allowing, of giving leave to do something: May I have *permission* to leave school early today?

per·son·al·i·ty [pûr′sən·al′ə·tē] *n.* The characteristics or qualities that make each person different from every other person: It takes many characteristics to make up a *personality*.

pes·ti·len·tial [pes′tə·len′shəl] *adj.* Causing a pestilence, a disease, such as a plague, that spreads rapidly and may be harmful or fatal to many persons.

phos·phor·es·cent [fos′fə·res′ənt] *adj.* Giving off light without heat: The light of fireflies is *phosphorescent*.

phys·i·cal weath·er·ing [fiz′i·kəl weth′ ər·ing] *n.* Destruction of rocks by the action of air, water, or ice.

pin·ey woods [pī′nē woodz] *n.* A large group of growing trees, the greatest number of which are pines. ■

ping [ping] *v.* To make a sound like that of a stone hitting a piece of metal: The stone from Don's slingshot *pinged* against the metal roof.

pin·ion [pin′yən] *v.* **pin·ion·ing** To prevent a bird from flying by cutting off the last joint of its wing or by tying the wings.

plait [plat *or* plāt] *n.* Three or more strands, as of hair, woven together; a braid. ■

ple·si·o·sau·rus [plē′sē·ə·sôr′əs] *n.* Any of a group of sea animals that are no longer living. They had small heads, long necks, four paddlelike flippers instead of legs, and short tails. ∎

plop [plop] *v.* **plopped** To drop, fall, or move suddenly, making a sound like that of an object striking water.

plot [plot] *n.* The main order of events in a play, a story, or a novel: The *plot* of the book I read last night was very exciting.

plough [plou] *n.* Another spelling of **plow,** a large tool for cutting into the soil and turning it over before seeds are planted.

pol·lute [pə·lōōt′] *v.* **pol·lut·ed** To make dirty or impure: Some industries *pollute* streams and rivers by pouring unsafe chemicals into them.

pol·y·es·ter [pol′ē·es′tər] *n.* Any of several artificially produced substances called resins that are used for making paints, plastics, and cloth.

port·a·ble [pôr′tə·bəl] *adj.* Capable of being easily carried or moved: I will take my *portable* typewriter with me on vacation.

por·ter [pôr′tər] *n.* Someone who is hired to carry baggage, as at an airport or train or bus station.

port·fo·li·o [pôrt·fō′lē·ō] *n.* A carrying case for drawings, manuscripts, and so on; by extension, the collection in such a case: Ken made up a *portfolio* of all the stories he had written.

pout [pout] *v.* **pouted** To push out the lips when feeling annoyed or ill-humored.

pre·cious [presh′əs] *adj.* Worth a great deal; valuable: Diamonds, rubies, sapphires, and emeralds are *precious* gemstones.

pre·scribe [pri·skrīb′] *v.* To order the use of something, as a treatment or a medicine: The doctor *prescribed* a syrup for my cough.

pre·vious [prē′vē·əs] *adj.* Happening or coming before something else; earlier: The corn crop had been larger the *previous* year.

pride [prīd] *n.* A sense of one's own worth and dignity; respect for oneself: She had *pride* in her ability to cook well.

proc·ess [pros′es] *v.* To put through a series of operations in order to produce something; to prepare or treat by some special method: This factory *processes* canned soups.

a	add	i	it	ōō	took	oi	oil
ā	ace	ī	ice	ōō	pool	ou	pout
â	care	o	odd	u	up	ng	ring
ä	palm	ō	open	û	burn	th	thin
e	end	ô	order	yōō	fuse	t̶h̶	this
ē	equal					zh	vision

ə = { a in *above* 　 e in *sicken* 　 i in *possible*　　 o in *melon* 　 u in *circus* }

pro·tein [prō′tēn′ *or* prō′tē·ən] *n.* Any of a large group of substances containing nitrogen that are needed in the diet of animals and people: Meat, eggs, beans, and dairy products contain *protein.*

pub·lic·i·ty [pub·lis′ə·tē] *n.* Articles or other information bringing something to the notice of the public.

pur·suit [pər·s(y)o͞ot′] *n.* The act of chasing something or someone: The dogs are in *pursuit* of the fox.

Q q

quill [kwil] *n.* A large, stiff feather from the tail or wing of a bird, used to make pens or other tools. ■

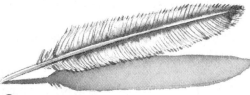

Qty. quantity

R r

ra·di·ant [rā′dē·ənt] *adj.* Shining; beaming: Tom has a *radiant* smile.

ram·page [ram·pāj′] *v.* **ram·pag·ing** To rush about violently; to behave wildly.

rare·ly [râr′lē] *adv.* Not often; seldom: I *rarely* go to movies, but I often attend basketball games.

raw·hide [rô′hīd′] *n.* The untanned skin, or hide, of cattle: Dogs love to chew *rawhide.*

rear [rir] *v.* **reared** To care for; to help bring up: They had *reared* their children to love classical music.

re·ceipt [ri·sēt′] *n.* A written statement of money paid or of a package, letter, or goods delivered: In case of doubt, a *receipt* can be proof that the letter was delivered.

reck·less·ly [rek′lis·lē] *adv.* In a careless, foolishly risky manner: He drove the pony cart *recklessly* and caused it to turn over.

re·flect [ri·flekt′] *v.* To express or to show as a mirror would: This letter to the editor *reflects* the writer's opinion.

re·flec·tive [ri·flek′tiv] *adj.* Capable of bouncing light back after it hits a surface: Silver is highly *reflective.*

re·form [ri·fôrm] *n.* A change meant to improve conditions or correct wrongs: *Reforms* have been made in the state's prison system.

reg·is·ter [rej′is·tər] *v.* To show an emotion by one's actions or by the expression on one's face: Her face *registered* the anger she felt.

re·gret·ful·ly [ri·gret′fəl·ē] *adv.* In a sorrowful or grieving manner: He resigned from his job *regretfully.*

reg·u·lar [reg′yə·lər] *n.* A professional soldier; a member of the permanent army of a country.

re·quire [ri·kwīr'] *v.* **re·quir·ing** To order or demand; to insist upon: The rules *require* that students get to class on time.

re·solve [ri·zolv'] *v.* **re·solved** To decide; to make up one's mind about something: After a family debate, we *resolved* on the red car.

re·spond [ri·spond'] *v.* To answer; to reply: Tell her I will *respond* to her letter soon.

re·sponse [ri·spons'] *n.* An answer or reply either in words or by one's actions: Her *response* to the unkind remark was total silence.

re·tire [ri·tīr'] *v.* **re·tired** To remove from or give up a job or period of service, usually because of long service or age: Uncle Jake *retired* at age seventy.

re·tort [ri·tôrt'] *v.* To reply sharply: "Mind your own business," I *retorted.*

rind [rīnd] *n.* A firm skin or outer coating of fruit, bacon, or cheeses: He peeled the *rind* from the orange.

ro·dent [rōd'(ə)nt] *n.* Any of a group of mammals that have large front teeth for gnawing: Rats, mice, squirrels, and beavers are *rodents.* ■

romp [romp] *v.* To play roughly and noisily: The children *romped* in the sand and waves.

S s

sa·chet [sa·shā'] *n.* A small pad or bag containing perfumed powder. It is used for scenting items of clothing.

sal·vage [sal'vij] *v.* **sal·vaged** To save property from ruin or destruction by fire, flood, shipwreck, or other disaster: They *salvaged* all the family linens from the fire.

sar·casm [sär·kaz'əm] *n.* The use of cutting, unpleasant remarks, aimed at hurting someone's feelings.

scale [skāl] *n.* One of many hard, thin, flat plates that make up the outer covering of some snakes, lizards, and fish.

scal·y [skā'lē] *adj.* Having scales like a snake or some fish.

scar·let [skär'lit] *adj.* Colored a very bright red, sometimes with a tinge of orange: Her lipstick was *scarlet.*

a	add	i	it	o͞o	took	oi	oil
ā	ace	ī	ice	o͞o	pool	ou	pout
â	care	o	odd	u	up	ng	ring
ä	palm	ō	open	û	burn	th	thin
e	end	ô	order	yo͞o	fuse	th	this
ē	equal					zh	vision

ə = { a in *above*　e in *sicken*　i in *possible*　o in *melon*　u in *circus* }

scene [sēn] *n.* A section of a movie or play, usually part of an act: The time and place of the action changes in every *scene* of this play.

scen·er·y [sē′nər·ē] *n.* The painted screens, hangings, and so on that are used on a theater stage to represent places in a play: The *scenery* shows a poor person's home during a time of trouble.

scoun·drel [skoun′drəl] *n.* A mean person without honor; a rascal or villain: The *scoundrel* who ran away with the pies has not been caught.

sea level [sē′ lev′əl] *n.* The level of the surface of the ocean, especially when it is halfway between high tide and low tide. The heights of land features, such as plains, mountains, hills, and so on, are measured from sea level.

sem·a·phore code [sem′ə·fôr′ kōd] *n.* A system of signals for sending messages by holding the arms or flags in different positions. ■

sem·i·cir·cle [sem′ē·sûr′kəl] *n.* One-half of a circle: The chairs were in a *semicircle* around the storyteller.

sen·sa·tion [sen·sā′shən] *n.* A feeling; an awareness of a feeling that results from the action of the senses, such as sight, hearing, touch, taste, or odor: Huddling near the stove, he felt a happy *sensation* of warmth.

se·vere·ly [si·vir′lē] *adv.* In a strict, harsh manner: Because I had not practiced my piano lesson, I was punished *severely*.

shawl [shôl] *n.* A large, oblong or square cloth, worn as a scarf around the shoulders or over the head.

she·bang [shə·bang′] *n. slang* Every part of a situation, an organization, or a set of facts or other things considered all together; used chiefly in the phrase *the whole shebang*.

shed [shed] *v.* To cast off; to get rid of: An umbrella *sheds* rain. The children *shed* their heavy coats when they came in out of the snow.

shield [shēld] *n.* A wide piece of armor carried on the arm and used to protect the body while fighting.

sim·u·late [sim′yə·lāt′] *v.* To imitate; to take on the appearance of: The praying mantis can *simulate* a twig.

sit·u·a·tion [sich′oō·wā′shən] *n.* A combination, or set, of circumstances; a place or position: Suddenly she found herself in an awkward *situation* and did not know what to do.

skel·e·ton [skel′ə·tən] *n.* The framework of bones and cartilage in a body that supports the muscles, internal organs, and skin.

skiff [skif] *n.* A light rowboat that sometimes has a small triangular sail.

slab [slab] *n.* A thick, flat, broad piece, as of stone, wood, cheese, and so on: He cut a huge *slab* of meat and laid it carefully on an equally large *slab* of bread.

slooch [slōōch] *v.* **slooch·ing** A made-up word imitating the sound of mud oozing through wet shoes.

small·pox [smôl′poks′] *n.* A very contagious disease that causes a high fever and skin sores that often leave scars: *Smallpox* is caused by a virus, but it can be prevented by vaccination.

so·ci·e·ty [sə·sī′ə·tē] *n., pl.* **so·ci·e·ties** An organized group of people joined for a purpose or a common interest: I am a member of a patriotic *society* and a scientific *society*.

so·pran·o [sə·pran′ō] *n., pl.* **so·pran·os** **1** The highest female singing voice. **2** A singer with such a voice.

source [sôrs] *n.* The person or thing from which anything comes or originates: The water pipes upstairs are the *source* of that leak.

spar [spär] *v.* To box; to make the motions of boxing.

spec·i·fy [spes′ə·fī] *v.* **spec·i·fied** To make definite; to state the details of something: Please *specify* the kind of uniform you want.

speech·less [spēch′lis] *adj.* Unable to speak: She was *speechless* with fright.

spell [spel] *n.* An indefinite period of time: We had a cold *spell* in late April.

spire [spīr] *n.* The tall, pointed top of a steeple or a tower.

spunk [spungk] *n.* An informal word for courage, pluck, spirit: When Alfonso got up from his fall and continued the race, he showed lots of *spunk.*

sput·ter [sput′ər] *n.* Spitting and popping noises. We heard a *sputter* from the frying pan.

stalk [stôk] *n.* The stem of a plant.

stamp [stamp] *v.* To bring the foot down heavily and forcefully: He *stamped* on the ants.

stock [stok] *n.* Butt or handle of a rifle: The *stocks* of rifles are usually wooden, while the barrels are metal.

stomp [stomp] *v.* To stamp the feet. The giant *stomped* over the countryside, making the trees shake.

strand·ed [stran′did] *adj.* Left on shore or in some other helpless position: There I was, a *stranded* tourist without a cent.

stray [strā] *adj.* Wandering and lost: The shepherd rounded up the *stray* sheep.

stream [strēm] *n.* A steady flow of something, as of people, words, and so on: A *stream* of ball fans moved into the stadium.

a	add	i	it	ōō	took	oi	oil
ā	ace	ī	ice	ōō	pool	ou	pout
â	care	o	odd	u	up	ng	ring
ä	palm	ō	open	û	burn	th	thin
e	end	ô	order	yōō	fuse	th	this
ē	equal					zh	vision

ə =	a in *above*	e in *sicken*	i in *possible*
	o in *melon*	u in *circus*	

601

stretch [strech] *v.* To draw out or extend the body as far as one can: Laura *stretched* her muscles and then relaxed.

stroke [strōk] *v.* To pass the hand over; to pat gently; to pet: She *stroked* the pony's glossy coat.

suave [swäv] *adj.* Polished; smooth in texture: The lake lay *suave* and blue, so unlike the choppiness of the day before.

suc·ceed [sǝc·sēd'] *v.* To get good results; to turn out well; to accomplish what one plans to do: Did you *succeed* in finding the rock sample you wanted?

sum·ma·ry [sum'ǝr·ē] *n.* A short statement giving the main points: This paragraph is a good *summary* of the entire article.

su·per·hu·man [sōō'pǝr·(h)yōō'mǝn] *adj.* More than merely human; above and beyond normal or ordinary in power, experience, and so on.

surf [sûrf] *n.* The waves of the sea or ocean as they break, roaring and foaming, onto the land. ■

sus·pense [sǝ·spens'] *n.* Doubt or uncertainty about what will happen: The *suspense* kept me on the edge of my chair.

T t

tel·e·scop·ic lens [tel'ǝ·skop'ik lenz] *n.* lens, as in a camera; *adj.* that like a telescope, makes far-off objects look nearby.

tel·e·vise [tel'ǝ·vīz] *v.* **tel·e·vised** To send by television: The afterschool special will be *televised* at 4 o'clock.

tempt·ing [temp'ting] *adj.* Attractive; appealing; inviting: I saw a *tempting* display of chocolates at the candy store.

ten·or [ten'ǝr] *n.* **1** High-pitched male singing voice. **2** A singer with such a voice.

tense [tens] *adj.* Tightly stretched; taut: His body seemed *tense* as he waited for his turn at the tryouts.

ter·race [ter'is] *v.* To form or build into terraces—flat, raised, level spaces, each with one or more sloping sides and each placed above another: We will *terrace* our garden so the water does not go straight down the hill.

thick·et [thik'it] *n.* A thick, dense growth of shrubs, bushes, or small trees: Small animals hide easily in a *thicket*.

threat [thret] *n.* A sign or indication of possible evil to come: Small rumbles were a *threat* that a large earthquake might occur.

tier [tir] *n.* A row of something, such as seats in a stadium or some theaters, placed one over the other.

top·sy·tur·vy [top'sē·tûr'vē] *adj.* Being in great disorder; being upside-down.

tor·na·do [tôr·nā'dō] *n.* A violent whirlwind, forming a twisting, funnel-shaped cloud that extends downward from dark storm clouds above and that moves over the land in a narrow, destructive path. ■

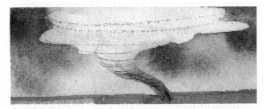

tou·sled [tou'zəld] *adj.* Untidy, mussed up: His hair was always *tousled;* it was never neat.

trans·port [trans·pôrt'] *v.* To carry from one place to some other place: Ships are used to *transport* oil from one country to another.

trap·per [trap'ər] *n.* A person who traps wild animals for their furs.

trick·ling [trik'ling] *adj.* Slow-moving, bit by bit, like drips of water from a spout.

tri·umph [trī·əmf] *n.* A victory; a success: The conquest of Mount Everest was a great *triumph* of adventure.

troll [trōl] *n.* In folklore, especially in Scandinavian folktales, a dwarf or giant that lives under the ground or in a cave.

ty·rant [tī·rənt] *n.* A ruler with great power that is used unfairly or in a cruel way.

U u

un·ed·it·ed [un'ed'i·tid] *adj.* Not corrected; not arranged or prepared for publication: The book was *unedited* and had been printed with many mistakes in it.

un·ex·plored [un'ik·splôrd'] *adj.* Not explored; not well traveled over or examined: Very little of the earth is *unexplored.*

un·re·li·a·ble [un'ri·lī'ə·bəl] *adj.* Not to be relied on; not to be trusted.

V v

val·id [val'id] *adj.* Sound; reasonable; supported by facts or reasons: Your reasons are adequate, and the conclusion is *valid.*

a	add	i	it	o͞o	took	oi	oil
ā	ace	ī	ice	o͞o	pool	ou	pout
â	care	o	odd	u	up	ng	ring
ä	palm	ō	open	û	burn	th	thin
e	end	ô	order	yo͞o	fuse	th	this
ē	equal					zh	vision

ə = { a in *above*   e in *sicken*   i in *possible*
 o in *melon*   u in *circus* }

val·u·a·ble [val′y(o͞o)ə·bəl] *adj.* Being worth money or usefulness; having value: Your idea is a *valuable* one, and it will help our class play a great deal.

van·i·ty [van′ə·tē] *n.* Conceit; having too much pride in one's appearance.

van·quish [vang′kwish] *v.* To defeat; to overcome or conquer: After heavy fighting, the knights *vanquished* the enemy.

va·ri·e·ty [və·rī′ə·tē] *n.* A number of different things or kinds: This store has a *variety* of garden tools.

va·ry [vâr′ē] *v.* **var·ied** To be different: The teddy bears in that window *vary* a great deal in quality.

ver·sion [vûr′zhən] *n.* A description of, or statement about, an event, usually from one person's point of view: Ruby's *version* of the story was different from Toby's.

vet·er·i·nar·i·an [vet′ər·ə·nâr′ē·ən] *n.* A doctor for animals.

W w

wa·ter·col·or [wô′tər·kul′ər *or* wot′ər·kul′ər] *n.* Paint for artists' use that mixes with water rather than with oil.

well [wel] *v.* **welled** Rose up, came to the surface, as in emotions: When she thought about him, all kinds of feelings *welled* up inside her.

whop·per [(h)wop′ər] *n. slang* Something very large, especially a big lie.

will [wil] *n.* The power of the mind to decide and to act on the decisions made: My grandmother was a person of very strong *will.*

wiz·ard [wiz′ərd] *n.* A man supposed to have magical powers; a magician.

wrought [rôt] *v.* An old past tense form of *to work,* used now in the sense of "made" or "brought about": The table was *wrought* of wood and iron.

Y y

yank [yangk] *v. informal* To pull suddenly; to jerk: The dog *yanked* on his leash.

yoke [yōk] *v.* **yoked** To attach a pair of animals together by means of a yoke, a crossbar with two U-shaped pieces around the necks: Please *yoke* these animals so that they can pull the plow.

Z z

zeal [zēl] *n.* Great interest or effort; enthusiasm for a cause: Danny worked with great *zeal* to promote the band concert.

ze·nith [zē′nith] *n.* The point in the sky directly over the observer's head.

Pronunciation Guide to Names, Words, and Phrases

Aesop [ē'sop]
Afa [ä'fä]
Allegheny [al'ə·gā'nē]
Audubon [ô'dōō·bon]

Babar [ba'bär']
Bellinis [bə·lē'nēz]
bobo [bō'bō]
Bora Bora [bô'rə bô'rə]
bravo [brä'vō]
buenas tardes [bwā'näs tär'des]

Calle [ka'lē]
Carlos [kär'lōs]
Carmelita [kär·mə·lē'tä]
carr [cär]
Ceylon [si·län']
Chameleon [kə·mēl'yən]
Chilean [chil'ē·ən]
Choctaw [chok'tô]
Cincinnati [sin'sə·nat'ē]

Danube [dan'yōōb]
deVarona, Donna [de və·rō'nə, don'ə]
Dia Wolo [dē'ə wō'lō]
Don Pedro [don pā'drō]
Duivenisse [dwē'və·nis·ə]

Edinburgh [ed'(ə)n·bûr·ō]
Everest [ev'ər·ist]

Floriana [flôr·ē·än'ä]

Gerez, Toni de [her'es, tō'nē də]
Gettysburg [get'ēz·bûrg]

Giles [jīlz]

Heidi [hī'dē]
Hiroshige [hir·ō·shē'ge]
Hita Kolorim [hē'tə kôl'ə·rim]
hodometron [häd'o·met'ron]
hodos [hō'dəs]
Hokusai [hok'·ōō·sī]

ibis [ī'bis]
Indianapolis [in·dē·ə·nap'ə·lis]

Jahdu [jä'dōō]
Jiya [jē'yə]
Juan [hwän]

Kees [kēz]
Kino [kē'nō]

LaFarge [lə·färj']
Lafayette [lə·fī·yet']
Lagos [lä'gōs]
La Vibora [lä vē'bôrä]
Lopez, Alonzo [lō'pez, a·lon'zō]

Mafatu [mä·fä'tōō]
Magdalena [mag·də·lā'nə]
Mako [mā'kō]
Mama Luka [mä'mä lōō'kä]
mañana [mä·nyä'nä]
Maria [mä·rē'ä]
matarile [mä·tä·rē'lä]
Miesje [mēs'yə]

Navajo [näv'ə·hō]
niña [nē'nyä]

605

Olivera [ō·li·vâr′ä]
Olympic [ō·lim′pik]
Oni [ō′nē]
Ontario [on·târ′ē·ō]
Opu Nui [op′o͞o no͞o′ē]

Papago [pä′pə·gō]
Patuxent [pə·tuks′ənt]
Perrault [pär′rō]
pesos [pā′sōs]
phoebe [fē′bē]
Phoenix [fē′niks]
Pinocchio [pi·nō′kē·ō]
plaza [plä′sä]
Pocahontas [pō·kə·hon′təs]
Polynesian [pol·i·nē′zhən]

Qingjiang [ching·zhäng′]
quetzal [kät·säl′]

Roosevelt [rō′zə·velt]
Rumplestiltskin [rum·pəl·stilt′
  skin]

sandia [san·dē′ə]
Señor Alcalde [sä·nyôr′
  al·käl′dä]

Serendip [ser′ən·dip]
Setsu [set′so͞o]
sí [sē]
Sioux [so͞o]
Sjaantje [syän′tyə]
sombrero [som·brâr′ô]
Sri Lanka [srē läng′kə]

Teresa [te·rä′sä]
Thames [temz]
Toronto [tə·ron′tō]
Totim [tō′tim]
Toto [tō′tō]
Tour de France [to͞or də fräns]
Tremain [trə′mān′]
Trui [tro͞o·wē′]
Tucson [too′son]
Tupa [to͞o′pə]

Uchida, Yoshiko [yo͞o·chē′də,
  yō·shē′kō]

Van Rhijn, Aleid [van rin, ä′lād]

Witje [wit′yə]

Yaquí [ya′kē]

Index of Titles
and Authors